BARRON'S

AMERICAN HISTORY THE EASY WAY

WILLIAM O. KELLOGG

St. Paul's School
Concord, New Hampshire

BARRON'S EDUCATIONAL SERIES, INC.

All inquiries should be addressed to:
Barron's Educational Series, Inc.
250 Wireless Boulevard
Hauppauge, New York 11788

Library of Congress Catalog Card No. 91-15327
International Standard Book No. 0-8120-4625-0

Library of Congress Cataloging-in-Publication Data

Kellogg, William O.
   American history the easy way / William O. Kellogg.
      p.   cm.
   Summary: Reviews the history of the United States, from
prehistory through 1990, and includes study questions.
   ISBN 0-8120-4625-0
   1. United States—History—Examinations, questions, etc.
2. United States—History—Outlines, syllabi, etc.   [1. United
States—History.]   I. Title.
E178.25.K39   1991
973—dc20   91-15327
                                               CIP
                                                AC

PRINTED IN THE UNITED STATES OF AMERICA

34   100   9876543

Table of Contents

Foreword

This book was written to serve as an introduction to American History. It is designed to include the reader as an historian and each chapter begins with a different "Approach to History" that some historians pursue. There are questions raised within the text which invite the reader to consider issues of significance without being given "an answer." Chapters are divided into sections. At the end of each section are presented "Links from the Past to the Present" to help link past events with today. Also included are key points summarizing the key idea in each section and a list of those "People to Remember" who appear in the section. Each summary includes several True-False and Multiple Choice questions to help the reader recall important information. Many words important for understanding American History are defined at the bottom of the page where they are used. All these devices are meant to help the student of whatever age to grasp more readily the content and significance of the history of the American people.

While my name alone is attached to this work and I am fully responsible for it, there are many people who have been influential in bringing the work to print. The book summarizes over 35 years of teaching, and my many students and colleagues during those years have greatly influenced my understanding of American History. When beginning this project, I contacted colleagues from around the country with a questionnaire to solicit their ideas on key people, dates, and events. Their responses were invaluable in confirming decisions as to what should or should not be included in the book. They have my deep appreciation. My editor, Jane O'Sullivan, has combined patience, criticism and support in a wonderful mix that has helped to make this endeavor an enjoyable one. Finally, I wish to thank the publisher. Barron's Educational Series provided me a rare opportunity to summarize my thoughts, generated over a third of a century, on teaching and the meaning of American History. It has been a very rewarding experience. My hope is that others will benefit from what I have learned about history as presented in this book. As in all of my writing, it could not have been accomplished without the support of my family and St. Paul's School.

St. Paul's School
Concord, N.H.
December 31, 1990

Acknowledgments

Photograph on page 23: Abraham Scuman Fund. Courtesy Museum of Fine Arts, Boston.

Photographs on pages 45, 105, and 132: Gift of Maxim Karolik for the M. and M. Karolik Collection of American Paintings, 1815–1865. Courtesy Museum of Fine Arts, Boston.

Photographs on pages 76 and 117: Gift of Mrs. Maxim Karolik for the M. and M. Karolik Collection of American Paintings, 1815–1865. Courtesy Museum of Fine Arts, Boston.

Photograph on page 77: Bequest of Charles Hitchock Tyler. Courtesy Museum of Fine Arts, Boston.

Photograph on page 86: Courtesy New Hampshire Historical Society.

Photograph on page 115: Bequest of Martha C. Karolik for the M. and M. Karolik Collection of American Paintings, 1815–1865. Courtesy Museum of Fine Arts, Boston.

Cartoon on page 294: Reprinted with special permission of North America Syndicate

Cartoon on page 312: Reprinted with permission of Mike Marland, *Concord Monitor*, Concord, New Hampshire.

Cartoon on page 319: Reprinted by permission, Tribune Media Services.

Cartoons on pages 322 and 331: TOLES COPYRIGHT 1989 *Buffalo News*. Reprinted with permission of United Press Syndicate. All rights reserved.

CHAPTER 1

A Nation of Immigrants

The Method of the Historian

Many people think history is a set of facts, explaining what happened in the past, that everyone should learn. They believe that by memorizing this material, they will know history. Unfortunately, this is only partly true. The truth is that history is a record of the past, and consists of information historians have gathered to explain, as best they can, what occurred before the present. You might ask, "What is the difference between these two statements?" The answer is that the latter statement avoids the word facts, and suggests the method historians use to gain an understanding of the past.

"Facts" come in all degrees of accuracy, something that can be hard for the inexperienced student of history to accept or understand. Part of the historian's method is to evaluate facts. For instance, you may be familiar with the statement "Columbus discovered America in 1492," and believe it to be a fact. Historians have considered the evidence and agree that Columbus came to the Americas in 1492—that is, 1492 according to the calendar used by most people in the United States but not 1492 according to the Jewish or Chinese calendars. Therefore, we must be clear what we mean when we state a "fact," because it may not be universally understood. More importantly, we know that there were Native Americans already in the Americas, and other Europeans had come here—they had all "discovered" America long before Columbus. So to be accurate, you need to rephrase the statement so it reads, "Columbus rediscovered America for the Europeans in 1492 AD."

The historian's method begins with the collection and questioning of so-called factual information. Once historians have collected a good deal of information—often referred to as data—they study it and develop explanations of how these facts relate. These explanations are hypotheses[1], since there is no way we can be certain just how the events, the facts, of the past were understood and related to each other.

The historian's method is very similar to the method used by scientists. Using the so-called scientific method, the scientist collects data, develops a hypothesis about why the observed data behaved the way it did, and then prepares experiments in the laboratory to prove the hypothesis by running the test over and over again to show the data will always perform the way the hypothesis states.

Unfortunately, once historians have developed a hypothesis as to why events occurred in a particular way, they cannot run an experiment over and over again to prove the hypothesis. Historians' hypotheses cannot be tested the way scientists' are. Therefore, there is always an element of uncertainty in what historians write.

Historians must rely on careful research and analysis of information. They must be aware of their own personal views and try to be objective.

Information such as the statement about Columbus becomes important only when used to support a hypothesis; it is of little significance alone. As you study history, you must learn the facts (data), but a fact is meaningful only when it helps to support a hypothesis about how past events occurred. As a student of history, you need to understand the hypotheses the writer of history is supporting, and judge how well they are proven by the facts presented. Then you need to ask if there are additional facts that might disprove the hypothesis.

In conclusion, historians do not think of history as a mere collection of facts but rather as a series of hypotheses or explanations of the past supported by factual evidence. Historians attempt to keep their personal biases out of their interpretation but it often is present. Because there is no way to finally prove what exactly happened in the past, there are often several explanations or interpretations of the past. Historians often disagree. Have you ever experienced a situation in which you and a friend, or you and your parents, disagreed and each presented an explanation with evidence that the other person would not accept? That can happen in history. As you read on, think what the hypotheses of the author are, and ask yourself how sound the evidence is to support the position presented.

---

[1]*hypotheses*   A calculated guess; an improved theory or explanation offered as a way to understanding.

Introduction

We are a nation of immigrants. Some of you reading this book may be immigrants yourselves; most of you will know people in your communities from Asia, Latin America, or Europe, who recently came to America as immigrants. All of us have ancestors who were immigrants—some voluntary, some forced. The immigrant experience is one that all Americans have shared from the earliest to arrive—the Native Americans—to the most recent arrivals from Cambodia, El Salvador, or East Germany.

We will begin this study of American History with a brief look at the first immigrants, the ancestors of today's Native Americans, and those who followed before the arrival of Christopher Columbus. By realizing we all share in some way this immigrant experience, and that it is still a current issue, the past will become closer and easier to understand.

I.   NATIVE AMERICAN IMMIGRANTS

The First Immigrants

The first immigrants who came to the North American continent were the nomadic[1] ancestors of the Native Americans. By the best estimates of historians, sometime around 50,000 years ago, several related groups began crossing the Bering Sea over a land bridge between Siberia and Alaska. From there they moved south and east, and their descendants populated the North and South American continents.

These first groups were nomads who hunted animals and gathered fruits and berries. During the last Ice Age they moved south away from the cold. Later, as the ice receded, the land bridge over which they had come was flooded, cutting the new arrivals off from their places of origin.

This pattern of separation from home, from all that was familiar, has been repeated over and over again in the history of the Americas. Can you think what it would be like to be completely cut off from all familiar places? All immigrants share this experience.

What would such immigrants bring with them, either now or 50,000 years ago? Many have brought just what they could carry. Often that is not much, and in the case of the first immigrants it may have been little more than furs for clothing, some crude hunting tools, and perhaps baskets or fur sacks for gathering food.

The most important thing immigrants brought with them was what they knew—the skills they had developed. For these first Native American immigrants it was hunting and tracking skills, knowledge of fire, and tools of stone and bone.

They also had language. After thousands of years of separation from their relatives in Siberia, the languages of the Native Ameri-

Native Americans arrive in North America over a land bridge.

---

[1]*nomadic*   Wandering; nomadic tribes are not settled and move from place to place usually in search of food or to find food for their animals.

cans throughout the western hemisphere became greatly varied, with little resemblance to each other, and none with that of Siberia.

In spite of this separation, it is interesting to note that the descendants of these earliest inhabitants living in Siberia and North America developed similar ways of dealing with their environment. At a museum of the native peoples in Irkurst, Siberia, in the Soviet Union, you can see snow shoes and leather mocassins very much like those developed by Native Americans. It is doubtful that the idea for these items came to America with the first nomads, but peoples in similar circumstances developed similar ideas to deal with their environment.

Differing Cultures

Native Americans develop different cultures.

All immigrants have had to adapt to their new environment. As the nomadic bands spread out to different parts of the two continents, they changed their ways of living and slowly developed different cultures. By 5,000 years ago the beginnings of many such cultural groupings could be identified in the Americas, and several of these developed into highly complex civilizations. The most famous of these are the Aztec and Mayan civilizations in Mexico and Central America, and the Inca civilization in Peru. In the United States there were many different Native American cultures[2]. The Pueblo culture of the southwest (Arizona, New Mexico, and Colorado), and the Algonquian culture of the northeast are significant examples. In each of these geographic areas, the Native Americans developed cultures and patterns of behavior that allowed for highly successful ways of life.

Mayan, Aztec, and Inca

Mayan, Aztec, and Inca cultures are all city based civilizations.

Mayan civilization was in decline by the time Spanish explorers arrived in the 16th century (1500s). It was an urban culture with cities dominated by large stone pyramid-temples. Large tracts of land were cultivated. Mayans had invented writing and a system of mathematics. The Aztecs, a more warlike civilization, had come to dominate Mexico and most of the areas of Mayan civilization by 1500. Their capital, Tenochtitlan, (Mexico City is built on the site) was one of the great cities of the age. The gold and silver of the empire was collected there. In Peru the Incas had a flourishing urban-based civilization that controlled large areas of the Andes.

These civilizations, while extremely important for understanding the history of Mexico and all of the Americas, are not as directly related to United States history as the cultures of the Pueblos and Algonquians.

Pueblo

The culture of the Pueblos revolved around their villages. Pueblos are villages of multi-storied buildings and were built with

---

[2]*culture* A set of beliefs and patterns of behavior developed by a group of people. These appear in their religious, artistic, social, and political attitudes and are supported by their material productions.

defense in mind. Some, such as Pueblo Bonito, stand in valleys as large isolated structures with windowless solid walls facing out. Connected houses and rooms built against these outside walls face a yard where outdoor life centered safe from attack. Other pueblos were built on the sides of cliffs or, as with the Hopis, on mesas[3].

Pueblo dwellers evolve very complex political, social, and religious organizations.

Often hundreds of people lived within one pueblo. Pueblo dwellers were dependent on agriculture, and not hunting, for survival. Men did this work while the women prepared the food and cared for children. Politically each pueblo was independent and was run by a man's council.

Religion centered around the cultivation of crops and there were elaborate ceremonies and rituals, often with dancing, to celebrate planting, harvesting, and to bring rain. Many of these ceremonies continue today as part of the rich culture of the various tribes who still live in pueblos in the southwest, and outsiders may attend these religious ceremonies.

As you watch the religious dances of, for instance, the Hopis, you are struck by the intricacy of the ritual, by the soberness and deep feelings of the participants, and by their great need for favorable conditions for their agriculture.

You can also appreciate how different these traditions seemed to the Spanish who entered the Southwest after 1500. Even today, when TV exposes us to all the cultures of the world, we often find it difficult to accept what is different. It is this experience of being different that all immigrants experience. The Spaniards found it difficult to accept the culture of the Pueblo peoples, yet it was a highly developed culture long before they came. That many pueblos still exist is a credit to the peoples of this earlier civilization in what became the United States.

Algonquian

The Native Americans who greeted the Europeans on the Atlantic coast also lived in villages. The Algonquian villages were built of wood and other perishable materials, and only archaeological evidence remains of them. The villages were often surrounded by wooden posts forming a wall for defense. An extended family lived in a single house. The female members remained in the home in which they were born, and males joined their wife's families. This arrangement is referred to as matrilineal.

The way societies form families—matrilineally or patrilineally— is important because it reveals how important males and females are within the society, how social power is distributed, and often how political and economic power is held. For instance, Algonquian women did the agricultural work for the tribe, could become political leaders of the tribe, and often were the religious leaders.

The religious beliefs of the Algonquians, as is natural with any agricultural people, focused on the crops. They worshipped the forces of nature involved with planting and harvesting. The Native

The Algonquians live in a close relationship with nature.

---

[3]*mesas* Flat plateaus with steep sides.

Americans had an understanding of a close relationship between humans and their natural environment.

One Iroquois chief—the Iroquois are a tribe of the Algonquian group—remarked that the Iroquois planned for the "seventh generation," and not just for the next year or two. Planning for the seventh generation suggests a realization that actions have long range effects that must be considered. As we face environmental crises, some scholars suggest we could have learned much if we had tried to understand the religious teachings of the agriculturally based Native American societies of the northeast, or of the Pueblos.

The Europeans did not understand, or appreciate, the complexity and significance to the Native Americans of their religious beliefs. The two cultures came into conflict, as often happens when two cultures meet or when immigrants from a different cultural tradition arrive. Usually the minority is persecuted by the intolerant majority, but as we shall see in the case of the Europeans coming to the Americas, the minority view triumphed. This was due to many factors, and has meant the loss to us of ideas from which we might have learned.

Evidence of Pre-Colombian Contacts

There is now evidence to support the idea that many Native American cultures had contacts with Africans and Europeans long before the "discovery" of America by Christopher Columbus. These contacts appear to have been peaceful. There is no evidence for continual trade. What ideas were exchanged is not clear, but the appearance of clay figurines with distinctly Negroid features in Aztec art before 1500 AD, and of inscriptions in Egyptian hieroglyphs and Celtic writing in New England, prove there were contacts.

Stories of the Great Bear (Big Dipper) suggest pre-Columbian contacts between Europe and America.

Another bit of information that is difficult to account for, except in terms of contact with Europe, is the fact that the arrangement of stars we call the Big Dipper was referred to as the Great Bear by the ancient Greeks, the Romans, and the Native Americans of New England. This is attested to by Cotton Mather, a minister in Boston in colonial days, who asked the natives in Boston what they knew of navigation. In their explanation they referred to the Big Dipper as the Bear, and described how they used the North Star and the Great Bear (Big Dipper) in finding direction. We can understand how different people would use the North Star but what makes this remarkable, and supports the idea of contacts, is the fact the stars in the Big Dipper are not arranged to look like a Bear except by the greatest stretch of the imagination.

KEY POINT TO REMEMBER

Native American peoples had developed sophisticated civilizations long before the arrival of European settlers or explorers.

LINKS FROM THE PAST TO THE PRESENT

1. All Americans or their ancestors share the immigrant experience, giving us all something in common.
2. Native-American religious beliefs provide insights that can be helpful in the environmental crisis.

QUESTIONS

Identify each of the following:

Mayan	Pueblo
Aztec	Algonquian
Inca	Pueblo Bonito

True or False:

1. The Mayans had conquered the Aztecs before the first Europeans arrived.
2. As we face environmental crises, we realize we could have learned how to treat our environment better from the Algonquians.
3. All Americans or their ancestors came to America as immigrants either voluntarily or under force.
4. Before the arrival of European immigrants, no cities were built by Native Americans.

Multiple Choice:

1. The Pueblos of the Southwestern United States were built
   - a. high up on mountains.
   - b. on islands.
   - c. on mesas, cliffs, and in valleys.
2. The first Native American immigrants to the Americas brought with them
   - a. only the ability to communicate.
   - b. fur clothing, hunting tools and baskets, hunting skills, fire, and communication.
   - c. their relatives and their tents and packages.
3. The religious beliefs of both the Pueblos and the Algonquians centered on
   - a. the forces of nature involved in the production of crops
   - b. successful hunting expeditions.
   - c. witchcraft involved in matrilineal descent.
4. The fact the Big Dipper is called the Great Bear by both Europeans and Algonquians suggests
   - a. the Big Dipper can be seen by both groups at night
   - b. the North Star is important for navigation
   - c. there was contact between Europe and America before Columbus.

ANSWERS

True or False: 1. F, 2. T, 3. T, 4. F.
Multiple Choice: 1. c, 2. b, 3. a, 4. c.

II.   EUROPEAN IMMIGRANTS

The first European immigrants to the New World, of whom we have any clear evidence, came from Northern Europe. They are usually referred to as the Vikings or Norsemen, and their visits and small settlements in Greenland, Nova Scotia, and New England are dated about 1000 AD. Contacts between the Norsemen and the Algonquian groups lasted for the next 400 years. Recently evidence has been found that long before the Vikings, immigrants from the Celtic[1] lands of Europe had settled in the area of New England.

The Celts and Vikings make contact with the New World.

The Celts

Two questions the historian would immediately ask on reading this last sentence are "What is the evidence?" and "Why is this information important?" The best way to answer the second question is to answer the first.

Celtic peoples visit the New World during the period of the Roman Republic.

Evidence of settlements during the period of the Roman Republic (509–31 BC) by the Celtic peoples comes from inscriptions found at a number of locations in the northeast, from Algonquian tales of ancestors who came from "across the sea" rather than on the overland bridge, from circles of stones in North America that are similar to Stonehenge in England, and from the facial features of the Algonquians, which are as much like European features as they are like the features of the western Native American tribes.

The latter point suggests that the Algonquians were a mixed group, and not pure descendants of those who came across the land bridge from Siberia. They probably exchanged ideas with other peoples when both were at an early stage of civilization. The Algonquians may well have learned about navigation and the use of the North Star and of the Great Bear from the Celts.

The Vikings

The story of the Vikings or Norsemen is more likely to be known by Americans than that of the Celts. It is often included in history textbooks because there is more evidence for their visits and settlements. There are written references to travel to North America in the archives[2] of Denmark.

A Norseman, Leif Ericson, explores the coast of North America, and colonies are established.

Eric the Red, who was exiled from Iceland, founded a settlement in Greenland about 1000 AD. According to the *Sagas* or old stories of Scandinavia, his son, Leif Ericson, explored the coast of North America. Several settlements were established, with some evidence suggesting the Norsemen penetrated as far as Minnesota either coming down from Hudson Bay or going west through the Great Lakes.

Contacts with the Northeast continued for many years. A Danish court record states that in 1354 a search party was sent to locate a settlement on the coast of Greenland. Apparently the settlement had been destroyed, or there had been no contact with it for some time. After that time, contacts between the Norse settlements in North America and Europe appear to have ceased, and the next immigrants came from Southern Europe.

---

[1]*celtic*   Civilization found in Western France, Southern England, and Ireland about 1000 BC. Stonehenge in England was built by the Celts.

[2]*archives*   Official government records.

Why was contact lost?

Why did these contacts cease, and why weren't they widely known throughout Europe? We do not know for certain, but historians have offered many hypotheses. These include the growth of new ideas during the Renaissance[3], and the rise and spread of Islam[4]. There is, however, no general agreement. Thus the answer, as so often in history, is hidden in mystery.

Historians have offered different hypotheses as to why contact was lost.

Reestablishing Contact

Slowly conditions changed and new views developed as they always do. The period we call the Renaissance replaced the Middle Ages. The Renaissance began in Italy around 1300 AD and slowly spread to Northern and Western Europe. Among the many philosophical ideas of the Renaissance, new attitudes toward the individual, and the concept of a secular[5] nation state were most important. The former encouraged individual initiative, manifested in the individual exploits of discoverers, explorers, and conquerors. The latter encouraged the growth of what we consider a modern nation.

Renaissance attitudes encourage new explorations.

The Renaissance provided impetus for the explorations of the Portuguese, and provided ideas and new sailing techniques which Christopher Columbus used on his voyages. Another impetus to Portuguese exploration was a response to new economic conditions brought about by both the earlier Crusades and the Renaissance.

The Crusades had directed attention away from Northern Europe towards the Eastern Mediterranean. Although the Crusades failed, and Christian Europe could not dislodge the followers of Mohammed from the Eastern Mediterranean, they did introduce new ideas and new goods from Asia to Europe. The Italians of Venice and Genoa traded with the Islamic peoples for goods like silks and spices, and developed a near monopoly[6] of the trade.

Portuguese explorers sail around Africa to establish a sea route to Asia.

After 1400 the Portuguese rulers began to look for a route to Asia along the African coast, but they had no idea as to how large Africa would be.

New instruments—the magnetic compass and the astrolade, which allows the sailor to determine latitude—helped navigators

---

[3]*Renaissance* The period of time in Europe between the Middle Ages and the Modern Era. The time of the Renaissance varied in different parts of Europe.

[4]*Islam* The religion of which Mohammed is the prophet. Mohammed lived and heard the word of God in Mecca and Medina, Saudi Arabia. From there the faith of Islam was spread by conquests from Spain to Indonesia. It is still the major faith in North Africa, the Near East, Pakistan, and Indonesia and is widespread throughout the world.

[5]*secular* Having to do with worldly as opposed to spiritual or religious concerns.

[6]*monopoly* Exclusive possession of anything; control of the supply of any commodity or service in a given market or area which permits the holder of the monopoly to set prices.

on these explorations. They were also aided by the development of a new type of ship, the caravel, which could sail against the wind.

As so often in history, inventions helped create change. Prince Henry the navigator, son of King John I of Portugal, is given credit for beginning these explorations, which became very profitable as the Portuguese brought African products to Europe. They introduced the first black slaves into Europe, thus beginning the era of Black Slavery. Eventually, in 1488 Bartolomeu Dias rounded the southern tip of Africa, and in 1498 Vasco da Gama sailed around Africa to India.

The Portuguese had found a new route to the riches of Asia. But this was not the only possible route. Christopher Columbus had another idea.

Christopher Columbus

Christopher Columbus was born in or near the Italian town of Genoa. His parents were wool weavers, but Columbus became a sailor and developed a vision that changed the course of history. Columbus' idea had been rejected by the Portuguese by whom he had been employed as a sailor. They were not as interested in financing an expedition across the ocean as they were finding success along the African coast. Columbus therefore went to Ferdinand and Isabella of Spain.

Ferdinand and Isabella of Spain agree to finance a voyage by Christopher Columbus.

After several years, the rulers of Spain agreed to help finance a voyage westward from Spain to Japan. The result is the famous first voyage of Christopher Columbus and his three sailing ships, the *Nina, Pinta* and *Santa Maria*. He touched land, probably in the Bahamas, and named the first island he touched San Salvador.

While many others had already come to the Americas, his trip was followed by an ever increasing number of voyages, the stories of which spread throughout Western Europe. Soon, the rapidly developing nation states of Western Europe—Spain, France, and England—were involved in a race to find a way through the Americas and on to Asia.

Columbus is often credited with "discovering a new world."

To the Europeans it seemed that Columbus had "discovered a new world." It changed history. We know, however, that many immigrants and discoverers had already come to this new world of the Americas. Columbus came at a time in which many technical developments in sailing techniques and communication made it possible to report his voyages easily, and to spread the word of them throughout Western Europe. It was also at a time of growing economic rivalries between the developing nation states. They were all seeking new wealth, and this eventually led to a rivalry for the establishment of colonies in the Americas.

Spanish Explorers

Spaniards explore the Americas and sail around the world.

Columbus made four voyages to the west, and explored the Caribbean and Latin American area extensively. He died in 1506, still certain he had arrived at the coast of Asia, and his Spanish settlement in Santo Domingo became the base for many expeditions.

Two important Spanish expeditions were those led by Ponce de Leon, who conquered Puerto Rico in 1508–9 and explored Florida in 1513, and by Vasco Nunez de Balboa, who crossed the Isthmus of Panama and saw the Pacific in 1513. After extensive explorations along the coast, the Spanish began the conquest of Central and South America.

In 1519 Ferdinand Magellan, a Portuguese sailing for Spain, started on an expedition around the world. Although Magellan was killed, the expedition returned to Spain in 1522. Magellan's expedition proved that the earth was round, and that the lands visited by Columbus were not Asia.

John Cabot

The first voyage west not sponsored by Spain was that of John Cabot, an Italian who lived in Bristol, England. His two voyages, in 1497 and 1498, were supported by English merchants and by an agreement with the English King, Henry the VII. John Cabot sailed along the coasts of Newfoundland and New England as far south as Delaware Bay, claiming this territory for England and providing the basis for English claims to North America.

English claims to North America are established by voyages of John Cabot.

KEY POINT TO REMEMBER
Christopher Columbus did not "discover" America. It was well known to the Native Americans, and had been known to the Celtic peoples and Vikings. His voyages reacquainted Europeans with the American continent.

LINKS FROM THE PAST TO THE PRESENT
1. The Renaissance inspired individualism, which has been a hallmark of American society.
2. Throughout history, inventions, ranging from the plow to the stirrup to the atomic bomb, have led to major historical changes.

PEOPLE TO REMEMBER
Christopher Columbus Italian explorer, reestablished regular contact between Europe and the Americas. His voyages from Spain to the Caribbean started in 1492.

QUESTIONS
Identify each of the following:

Crusades	Vasco de Gama
Middle Ages	Ferdinand and Isabella
Renaissance	Christopher Columbus
Islam	John Cabot

Multiple Choice:
1. Evidence of Celtic settlement in North America includes
    a. facial features of the Algonquians and inscriptions
    b. circles of stones like Stonehenge in England
    c. both of the above

2. Viking contacts with America
   a. lasted for many years
   b. were very limited
   c. came only on the island of Greenland
3. Portuguese explorations were helped by
   a. the Italians of Genoa and Venice
   b. African slaves who sailed the ships
   c. new instruments—the compass and astrolade—and a new ship design—the caravel
4. The rulers of Spain agreed to
   a. finance Christopher Columbus' voyage westward
   b. repay Christopher Columbus for any expenses he had on his voyage
   c. send immigrants to America
5. News of Christopher Columbus' voyages spread throughout Europe because of
   a. the invention of the steamship
   b. the conquest of Western Europe by Islam
   c. recent inventions in communication and the ideas of the Renaissance

ANSWERS
Multiple Choice: 1. c, 2. a, 3. c, 4. a, 5. c.

CHAPTER 2

European Settlements in North America

APPROACHES TO HISTORY
Explaining History by Multiple Causes

Usually the most satisfactory explanation of past events is one that includes many different reasons or causes. This approach to past events is known as a multi-causal approach. However, as we will see in future chapters, a historian will often concentrate on one explanation for past events.

The multi-causal approach is one that most of us use all the time in explaining events in our lives. For instance, if you tell friends from school that you will meet them at the movies, three miles from home, and you do not show up, your explanation the next day will often be multi-causal.

The story might include 1) you could not find your wallet and your mother would not lend you the money, 2) you could not call because the telephone wasn't working, and 3) you could not take the car because your license was in the wallet. Therefore, you could not get to the movie house even though you knew your friends would pay for you if you got there.

That simple story involves three major categories of explanations—1) economics (no money), 2) fate (broken phone), and 3) ideology or belief (will not drive without a license).

We'll look at each of these explanations in greater detail in later chapters, but they provide reasons we often use to explain our own actions. These are also explanations used by historians to provide understanding of past events. All three explanations have been used to explain the establishment of settlement by Europeans in North America.

I. THE SPANISH IN THE AMERICAS— THE EARLY YEARS

In the late 15th and throughout the 16th centuries, England and France were involved in domestic issues centering on nation building and a conflict over religion. While some exploration of the New World was done, no settlements were attempted by England and France until late in the 16th century. The Reformation[1] in Europe, which destroyed the unity of the Christian Church in Western Europe, was the central concern of the Northern Europeans in the 16th century. Spain, however, remained strongly Roman Catholic. Free of religious conflict in the 16th century, the Spanish were free to explore, conquer, and bring Roman Catholicism to the Americas.

The Reformation disrupts the unity of the Christian Church.

Spanish Cultural Developments

The Spanish sought wealth and found it in Mexico, which was conquered by Ferdinand Cortez in the 1520s, and in Peru, which was conquered by Francisco Pizarro in the 1530s. The Spanish established their rule over these areas creating a huge empire that was kept under the tight control of the King of Spain.

The Spanish conquer Mexico and Peru, seize wealth and force the natives to convert to Roman Catholicism.

Governors were sent to rule the new territories and settlers, mainly males, came to exploit the riches. Slaves were soon imported from Africa to aid in the development of the wealth of the colonies. The Spanish settlers married both native women and slaves.

In their devotion to Christianity, the Spanish destroyed both written records and buildings of the Incas and Aztecs. They built Christian churches and worked to convert the natives to Roman Catholicism. They melted down most of the gold and silver artifacts[2] they seized into ingots for shipment to Spain. Their reasons for settlement are considered both economic and ideological, thus providing a clear example of a multi-causal explanation.

St. Augustine, Santa Fe and San Diego

Spanish explorers traveled into Florida, explored the Mississippi River delta, and conquered several of the pueblos of the Southwest. These explorations later led to the founding of cities by the Spanish in what is now the United States. St. Augustine, Florida, the oldest surviving European settlement in the United States, was established in 1565 as a military fort to block the French exploration in Florida. The Spanish founded Santa Fe in New Mexico in 1609, just after Jamestown and Quebec had been founded, and the first

St. Augustine, Florida, is established in 1565.

---

[1]*Reformation* The religious movement in Western Christendom precipitated by Martin Luther in 1517 which resulted in the formation of various Protestant churches and which ended the unity of Europe under the Roman Catholic faith.

[2]*artifact* An object, product of human workmanship, such as carvings, bowls, etc. We often use *artifact* to refer to objects found by archaeologists while digging.

settlement in California in San Diego in 1769. As their names suggest, many of the early Spanish settlements were missions, established to bring Christianity to the natives.

Native American/Spanish Interactions

The impact of Spanish settlement on the Native American culture was overwhelming. While a few Spaniards tried to preserve records, the majority of settlers were driven by dreams of wealth and their leaders by religious zeal. In establishing their control, they destroyed much of the culture of the Native American. This destruction of the material products of the culture, and the knowledge it represented, is a great loss for all people.

An even greater loss, however, was in the number of natives who died as a result of diseases introduced by European explorers and settlers throughout North and South America. The natives had no immunity to such European diseases as smallpox. Natives everywhere died. One source estimates that of a million natives on the Island of Hispaniola when Columbus arrived, 500 were left by 1550. Europeans did take a new, severe form of syphilis back from the Americas and it spread throughout the continent but did not wipe out the European population.

The Spanish bring new diseases which kill many of the natives.

One positive result of the opening up of the Americas was an exchange of products. Beans and potatoes were introduced to Europe, and cattle and horses to the Americas. The horse totally changed the life style of the Native Americans on the Great Plains. Tobacco, first grown in the Americas, likewise changed the life, wealth, and ultimately the health of the Europeans.

Non-Spanish Explorations

Despite their involvement in nation building and religious wars during the 16th century, Northern Europeans did manage to send explorers to seek a passage through the North American continent. A Frenchman, Jacques Cartier, explored the St. Lawrence River, the Great Lakes, and finally the Mississippi River area. The French made an attempt at a settlement in Florida but were stopped by the Spanish. It might have changed the history of the Americas if they had succeeded. The French also explored the coast of New England.

The French, English and Dutch explore areas of North America.

In the early 17th century Henry Hudson, sailing for the Dutch, explored the East Coast from Hudson Bay to the Carolinas. He gave his name to the Hudson River, which he hoped might be the long-sought passage to the Pacific Ocean. His discoveries gave the Dutch a claim to what became New York.

The English Sir Francis Drake explored the Pacific coast of the Americas, raiding Spanish ships and discovering San Francisco Bay (1579), which he claimed for England. He went on to sail around the world—the second European expedition to do so. He is a hero to the English, but he was a pirate to the Spanish.

We look back on these early explorers as great adventurers who opened up a new world. We often overlook the view Native Americans had of their exploits, or how peoples from other nations viewed them. They are the individuals who made later settlement possible. They were daring and in many ways exciting people, but their activities need to be viewed from different perspectives. This is another aspect of a multi-causal approach. To the Native Americans the Europeans were not explorers but conquerors.

KEY POINT TO REMEMBER

European nations explored and claimed lands in the Americas after 1492 even though the land was already inhabited by Native Americans.

LINKS FROM THE PAST TO THE PRESENT

1. Spanish influence in the South and Southwest was established early in our history and is still important today.

QUESTIONS

Identify each of the following:

Jacques Cartier   Sir Francis Drake
Hispaniola   St. Augustine
Santa Fe

True or False:

1. The Spanish in the Americas overwhelmed the Native American culture.
2. Tobacco, beans and potatoes were all brought to Europe from the Americas.
3. The English, French, Spanish and Swedes all claimed territory in New England.
4. The horse introduced from Europe changed the life style of Native Americans on the Great Plains.
5. Jacques Cartier and Henry Hudson claimed lands in North America for the Dutch.
6. The Reformation destroyed the unity of the Christian Church in Western Europe.
7. Christopher Columbus did not establish a colony in the Americas.

Multiple Choice:

1. In the Spanish colonies in the Americas
    a. governors were elected by the settlers
    b. the settlers married both native women and slaves
    c. the settlers quickly adopted the natives' religion
2. The oldest surviving European settlement in the United States is
    a. San Diego
    b. Santa Fe
    c. Fort Augustine
3. The early European explorers made claims to areas such as
    a. Francis Drake's claim to San Francisco Bay for England
    b. Jacques Cartier's claim to Hudson Bay for France
    c. Henry Hudson's claim to the Hudson River for England

ANSWERS

True or False: 1. T, 2. T, 3. F, 4. T, 5. F, 6. T, 7. F.
Multiple Choice: 1. b, 2. c, 3. a.

II. EUROPEAN COLONIES IN NORTH AMERICA

Jamestown

These explorations set the stage for the Europeans to begin the period of rapid colonization in the 17th century. The Spanish had already established the first colony in the future United States when the English made their first attempt at Roanoke Island on the North Carolina coast. This attempt organized by Sir Walter Raleigh failed, and the settlers all disappeared. This famous "lost colony" of 1584 has been the focus of many studies, but to this day no one is certain what happened to the first English immigrants in North America.

The first successful English settlement was established on an island in the James River in Virginia in 1607. Jamestown, named for the English king, James I, was founded by the London Company. Several of the original settlements were established by companies chartered by the King. Their goal was to make money.

English settlers establish the colony of Jamestown in Virginia in 1607.

The settlers at Jamestown suffered greatly at first until they learned to grow tobacco and ship it to England. Tobacco became the source of wealth for Virginia and affected its history.

The first African-Americans to arrive in North America were brought to Jamestown as bound servants in 1619 to help raise tobacco. By 1680, it is estimated, there were roughly 3000 blacks in bondage in Virginia.

The majority of workers were English, many of whom came over as indentured servants. Passage to the colonies was expensive so many signed contracts to work for a set number of years, usually seven, in return for passage and board. Bound servants, on the other hand, were committed to work for life, but they could buy out of the contract. Slavery in America began as a system of bondage that grew more and more harsh over the years. While Jamestown is remembered for the introduction of tobacco and the arrival of the first African-Americans as slaves, it should also be remembered for having the first elective legislature in North America, thus establishing our tradition of democracy. Twenty-two Burgesses—two chosen by each town or plantation—met in 1619 to establish the tradition of an elected house of representatives.

The House of Burgesses played an important but varied role throughout colonial history and particularly at the time of the Revolution. It was traditions of this type that laid the foundation for our nation.

Non-English Colonies

In 1608 the French established their first permanent settlement in North America at Quebec. Again the purpose was to make money, in this case by developing the trade in furs with the Native Americans. There was a large market for fur in Europe, and along with the fish caught in the Gulf of St. Lawrence and the North Atlantic, this trade brought some prosperity to the French settlers.

French settle in the St. Lawrence Valley, Dutch in New York and Swedes in Delaware.

The Dutch followed up on the explorations of Henry Hudson in the area of New York by founding a colony. Companies were formed in Holland to further the exploration and settlement of the area. In 1624 the Dutch established a permanent settlement in New York Harbor on Governors Island. Later the Dutch worked with some Swedish investors to establish a settlement at what is now Wilmington, Delaware.

By 1640 there were Spanish, English, French, Dutch, and Swedish colonies established along the coast of North America. The latter four nations had established their first colonies for economic reasons, and while the Spanish established Fort Augustine for military reasons, they were also motivated by economics.

While this suggests a single cause for settlement, members of each colony had different reasons for being there. Many settlers were interested not only in making money but in converting the native population to Christianity. Some were there to escape conditions at home, and others had very personal reasons for leaving their homelands.

The Pilgrims at Plymouth

The later English colonies were founded for several different reasons. The second English colony, that at Plymouth Bay in Massachusetts, was founded by an English company, but the settlers, the Pilgrims, had religious (that is, ideological) reasons for coming.

During the reign of Queen Elizabeth I, the Protestant Church of England was firmly established as England's official religion. Immediately, differing groups began protesting. Each of these wished to change the newly established church in some way. With the death of Elizabeth I in 1603 and the accession of James I, protest grew.

One group, the Pilgrims, went to Holland but did not wish to bring their children up as Dutch. Their leaders arranged with the Virginia Company to go to America. They joined a group of non-Pilgrims and sailed on the *Mayflower*, landing on Cape Cod.

The Mayflower Compact is signed and establishes a plan of government for Plymouth colony.

Before landing and settling in Plymouth, 41 adults on the Mayflower signed an agreement, the Mayflower Compact. This plan of government, drawn up by a few and agreed to by all, formed the basis of the government of the colony. This concept of government by compact or written agreement became a cornerstone of our democracy.

The Puritans at Massachusetts Bay

Massachusetts Bay colony becomes the center of Puritanism in America.

Other colonies were soon established in the Massachusetts Bay area. The most important was the Massachusetts Bay Colony founded in 1629. It was founded by another group of religious reformers, the Puritans, whose ideas have been very important throughout our history.

The founders had a company charter, taken to America, and annual meetings were held there. This provides a third idea (the first being the elected House of Burgesses and the second the compact theory) that influenced our democratic ideas and that appeared early in the English speaking colonies.

Annual meetings allowed America to develop its own Parliamentary tradition, and later led the colonists to reject offers from the English that would allow the colonists to send representatives to England's Parliament.

The first governor, and one of its most distinguished citizens, was John Winthrop, a devout Puritan. He helped make Massachusetts Bay a "Bible Commonwealth," which he believed would serve as a "shining city on the hill"—that is, as an example for all people.

Massachusetts Bay Colony flourished as King James I increasingly enforced on his subjects conformity to the Church of England. Many protesting Puritans fled to America for freedom of worship. This has occurred many times in our history as different governments have persecuted their subjects for their religious beliefs. In fact, it happened in New England when Massachusetts' Puritans prosecuted Roger Williams and exiled him. He founded a colony at Providence in Rhode Island, which was noted for religious toleration and fair treatment of the Native Americans.

Settlements in Connecticut and New Hampshire were also established before 1640. These settlers had religious as well as economic motives for settlement.

The Other English Colonies

The Puritan protesters wished to move the Church of England even further from the Roman Catholic position. Meanwhile, the Catholics in England also suffered under the policies of King James. The Catholic Lord Baltimore acquired from the King the right to establish a colony in what is now Maryland. He was named the proprietor, or owner, of the colony in the charter, which did not state what church had to be set up as the official church of the settlement. Lord Baltimore encouraged Catholics to come to Maryland to escape religious persecution.

Roman Catholics find toleration of their religious beliefs in Maryland.

Pennsylvania was given to William Penn, a Quaker, as his personal property. It became a refuge for those of the Quaker religious persuasion as well as a place for those who wished to prosper economically.

Pennsylvania is founded as a refuge for Quakers.

Thus from the start America became a refuge for individuals wishing to escape persecution for their beliefs, regardless of what they were. The country has remained a haven for the persecuted to this day.

The last colony, Georgia, was founded as a military buffer between the Spanish in Florida and the other English colonies, and as a penal location for English criminals. It soon became an area of plantations.

The final colony, Georgia, is established as a penal colony and buffer between Spanish and English colonies.

By 1740 the English had established thirteen distinct colonies along the North American coast. It should be clear they were established for different reasons, and the settlers had various personal reasons for coming, ranging from a desire to worship as they wished to making money quickly. Some settlers were forced to come, as were the Afro-Americans and the criminals who were sent to Georgia instead of being put in English jails.

KEY POINTS TO REMEMBER

Settlements in the Americas were established by the Spanish, English, French, Dutch and Swedes primarily for economic and religious reasons. Individuals, however, had many other motives for coming.

LINKS FROM THE PAST TO THE PRESENT

1. Many democratic ideas incorporated in the United States system of government have their roots in the governments of different colonies.
2. Many colonists were intolerant of those who held a different religious belief, and this attitude has surfaced often in United States history.

PEOPLE TO REMEMBER

John Winthrop Puritan; first Governor of Massachusetts Bay Colony; tried to build the perfect Christian community based on the Bible.

William Penn Quaker; Proprietor of Pennsylvania; established religious toleration in the colony.

Roger Williams persecuted by Massachusetts Bay Puritans; he founded Providence in Rhode Island on the basis of religious toleration and fair treatment of the local inhabitants.

QUESTIONS

Identify each of the following:

Lord Baltimore   Quebec
William Penn   New Amsterdam
Jamestown

True or False

1. African-Americans first arrived in the English colonies in America at Jamestown.
2. The House of Burgesses was the first elective legislature in North America.
3. French settlers in Quebec relied on agriculture to make a living.
4. The Mayflower Compact signed between the settlers of Plymouth and the Native Americans was an agreement to help each other.
5. The only religion acceptable in the English colonies was the Church of England.
6. John Winthrop believed Massachusetts Bay Colony would serve as a "shining city on a hill."
7. William Penn made Roman Catholicism the official religion of Pennsylvania.

Multiple Choice

1. Settlers at Jamestown suffered until they learned to grow
   a. corn
   b. cotton
   c. tobacco

2. The Dutch established a colony in
   a. Governors Island, New York
   b. Fort Augustine, Florida
   c. Plymouth, Massachusetts
3. Roger Williams established a colony in
   a. Rhode Island
   b. Connecticut
   c. New Hampshire

ANSWERS

True or False: 1. T, 2. T, 3. F, 4. F, 5. F, 6. T, 7. F
Multiple Choice: 1. c, 2. a, 3. a.

Founding of Colonies in North America
First National Settlements

Date	Name	Founding Country	Primary Reasons For Founding	Important Leader
1565	St. Augustine, FL	Spain	Military Fort & Missionary base	—
1607	Jamestown, VA	England	Missionary base to convert Indians	Capt. John Smith
1608	Quebec, Canada	France	Export Fur Trade	Samuel de Champlain
1624	Manhattan, NY	Holland	Develop Farming & Trade	Peter Minuit
1638	Wilmington, DE	Sweden/Holland	Develop Farming & Trade	—

First English Settlement in each of the 13 States

Date	State	Reason for Settlement	Important Leader
1607	Virginia Jamestown	Economic & Religious	John Smith
1620	Massachusetts Plymouth	Religious	Wm. Bradford
1631	Connecticut	Religious & Economic	Thomas Hooker
1634	Maryland	Religious & Economic	Lord Baltimore
1636	Rhode Island	Religious	Roger Williams
1638	New Hampshire	Economic	John Wheelwright
1654	North Carolina	Economic	—
1664	New York—Conquered from the Dutch	Economic	Duke of York
1664	New Jersey—Conquered from the Dutch	Economic	Sir George Carteret
1680	Pennsylvania	Religious & Economic	Wm. Penn
1680	South Carolina	Economic	Anthony Cooper
1682	Delaware—Conquered from the Dutch in 1664–separated from Pennsylvania in 1682		—
1732	Georgia	Penal colony, Economic & Military	James Oglethorpe

III.   THE ENGLISH COLONIES TO 1763

Ideas From The Past

Whenever we tell a story, we must decide what to include and what to leave out. We do this all the time. When someone asks you, "What happened at school or work today?" you pick certain things to tell. You leave out many details and sometimes major events.

We must do the same as we write an account of American history. We make decisions about what is important. In determining what to include from the history of the English colonies to 1763, we decided that three points are particularly important:
- first, experiences or traditions shared by all the colonies:
- second, geography and how it influenced the development of different lifestyles;
- third, developments that established ideas or principles that have become the foundation of the independent American nation and still affect us today.

In the previous section we indicated three colonial developments that became important foundations of the American nation:
- first, the idea of a written compact or constitution as the basis for government, which was first done by the Pilgrims when they signed the Mayflower Compact;
- second, the idea of a legislative body elected by the people living in an area, which would make laws for governing those people;
- third, annual meetings of the legislative body to make laws for the territory.

This connection between the colonial past and today is the most important point to understand about this 170-year period of our history.

Geographic Differences

Geographic similarities have led scholars to group the 13 English colonies in three divisions: New England, Mid-Atlantic and Southern.

For purposes of analysis, the thirteen English colonies are often grouped into three divisions: first, the New England colonies of New Hampshire, Massachusetts, Rhode Island, and Connecticut; second, the Mid-Atlantic colonies of New York, New Jersey, Pennsylvania and Delaware; third, the Southern colonies of Virginia, Maryland, North Carolina, South Carolina and Georgia.

This division is based on geographic variations that led these colonies to develop in different ways. Geography is an important tool of historians since geography affects so many parts of our lives. In fact, some historians view geography as the all-important factor in history.

Consider how important where you live is to you. How does your neighborhood, your geographic location in this world, affect what you can and can not do?

Land and Climate

An area's geography helps determine its agricultural and economic life.

The geography of each of these three regions helped determine the area's lifestyle. The Southern states were blessed with rich soil, warm climate and many rivers that were navigable far inland. This combination of geographic factors helped the South become a major agricultural area. At first tobacco was the cash-producing crop, and later indigo, rice, and cotton, became important.

Tobacco cultivation was best done on large farms or plantations, and would not grow easily in the rocky soil and colder climate of Massachusetts. However, New England was covered with fine forests that provided lumber for ship building, and the ocean off the coast was full of fish. Therefore, a seafaring lifestyle developed quickly. New England farmers raised food for the area near them, but there was no large agricultural export crop, and the farms in New England remained small.

In the Middle Atlantic states, especially Pennsylvania, there was good soil but a cooler climate than that of Virginia. The Pennsylvania settlers, especially the Germans, developed large farms and raised staple crops such as wheat and corn for all the colonies.

Cities and Towns

Cities and towns, an important part of the trade and life of New England, grew up first along the sea coast and later throughout

Isaac Winslow and his Family by Blackburn
This family portrait done about 1755 by the American painter,
Joseph Blackburn, shows the Isaac Winslow family in a typical
formal pose of the period. The clothing worn by the family is typical
of that worn by wealthy Americans and Englishmen before the
Revolution. The Founding Fathers wore similar clothing during
the hot summer in Philadelphia when they wrote the Constitution.
Do you think the children would be comfortable in such clothes?

Boston, New York and Philadelphia grew into major cities before the Revolution.

New England. Boston with its excellent harbor became a thriving seaport. The cities of Philadelphia and New York—both located on rivers—became important trade centers and harbors for the Mid-Atlantic colonies. The produce from the immediate inland area came to those cities and was transported overseas or shipped to other colonies. The tidal rivers of the South allowed ships to go far inland to pick up tobacco at the docks of the plantations. There was thus no need for commercial cities in the South, and before the Revolution, Charlestown and Savannah, the largest cities of the region, were still small towns compared to Boston, New York, and Philadelphia. Thus geography affected the development of the colonies and helped establish the lifestyle of the three regions.

Economic Growth

Close to 170 years elapsed between the establishment of the first permanent English colony at Jamestown and the signing of the Declaration of Independence by the thirteen English colonies. In those years many changes occurred in the colonies and in the relations between them and the "Mother Country," England.

The 13 colonies grew in prosperity and population in the 170 years between 1607 and 1776.

Each colony grew in population, and several had immigrants who were not from England. Germans came to Pennsylvania. African-Americans were brought especially to the southern colonies.

The government structure of each colony underwent changes. By 1763 all thirteen colonies were Royal Colonies under the supervision of the King, or were under the supervision of private proprietors or owners. Life in the colonies ranged from the rather austere, church-focused life of Massachusetts merchants to the more relaxed, plantation-centered life of the Virginia aristocracy.

Prosperity grew for all the colonies, though not at an even rate. Trade increased, and each colony or region developed its own specialties just as today. New England developed her forests and fisheries as well as some manufacturing such as the making of rum. The Mid-Atlantic colonies developed agriculture, and people on the frontier in that region relied on the fur trade. Virginia and North Carolina relied on tobacco, and the more southern colonies added indigo and rice as sources of wealth. By the middle of the 18th century there were thirteen distinct colonies, but they shared many points in common.

Trade

Following mercantilist theory, the Acts of Trade and Navigation set controls on colonial trade.

Although the colonies were all under the supervision of the King or their proprietors, the colonists all shared the rights and privileges that the citizens of England had won over the years. The colonies all followed English law, and while each had an appointed governor, each also had some form of elected legislative body to check his power. The English Parliament, following the theory of mercantilism[1], passed laws to control manufacturing and trade in

---

[1]*mercantilism* A system of economic organization based on the theory that gold is wealth. A mother country attempted to control its trade with its colonies so that it achieved a greater amount of gold than the colonies. Acts of Trade and Navigation controlled trade relationships.

the colonies, but from the 1650s when the first Acts of Trade and Navigation were passed until the end of the French and Indian War in 1763, the colonists largely ignored—and the British only fitfully enforced—these laws.

New England merchants were able to develop a triangular trade system in which molasses made from sugar cane grown in the French and English colonies in the West Indies (Caribbean) was brought to New England, distilled into rum, shipped to Africa, sold for natives who were in turn sold as slaves in the West Indies in order to purchase more molasses or sugar. There were many other opportunities for trade such as selling dried fish or furs in the European market and buying manufactured goods—fancy cloth, furniture, china—to sell in the colonies.

The Southern colonies sold their agricultural products in England and bought manufactured goods there, so the Southern colonies were much more closely tied to England in their trade.

The English Acts of Trade stipulated what could be manufactured and traded. They also required that all goods go to England before being shipped to other countries. When the British began to enforce these laws after 1763, they antagonized the colonists who had grown accustomed to little control by the English government.

Military Conflict

During the 150 years after the founding of the Jamestown colony, the thirteen colonies also shared several military experiences. All the colonies shared the frontier experience of opening up new land for European settlement. This created conflicts with the Native Americans and led to several bloody encounters in different colonies. Also, all the colonies were threatened directly or indirectly by the Spanish colonies in Florida and the French colonies in Canada.

In the 18th century the French, Spanish, and English were all interested in gaining control of the area west of the 13 original English colonies. These three nations were also in conflict in Europe, and they fought a series of wars between 1689 and 1763, each of which involved the American colonies to some extent. Fortunately for the English colonies, the English either won or fought to a draw in all these conflicts.

Wars provide shared experiences for the colonists.

These shared experiences of trade, language, English law and military activity laid the foundation for the union of the colonies in 1776.

Education in the Colonies

The connection with the colonial past that probably most directly affects you at this moment is the importance placed upon education in society. Schooling was a major concern of the Puritans of Massachusetts. To ensure that the church members could all read the Bible, the colony's legislative body passed a law, "Ye Olde Deluder Satan Act," in 1642 requiring that each town provide schooling for its youth. The college of Harvard was founded in 1636 to ensure an educated leadership, especially clergy, for the colony. In New York and Pennsylvania laws encouraging schooling were

Some colonies recognize the importance of education and some establish religious toleration.

passed in the late 17th century, and apprentices were generally required to be given a certain level of formal education which was then referred to as "book learning." Today we believe education is essential in order for our citizens to participate in democratic government.

Religious Toleration

Another important link to the colonial past is our religious toleration, which can be traced back to the Act of Toleration in Maryland in 1649 and the New York Chapter of Liberties of 1683, granting freedom of religion to all Christians. Pennsylvania's laws were also very tolerant. However, other colonies such as Massachusetts were intolerant of religious diversity, and the government enforced a particular religious worship. This view was overcome in the course of our history, and our Bill of Rights established a separation of church and state.

Links to the Bill of Rights

American rights "to bear arms and freedom of the press" are rooted in colonial traditions.

Another right found stated in our Bill of Rights is that of bearing arms. Throughout colonial history the colonists were under continual military threat from other European nations and from the Native Americans. As they pushed westward into the land of the native inhabitants, the colonists had to be prepared to fight. Thus an attitude was developed about self-defense that was written into the Bill of Rights as the personal right to have a weapon.

Another right incorporated in the Bill of Rights and based on colonial experience is freedom of the press. In a famous trial in New York in 1735 Peter Zenger, a publisher, was acquitted of seditious[2] libel against the government. His paper, *The Weekly Gazette*, had published articles criticizing the government of the colony, and Zenger was arrested. His acquittal was a landmark in the history of the free press—a right we often take for granted but which is considered basic to a democratic and free society.

Control of the Purse

Another very important connection with the colonial past is summed up in the expression, "the legislative power of the purse." This phrase means that the legislative body has control of the government's budget. It appropriates money and passes tax laws. Almost all colonial legislators worked on this basis, particularly the Virginia House of Burgesses. When the English government curtailed the "power of the purse" in Virginia, the struggle for independence was not far away.

Summary

All of these important ideas that affect us today grew out of the tradition of English Common Law. Common Law was and is based

---

[2]*seditious* Attempting to undermine or overthrow a government; opposition to government power.

on the tradition of past cases and experiences. The English have never written a Constitution, but at times they forced the King to sign documents giving specific rights to his subjects. All the English colonists believed these rights extended to them—rights such as trial by a jury, bearing arms, and regular meetings of Parliament to allow the people's voice to be expressed. When the French and Indian War ended in 1763, the English government began to change its policies towards the colonies, and many colonists believed these changes threatened their traditional rights as Englishmen. This finally led to the revolt of the English colonies in America.

Colonists believe they share all the rights won by Englishmen.

Important Connections Between Colonial History and the Present

1. The importance of education.
2. Religious toleration.
3. The right to and need for self-defense.
4. Freedom of the press.
5. The power of the people to control the purse, i.e. taxation and the budget.
6. The rights of Englishmen as seen in the English Bill of Rights and Petition of Rights, for example, trial by jury.
7. The concept of a contract or written agreement as the basis of government.
8. An elected legislature chosen by the people in an area.
9. Annual meetings of the legislative body.

KEY POINT TO REMEMBER

There are important connections or links between colonial times and today especially in education, the Bill of Rights and governmental structure.

LINKS FROM THE PAST TO THE PRESENT

1. The shared experiences of the colonists tied them together; shared experiences still tie people together today.
2. The rights stated in the Bill of Rights, which we all share, are based on colonial experiences.

Questions

Identify each of the following:

Mercantilism	Peter Zenger
Boston	"Ye Olde Deluder Satan Act"
"Power of the Purse"	Maryland Act of Toleration

True or False:

1. The most important crops of the Southern colonies were tobacco, indigo and rice.
2. Geography is of little importance in the study of history.
3. Although some colonies were very tolerant of religious differences, Massachusetts was intolerant of views other than Puritanism.
4. The "power of the purse" referred to the power of the legislative body to control the budget and taxation.
5. The Acts of Trade passed by the English government were meant to control the trade of the colonies following the theory of Mercantilism.
6. The most important colonial cities were all in the Mid-Atlantic and Southern colonies.

Multiple Choice:

1. The Mid-Atlantic colonies included
    a. Massachusetts, New York, Delaware
    b. Pennsylvania, New York, Delaware
    c. Virginia, Maryland, Connecticut
2. By 1763 all thirteen colonies were either controlled by proprietors or were under the supervision of the King as
    a. his private estate
    b. economic centers of royal power
    c. royal colonies
3. All thirteen colonies had in common
    a. good harbors with large port cities
    b. the frontier experience
    c. rich soil
4. There are many connections between colonial times and the present. Two important connections are
    a. interest in schooling and the right to bear arms
    b. free press and the right to have slaves
    c. legislative control of the budget and the right of the government to control religion
5. The colonists believed they had
    a. no need to fear the French in Canada or the Spanish in Florida
    b. to obey the acts of trade and navigation
    c. the rights of Englishmen

ANSWERS

True or False: 1. T, 2. F, 3. T, 4. T, 5. T, 6. F.
Multiple Choice: 1. b, 2. c, 3. b, 4. a, 5. c.

CHAPTER 3

The American Revolution

APPROACHES TO HISTORY

Understanding the Past Through Cause and Effect Analysis

We in the western tradition of civilization are continually seeking the causes of actions. We understand the past—that is, our history—as a series of happenings, each with causes and each having an effect. Just as in personal relations we believe you are who you are because of your past, so we believe the United States as a nation is what it is because of past events, all of which had effects that in turn became the causes for other events. It is for this reason that history textbooks start far in the past and trace the cause and effect of events to the present.

Students sometimes are uninterested in the distant events, and fail to understand there is a chain connecting all of the past to the present. Some would rather study more recent or current events, but because of the cause-effect relationship, you cannot understand the present without looking at the past causes.

In our own lives we all seek causes for events, sometimes more consciously than at other times. For instance, if we lose a game, we often seek the causes—lack of practice, poor conditioning, a better coached opponent—and we plan ways to avoid our mistakes the next time. The historian does the same with the past, seeking the causes of events and trying to determine how one event led to another.

In the last chapter we saw that an event, colonization, had several different causes. In this chapter we will consider an event, the American Revolution, and trace how one event led to another in a series of actions and reactions.

While history may seem inevitable as described in the textbook, the progression of events was not inevitable since at any time people could have reacted differently than they did. However, the historian, looking back at events and putting them in order, can create what appears to be an inevitable series of causes and effects, of actions and reactions, that led in this case to American independence.

I. STEPS LEADING TO THE AMERICAN REVOLUTION

French and Indian War

The English and French fought a series of wars between 1689 and 1763.

The French and Indian War (1754–1763) was one of a series of four wars fought between England and France, and their different European allies between 1689 and 1763. These wars involved fighting both in Europe and overseas as the Europeans struggled for hegemony[1] in Europe, and control of an overseas empire. America was involved to some extent in all the wars, as the colonists fought the French in Canada and repulsed attacks on frontier settlements. The English prevailed in the first four wars and the treaties ending them either restored the status quo[2] or granted new territories to England.

The French and Indian War, called the Seven Years War in Europe (1754–1763), was the fourth of these wars. For Americans, the most famous battle in this war was the capture of Quebec in Canada by the English General Wolfe, whose British troops successfully assaulted the cliffs of Quebec and defeated the French General Montcalm at the Citadel. The most important event of the war, however, was the ambush and defeat of the English General Braddock by combined French and Indian forces near modern Pittsburgh. George Washington, a member of the Virginia militia and a surveyor who knew the area, helped save the British forces in their retreat and thus gained wide reputation—to say nothing of a lesson in tactics. It was largely because of this event that Washington was chosen to lead the colonial forces in the Revolution.

The English won a great victory over the French in the French and Indian War, but it was very costly.

The French and Indian War was very costly for the English. Besides fighting in the Americas, there was fighting in India and on the European continent. At the start of the war, the English suffered several defeats, but under the leadership of William Pitt, the King's first minister, they finally won. In the Peace of Paris signed in 1763, the French ceded to England its claim to Canada, Cape Breton, and the islands in the St. Lawrence River, as well as all territory east of the Mississippi River except the city of New Orleans. Spain, who had fought as an ally of France, ceded East and West Florida to the English, who in turn restored Cuba to Spanish rule.

The French and Indian War thus ended with the English in control of North America east of the Mississippi from Hudson Bay to the Florida Keys. The English became the dominant power in the world, but domestically they faced a huge war debt. How to pay the debt and how to govern the newly acquired territory of Canada became pressing problems for the English government. The steps they adopted to handle these two issues became the first steps in the series of events that led to the Revolution.

---

[1]*hegemony* Domination or control over another area by one country.

[2]*status quo* A situation remaining the same without change.

Wars Between England and France—1689 to 1783

Dates	Name of the War in the Americas and (Europe)	Name of Treaty	Main Terms of Treaty
1689–1697	King William's War (War of the League of Augsburg)	Treaty of Ryswick	Status Quo
1702–1713	Queen Anne's War (War of the Spanish Succession)	Treaty of Utrecht	England gains Newfoundland, Acadia, Hudson Bay
1739–1748	King George's War (War of the Austrian Succession)	Treaty of Aix-La-Chapelle	Status Quo
1754–1763	French & Indian War (Seven Years War)	Treaty of Paris	England gains Canada
1775–1783	American Revolution (War of the American Revolution)	Treaty of Paris	13 Colonies gain independence

Proclamation Line of 1763

The first step taken by the English after the war was the issuing of the Proclamation Line of 1763, declaring that there was to be no English settlement west of the Appalachian Mountains—that is, in the Northwest Territory from which Ohio, Indiana, Illinois, Wisconsin, and Michigan, were later created. The English believed conflict over this area had brought the Native Americans to the side of the French in the war. Many of the native inhabitants had followed Chief Pontiac of the Ottawa Tribe in attacks on English forts in the frontier area.

The Proclamation Line of 1763 forbids colonial settlement west of the Appalachians and antagonizes the colonists.

To the English, the Proclamation seemed a good solution to the problem of Indian rights. To the colonists, who had already begun to settle the area in small numbers, it appeared an infringement of their rights. Men such as George Washington and Benjamin Franklin—both of whom became important leaders of the Revolution—were involved in plans for land development in the Northwest Territory.

The Proclamation also stated that English law would prevail throughout the territory, including Quebec. This annoyed the French.

The effect of the Proclamation was thus to antagonize important colonial leaders, those colonists who were already settled in the area, and the French settlers of Quebec. These effects later became important causes of unrest which led to revolution.

Paying for the war

The English next faced the problem of how to pay their war debt. The war had been expensive. English taxes were already high, and the government had to keep an army in the colonies to protect the frontier and control their new Canadian possessions. The government, led by the Chancellor of the Exchequer, i.e. treasury, George Grenville, decided to raise money in the colonies by means of import duties on a number of items including molasses and sugar. The law quickly became known as the Sugar Act—the first act pased by the English Parliament[3] for the specific purpose of raising tax monies in the colonies.

The English pass the Sugar Act to raise revenue to pay for the war.

Parliament also passed a Currency Act, which forbade the issuing of paper money in the colonies and required the use of gold in business transactions. The Acts of Trade and Navigation, first passed in the 1650s had regulated trade using import duties but their purpose had not been to raise money, and the acts had never been strictly enforced. Now the English government was prepared to enforce the Acts of Trade as well as the Sugar and Currency Acts.

The colonists were shocked by these measures. They were suffering from a business recession and believed the new import duties, the required payment in gold, and the enforcement of the trade acts would further deflate their business opportunities. A town meeting in Boston denounced the laws as "taxation without representation," a slogan that became the rallying cry of colonial opposition.

The colonists react with the cry, "no taxation without representation."

Boston proposed united action. Protest spread to the other colonies. This protest took the form of non-importation agreements in which colonists agreed not to use certain goods imported from England, such as lace, and to wear only colonial made clothes. A non-importation agreement is similar to an embargo and is meant to have an impact on the economic life of a nation.

The British did not respond directly to the colonial protest but rather passed two more acts designed to alleviate their domestic economic problems. The first act, the Quartering Act of 1765, required the government of the colonies to provide barracks and supplies as needed by the English forces in the colonies. In 1766 the act was extended to require putting the soliders in inns or taverns, where they would be paid for by the colonists. The colonists saw this as an invasion of their personal privacy and of their homes. The Quartering Acts angered many colonists not affected by the revenue acts.

The Stamp Act of 1765

The second act of 1765, the Stamp Act, affected almost everyone in the colonies. To raise money to be used for the defense of the colonies, the Stamp Act required that every paper document from newspapers to playing cards carry a stamp on it. The stamps were to be purchased from colonists who were designated as stamp

---

[3]*Parliament* The Legislative, i.e. lawmaking, branch of the English government.

agents. Any lawbreakers were to be tried in vice admiralty courts, where there were no juries.

The reaction of the colonists to the Stamp Act was immediate. The act broadened the base of the opposition to England—lawyers, land speculators, publishers, merchants, tavern owners, everyone was affected—and all feared this would be only the first of many direct taxes on the colonists. The colonial economy was still suffering from the war, and leaders believed they should pay no new taxes—a cry that still resounds in American political life and that is deeply rooted in our past. Some feared that the use of vice admiralty courts would change the colonial legal system, based on the traditional rights of Englishmen to a trial by a "jury of one's peers." [4]

In reaction to these laws, several leaders of colonial opposition attacked the English in written statements incorporating new political theories on the relationship between the colonies and England. Some argued that the English Parliament could not tax the colonists but could levy import duties. Other leaders, such as Patrick Henry, turned to speech making. Patrick Henry of Virginia led a successful fight in the House of Burgesses to pass resolutions stating the English king had always acknowledged Virginia's right to govern her internal affairs, and supporting the concept of no taxation without representation.

The colonists support non-importation agreements as colonial opposition to the English government grows after the Stamp Acts.

Another effect of the laws was the formation of secret organizations, usually called the Sons of Liberty, in many towns. They often turned to violence, as they did in Boston, where the records of the vice admiralty courts were burned.

A third reaction was the calling of an intercolonial meeting, the Stamp Act Congress, which met in New York in October of 1765 with eight colonies represented. They passed a "Declaration of Rights and Grievances," claiming for the colonists all the rights of English citizens and declaring that taxation without representation in the legislature was a violation of these rights.

Non-importation gained further support, and English merchants whose exports had suffered called for repeal of the Stamp Act. Yielding to the pressure, the English government repealed the act in March 1766. At the same time Parliament passed the Declaratory Act, which claimed Parliament had the authority to pass laws for the colonies "in all cases whatever." This proved that in spite of the effect of the Stamp Act on the colonies and their reactions, the English were not ready to admit the need for a change in the relationship between colony and Mother Country. The progression of actions and reactions continued.

KEY POINT TO REMEMBER
The English after the French and Indian War had a large war debt and sought ways to get the colonists to pay some of it.

---

[4]*peer* A person of equal rank with you.

LINKS FROM THE PAST TO THE PRESENT

1. America's attitudes towards taxes, as illustrated in the pre-Revolution slogan "no taxation without representation," reflects a basic distrust of taxation and government power that runs throughout our history, including George Bush's 1988 campaign pledge, "No new taxes."

PEOPLE TO REMEMBER

Benjamin Franklin Inventor, businessman, diplomat; a resident of Philadelphia. Franklin had interest in western lands, represented the colonies in London before the Revolution, and was considered a senior statesman at the Constitutional Convention. His *Poor Richard's Almanac* is full of wisdom that has appealed to Americans throughout history.

QUESTIONS

Identify each of the following:

Proclamation Line	Quartering Act
Sugar Act	Stamp Act
Currency Act	Sons of Liberty
Non-importation Agreement	Declaratory Act

True or False:

1. Historians in the western tradition seek a cause-and-effect relationship to explain past events.
2. The English won a great but expensive victory in the French and Indian War.
3. Chief Pontiac of the Ottawa tribe refused to attack settlements in the Northwest Territory.
4. The English Parliament viewed the Sugar Act as a way of raising revenue in the colonies.
5. The Acts of Trade and Navigation had all been revenue-raising acts.
6. The cry of the colonists, "No taxation without representation," was first used by Patrick Henry in the House of Burgesses.
7. The Stamp Act affected almost every person in the colonies.
8. One colonial reaction to the Stamp Act was the formation of secret organizations such as the Sons of Liberty, who used violence.

Multiple Choice:

1. The French and Indian War ended by a treaty signed at
    a. Ghent
    b. Vienna
    c. Paris
2. The colonial response to the Sugar and Currency acts and the enforcement of Acts of Trade was to adopt
    a. non-importation agreements
    b. the Quartering Act
    c. payment in gold for all debts

3. To the English the Proclamation Line seemed a good way to
   a. gain the support of Benjamin Franklin and George Washington
   b. support French law in Quebec
   c. solve the problem of Indian rights

ANSWERS

True or False: 1. T, 2. T, 3. F, 4. T, 5. F, 6. F, 7. T, 8. T.
Multiple Choice: 1. c, 2. a, 3. c.

II   THE BEGINNING OF VIOLENCE

The Townsend Act

The English government still felt the need to raise revenue in the colonies. During this period in English history the government leadership changed quite often, and the next acts bear the name of the new Chancellor of the Exchequer, Charles Townsend. While Townsend denied the latest argument of some colonists that Parliament could not place internal taxes[1] on the colonists but could place external taxes[2], the Townsend Acts of 1767 were all external taxes—import duties on glass, lead, paints, paper, and tea. The income was to be used for the defense of the colonies and in "support of the civil government." New vice admiralty courts, again without trial by jury, were established to enforce the Townsend Acts.

Massachusetts led the way in protesting against the Act. A circular letter[3] written by Samuel Adams was sent to the other twelve colonies telling of their opposition to the Townsend Acts and calling for a renewal of non-importation agreements. English customs officials in Boston were attacked after they had seized a ship belonging to John Hancock, a merchant they suspected of not paying the duties. The custom officials requested protection, and English troops were sent to occupy Boston.

Throughout 1768 and 1769 support grew for non-importation in every colony except New Hampshire. In 1769 Virginia, again led by Patrick Henry, adopted a strong non-importation agreement—the Virginia Association—and in reaction the Royal Governor dissolved the House of Burgesses.

The colonies were quite united in their opposition to the Townsend Acts. There was general agreement that the English Parliament had no right to raise revenue in the colonies in any way. Finally, in April 1770, responding to the economic pressure, Parliament repealed the Townsend duties except for the tax on tea. Again, acts of the English met with strong reactions from the colonists, and the cause-and-effect pattern continued.

British Troops are sent to Boston to protect customs officials after violence breaks out over the Townsend Acts.

---

[1]*internal taxes*   Taxes paid by the citizens within a country, example, income or sales tax.

[2]*external taxes*   Taxes paid on goods imported to a country and paid at the point of importation, import duties.

[3]*circular letter*   A letter that is circulated or sent to several recipients.

Violence in New England

As a result of the English action, the non-importation agreements were all abandoned by mid 1771. Agitation against the British quieted. It appeared the crisis might be over, but three incidents in New England showed it was not. On March 5, 1770, an English soldier seeking part-time work and a colonial worker got into a fight. That evening bands of colonists roamed the streets in protest. Feeling threatened by these colonists, British troops fired on a crowd and five colonists died, including Crispus Attucks, a mulatto and one of the leaders of the protest.

The Boston Massacre and Gaspee incident increase tensions.

This incident, known as the Boston Massacre, raised tensions. The English soldiers were put on trial and were defended by John Adams and Josiah Quincy, both of whom were strong patriots but who also were strongly committed to the rule of law in the struggle against England. All but two of the soldiers were acquitted. The two were found guilty of manslaughter, branded on the hand, and released. Bostonians accepted the verdict but tensions remained.

The next incident occurred in June, 1772. The customs schooner *Gaspee* ran aground in Naragansett Bay. That night, armed men from Providence, Rhode Island, boarded the *Gaspee*, wounded the captain, and after removing the crew, burned the boat. It was announced that any suspects in the incident would be sent to England for trial. Soon thereafter the Governor of Massachusetts announced that he and the colony's judges would be paid by the English government and not by the colonial assembly.

The Boston Massacre, the *Gaspee* incident, the threat of trial without a jury of peers, and the loss of the "power of the purse" that gave colonial legislatures some control over the royal governors all struck at the traditional rights of Englishmen and colonial rights. Samuel Adams, a leader of the patriots' cause in Massachusetts, called for meetings to discuss this loss of rights and to establish Committees of Correspondence in each town and colony to keep the colonists informed of what was happening. The English response was to pass still another act that agitated the colonists.

Boston Tea Party

In 1773 the only duty remaining from the Townsend Acts was the tax on tea. The East India Company was the chief English producer of tea. The company was important to the government since it had extensive influence in India, but the company was close to bankruptcy. To save the company, parliament decided to take several measures. They dropped the tax on tea paid in England but kept the import tax on tea in the colonies. Then they allowed the company to sell tea directly to agents at a set price rather than at public auction.

Colonial merchants saw these actions as arbitrary. They believed that with no public auction to set the price of tea, the East India Company had in essence been given a monopoly. They also believed their profits had been undercut.

Reaction was immediate. The Committees of Correspondence spread the word quickly. Meetings in New York and Philadelphia condemned the Tea Act. In December 1773, when the Governor of Massachusetts refused to send recently arrived tea ships back to England, men dressed as Indians boarded the ships and dumped 342 chests of tea into the harbor.

The English in turn reacted strongly with a series of Coercive Acts referred to by the colonists as the Intolerable Acts of 1774. These acts were meant to punish the Bostonians for the "Tea Party." One act, the Boston Port Bill, closed the port of Boston by forbidding the unloading of all ships in the harbor. The government of Massachusetts was changed to bring it more under the King's direct control. Finally, the Quebec Act set up a permanent, highly centralized government for Canada in which Parliament was given the power to tax Quebec and the border of Canada was extended south to the Ohio River.

The colonists believed the Quebec Act threatened both their claim to "no taxation without representation" and their claims to the Northwest Territory. The stage was set for further action to unite the colonies.

The English close the port of Boston after the Boston Tea Party.

First Continental Congress

Rhode Island, New York, and Pennsylvania called for a meeting or congress of all the colonies, and Massachusetts suggested that a meeting take place in Philadelphia in September 1774. At this first Continental Congress, fifty-six leaders from twelve colonies (Georgia was not represented) gathered. Some, like Patrick Henry and Richard Henry Lee of Virginia, Sam and his cousin John Adams of Massachusetts, and Christopher Gadsden of South Carolina, were considered radicals[4] and were the leaders of the patriot[5] cause. There were, however, many outstanding conservatives[6] like Joseph Galloway of Pennsylvania, who desired to heal the growing division between England and the colonies and who later became a leader of the Loyalists[7].

The delegates decided to keep their deliberations secret and to allow each colony only one vote. These two decisions set the pattern for later colonial meetings. The Patriots introduced a series of resolutions, the Suffolk Resolves from Massachusetts, which called for the people to arm, not to obey the Coercive or Intolerable Acts, and to collect their own colonial taxes. The conservatives countered with a plan of union between England and the colonies written by Joseph Galloway.

Debate followed; Galloway's plan was defeated six to five with one abstention. A modification of the Suffolk Resolves was then

Increased violence, the Intolerable Acts and the Quebec Act lead the colonists to call the First Continental Congress.

[4]*radical*   One who favors major changes in the structure of society.

[5]*patriot*   Those colonists who supported the cause of opposition to England and eventually supported the concept of independence.

[6]*conservative*   In politics, one who wishes to keep conditions basically as they are with little or no change.

[7]*Loyalist*   Those colonists who remained loyal to the King and Parliament of Great Britain throughout the war.

While Massachusetts organizes a militia, the Minute Men, the Continental Congress organizes a non-importation embargo to force repeal of Acts of the English Parliament.

adopted. The Declaration and Resolves that the congress passed declared the Coercive Acts and Quebec Act unconstitutional, and called on the colonies to reinstate the non-importation agreements until Parliament repealed the acts.

An association to enforce non-importation was established, and the delegates agreed to meet the following May if Parliament had not changed the laws.

The colonists had resorted to an economic boycott to make Parliament change its policy, but their reaction was still peaceful.

During 1774 Thomas Jefferson in a pamphlet, *Summary View of the Rights of British America,* and John Adams in his "Novanglus" letters developed the concept of a dominion status or relationship between England and the colonies. They argued that the colonies should have their own government, and simply acknowledge the king as the head of state. This concept was later adopted by England in dealing with other colonies—Canada, South Africa, and India—but the idea was too radical at the time.

The English government offered a plan of conciliation in 1775, but it was rejected by the House of Lords, the upper house of the English Parliament. Parliament then declared Massachusetts to be in rebellion. In the meantime, Massachusetts colonists had begun to arm themselves and to organize special groups of militia, the Minutemen, who would be prepared to defend the colony at a minute's notice.

Fighting: Lexington and Concord

The Revolutionary War begins at Lexington and Concord in April 1775.

In April 1775 General Gage, commander of the English forces occupying Boston, decided to seize the weapons the Minutemen were gathering at Concord, twenty-one miles west of Boston. On the night of April 18, he secretly sent forces to seize these stores, but his plan was discovered. Paul Revere and William Dawes rode out from Boston to alert the Minutemen. Some gathered on the village green in Lexington, where they confronted the English troops. There was considerable confusion, shots were fired, and eight colonists were killed and one English soldier wounded. The British went on to Concord, where some supplies were destroyed. Then the British began the march back to Boston.

The colonists were now fully alerted, and there was fighting along the return route. Seventy-three British were killed; the Minutemen's losses were considerably less. A war had begun. Massachusetts was truly in rebellion.

The English attempt to have the colonists help pay for the costs of the French and Indian War, which seemed so logical to them, had had a devastating effect on English colonial relations and had led to another war. None of the events was inevitable, but as we look back at the period 1763–1775, we can see how colonial reactions to specific English acts, and vice versa, led in a cause-and-effect progression to war. It is this logical progression of events that the historian seeks to discover when writing history. As a student, if you look for this progression, you will become your own historian and events should be easier to understand.

Organizing for War

The Second Continental Congress met on May 10. On the same day, Massachusetts' colonists under the leadership of John Hancock seized Fort Ticonderoga on Lake Champlain. They captured a large number of cannons and other supplies from the English. The war was under way. The Congress quickly agreed to put the colonies in a state of defense and sent an appeal to the people of Canada to join them. On June 15, at the suggestion of John Adams of Massachusetts, Congress named George Washington of Virginia as Chief of the Continental forces and called for soldiers to join him.

Washington accepted the post and headed for New England to take command of the Massachusetts Minutemen, who had now become part of the Continental Army. Before Washington could arrive in Boston, General Gage declared the Americans to be in arms and rebels and offered amnesty to all who would surrender except Sam Adams and John Hancock. Instead, the Americans moved to occupy heights overlooking Boston Harbor. On June 17th General Gage attacked the colonists on Breed's Hill (known through history as the Battle of Bunker Hill) and dislodged them, but at the loss of over 1000 men.

Although hostilities had begun, the Continental Congress made one more effort at reconciliation with the King. They sent a petition, the Olive Branch Petition. The Congress rejected a proposal of the British government that still asserted the supremacy of the English Parliament over the colonies, and moved rapidly to set up a government. A post office department was established, and a commission to negotiate with Native American tribes. The non-importation agreements were changed to allow importation of arms from other countries.

In September delegates from Georgia joined the Congress. The King rejected the Olive Branch Petition and declared the colonies to be in rebellion. The Congress authorized a navy, and in December, Virginia and North Carolina militia defeated the Governor of Virginia and his Loyalist forces at Great Bridge, Virginia, and later destroyed his base at Norfolk.

The Second Continental Congress appoints George Washington chief of the colonial army and makes a final plea for peace to the English Government.

Independence

The rebellion had begun in 1775, but the goal of the colonists was not yet determined. In January 1776 a pamphlet, *Common Sense*, written by Thomas Paine, called for independence as the goal and claimed it was ridiculous to have such a little country as England ruling such a large area. Thomas Paine also blamed the King for all the problems between Mother Country and colonies. The pamphlet became very popular. By June the move for independence was strong, and the Continental Congress appointed a committee to draft a Declaration of Independence. Conress voted for independence 12–0, with New York abstaining. On July 4 the Continental Congress approved the Declaration essentially as written by Thomas Jefferson. The united colonists now had a goal for the war.

The Continental Congress votes for independence on July 4, 1776.

Articles of Confederation

The Congress adopts the Articles of Confederation as the form of government for the independent states.

A form of governmental organization was needed. The Continental Congress appointed a committee to draft a frame of government, an idea that finds its roots in the Mayflower Compact. The Committee's report, the Articles of Confederation, was not adopted by Congress until November 1777. The Articles were then sent to the individual colonies—now states—for ratification. Final approval did not come until March 1781, so throughout most of the Revolution, the Americans had no officially approved government.

This did not prevent the Continental Congress from waging a full scale war, including gaining allies. France recognized American independence in December 1777 and signed a Treaty of Alliance in 1778. Soon after, England and France were at war again, greatly helping the American cause. The War of American Independence thus became another in that long series of wars between England and France for world domination. In that series, it became the only war the English lost.

Declaration of Independence
The Unanimous Declaration of the
Thirteen United States of America

The Declaration of Independence can be divided into three sections. The first is a statement of philosophy which is based on John Locke's theory of government. The second part is a list of grievances against the King of England which provided the reasons for taking action and declaring independence. The third part is a declaration that the thirteen colonies are independent states. All Americans should be familiar with the statement of philosophy and the declaration. These form the basis of our national philosophy. They are presented here. They are followed by a set of questions to help you identify the important points in the document.

"WHEN IN THE COURSE OF HUMAN EVENTS it becomes necessary for one people to dissolve the political bands which have connected them with another, and to assume among the powers of the earth the separate and equal station to which the laws of nature and of nature's God entitle them, a decent respect to the opinions of mankind requires that they should declare the causes which impel them to the separation. We hold these truths to be self-evident: (1) that all men are created equal, (2) that they are endowed by their Creator with certain inalienable[1] rights, that among these are life, liberty, and the pursuit of happiness; (3) that to secure these rights governments are instituted among men, deriving their just powers from the consent of the governed, (4) that whenever any form of government becomes destructive of

---

[1]*inalienable*   Incapable of being surrendered or transferred.

these ends, it is the right of the people to alter or to abolish it and to institute a new government, laying its foundation on such principles, and organizing its powers in such form, as to them shall seem most likely to effect their safety and happiness.

"Prudence, indeed, will dictate that governments long established should not be changed for light or transient causes; and accordingly all experience hath shown that mankind are more disposed to suffer, while evils are sufferable, than to right themselves by abolishing the forms to which they are accustomed. But when a long train of abuses and usurpations[2], pursuing invariably the same object, evinces a design to reduce them under absolute despotism, it is their right—it is their duty—to throw off such government and to provide new guards for their future security.

"Such has been the patient sufferance of these colonies, and is now the necessity which constrains them to alter their former systems of government. The history of the present King of Britain is a history of repeated injuries and usurpations, all having in direct object the establishment of an absolute tyranny over these states. To prove this, let facts be submitted to a candid world:...[a list of grievances follows]

"In every stage of these oppressions we have petitioned for redress in the most humble terms; our repeated petitions have been answered only by repeated injury. A prince [King of England] whose character is thus marked by every act which may define a tyrant is unfit to be the ruler of a free people.

"Nor have we been wanting in attentions to our British brethren. We have warned them, from time to time, of attempts by their legislature to extend an unwarrantable jurisdiction over us. We have reminded them of the circumstances of our emigration and settlement here. We have appealed to their native justice and magnanimity[3]; and we have conjured[4] them, by the ties of our common kindred, to disavow these usurpations, which would inevitably interrupt our connections and correspondence.

"They, too, have been deaf to the voice of justice and consanguinity[5]. We must, therefore, acquiesce in the necessity which denounces our separation, and hold them, as we hold the rest of mankind, enemies in war, in peace friends.

"We, therefore, the representatives of the United States of America, in general congress assembled, appealing to the Supreme Judge of the world for the rectitude of our intentions, do, in the name and by authority of the good people of these

---

[2]*usurpations*   The illegal seizure of political power or authority.

[3]*magnanimity*   Quality of being honorable or exhibiting nobleness.

[4]*conjured*   To charge or call upon in a solemn manner.

[5]*consanquinity*   Blood relationships or any close relation or connection.

colonies, solemnly publish and declare that these united colonies are and of right ought to be FREE AND INDEPENDENT STATES; that they are absolved from all allegiance to the British crown, and that all political connection between them and the state of Great Britain is and ought to be totally dissolved; and that as free and independent states they have full power to (1) levy war, (2) conclude peace, (3) contract alliances, (4) establish commerce, and (5) to do all other acts and things which independent states may of right do. And for the support of this declaration, with a firm reliance on the protection of Divine Providence, we mutually pledge to each other our lives, our fortunes, and our sacred honor."

QUESTIONS

1. What are the four self-evident truths stated in the Declaration?
2. What are the three inalienable rights listed in the Declaration?
3. When does it become the "duty" of a people "to throw off" a government?
4. What is stated as the object of the acts of the King of England?
5. What do the colonists claim they have done in response to the King's "oppressions?"
6. What five powers do the "free and independent states" claim they now have?
7. Upon whom does the writer call for protection?

ANSWERS

1. The four truths are numbered one through four in paragraph two.
2. "Life, liberty, pursuit of happiness."
3. "When a long train of abuses and usurpation reveals a design or plan to reduce or bring them (meaning the people) under absolute despotism or tyranny."
4. The establishment of an absolute tyranny over the states.
5. "Petitioned for redress," meaning begged or asked for a change in the policy.
6. The five powers are numbered in the last paragraph.
7. "Divine providence," meaning some concept of a higher being or a God.

KEY POINTS TO REMEMBER

Neither the English nor the colonists truly understood the other's view or concerns, and the actions and reactions of each side steadily escalated until they found themselves at war.

LINKS FROM THE PAST TO THE PRESENT

1. Throughout America there has been a distrust of monopolies and the control of business opportunities by one company or group of companies, as seen in the opposition to the tea tax, anti-trust legislation, and regulation of industry.
2. The philosophy expressed in the Declaration of Independence concerning equality, inalienable rights, the purpose of government, and the right of revolution and dissent forms the core of America's beliefs and, while questioned at times during the past 200 years, still provides the basic ideology of the nation.

QUESTIONS

Identify each of the following:

Townsend Acts	Coercive or Intolerable Acts
Internal Taxes	Quebec Act
External Taxes	Continental Congress
East India Company	Olive Branch Petition

True or False:

1. George Washington had no military experience before being appointed chief of the Continental forces.
2. Thomas Paine's *Common Sense* urged independence as the goal of the struggle with England.
3. Patrick Henry was a Loyalist leader of the House of Burgesses.
4. The colonists believed the Parliament had granted the East India Company a monopoly over tea in the colonies.
5. The Boston Massacre helped to quiet the agitation and turmoil in Boston.
6. After the customs officials in Boston were attacked, they requested the protection of English troops.

Multiple Choice:

1. At the first Continental Congress the delegates
   a. were all radical leaders of the Patriots' cause
   b. decided to keep deliberations secret and to allow each colony one vote
   c. voted to approve Galloway's Plan of Union.
2. The English repealed the Townsend Acts as a result of
   a. the request of English and French merchants
   b. the urging of the East India Company
   c. the effectiveness of the non-importation agreements.
3. John Adams and Josiah Quincy defended the English soldiers accused of killing colonists in the Boston Massacre because
   a. they were forced to do so by the British
   b. they were both supporters of the English
   c. they were commited to the rule of law in the struggle against England.
4. In the fighting on Lexington Green, the Minutemen
   a. killed the English commander
   b. had been alerted the English were coming
   c. fled before the English troops arrived.

III.   THE AMERICAN REVOLUTION

To make the study of the American Revolution simpler, we will divide the conduct of the war into three regions: New England, the Middle States, and the South. We will mention only the most important battles in each region.

The Fighting in New England

The English withdraw from Boston and occupy New York.

We have mentioned the fighting at Lexington and Concord, where, according to tradition, the war began, and at Breed's Hill, which is traditionally called Bunker Hill. Both these battles occurred outside Boston. The battle at Breed's Hill provided the first real test of the ability of the colonial militia to stand up to regular English forces, which they did well. The army under Washington laid siege to Boston, and on March 17, 1776 the British withdrew their forces, sending them to New York. Washington moved his army to New York but could not stop the English from occupying the city. Washington escaped with his army across New Jersey into Pennsylvania. Matters were bleak for the Americans at that point, but the fighting had moved out of New England.

The Fighting in the Middle States

Victories at Trenton and Princeton encourage the colonists.

A victorious surprise attack on the British at Trenton, New Jersey, in December 1776, and another victory at Princeton in January, 1777 gave hope to the Americans who spent the rest of the winter camped near Morristown, New Jersey. The British planned a major attack for 1777 to cut New England off from the other states. The plan was to have three armies meet at Saratoga, New York. One army was to come up from New York City, one army was to move east from Lake Erie, and one army was to move south from Canada. The British General Howe, who was now the British Commander in New York, decided to first attack Philadelphia, the American capital. Although Washington lost battles, he delayed Howe's move north to Saratoga, and the Americans defeated the army coming from Canada at the Battle of Saratoga.

After the Battle of Saratoga, the French sign a Treaty with the colonists.

This was the turning point of the war. Although the British had occupied Philadelphia, when the French heard of the victory at Saratoga, they recognized America's independence, signed a Treaty of Alliance, and joined the war the next year. This was decisive for America.

Meanwhile, Washington spent the winter of 1777–78 at Valley Forge in Pennsylvania. The conditions were miserable in his camp, while the British enjoyed the pleasures of Philadelphia and New York, but the British withdrew from Philadelphia to New York in June of 1778 upon hearing that a French fleet was heading for New York.

For the next several years fighting in the middle Atlantic states focused on New York and on the frontier, where the English, allied with Native American tribes, perpetuated several massacres. These frightened the American frontiersmen, who organized successful attacks on British forces in the Northwest Territory. These victories allowed the Americans to claim the area at the peace conference.

An Incident of the Revolution by Jacob Eichholtz
Jacob Eichholtz (1776–1842), an American artist, painted this Incident of the American Revolution *many years after the revolution. The work of artists was the only source of visual information about war prior to the invention of the camera. The Civil War was the first war in which civilians were given direct information on what the battlefield looked like. In this painting Eichholtz has created a dramatic moment but also has provided us with information about the clothing, housing and uniforms of the time. Note particularly the source of water, the hatchet for chopping firewood, and the place of the African-American in the scene. Who do you think the person on the white horse is? Are the people surprised at seeing Washington?*

The Fighting in the South

Fighting in the South had begun in Virginia in 1775 and continued in the different southern states until the last major battle of the war at Yorktown, Virginia, in October, 1781. Lord Cornwallis, the English commander in the south, had been fighting in the Carolinas but was unable to defeat the Americans, who got supplies and recruits from Virginia. So Lord Cornwallis moved his attack into Virginia. Washington then moved south from New York, joined by a French army that had been in Newport, Rhode Island. These two armies joined the southern army led by General Lafayette, the most famous European to join the American cause, and General Von Steuben.

Lord Cornwallis established a base at Yorktown, where the English fleet could supply him. Fortunately the American and French land attack was coordinated with the French fleet, which sailed into Chesapeake Bay blocking escape or reinforcement from the sea for Lord Cornwallis. After several successful American attacks on his lines, including one led by the young Alexander Hamilton, aide-de camp[1] to Washington, Lord Cornwallis surrendered his army to Washington's forces on October 19, 1781.

General Cornwallis surrenders to Washington's forces at Yorktown on October 19, 1781, bringing the war to an end.

NORTH AMERICA 1783

- The United States of America.
- British claims not finally ceded to U.S. until the Jay Treaty of 1795.
- British possessions.
- Spanish possessions.
- Disputed and unsettled frontiers

1784 Russian settlement founded

By the Treaty of Paris, 3 September 1783, Britain recognised the independence of the United States, withdrew all military and naval forces, agreed to fix the boundary of Canada by negotiation and returned Florida to Spain.

0   1000
Miles

[1]*aide-de-camp*   A military term for a person of rank who assists a higher ranking officer.

Several British defeats by the French in the West Indies followed the American victory at Yorktown. In March 1782, the English House of Commons voted to no longer pursue the war in the colonies and the government of Prime Minister Lord North, which had run the war, resigned. Peace negotiations began, and the terms of the Peace of Paris were finally agreed upon in January 1783, ending the American War for Independence.

Terms of the Peace of Paris, 1783

The terms of the Peace of Paris were very generous for the Americans. The English recognized the independence of the thirteen colonies, gave the United States rights to fish off Newfoundland and to dry fish there, and agreed to withdraw all troops as quickly as possible. The boundaries were generous also: the United States received all the land east of the Mississippi River, south of the watershed of the St. Lawrence River, and north of Florida, which was given to Spain. Debts owed by citizens of the two countries were recognized, and it was agreed the Congress would ask the states to return properties seized from any Loyalists and restore their rights. The English were to give their forts in the Northwest Territory to the United States.

The Peace of Paris recognizes an independent United States of America.

Summary

The Peace of Paris of 1783 ended twenty years of conflict and created a new nation with a very large territory to rule. The early years of the conflict were non-violent and centered on issues of the rights of the colonists as Englishmen and on taxation without representation. Because neither side truly understood the other, the action escalated into violence by 1775 and full scale war when the colonists declared independence in 1776. With aid from the French, the United States finally forced the English to recognize their independence in 1783.

Steps Leading to the American Revolution
Action and Reaction—Cause and Effect

1763—Proclamation of 1763
1764—Sugar Act and Currency Act
1764-5—Non-importation Agreements
1765—Stamp Act
1765 and 1766—Quartering Act
1765—Sons of Liberty Organizations
1766—Repeal of the Stamp Act
1766—Declaratory Act
1767—Townsend Acts
1769—Virginia House of Burgesses dissolved
1770—Boston Massacre
1772—Committees of Correspondence
1772—Gaspee Incident
1773—Boston Tea Party
1774—Coercive or Intolerable Acts

```
1774—Quebec Act
1774—Summary View of the Rights of British America and
      "Novanglus" Letters
1774—First Continental Congress
1775—Battle of Lexington and Concord
1775—Declaration and Resolve of the Continental Congress
1775—Second Continental Congress
July 4, 1776—Declaration of Independence
```

KEY POINT TO REMEMBER
The French recognized United States' independence and joined the war after the Battle of Saratoga in 1777, and the war ended through the combined French and American victory over Lord Cornwallis at Yorktown.

LINKS FROM THE PAST TO THE PRESENT
1. Successful military operations are complex and require extensive planning, as illustrated at Yorktown.

PEOPLE TO REMEMBER
George Washington   Virginia planter; Commander of Colonial forces in the Revolution, victor at Yorktown; later President of the Constitutional Convention and first President of the United States under the Constitution; most noted of the "Founding Fathers" of the United States.

QUESTIONS
Identify each of the following:

Battle of Lexington and Concord   George Washington
Battle of Breed's Hill   Lord Cornwallis
Battle of Saratoga   General Lafayette
Battle of Yorktown   General Burgoyne

True or False:

1. Lord Cornwallis surrendered to General Washington after the Battle of Saratoga.
2. Colonel Alexander Hamilton served as aide-de-camp to General Washington at the Battle of Yorktown.
3. Valley Forge served as General Washington's winter camp while the English occupied Philadelphia.
4. The Treaty of Paris of 1783 gave to the United States all land north of Florida, east of the Mississippi River, and south of the Great Lakes and the watershed of the St. Lawrence.
5. The Treaty of Paris of 1783 was a treaty with both England and Spain.

Multiple Choice:

1. The American Revolution was fought in the following regions:
    a.   only the South and New England
    b.   New England, the Great Lakes, and the middle states
    c.   New England, the middle states, and the South

2. The British plan for the campaign that led to the Battle of Saratoga was to have
    a. three armies meet at Saratoga, splitting the colonies
    b. General Howe lead General Washington away from Saratoga
    c. the French withdraw from the war
3. The victory at Yorktown demonstrated close cooperation between
    a. the English fleet and General Lafayette
    b. the French fleet, the French army, General Washington, and General Lafayette
    c. the French and English fleets
4. What is the correct order of events leading to the American Revolution?
    a. Stamp Act, Sugar Act, Townsend Act, First Continental Congress
    b. Sugar Act, Townsend Act, Stamp Act, First Continental Congress
    c. Sugar Act, Stamp Act, Townsend Act, First Continental Congress

ANSWERS

True or False: 1. F, 2. T, 3. T, 4. T, 5. F.
Multiple Choice: 1. c, 2. a, 3. b, 4. c.

CHAPTER 4

The Constitution and the Establishment of the New Nation

APPROACHES TO HISTORY:

The Influence of Individuals

When we consider who we are and how we got that way, one factor we must consider is the influence of individuals on our lives. From our births we are influenced by other people—sometimes positively, sometimes negatively.

Think about people who have influenced you—parents, teachers, and friends you know personally; or sports heroes, political leaders, or rock and roll stars. Some of these you would like to know and be like, while others you detest and wish they would drop dead. All these people have helped to make you who you are.

The same is true in the history of a nation. There are always people who influence a nation's history and have a positive or a negative impact. Some historians explain all history as the result of the influence of individuals. What do you think? Have individuals been important in your life? Can you relate this to your study of history?

So far we have mentioned many individuals whose actions were important in the history of the United States, like John Cabot sailing to North America for England or George Washington at Yorktown. Without them, our history would have been very different.

In the first years of United States independence, the nation benefited from the leadership of many great men who have been referred to as "The Founding Fathers." These men wrote the Constitution and provided the leadership of the nation during its first twenty years of independence. If we think of them as people like us with similar strengths and weaknesses, passions and concerns, it may be easier to appreciate their contributions to United States History.

I. POST-REVOLUTION GOVERNMENT UNDER THE ARTICLES OF CONFEDERATION

The Articles of Confederation[1] provided the first government for the independent United States. The Articles were written in 1777 but were not finally approved by all the states until 1781. Maryland delayed ratification until each state that claimed land in the Northwest Territory agreed that the area would not be controlled by any existing state.

A method of government, with a plan for entrance into the union, is designed for the Northwest Territory.

Designing a method of government for the Northwest Territory was, after the winning of the war, the greatest success of this government. The Land Ordinance of 1785 required that the Northwest Territory be surveyed and divided into six-square-mile townships and that these be subdivided into thirty-six sections each. This pattern of surveying and eventual settlement can still be seen, especially in Ohio, where the rural roads follow the straight township lines surveyed after 1785, and it now seems strange to find a right angle turn in a road in the midst of a cornfield.

It was this pattern that the United States followed throughout the westward expansion. Lots were sold and the proceeds went to the United States treasury.

The Northwest Ordinance of 1787 required that three to five new states be created from the territory. Each state was to be given self government when the population reached 5,000 free adult males. When there were 60,000 free inhabitants, the new state would be admitted to the union "on an equal footing with the original states." Thomas Jefferson (as with the Declaration of Independence) was the individual behind the Northwest Ordinance, which established the policy the United States followed as it grew from thirteen to fifty states, all equal in rights. This far-sighted policy eliminated the Mother Country-Colony relationship that had plagued the English colonies until independence in 1783.

Weaknesses of the Articles

Despite that success, the Articles of Confederation proved to be a weak and ineffective frame of government. In fact, the time during which they were in operation was called the "critical period" by an early American historian, John Fisk, and the name has stuck. The writers of the Articles of Confederation, reacting against the power of the English King and Parliament, wanted to be certain the central government would be weak compared to that of each of the thirteen states. The central government was given no power to tax or to control commerce—powers the colonies had objected to in Parliament. There was no court to enforce federal laws. Executive authority was exercised by a committee of the legislature. It was difficult for the central government to conduct foreign policy. For example, it was impossible for the central government to get the

The government, under the Articles of Confederation, is unable to enforce federal law.

---

[1]*confederation*　A body of independent, separate states more or less united for joint action.

states to honor the debts owed to the Loyalists. As a result, the English refused to withdraw from some of the forts in the Northwest Territory as required by the Treaty of Paris. The central government had no way to force the states to obey its orders; the states could only be requested to provide militia and monetary contributions.

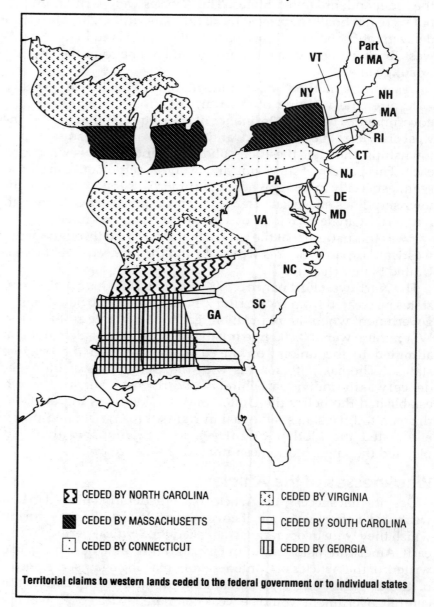

CEDED BY NORTH CAROLINA
CEDED BY VIRGINIA
CEDED BY MASSACHUSETTS
CEDED BY SOUTH CAROLINA
CEDED BY CONNECTICUT
CEDED BY GEORGIA

Territorial claims to western lands ceded to the federal government or to individual states

Responses to Economic Problems

Shays' Rebellion reveals the economic distress of farmers.

The economic situation in the United States had deteriorated badly during the war and continued to decline after 1783. Again the the central government was powerless, as each state developed policies for its own benefit. The frontier farmers were particularly hard hit. To avoid bankruptcy, many banks were forced to foreclose on their mortgages. Finally, in 1786, disgruntled farmers led by Daniel Shays rose in rebellion against the government of Massachusetts. While Shays' Rebellion was crushed, it frightened many people in the United States and encouraged a movement towards revision of the Articles of Confederation.

Just as during the American Revolution the country had split into Loyalists and Patriots with many individuals undecided, so did the country split over support for the Articles of Confederation.

Responding to economic problems between Virginia and Maryland, in 1785 James Madison and George Mason of Virginia arranged for a conference hosted by George Washington at his home, Mount Vernon. These individuals led the way in finding solutions to some immediate economic problems between Virginia and Maryland, and they also suggested that all the states gather at Annapolis, Maryland, in September 1786, to discuss commerical problems. Meanwhile, in Congress, Charles Pinckney of South Carolina proposed a reorganization of the federal government.

Many men who had been Patriot leaders were speaking out on the need for changes in the Articles. Only twelve individual delegates arrived at Annapolis so they could not accomplish much, but they sent a proposal, drafted by Alexander Hamilton, to all the states proposing a convention in Philadelphia in May 1787 to discuss commercial and all other matters. The Congress of the Confederation government finally endorsed the proposal, and the stage was set, thanks to the work of these individuals, for a major revision in the frame of government of the United States.

Patriot leaders support changes in the Articles.

Constitutional Convention

The Constitutional Convention officially opened on May 25, 1787 in Philadelphia. Fifty-five delegates, many already famous for their contributions to American independence and government, eventually participated in the Convention. George Washington was elected president. His fairness and patience contributed greatly to its success. Some of the delegates wanted merely to revise the Articles of Confederation, but Edmund Randolph introduced a plan, the Virginia Plan, which would create a new central government with a bicameral[2] legislature, an executive[3] elected by the legislature and a separate judiciary[4]. In Randolph's plan, representation in the bicameral legislature would be based on each state's population. This raised concern among the smaller states. William Patersen then introduced a plan, the New Jersey Plan, which basically retained the Articles of Confederation and gave the states equal power in the legislature but added a supreme court.

Virginia Plan introduced at the Constitutional Convention calls for a new central government.

Debate was long. We can follow the debates of the Convention through the invaluable notes taken by James Madison. The Convention operated in secrecy, which allowed delegates to discuss their opinions openly and to change their position without publicity—

---

[2]*bicameral*   A legislature (lawmaking body) that has two chambers or houses. The United States Congress is bicameral with the Senate and the House of Representatives making up the two chambers.

[3]*executive*   The branch of government which is responsible for executing the laws.

[4]*judiciary*   The branch of government responsible for judging the laws and those accused of breaking them.

something no longer possible in the U.S. government. Madison's notes were not published until 1840, four years after his death.

Debate on the Virginia and the New Jersey Plans continued until Roger Sherman of Connecticut offered a compromise, which is often referred to as the Great or Connecticut Compromise. Sherman's plan was accepted by both the large and the small states because it had something for each. His plan called for a bicameral legislature: in the upper house of the legislature, to be called the Senate, each state would have equal representation; in the lower house, to be called the House of Representatives, each state would have representation based upon its population.

Through compromises a new Constitution is accepted by the Convention.

It was through many compromises of this type that the delegates were able to finally agree upon a new frame of government for the United States—the United States Constitution. A committee of five individuals—William Johnson as Secretary of the Convention, Alexander Hamilton, James Madison, Rufus King, and Governeur Morris—actually wrote the document, incorporating all the compromises and points that had been approved in the three and one half months of debate. Finally thirty-eight of the fifty-five convention members signed the Constitution. The Convention sent the new document to Congress, which in turn submitted it to the states with the recommendation that special ratifying conventions be called in each state.

Ratification Debate

The Federalist Papers *explain the new Constitution and win votes for ratification.*

Debate immediately began on the merits of the Constitution. Those supporting the Constitution were called Federalists and those opposed were called Anti-Federalists. Many were undecided, and how they voted would determine the future of the United States.

To help persuade them, James Madison, John Jay, and Alexander Hamilton wrote a series of papers, *The Federalist Papers*, which explained and analyzed the Constitution. *The Federalist Papers* are considered the best analysis of our Constitution and of the process of democratic government ever written. These three men helped to win votes in several states such as New York and Virginia, where the debate over ratification[5] became intense. In Virginia, Patrick Henry, the Patriot and hero of attacks on the power of the English Parliament, led the Anti-Federalists while James Madison, who because of his many contributions at the Convention has been called the "Father of the Constitution," led the Federalists.

One of the strong arguments of the Anti-Federalists was that the Constitution did not protect the individual rights of the people—those same rights that had been at the heart of the struggle against England. Virginia finally ratified the Constitution 89–79 but only after a proposal to add a Bill of Rights to the Constitution was agreed to.

In New York, where Alexander Hamilton led the Federalists, defeat appeared certain. However, George Clinton, the Anti-

---

[5]*ratify* To approve or confirm formally.

Federalist leader, was out-maneuvered by Hamilton, and New York approved the Constitution 30–27.

Before Virginia and New York's ratification, the required nine states had ratified the Constitution. With the approval of nine states the Constitution was to go into effect. However, the government could never have functioned effectively if New York and Virginia had not joined the Union. The work of Hamilton and Madison was crucial for establishing the new government.

Delaware was the first state to ratify the Constitution, doing so in December 1787; Rhode Island was the last. Rhode Island first rejected the Constitution in a popular referendum[6]. However, after the other twelve states ratified and the new government was functioning, Rhode Island reconsidered and entered the Union in May 1790. The vote was 34–32 and with that close vote, the Union of the thirteen states was complete.

Narrow victories in New York and Virginia bring those states into the new government.

KEY POINT TO REMEMBER

Through a series of compromises, the Founding Fathers were able to agree on a new frame of government, the Constitution of the United States of America.

LINKS FROM THE PAST TO THE PRESENT

1. We still live under the Constitution, and if we did not, we would not be the United States we have been known as for 200 years.

PEOPLE TO REMEMBER

James Madison Virginian, called "Father of the Constitution"; his notes give us invaluable information on the Convention; later he was one of the authors of *The Federalist Papers*, which is one of the finest analyses of constitutional republican government; he introduced the amendments known as the Bill of Rights in Congress in 1789 and served as President of the United States from 1809 to 1817.

QUESTIONS

Identify each of the following:

Founding Fathers	Critical Period
Daniel Shays	Virginia Plan
Alexander Hamilton	Federalist Papers
Northwest Ordinance	Anti-Federalists

True or False:

1. The leaders of the past were people like us with emotions and personalities.
2. The Land Ordinance established a method of surveying and dividing into lots the land in the Northwest Territory.
3. The Articles of Confederation established many courts to enforce the laws passed by Congress.

---

[6]*referendum* The process of referring measures passed by a legislature to the voters for their approval or rejection in a general election.

4. Many men who had been leaders of the Patriot cause in the Revolution spoke against the Articles of Confederation.
5. George Washington served as President of the Constitutional Convention.
6. Alexander Hamilton is called the "Father of the Constitution."
7. Rhode Island was the first state to ratify the Constitution.
8. The Constitutional Convention met in Philadelphia from May to September 1787.
9. Women deliberately refused to take part in the Constitutional Convention because George Washington was a military hero.
10. Thomas Jefferson was important in the writing of the Declaration of Independence and the Northwest Ordinance.
11. The Critical Period in American history refers to the period when the ratification of the Constitution was being debated.
12. A Constitutional Convention was the idea of the Congress of the Confederation which first proposed the idea.

Multiple Choice:
1. After the winning of the war, the greatest success of the government under the Articles of Confederation was
    a. writing the Constitution
    b. creating five new states
    c. designing a method of government for the Northwest Territory
2. Economic conditions declined after the war, and particularly hard hit were
    a. farmers
    b. bankers
    c. James Madison and George Mason
3. Edmund Randolph's Virginia Plan called for
    a. a bicameral legislature based on population
    b. a Senate with equal representation for each state
    c. no judiciary
4. The Great or Connecticut Compromise called for
    a. an executive of five individuals
    b. a Senate with equal representation for each state and a House of Representatives with representation based on population
    c. the convention to operate in secrecy

ANSWERS
True or False: 1. T, 2. T, 3. F, 4. T, 5. T, 6. F, 7. F, 8. T, 9. F, 10. T, 11. F, 12. F.
Multiple Choice: 1. c, 2. a, 3. a, 4. b.

II.   THE NEW GOVERNMENT

Once the Constitution was ratified by nine states, it was to go into effect. The old congress of the Articles set the dates when the new government would begin to function and chose New York City as the temporary capital. The first elections for the House of

Representatives and the Senate were held in February 1789, and at the same time the presidential electors cast their ballots. George Washington was unanimously elected President and John Adams, Vice President. George Washington was inaugurated as the first President on April 30, 1789, in New York City.

Several executive departments were quickly created. Thomas Jefferson was named Secretary of State; Henry Knox, Secretary of War; Alexander Hamilton, Secretary of the Treasury; Samuel Osgood, Head of the Post Office; and Edmund Randolph, Attorney General. According to the Constitution it was the responsibility of the Congress to establish a court system under the Supreme Court, which they did in the Judiciary Act of 1789. John Jay was named the first Chief Justice of the Supreme Court.

George Washington is elected President, executive departments are established and a federal court system is set up.

These men, all of whom had been active in state and national government, worked together to set the basic policies for the new government. Many precedents were established that still apply today. For instance, the Constitution does not mention a presidential cabinet[1] but, by regularly meeting with his department heads, George Washington established the idea of a cabinet.

Bill of Rights

During the ratification of the Constitution, four states, in addition to Virginia, indicated the need for amendments to the Constitution to protect individual rights. Constitutional amendments to form a Bill of Rights was one of the first issues considered by the newly elected House of Representatives. Again it was James Madison who led the debate. The Federalists did not want to go through another Constitutional Convention so they responded quickly to the suggestions of the Anti-Federalists. Twelve amendments were offered to the states and ten were ratified by the requisite nine states by December 15, 1791.

The Bill of Rights, the first Ten Amendments to the Constitution, is adopted.

These ten amendments formed the United States Bill of Rights. They are the guarantee of our liberty. For over 200 years they have been interpreted by the Supreme Court. These interpretations have extended our original rights. These decisions have extended the freedoms guaranteed in the Bill of Rights to incorporate inventions such as the telephone, which was never anticipated by the Founding Fathers. The Supreme Court has said that freedom of speech forbids wire tapping. Of course, there are limits and times when wire tapping would be legal, just as there are some limits to the freedom of speech. But these limits are carefully guarded by the court and the executive branch.

The Supreme Court's interpretation of the Bill of Rights keeps it a living document.

Because of such careful decisions, the Bill of Rights of 1791 is a vital and living document, which provides Americans with freedoms enjoyed by few other people in the world. James Madison and the other individuals who worked for the adoption of these ten Constitutional Amendments deserve our respect and admiration.

---

[1]*cabinet* The leaders of executive departments who meet regularly and share responsibility of government. They give advice to the President who makes final decisions.

DOCUMENT

The Bill of Rights:
The First Ten Amendments to the Constitution

The first ten amendments adopted by the states in 1791 guarantee our individual rights as United States citizens. They reflect the period of colonial opposition to England when the colonists believed many of these rights were threatened by English action. One reason for opposition to the Constitution by the Anti-Federalists was its lack of a statement of rights. The first congress under the leadership of James Madison wrote and sent to the states these ten articles, and the states ratified them quickly. These amendments and their interpretation by the Supreme Court are important to all United States citizens. Which ones are most important to you personally?

ARTICLE I
[Basic Liberties: Religion, Speech, Press, Assembly, Redress]
Congress shall make no law respecting an establishment of religion, or prohibiting the free exercise thereof; or abridging the freedom of speech, or of the press; or the right of the people peaceably to assemble and to petition the government for a redress of grievance.

ARTICLE II
[Right to Bear Arms]
A well-regulated militia being necessary to the security of a free state, the right of the people to keep and bear arms shall not be infringed.

ARTICLE III
[Quartering of Troops]
No soldier shall in time of peace be quartered in any house without the consent of the owner, nor in time of war but in a manner to be prescribed by law.

ARTICLE IV
[Search and Seizure: Warrants]
The right of the people to be secure in their persons, houses, papers, and effects against unreasonable searches and seizures shall not be violated; and no warrants shall issue but upon probable cause, supported by oath or affirmation, and particularly describing the place to be searched and the persons or things to be seized.

ARTICLE V
[Rights of the Accused]
No persons shall be held to answer for a capital or otherwise infamous crime unless on a presentment or indictment of a grand jury, except in cases arising in the land or naval forces or in the militia, when in actual service in time of war or public danger; nor shall any person be subject for the same offense to

be twice put in jeopardy of life or limb, nor shall be compelled in any criminal case to be a witness against himself, nor be deprived of life, liberty, or property without due process of law; nor shall private property be taken for public use without just compensation.

ARTICLE VI
[Protection for the Accused in Criminal Trials]
In all criminal prosecutions the accused shall enjoy the right to a speedy and public trial by an impartial jury of the state and district wherein the crime shall have been committed, which district shall have been previously ascertained by law, and to be informed of the nature and cause of the accusation; to be confronted with the witnesses against him; to have compulsory process for obtaining witnesses in his favor; and to have the assistance of counsel for his defense.

ARTICLE VII
[Suits at Common Law]
In suits at common law, where the value in controversy shall exceed twenty dollars, the right of trial by jury shall be preserved; and no fact, tried by a jury, shall be otherwise reexamined in any court of the United States, than according to the rules of the common law.

ARTICLE VIII
[Bails and Punishments]
Excessive bail shall not be required, nor excessive fines imposed, nor cruel and unusual punishments inflicted.

ARTICLE IX
[Other Rights]
The enumeration in the Constitution of certain rights shall not be construed to deny or disparage others retained by the people.

ARTICLE X
[Powers Reserved to the States or to the People]
The powers not delegated to the United States by the Constitution, nor prohibited by it to the states, are reserved to the states respectively, or to the people.

QUESTIONS
1. Can Congress make a law limiting the freedom of the press?
2. Under what conditions may soldiers be housed in a person's house?
3. Under what conditions may a search warrant be issued?
4. When may private property be taken for public use?
5. What type of trial is guaranteed to all citizens?
6. Do people have any rights not listed in the Bill of Rights?
7. Who holds the powers not delegated to the federal government?

ANSWERS
1. No, see Article I.
2. Only with the consent of the owner or in time of war as prescribed by law.
3. Only upon probable cause when the cause is supported by an oath and the place to be searched and the person or things to be seized are described.
4. Only when just compensation or payment is given.
5. All citizens are guaranteed a speedy and public trial by impartial juries.
6. Just because a right is not listed in the Bill of Rights does not mean it is not held by the people. The Bill of Rights is not meant to limit citizen rights.
7. The powers not delegated to the federal government or denied to the states are held by the states or the people.

Hamilton's Economic Program

The greatest failures under the Articles were in the area of commercial and financial matters. The Constitution gave the new government the power to both tax and regulate commerce. Alexander Hamilton, as Secretary of the Treasury, developed a financial program for the new nation. He proposed that the United States pay at par[2] both the foreign and domestic debt acquired by the central government under the Articles and that the state's war debts be taken over and paid by the federal government.

Hamilton's economic program is designed to encourage national unity and provide security for economic activity.

Hamilton's goal was to encourage a sense of national unity and support for a government that was financially reliable and responsible. He believed such responsibility would improve business and commerce and would ultimately help the new nation.

Opposition to Hamilton's plan came from southern states that had made arrangements to pay off their debts and from those individuals who had sold their government bonds at less than par value. Support came from New England states that had large debts and from those people who had bought government bonds[3]. The House of Representatives, led by James Madison, voted down the proposed assumption of state debt by the federal government. Government was at a standstill and some resolution of the crisis was needed.

Hamilton and Madison compromise and Hamilton's economic plan is accepted.

What occurred illustrates how individuals can change history. Thomas Jefferson arranged a dinner party for Madison and Hamilton. At the dinner Madison agreed to support the assumption of state debts and in return, Hamilton agreed to support the establishment of a new capital city on the Potomac. Both had to give up something, but both gained—Hamilton, who was from New York, lost the national capital, but he got his economic plan

---

[2]*par* Equal to the value stated on a bond.

[3]*bond* Any interest-bearing certificate issued by a company or government.

accepted; Madison got the capital in his area of the country but had to accept the fact that the federal government would pay the states' war debts. It is through compromises of this type, often arranged in a personal way, that the federal government has operated since that date. The House of Representatives voted in favor of both measures.

Southerners led by Patrick Henry still objected, but Hamilton's economic plan went into effect. To provide money to pay off the debt, the plan included a tariff on many imports. Later in 1791, in order to collect more money, Hamilton imposed an excise tax on whiskey. In the years following, there was considerable opposition to the whiskey tax on the frontier, and there were cases of violence. Whiskey was important to the farmers, who turned their excess grain into whiskey that could then be sold or saved for later consumption. The farmers who objected to the tax later strongly supported Thomas Jefferson in his disagreements with Hamilton.

Arguments over the Bank of the United States

The next proposal of Hamilton's was for the establishment of a Bank of the United States. Congress approved the proposal and before signing the bill, George Washington asked his cabinet members to give him their written opinions on whether the Bank of the United States was constitutional or not. The responses represented two interpretations of the Constitution—two interpretations that still divide Americans. The first, articulated by Thomas Jefferson, supported "strict construction." This view emphasizes the 10th Amendment, which states that powers not delegated to Congress are held by the states. Nowhere in the Constitution is a bank mentioned. Therefore, according to Jefferson's view of strict constructionism, a national bank is not constitutional.

Hamilton and Jefferson disagree over a Bank of the United States and offer two interpretation's of the Constitution.

The second view, stated by Alexander Hamilton, supported "loose construction" and the ideal of "implied powers." This view of the Constitution emphasizes that every idea could not be anticipated by the Founding Fathers, and therefore everything could not be listed in the Constitution. The Constitution does give the federal government the power to tax. According to Hamilton's interpretation, implied in the power to tax is a place to keep the tax money. Therefore, a national bank is constitutional since it provides that place to keep the tax money and is thus needed in order for the government to exercise one of its stated powers.

Washington accepted Hamilton's argument. The disagreement between Jefferson and Hamilton is one base upon which the American two-party system of government is built. These two conflicting views towards government and the Constitution still guide the view of Americans. They have been combined in different ways over our history, but the attitudes of the Jeffersonians and Hamiltonians that developed during Washington's first term are still with us.

Washington accepts Hamilton's view of "loose construction" based on implied powers.

What are your opinions about government? Would you have followed Jefferson or Hamilton in 1791?

Two Views of Government—Jeffersonian and Hamiltonian

Jeffersonian

Jeffersonians distrusted strong central government. Their sympathies were with the debtors and the agrarian (farming) order, based on individuals who own their own farms. They supported a broad distribution of wealth and disliked industrialism and organized finance. They believed in the perfectability of man and that the people using representatives knew best how to govern themselves. In summary, Jeffersonians believed that the less power the federal government has, the better.

Hamiltonian

Hamiltonians supported a strong and active central government, which would encourage industry, commerce, and finance. Their sympathies were with creditors and business interests. They distrusted the people's ability to govern themselves and supported a powerful executive with an elite following. In summary, Hamiltonians believed in a strong and active government, which acted to benefit certain interests.

Differences between Hamilton and Jefferson over the role of government lead to the first political parties—Federalists and Democratic-Republican.

The Start of Political Parties

In spite of their differences, both Hamilton and Jefferson supported George Washington for a second term. It was clear, however, that their differences on government policy were leading to a personal feud. George Washington tried to reconcile the two individuals but failed. After George Washington and John Adams were re-elected, Jefferson resigned from the government. In the vice presidential election of 1792, George Clinton, the old Anti-Federalist, had won fifty votes. The Federalist, John Adams, was re-elected with seventy-seven votes. This vote, the resignation of Jefferson, and the disagreements over the role of government between Jefferson and Hamilton mark the beginning of the two-party system in the United States. The first two parties that developed under the government of the Constitution were known as the Federalists and Democratic-Republicans.

Summary

During George Washington's first term the basic structure of the U.S. government was put into place. It included executive departments, a cabinet, and the judicial structure. The Bill of Rights was added to the Constitution. The basis of the two-party system can be found in the disagreements between Alexander Hamilton and Thomas Jefferson over the Bank of the United States, their understanding of the role of government and their interpretation of the Constitution. The main concerns of George Washington's first term were the financial issues of war debt payment and a Bank of the United States. During his second term foreign policy issues became the major concern.

KEY POINT TO REMEMBER

Under the presidency of George Washington, precedents such as the cabinet were established, arguments over loose and strict construction of the Constitution were developed, and a written Bill of Rights guaranteeing individual rights was adopted.

LINKS FROM THE PAST TO THE PRESENT

1. The basic theories of loose and strict construction are still referred to in political debate, although these terms are not always used.
2. The Bill of Rights still guarantees Americans' basic liberties.
3. The structure of the government of the United States, such as the executive cabinet and departments, the powers of Congress and the states, as it was written in the Constitution or established during Washington's presidency, is still in place.

PEOPLE TO REMEMBER

Alexander Hamilton New Yorker, Aide-de-camp to George Washington at Battle of Yorktown; argued for stronger central government at Constitutional Convention; first United States Secretary of the Treasury, whose economic plans, including a Bank of the United States, supported a strong government and loose construction of the Constitution.

QUESTIONS

Identify each of the following:

Judiciary Act of 1789   Cabinet
Bill of Rights   Strict Construction
Bank of the United States   Hamiltonian view of government

True or False:

1. The first ten Amendments to the Constitution are referred to as the Bill of Rights.
2. Hamilton believed a Bank of the United States was unnecessary.
3. Jeffersonians believed the less power the federal government has the better, while Hamiltonians believed in a strong and active federal government.
4. George Washington was inaugurated as first President of the United States in 1789.
5. In a compromise between Madison and Hamilton it was agreed New York would remain the United States capital for 100 years.
6. The Founding Fathers listed every power Congress might need in the Constitution.

Multiple Choice:

1. Among the actions taken in George Washington's first term were
    a. the establishment of several executive departments
    b. a declaration of war against France
    c. the passage of the Judiciary Act of 1801

2. Hamilton's economic plans included
   a. a tax on cigarettes and gasoline
   b. a tax on whiskey
   c. forcing the states to pay their war debts
3. The beginning of the two party system in the United States can be seen in
   a. the vote over the Bill of Rights
   b. the resignation of Jefferson from Washington's cabinet and his disagreement with Hamilton over the role of government
   c. the Anti-Federalists' dislike of Washington's authority
4. Among the members of the first United States cabinet were the following:
   a. John Jay, Alexander Hamilton, James Madison
   b. Alexander Hamilton, Thomas Jefferson, John Jay
   c. Thomas Jefferson, Henry Knox, Alexander Hamilton

ANSWERS

True or False: 1. T, 2. F, 3. T, 4. T, 5. F, 6. F.
Multiple Choice: 1. a, 2. b, 3. b, 4. c.

III   THE FRENCH REVOLUTION'S IMPACT ON AMERICA

United States Reaction to the Start of the French Revolution

The French Revolution began in 1789, and most Americans seemed to support it. The Revolution appeared modeled on our own revolutionary fight for individual rights. The French Revolution began with protests but gradually grew more violent. In 1792 the French established a repubican government and in January of 1793 beheaded their King, Louis XVI. In February, France declared war on Great Britain, Spain, and Holland. The final war in the 150 year series of wars between the English and the French had begun.

American attitudes toward the French Revolution began to change. Again Thomas Jefferson and Alexander Hamilton represented the two opposing views. Thomas Jefferson, who had served as United States representative to France, supported the revolution and viewed it as a fight to extend individual rights. Alexander Hamilton saw the revolution as a threat to established government. He sympathized with the English and supported economic ties with our former enemy. Neither Jefferson nor Hamilton wanted the United States to become involved in the war. Both supported American neutrality[1].

As you recall, however, in 1778 the United States had signed a treaty of mutual support with France. France had supported the United States in the war for independence. This treaty was still in

Hamilton supports England and Jefferson supports France at the start of the war between England and France.

---

[1]*neutrality*   The state of being neutral or uncommitted, not taking sides.

effect. Technically it had been signed with the Royal Government of France, which had been overthrown. George Washington used this technicality to proclaim United States neutrality, stating that we were at war with neither England nor France. United States citizens were warned not to support either side.

Washington declares United States' neutrality.

It was a wise move for the young republic not to become involved in the war yet it clearly indicated how national needs often take precedent over written documents when individual leaders make decisions affecting national policy. Commitments to a nation such as a treaty are often disregarded by later leaders.

Negotiations with England and Spain

Actions of both the English and the French during the War of the French Revolution affected the United States. First, the French government's representative, Citizen Genet, commissioned privateers to attack English shipping. Washington asked for his recall to France, but Genet remained in America as a private citizen and married a daughter of George Clinton.

Second, the English issued orders in council in 1793 whose enforcement led to the impressment[2] of United States ships and sailors. We were close to war with England, yet George Washington's government needed the trade with England to maintain its financial stability. Import duties on imported English goods were the main source of revenue for paying off the national debt.

There were other disagreements with the English, such as the British failure to evacuate their forts in the Northwest Territory as was stated in the Peace of Paris. Washington decided to send a special envoy[3], John Jay, then Chief Justice of the United States, to England to negotiate the issues and avoid war. The result, Jay's Treaty of 1795, was not popular. Jeffersonian Republican members of the House of Representatives attempted to block the treaty, but Washington established another important precedent for later presidents when he refused to provide the House with all of the legal papers involving the Treaty negotiations.

Jay's Treaty resolves differences between the United States and England.

By the terms of Jay's Treaty the British agreed to withdraw from the Northwest forts, opening the area to United States settlement and giving the United States control over the area's valuable fur trade. Other issues of concern, such as impressment, were to be resolved by commissions or were not mentioned. Alexander Hamilton strongly supported the Treaty and wrote papers arguing for its passage. The Jeffersonian Republicans opposed it, but it was ratified by the Senate.

The United States also had continuing disagreements with Spain over the terms of the Peace of Paris of 1783. By the efforts of Thomas Pinckney, United States Minister to England, these were resolved in Pinckney's Treaty. In Pinckney's Treaty, Spain and the United

---

[2]*impressment* The practice of the British forcing American sailors into service on British warships under the assumption that they were escaped British seamen and not accepting the fact that they were American citizens.

[3]*envoy* An official representative from one country to another.

Pinckney's Treaty with Spain provides the United States free navigation on the Mississippi River.

States reconfirmed the Mississippi River and the 31st Parallel as the United States boundary.

The Treaty also granted the United States free navigation on the Mississippi and the "right of deposit" in New Orleans. This allowed settlers in the area west of the Appalachians to have a water route to ship their produce abroad. It was an important development for the west whose population was growing. It also tended to tie the west to the south. This alignment remained until the Erie Canal and railroads made it possible for those in the Northwest Territory to ship their produce east.

By the end of Washington's second term, the terms of the Peace of Paris were honored, and the United States had established her neutrality in the War of the French Revolution.

Washington's Farewell Address

Washington retires and gives advice for the future in a Farewell Address.

In September 1796 a Philadelphia paper published what has become one of the most often quoted documents in United States history, Washington's Farewell Address. In it Washington explained why he would not seek a third term as President, a precedent followed until World War II, and now incorporated into the United States Constitution as Amendment XXII. He also gave three other often quoted bits of advice to the American public based on his own individual perceptions.

First, he argued the dangers of political parties, particularly if they were to follow geographic divisions. The nation has ignored his advice on parties only once. In 1860, just before the Civil War, our parties divided on strictly geographic lines. Washington's advice was good.

Second, he urged the nation to rely on "temporary alliances for extraordinary emergencies" and to avoid permanent alliances with foreign powers. Again, the policy was followed until after World War II. Some people still believe we should not join alliances as we did in the post-war period but instead remain isolated.

Third, Washington argued that the credit or reliability of debt payment by the United States must be cherished. We still acknowledge this concept, but since World War II we have had more and more difficulty controlling the debt of the United States.

Washington's advice is still quoted by political leaders. It again illustrates the important role an individual can play in history and illustrates what an important contribution George Washington made to the history of the United States—Commander of the Revolutionary Army, President of the Constitutional Convention, and first President of the United States.

The Presidential Election of 1796

The Presidential Election of 1796 illustrated how divided the country had become and how the party system, deplored by Washington, was already established. John Adams, the Federalist, was elected with 71 votes in the Electoral College[4] and Thomas Jefferson, whose followers would soon be designated as members of the Democratic-Republican party, was elected Vice President with 68 votes. Thus we had a president and vice president from different political parties.

John Adams is elected the second President.

The main issues of John Adams' presidency dealt with foreign policy and United States attempts to avoid involvement in the European war between France and England.

XYZ Affair

In reaction to Jay's Treaty and the apparent closeness of the United States to England, the French began interfering with United States shipping. In 1797 President John Adams sent three envoys to negotiate the United States-French differences. In Paris the French Foreign Minister, Talleyrand, delayed negotiations and sent three representatives, who were later designated as X, Y, Z, to seek bribes and a loan for France. Two American envoys immediately returned home.

A record of the French actions, which became known as the XYZ Affair, was made public early in 1798. There was a strong reaction against France and talk of war. Defense measures were taken including the establishment of the Department of the Navy. There were several naval skirmishes between 1798 and 1790. The Federalist Party split into two factions—one anti-war group led by Adams and a pro-war group led by Alexander Hamilton. Adams decided to negotiate with France. The resulting Convention of 1800 ended the Treaty of 1778. The Senate approved the Convention, which ended the threat of war.

The XYZ Affair splits the Federalist Party.

Alien and Sedition Acts

The threat of war with France had led to a fear of foreigners. Many leading Democratic-Republican writers were foreign born, and they were pro-French. The Federalists, feeling threatened by the Democratic-Republican writers and fearing France, passed four laws known collectively as the Alien and Sedition Acts. These Acts increased from five to fourteen years the period of residence required to become a citizen and allowed the President (1) to send from the country aliens considered dangerous, (2) to arrest aliens in case of war, and (3) to punish anyone forming groups to oppose

The Alien and Sedition Acts reflect American fear of foreigners.

---

[4]*Electoral College* The Electoral College elects the President and Vice President of the United States. It was established in the Constitution to avoid direct elections of the president. Every state has as many electors in the Electoral College as it has Senators and Representatives combined. The process by which electors are chosen have shifted over the years. The electors were originally voted for by state legislatures. Today they are voted for by the people in the general election in November every four years. The electors together make up the Electoral College. They vote for president and vice president. Today they vote as the people in their state voted but at the beginning of United States history they voted for whomever they wished. The original idea was to take the election of the president out of the control of the masses and put it in the control of specially elected state leaders who would be able to pick the best person for the presidency.

The Democratic-Republicans disagree with the Alien and Sedition Acts in the Kentucky and Virginia Resolutions and set forth a Theory of Nullification.

national laws or publishing writings that brought disrepute on the government or congress. The latter provisions would stifle opposition to the government, and the Democratic-Republicans attacked the laws as unconstitutional and an infringement on the Bill of Rights.

As an individual, how would you have reacted to the Alien and Sedition laws?

Kentucky and Virginia led the attack on the Alien and Sedition Acts. Both state legislatures (Kentucky had become a state in 1792) adopted resolutions calling the Acts unconstitutional.

Thomas Jefferson wrote the Kentucky Resolutions and James Madison the Virginia Resolutions. Both the Kentucky and Virginia Resolutions argued that the Constitution was a contract between states, and when laws passed by the federal government were unconstitutional, it was the duty of the states to stop the evil and to nullify the law. This argument is known as the Theory of Nullification[5].

The Theory of Nullification was resorted to on several other occasions before the Civil War to object to federal government actions that some groups felt infringed upon the rights of the states. The Theory of Nullification formed an important part of the concept of states rights. States rights are still invoked by many American leaders. The basis of the nullification argument is the idea that the states created the union, and as the 10th Amendment states, powers not "delegated to the United States" are reserved to the states respectively or to the people.

The Theory of Nullification and the concept of a strict construction of the Constitution form the cornerstone of the States Rights argument. They were both firmly stated by Thomas Jefferson, who believed in the rights of the individuals and the states over the rights of a powerful federal government.

Presidential Election of 1800

After a tie in the Electoral College, Thomas Jefferson is elected the third President by the House of Representatives.

The Alien and Sedition Acts became a major issue in the Presidential Election of 1800. The Electoral College vote ended in a tie between Thomas Jefferson and Aaron Burr. Both were Democratic-Republican candidates, and each had 73 votes. John Adams had 65; C. C. Pinckney, 64; and John Jay, 1.

The Federalists controlled the House of Representatives, where the final decision between the leading candidates had to be made. In spite of his personal feud with Thomas Jefferson, Alexander Hamilton supported Jefferson, who won the election on the 36th ballot cast in the House of Representatives. Aaron Burr became the Vice President. Burr, who was also from New York, never forgave Hamilton, with dire consequences. In 1804 Aaron Burr shot Hamilton in a duel.

After the election of 1800 congress proposed the 12th Constitutional Amendment, which established separate voting by the electors for President and Vice President.

---

[5]*nullification* Making invalid or inoperative.

Before leaving office John Adams had the opportunity to appoint a Federalist, John Marshall, Chief Justice of the Supreme Court. His leadership and decisions over the next years provide another important example of the role of the individual in shaping history. Also in 1801 a Judiciary Act was passed, enabling Adams to appoint a number of new judges. He appointed Federalists to these posts. This meant that the Federalist Party would have considerable power even though the new president was from the Democratic-Republican party.

These two acts, the appointment of Marshall and the appointment of federal judges, illustrate the significance of the federal court system in our nation. Today it is as important as it was in 1801, and a President's appointments to the courts can assure a continuation of his, or his party's, policies long after he is out of office.

Summary

The period of United States history from 1783–1801 particularly illustrates the theory that history is made by individuals. These two decades were dominated by our Founding Fathers. The individual contributions of these men to our history is so great and so complex that it cannot be calculated. Their understanding of human nature, their philosophy of government, their reactions to crisis, their feuds and disagreements helped shape the nation we have today. What kind of a country would have developed if there had been no George Washington, Thomas Jefferson, Alexander Hamilton, John Adams, James Madison, or Edmund Randolph?

That no women have been mentioned in this chapter may seem unfortunate but reflects the realities of political and economic life of the period. The wives, Martha Washington and Abigail Adams particularly, played important roles but not on the center stage.

KEY POINT TO REMEMBER

During the first twelve years under the Constitution, ideas were developed—such as nullification and states' rights—and a philosophical foundation of individual rights was established, all of which are still part of our government and affect each of our lives today.

LINKS FROM THE PAST TO THE PRESENT

1. The tension between national needs and treaty obligations must always be considered in foreign policy decisions.
2. The advice of George Washington in his Farewell Address has been quoted throughout our history to support isolation and to deplore partisan politics.
3. Supreme Court justices often remain on the Court for many years and so have a great influence on the nation.
4. The argument for states rights as dominant over the power of the federal government (the basis of the Theory of Nullification) is still used today.

PEOPLE TO REMEMBER

John Adams Massachusetts Patriot and lawyer; defender of English troops accused of the Boston Massacre; first Vice President and second President (1797–1801) of the United States, avoided United States' involvement in wars of the French Revolution.

QUESTIONS

Identify each of the following:

Jay's Treaty

12th Amendment

Washington's Farewell Address

Kentucky and Virginia Resolutions

Alien and Sedition Acts

Convention of 1800

True or False:

1. The French Revolution had little impact on the United States.
2. In his Farewell Address Washington urged the United States to sign alliances with European nations.
3. The XYZ Affair almost led to war with France.
4. Thomas Jefferson and Aaron Burr received an equal number of electoral votes for president in 1800.
5. The Judiciary Act of 1801 allowed the new president, Jefferson, to appoint new judges in all federal courts.
6. Although the United States had a Treaty of Alliance with France, George Washington proclaimed our neutrality.
7. The farmers of the West benefited from the "right of deposit" obtained in Pinckney's Treaty.
8. The Theory of Nullification is based on the idea the United States was created by the people, not by the states.

Multiple Choice:

1. The theory of states rights includes
    a. a strict construction of the Constitution
    b. the idea that the Constitution is a compact between the states
    c. both of the above.
2. During the Washington and Adams administrations the United States
    a. almost went to war with England, then with France
    b. was not affected by the French Revolution
    c. proclaimed neutrality, which was respected by both the French and English.
3. The Alien and Sedition Acts
    a. allowed the government to punish anyone forming groups to oppose national laws or publish writings bringing disrepute on the government
    b. decreased the period of residence required for citizenship from fourteen to five years
    c. were directed at Federalists and their friends.

4. The terms of the Peace of Paris of 1783 finally were honored after the United States
    a. threatened to go to war with England again
    b. began the impressment of English seamen
    c. negotiated and ratified Jay's Treaty and Pinckney's Treaty.

ANSWERS

True or False: 1. F, 2. F, 3. T, 4. T, 5. F, 6. T, 7. T, 8. F.
Multiple Choice: 1. c, 2. a, 3. a, 4. c.

CHAPTER 5

Sectionalism and Nationalism: 1801–1850

In the 19th century several famous American historians wrote histories of the United States assuming the young nation was particularly blessed. The idea is still a popular way of looking at our history. As we grew as a nation, it certainly seems we were unusually blessed or lucky, whether it was in establishing the original colonies, winning the American Revolution, or writing the Constitution. Good fortune generally continued to bless the American nation in the first half of the 19th century.

I. THE REVOLUTION OF 1800 AND JEFFERSON'S PRESIDENCY

The election of Jefferson as President in 1801 has been considered by some a peaceful revolution. After twelve years of Federalist rule, a new party, the Democratic-Republicans, moved into power. In his inaugural address, Jefferson spoke of continuity and reconciliation after the prolonged voting procedure in the House of Representatives. The Judicial Act of 1801 was repealed and attempts were made to remove Federalist judges, but the country weathered the transition of power easily. The Constitution worked. There was a lot to be proud of as an American.

Jefferson's election marks a peaceful revolution.

Barbary Pirates

In spite of the foreign policy successes of John Adams, the United States was not fully respected by other nations. For years, pirates had disturbed commerce along the Barbary Coast of North Africa, which includes modern Algeria, Morocco, Tripoli, and Tunisia. Safety could be purchased through paying tribute or bribes to the pirate states. Washington and Adams had done so. In 1801 the Pasha of Tripoli increased his demands, and declared war on the United States.

Jefferson provides strong presidential leadership in his attack on the Barbary Pirates.

Jefferson had opposed a navy and wanted peace, but he was determined to confront the pirates of Tripoli to defend American commerce. This support of the free passage of all ships on the open seas has been a continuing policy throughout United States history.

A blockade of the pirates proved successful. A treaty was signed with Tripoli in 1805, which freed United States commerce from the payment of tribute although we continued to pay tribute to the other Barbary states. This incident gave a boost to national pride and provides an important line in the United States Marine Hymn: "From the Halls of Montezuma (in Mexico) to the shores of Tripoli."

In this situation, Jefferson had gone against his party's sentiments for peace in order to pursue what he perceived to be the good of the nation. He thus provided a precedent for strong presidential leadership.

The Louisiana Purchase

The Louisiana Purchase doubles the size of the nation.

In another incident of nationalism Jefferson again went against his former ideas. Given the opportunity to purchase the Louisiana Territory—the area between the Mississippi River and the Rocky Mountains—from France, which had recently acquired it from Spain, Jefferson supported the purchase.

Jefferson believed French control of the territory and particularly of the city of New Orleans, which could block transport on the Mississippi River, was a threat to the United States. Jefferson believed control of the Mississippi River would provide an opportunity for the yeoman farmers, whom he supported, to move further west and have free transport to the sea.

Such a purchase was not mentioned in the Constitution, so Jefferson had to abandon his "strict construction" on this issue. Such flexibility was deplored by some of his supporters, but Jefferson's purchase greatly increased the size of the United States and removed a potential French threat. It provides another precedent for presidential leadership and an example of flexibility in response to different situations.

Lewis and Clark explore the Louisiana Territory.

Much of the Louisiana Territory was unexplored when it was purchased. To develop relations with the Native Americans and to develop routes to the west, Jefferson sent Merriwether Lewis and William Clark on a three-year, very successful exploratory trip through the northern part of the territory. Lewis and Clark's trip opened the territory for settlement and inspired future explorers. In turn, these added to the United States sense of nationhood.

New states enter the Union as the frontier moves west.

Since the first settlements in Virginia and Massachusetts, there had always been individuals moving west. Life on the frontier was always a challenge. Men led the movement westward, and the few women who came were "quickly married." Life was often lonely and quite isolated, but those on the frontier moved quickly to establish communities. By 1803, with the admission of Ohio, the union had grown to seventeen states—Vermont, 1791; Kentucky, 1792; Tennessee, 1796; Ohio, 1803. By 1821 there were twenty-four states. These new states were to play an important role in the development of national policy.

Napoleonic Wars: Non-Importation and Embargo

The Napoleonic War impacts on American shipping and freedom of the seas.

After a brief peace in 1802, the English-French conflict in Europe—known during its first years as the War of the French Revolution and after Napoleon took power as the Napoleonic War—broke out again in 1803. Unable to defeat the other nation decisively, both sides turned to attacks on commerce of noncombatant[1] nations. In spite of attempts by Jefferson and his successor, James Madison, to remain neutral, American commerce was affected.

---

[1]*noncombatant*   A neutral nation or person not involved in the war or conflict.

Buckland, Mass.
This View of Buckland, Massachusetts *by an anonymous American painter shows a typical small New England town of the early 19th century. What buildings can you identify? What would you expect to see at a small town crossroads today?*

The English again impressed American seamen. A legal precedent, the "broken voyage," which allowed goods from the West Indies to be landed in the United States, go through customs, and then be shipped to France as American goods, was reversed by an English judge in 1805. After the judge's decision, ships carrying such goods were seized by the English in their blockade of the French ports. The United States retaliated with a Non-Importation Act listing many goods that were not to be imported from England. An attempt to negotiate with the English failed.

In June 1807 a British warship in United States territorial waters attempted to take four sailors from a United States navy frigate, the *Chesapeake*. When the United States officers refused, the British fired on the ship, killing three Americans. The nation was close to war, but Jefferson avoided it and retaliated with an embargo to be effective in December 1807.

Non-importation and embargoes have little effect.

The Embargo of 1807 won Jefferson support in the West and the South but upset many East Coast merchants. The embargo stopped all trade in United States ships with any foreign nation, and restricted our coastal shipping. Smuggling quickly began and Napoleon, suggesting he was aiding the United States, began to seize all United States ships, saying that since the embargo forbade them to leave the United States, they must actually be English ships. United States trade suffered greatly and opposition to the embargo grew, particularly in New England. The sense of national unity was threatened.

Fighting on the Frontier

Westward expansion and the frontier area added another dimension to the growing national tension. Two Native American leaders, Chief Tecumseh and his twin brother, the Prophet, realized that the white settlers would keep coming and wanting more land in spite of treaties. Chief Tecumseh organized tribes in the old Northwest Territory in a defensive alliance.

Chief Tecumseh organizes Native American opposition to westward expansion and is defeated at Tippecanoe.

Settlers were certain the English supplied weapons and encouraged Tecumseh's attacks. New leaders in Congress, particularly Henry Clay from Kentucky and John C. Calhoun of South Carolina, helped stir up sentiment against England. This created a greater regional split. The West wanted war with England, while New England disliked the embargo against England and wished to open up trade. Both regions believed they were supporting what was best for the national interest. Those Congressmen who supported a war with England were referred to as War Hawks—the term *hawk* has been used often in United States history to describe individuals who want to use military strength in a crisis.

Taking pre-emptive action, General William Henry Harrison, in 1811, attacked Tecumseh's forces at Tippecanoe, burned his village headquarters and ended the Indian threat, but the attack did not stop the anti-English sentiment of the westerners.

Economic Warfare

In the meantime, opposition to the embargo had grown and it was repealed in 1809. Jefferson still wished to pursue an economic policy against England. A Non-Intercourse Act replaced the embargo. The Non-Intercourse Act opened trade with all nations except England and France. The Act stated that if either England or France stopped harassing United States shipping, trade would be opened with that nation. At this point James Madison became President. Jefferson, following Washington's precedent, refused to seek a third term. Madison continued Jefferson's attempts to avoid war through economic pressure just as the colonists had used it against England in response to the Stamp Act.

Economic measures appear to fail, and the War Hawks from the West push Madison to ask Congress to declare war on England.

In the next three years, 1809–1812, both England and France agreed verbally to change their policies towards United States shipping but failed to follow through. The War Hawks scored election victories in November 1810 and Henry Clay was elected Speaker of the House of Representatives. Continued impressment, which was viewed as an outrage on the national honor, and the Native American threat on the frontier played into the hands of the War Hawks. Finally, Madison asked Congress to make defense preparations.

He still continued to negotiate with the English, who insisted the United States interpretation of French actions was wrong. The English were facing economic distress and on June 16, 1812 finally agreed to accept the United States position. Unfortunately Madison had asked Congress for a declaration of war on June 1, 1812, and war was voted on June 18. The War of 1812 had begun.

Diplomacy and economic pressure appeared to have failed, yet if there had been faster communication across the Atlantic, it would have been otherwise. The War of 1812 should never have been fought, since the English had accepted the United States position two days before war was voted by Congress. The war, as do wars generally, created strong nationalist sentiment among some Americans. The West and South strongly supported the war; however, New York and New England were not as enthusiastic.

The War of 1812

There were three major areas of fighting during the war. The United States mounted an unsuccessful attack on Canada (Quebec)

Constitution vs. Guerriere
This scene of the battle between the U.S. Constitution and the British ship, Guerriere, was painted by an anonymous American after the battle. What can you learn from this painting about the battle and the way ships were armed and rigged?

but did win some successes on the Great Lakes; the English attacked Baltimore, Maryland, and burned the capitol, Washington, in a raid; the United States fought successfully in the southwest, where the great hero of the war, Andrew Jackson, defeated the English at the Battle of New Orleans on January 8, 1815.

Andrew Jackson wins fame at the Battle of New Orleans.

Unfortunately, this battle was fought two weeks after the United States and England had signed the peace treaty. Thus, in the war that should not have been fought, the greatest United States victory came after the war was over. Again we have an illustration of the slowness of communication in the era.

Treaty of Ghent

The Treaty of Ghent restores the status quo.

The terms of the Treaty of Ghent restored the prewar conditions. Prisoners were released, territory restored, and a commission of arbitration established to settle the United States-Canada boundary. No mention was made of impressment or other matters of maritime law that had been the major cause of the war.

Some historians have referred to the war as the second American War of Independence. The United States fought the English to a draw and lost no territory. The war confirmed the integrity and viability of the new nation. It enhanced the sense of nationalism in most of the country. The Federalists of New York and New England who opposed the war lost their national support and died as a political party.

The Hartford Convention

The Federalists lose political influence after the Hartford Convention.

The final act of the Federalists, one that sealed the fate of the party, was the calling of the Hartford Convention, which met from December 1814 into January 1815. The Convention was called because the Federalists were upset by the use of economic warfare and the declaration of war in 1812.

While its proposals for change were not radical, the meetings were held in secret, following the tradition of the Constitutional Convention. This made the Convention appear a secret plot to destroy the nation. The Democratic-Republican opponents accused the members of the Hartford Convention of sedition and treason. In reality, its program was a restatement of Jefferson's and Madison's ideas expressed in the Kentucky and Virginia Resolutions calling for the nullification of "infractions of the Constitution."

Thus a truism of American political life was established—those out of office call those in office to strict accountability to the Constitution, while those in office, for example Jefferson making the Louisiana Purchase, will stretch the meaning of the Constitution.

KEY POINT TO REMEMBER

The United States under Presidents Jefferson and Madison used economic measures to avoid being pulled into the Napoleonic War.

LINKS FROM THE PAST TO THE PRESENT

1. Freedom of the seas has always been one of the United States' foreign policy goals.

2. The United States has resorted to a hawkish approach to solving international problems many times from the War of 1812 to the invasion of Panama in 1989.
3. Economic boycott as a way to force other nations to change their policy has been used by Americans from the nonimportation agreement of the pre-Revolutionary period to the United Nations sanctions invoked during the Persian Gulf crisis in 1990.
4. Usually the party in power has supported loose construction, and the party out of power has supported strict construction.

PEOPLE TO REMEMBER

Thomas Jefferson Virginia planter and gentleman, author of the draft of the Declaration of Independence and Land Ordinance upon which the Northwest Ordinance was based; Washington's first Secretary of State; supporter of strict construction of the Constitution and Theory of Nullification (Kentucky Resolutions); third President of the United States (1801–1809); founder of the University of Virginia; author of Virginia Statute for Religious Freedom.

QUESTIONS

Identify each of the following:

Pirates of Tripoli	Chief Tecumseh
Louisiana Territory	Henry Clay
Embargo of 1807	James Madison
Battle of New Orleans	Treaty of Ghent

True or False:

1. The rhetoric of nationalism often includes references to the special qualities of one's nation.
2. Thomas Jefferson's election in 1801 has been considered an example of violent revolution.
3. Nowhere can one find in the Constitution a statement giving permission for the President to purchase territory for the country.
4. The Napoleonic War in Europe had a direct effect on United States' commerce.
5. General William Henry Harrison won the support of Chief Tecumseh and his brother the Prophet through negotiation.
6. Jefferson's use of the embargo had a bad impact on New England commerce.
7. Economic pressure was used by the United States before both the Revolution and the War of 1812 in an attempt to achieve goals without war.
8. The Federalists' Hartford Convention gave them new strength as a political party.
9. The Non-Importation Act under Jefferson forbade the importation of any goods from England, France, or any noncombatant nation.

10. The United States' victory at the Battle of New Orleans forced the English to sign the Treaty of Ghent.

MULTIPLE CHOICE

1. Which one of the following opened United States' trade to all nations except England and France?
   a. Non-Intercourse Act of 1809
   b. Embargo of 1807
   c. Non-Importation Act of 1806.

2. The fighting in the War of 1812 took place in the following major areas:
   a. Canada and the Great Lakes, Baltimore/Washington, the Southwest/New Orleans
   b. The Southwest/New Orleans, the Great Lakes, the West Indies
   c. Canada and the Great Lakes, the Southwest/New Orleans, the Oregon Territory.

3. Leaders of the War Hawks were
   a. James Madison and Thomas Jefferson
   b. Merriwether Lewis and William Clark
   c. Henry Clay and John C. Calhoun.

4. The War of 1812 need never have been fought because
   a. the Treaty of Ghent basically reaffirmed the status quo
   b. the British government accepted United States' terms before the Congress declared war
   c. the Battle of New Orleans was fought after the treaty was signed.

ANSWERS

True or False: 1. T, 2. F, 3. T, 4. T, 5. F, 6. T, 7. T, 8. F, 9. F, 10. F.
Multiple Choice: 1. a, 2. a, 3. c, 4. b.

II.   THE ERA OF GOOD FEELINGS AND THE JACKSON PRESIDENCY

The political issues of the Era of Good Feelings were the Bank of the United States, tarriffs, and internal improvements.

With the demise of the Federalist Party, James Monroe was overwhelmingly elected to the Presidency in 1816. It took time for new political combinations to be developed. This period immediately after the War of 1812 has been called the Era of Good Feelings. In 1820 when James Monroe was re-elected to a second term, he won by 231 votes to 1 in the Electoral College.

Domestic issues during the so-called Era of Good Feelings focused on the need for a Bank of the United States, since the first bank's charter was due to expire, on tariffs, and on improvement of internal transportation. These three issues eventually led to conflict over sectional needs and Constitutional interpretation. The Southern states preferred low tariffs because they imported many goods while exporting agricultural products. The East desired higher tariffs to protect its growing industries. The West desired better transportation routes, particularly between the West and the growing markets in the East.

Domestic Affairs

During Monroe's presidency the Republicans reversed their stand from Jefferson's original view on the bank and voted to recharter it in 1816. President Monroe would not accept the loose interpretation argument that the phrase in the Preamble of the Constitution, to "promote the general welfare," permitted the federal government to build roads, even if they would aid military defense. A tariff was voted in 1816, which helped the Northeast, but Monroe vetoed several road building bills pushed through Congress by the new leaders from the West, Clay and Calhoun. Henry Clay in 1824 coined the expression "the American System" to refer to the combination of high tariffs and internal transportation improvements in roads and canals that he and his fellow Westerners supported.

President Monroe will not change the traditional policies of the Democratic-Republicans and vetoes bills for internal improvements.

Monroe's Foreign Policy

Between 1816 and 1824 President Monroe had several foreign policy successes that established our national borders and gave the nation a sense of unity and strength. Under the leadership of Secretary of State John Quincy Adams from Massachusetts, after the War of 1812 the United States quickly negotiated the Rush-Bagot Agreement and the Convention of 1818 with England and the Adams-Onis Treaty with Spain. The English treaties established the United States' border with Quebec and set the precedent for a non-fortified border with Canada by reducing the number of warships on the Great Lakes. In the Adams-Onis Treaty, Spain ceded eastern Florida to the United States, and the United States renounced its claims to Texas. The border of the Louisiana Territory was also finally set.

Treaties with England and Spain adjust United States borders with Canada, Florida, and Mexico.

At the same time in the Far West, Russia was claiming the California coast as far south as San Francisco Bay. Adams contested the Czar's attempt to exercise Russia's control, and a treaty was signed by which Russia withdrew north of the 54° 42' line but kept her claim to Alaska.

The Monroe Doctrine

There had been revolutions in the Spanish colonies of South America during the Napoleonic War, and they had all declared independence. With peace re-established in Europe, there was talk after 1815 of reestablishing Spanish rule in the area. The British were opposed, as they enjoyed trade benefits with the newly independent countries. The English asked Adams to join them in preventing European interference with the new states. Adams and President Monroe preferred to handle the matter without the English.

Secretary of State J.Q. Adams and Monroe announce a basis for United States' relations with South America and Europe in the Monroe Doctrine.

In his 1823 message to Congress, Monroe stated four principles which, since that time, have been known as the Monroe Doctrine — a doctrine honored by every United States president since then. The Monroe Doctrine is the cornerstone of United States policy toward Central and South America. The four points Monroe made were:

1. The American continents were no longer available for colonization.
2. In the Americas there was a political system different from that of Europe.
3. The United States would consider dangerous to its peace and safety any interference by European powers in the Americas.
4. The United States would not interfere with existing colonies nor interfere in internal affairs of Europe nor take part in European wars.

While the European nations paid little attention to the Monroe Doctrine in 1823, they did not interfere in the Americas. These foreign policy successes of John Quincy Adams reinforced an American sense of nationhood and gave her greater national pride.

Panic of 1819

Henry Clay's American System was an attempt to unite the nation and encourage nationalism. It was not successful in doing so, since the American System included nothing of appeal to Southern interests. The election of 1824 reflected growing sectional interests that had been brought into focus by two earlier events: the Panic of 1819 and the Missouri Compromise of 1820.

The Panic of 1819 was the first of many in United States history. During the 19th and early 20th centuries, the American capitalist system experienced major economic difficulties approximately every twenty years. The causes were often similar, and those who suffered were the same groups.

The Panic of 1819 was brought on mainly by the rapid westward expansion, which led to extensive land speculation that in turn forced up land prices, and by a Congressional act that required the repayment in specie[1], rather than paper money, of any loans or mortgages involving the purchase of public lands.

The second Bank of the United States enforced this act, which led Senator Thomas H. Benton of Missouri to refer to the bank as "the Monster." Specie was never in great supply for farmers. Farmers often had to borrow from banks to get funds for spring planting and were dependent on fluctuating crop prices to get funds for repayment; frontiersmen struggling to establish new farms seldom had cash. When farmers and land speculators could not pay on loans, the bank had to foreclose[2] on them.

Several western states passed laws against mortgage foreclosures, but still the economy suffered. Manufacturers suffered since as farmers and banks went bankrupt, there was less money

The United States experiences its first major economic recession in the panic of 1819.

---

[1]*specie* Coined money, usually gold or silver.

[2]*foreclose* To take mortgaged land when the owner can no longer make payments on the mortgage (loan).

to buy manufacture goods. The worst of the crisis passed in 1819, and the economy slowly recovered, but a deep resentment towards "the Monster" persisted in the west and agricultural south.

The Missouri Compromise

The Missouri Compromise of 1820 was the first of many attempts to resolve the issue of the expansion of slavery into new states. The Constitutional Convention had sidestepped the issue of slavery. The Founding Fathers compromised. First, they allowed each slave to be counted as three fifths of a person in determining a state's population for representation in Congress. Second, they postponed action on the slave trade for twenty years.

During those years slavery was abolished in some northern states but southern agriculture became more dependent on slave labor. Congress outlawed the slave trade in 1807, but smuggling continued. As settlers moved west, those from the south took their slaves with them. As new states wanted to enter the union, slavery became an issue. Southern leaders wished to keep their number of votes in the Senate equal to that of the Northern states.

Growing Sectional interests are reconciled in the Missouri Compromise of 1820.

The United States in 1821 after the Missouri Compromise

Slavery had been outlawed in the Northwest Territory under provisions of the Northwest Ordinance of 1787, passed under the Articles of Confederation. This meant that each of the five states created in that area would enter the union without slavery. This set a precedent for the federal government to outlaw slavery in a territory. In 1820 Missouri applied for admission as a state to the union.

The acceptance of slavery in Missouri immediately became an important issue. It had the potential for splitting the nation. A compromise was needed. There was much negotiation in Congress. Henry Clay, with his strong national feelings, led the way in resolving the problem.

Henry Clay became known as the Great Compromiser because during the next thirty years he worked out several compromises between sectional interests that threatened to destroy the union. The Missouri Compromise of 1820 stated:
1. Maine would enter as a free state (number 23).
2. Missouri would enter as a slave state (number 24). This kept the balance in the Senate.
3. Slavery would be excluded from the territory of the Louisiana Purchase north of 36°30'.

This solution postponed the resolution of the issue of slavery for another generation.

The Election of John Quincy Adams

The Era of Good Feelings had been slowly dissolving as these sectional interests arose. No new party had yet emerged by the 1824 presidential election, but there were several strong individual candidates representing different views within the Republican Party.

Traditionally, members of the party in Congress had nominated the party's presidential candidate. Now, with divisions within the Republican Party, several state legislatures nominated candidates. Tennessee and Pennsylvania nominated Andrew Jackson, the military hero of the Battle of New Orleans. Kentucky nominated Henry Clay, the Great Compromiser. Massachusetts nominated John Quincy Adams, the successful Secretary of State. Congress nominated William H. Crawford.

In the electoral college voting, Jackson received 99 votes, Adams 84, Crawford 41, and Clay 37. Calhoun received 182 votes as Vice President and was elected, but since no one running for president had a majority, the House of Representatives had to pick the next president from the three top candidates. An illness made Crawford's candidacy unimportant, so the race was between Jackson and Adams.

Adams had supported Clay's American System. Clay threw his support to John Quincy Adams, who was elected President to the dismay of Andrew Jackson. Henry Clay was then appointed Secretary of State by Adams. Jackson supporters suggested that a corrupt bargain had been struck, but there is no proof. The supporters of Jackson became known as the Democrats, while Clay's supporters were referred to as National Republicans. Thus, the old Jeffersonian Democratic-Republican Party split, creating two new parties.

Andrew Jackson Becomes President

In the election of 1828 the Democratic candidate was Andrew Jackson. Jackson was nominated for the Presidency by the Tennessee legislature in October 1825, three years before the next election. He resigned from the Senate to organize his campaign. Jackson's support came from the South and the West, where he was a

The House of Representatives picks J.Q. Adams as president which upsets A. Jackson and ends the Era of Good Feelings.

war hero and a supporter of the American System of internal improvements. He was also billed as a "common" man, a symbol of the new American—not an aristocrat from an old Virginia or Massachusetts family. Actually, Jackson was wealthy and owned a fine plantation, the Hermitage, in Tennessee, but campaign slogans emphasized other aspects of his background.

In the years prior to 1828 many states had extended the vote to all white males and not just property owners. In the presidential election of 1828, 22 of 24 states allowed the people to vote directly for the electors rather than have them chosen by state legislatures. This move towards greater democracy was reflected in the election of that symbol of the common man—Andrew Jackson.

The election of 1828 was a mudslinging election—the first but not the last in American history. Mrs. Jackson died before Andrew Jackson's inauguration, and it has been suggested her death was in part due to accusations made against her in the campaign. The country was quite sectionally divided in the election, with the South and West plus New York and Pennsylvania supporting Jackson, and New England supporting Adams.

Andrew Jackson wins the mud-slinging election of 1828.

In his inaugural address Jackson made no reference to what became the major issues of his presidency: the tariff, national unity, internal improvements, and the second Bank of the United States. In the eight years Jackson was president, sectional issues threatened national unity. Through his decisive acts, Jackson emphasized national unity and strengthened the presidency.

To assure that his party's policies would be followed by government agencies, Jackson used the spoils system[3] extensively to place his supporters in government offices, replacing Federalist office holders. This policy was one further manifestation of the growing democratic ideas in the country. The spoils system is based on the idea that anyone can govern—no experience is necessary in a democratic society where all are equal.

The spoils system is used by Jackson to assure his policies will be followed by the bureaucracy.

The spoils system was first used by Jefferson, and it remained an important part of American political life until Civil Service Reform at the end of the 19th century. Today, many political leaders use the spoils system as much as the law allows since it permits them to reward their supporters and to get advice from people who think as they do. It assures that their party's policies will be followed.

Jackson also relied on friends, his "Kitchen Cabinet," rather than the cabinet of the heads of government agencies. This policy of relying on personal friends for advice has been followed in varying degrees by all presidents.

The Tariff Issue, Nullification, and National Union

The struggle over the tariff issue began before Jackson became president. In 1828, a tariff raising import rates on many goods was passed. It was quickly dubbed the Tariff of Abominations by its Southern opponents. The South Carolina legislature adopted

---

[3]*spoils system* The awarding of government jobs or the granting of favors or advantages by government officials to political supporters and workers.

resolutions calling the tariff oppressive and issued the *South Carolina Exposition of Protest*, written by the Vice President of the United States, John C. Calhoun.

View of State St., Portsmouth, N.H.
This print of the Main Street of Portsmouth, New Hampshire in the 1830's illustrates the building style, the Greek Revival, that was popular. It went with the Jacksonian period with its emphasis on democracy. Athens in ancient Greece was the first democracy recorded in history, and its temples were built with columns in front as are two of the buildings in this scene. The print also illustrates the condition of the streets, the dress and the style of transportation. How would the streets be lit at night?

Because the Tariff of 1828 is seen as unfair to the South, John C. Calhoun argues for the right of nullification.

In the *South Carolina Exposition*, Calhoun argued the right of nullification by one state. It was the same theory advanced by Thomas Jefferson and James Madison in the Kentucky and Virginia Resolutions of 1798. In 1832, a new tariff reduced some import duties but still maintained the principle of protection, which the South opposed.

A state convention in South Carolina met and nullified the Tariff Acts of 1828 and 1832 and forbade the collection of duties in South Carolina or any appeal of the issue to the Supreme Court. The state threatened to secede if the federal government were to use force. South Carolina issued a call to the other states for a national Constitutional Convention but received no support.

Jackson asked Congress for authority to enforce the tariff laws, which was given in the Force Bill of 1833. Secession and war seemed imminent when Henry Clay introduced in the House of Representatives a compromise tariff. At its passage, South Carolina suspended its nullification decree on the tariffs but nullified the Force Bill, which was, by then, unnecessary.

The crisis over tariffs and possible secession was averted, and national unity was preserved. Jackson was clearly a strong and national president. He had held the South in line, but the issue of secession and nullification would return in the future.

The second major issue of Jackson's presidency involved nationalism and internal improvements. It first took the form of debates in the Senate on the question of the nature of the union. Was it a compact between states or a popular government created by the people? The debate moved to the issue of union versus liberty. Daniel Webster of Massachusetts spoke firmly for the union of the states and made an often quoted statement—"Liberty and Union, now and forever, one and inseparable"—in concluding one of his speeches. Senator Robert Y. Hayne from South Carolina spoke for the Southern view and emphasized state sovereignty and liberty over union.

Jackson became involved after these Hayne-Webster debates when he appeared at a dinner honoring Jefferson. In a famous toast Jackson made his position clear, stating, "Our union, it must be preserved." In spite of this nationalistic viewpoint, Jackson vetoed several measures that would have allowed for internal improvements in the states. However, he did support harbor and river improvements paid for by federal funds.

Jackson makes his nationalism clear in a toast stating, "Our union, it must be preserved."

The End of the Bank of the United States

The third major issue, the rechartering of the Bank of the United States, arose in 1832. The charter was not to expire until 1836, but the head of the bank, Nicholas Biddle, requested a renewal of the charter in 1832 as a political move. The Bank had been quite successful in helping business and controlling the currency, but opposition was widespread. Debtors, again largely in the South and West, opposed the strict monetary policies of the Bank; state banks wanted to have some, or all, of the federal government deposits that went to the Bank of the United States. Many Southerners believed the Bank was unconstitutional. Nicholas Biddle's policies of support for business and his strong personality worked to his disadvantage as many viewed him as an arrogant supporter of an elitist minority. Congress voted to recharter the Bank, but Jackson vetoed the measure and the Senate failed to override the veto.

Congress votes to re-charter the Bank of the United States, but Jackson vetoes the measure.

Jackson's arguments against the bank reflect a limited understanding of banking, but a strong dislike of monopoly. It is the same American viewpoint that was seen in the colonists' opposition to the English support of the East India Tea Company's monopoly. The Bank became an issue in the election of 1832, which Jackson won easily.

Beginning in 1833, Jackson ordered the government to begin depositing government money in selected state banks that were quickly called "pet banks." These pet banks were not controlled by any regulations, and many loaned the money for speculation. Land speculation especially grew dramatically in the next four years.

In 1836, concerned about the situation, Jackson issued the Specie Circular, which required payment for public land to be made in specie. This curtailed land speculation but put a strain on the pet banks and eventually led to the second major panic of United States' history, the Panic of 1837. Jackson's intentions with the specie circular were sound, but there was not enough specie available to keep the entire economy working smoothly.

The Specie Circular is issued to curtail land speculation in the West, but it leads to the Panic of 1837.

Jackson also supported the removal of the Native American populations to reserved areas west of the Mississippi. The forced march to the West has been called "The Trail of Tears," a suitable name for the tragedy it brought. The South gave him strong support for this policy, which opened up large areas of valuable land to white settlement. Jackson ignored Supreme Court decisions favorable to the Native Americans in pursuing this nationalistic policy.

Personality Conflicts and the Emergence of Van Buren

During Jackson's presidency there were personality conflicts that provide an interesting background to many of the political decisions. Jackson discovered that Vice President Calhoun, as Secretary of War in 1818, had not supported his attack on the Cherokee Indians. This, combined with Calhoun's views on nullification, led to his resignation as Vice President. Jackson's attempts to force Washington society to accept Peggy Eaton, a former barmaid and the second wife of his friend the Secretary of War, ended in a standoff. Cabinet intrigues led to the resignation of all but one cabinet member in 1831. Finally, Martin van Buren of New York emerged as Jackson's closest political ally and logical successor as president.

Political parties adopt nominating conventions as the method for choosing presidential candidates.

Following the precedent they had set in 1832, in 1836 the Democrats held a party convention to nominate their candidate for president. The convention nominated Martin Van Buren. Party nominating conventions became the accepted method and are still used today.

Opposition to the Democrats was offered by the former National Republicans now loosely grouped as the new Whig Party. The Whigs backed several candidates. The first organized third party in American history, the Masonic Party, also offered opposition.

Van Buren easily won election but no vice presidential candidate won a majority of electoral votes. Following the Constitution, the Senate then voted and elected Richard Johnson vice president.

KEY POINT TO REMEMBER

Sectional differences were balanced by a sense of nationalism during the 1820s and 30s, and the issues of Andrew Jackson's presidency reflected both of these concerns.

LINKS FROM THE PAST TO THE PRESENT

1. Use of the spoils system to reward political supporters has been a common practice.
2. Party conventions to nominate presidential candidates are an established part of American politics.
3. Americans have opposed the formation of monopolies since before the Revolution.
4. The Monroe Doctrine has been a cornerstone of United States foreign policy since 1823 and has been invoked often in the 20th century.

PEOPLE TO REMEMBER

Andrew Jackson   Lawyer and general; commanded United States forces at Battle of New Orleans, 1815, and in attacks on Indians in Florida; lost presidential election of 1824 in the House of Representatives; seventh President of the United States, 1829–1837; vetoed Second Bank of the United States re-charter bill and countered South Carolina Tariff nullification, 1832, with show of force.

QUESTIONS

Identify each of the following:

The American System	Monroe Doctrine
Panic of 1819	John Quincy Adams
Compromise of 1820	Daniel Webster
Era of Good Feelings	South Carolina Exposition
Democratic-Republicans	and Protest
Second Bank of the United States	

True or False:

1. The Rush-Bagot Agreement and the Convention of 1818 established the border of the Louisiana Territory.
2. The Panic of 1819 was minor and had little impact on the United States' economy.
3. The Era of Good Feelings was a period in which one political party dominated political activity.
4. A Jackson veto of the second Bank of the United States was overridden by the Congress.
5. South Carolina led the opposition to the tariffs of 1828 and 1832.
6. Daniel Webster's statement, "Liberty and Union, now and forever, one and inseparable," was a statement in favor of national unity.
7. During Jackson's presidency, cabinet intrigues and social issues rocked Washington.
8. Andrew Jackson refused to use the spoils system.

Multiple Choice:

1. The Monroe Doctrine, the cornerstone of United States policy towards Central and South America, stated that
   a. any colonization in the Americas had to be approved by the United States
   b. the United States was available to fight in European wars
   c. the Americas had a political system different from Europe

2. The American System proposed by Henry Clay consisted of
   a. high tariffs and internal transportation improvements paid for by the national government
   b. roads built for American defense
   c. high tariffs and subsidies for southern farmers.
3. A party convention for the nomination of the party's presidential candidate was used by
   a. the Republicans to nominate James Monroe in 1820
   b. the Democrats to nominate Andrew Jackson in 1828
   c. the Democrats to nominate Martin Van Buren in 1836
4. The Missouri Compromise of 1820 stated that
   a. both Maine and Missouri would enter the union as free states
   b. slavery would be excluded from land north of 36°30′ in the Louisiana Purchase
   c. slavery would be excluded in the Northwest Territory
5. *The South Carolina Exposition of Protest*, written by John C. Calhoun,
   a. nullified the Tariffs of 1828 and 1832
   b. argued the right of nullification by one state
   c. was declared illegal by the Force Bill of 1833

ANSWERS

True or False: 1. F, 2. F, 3. T, 4. F, 5. T, 6. T, 7. T, 8. F.
Multiple Choice: 1. c, 2. a, 3. c, 4. b, 5. b.

III. NATIONALISM AND TERRITORIAL EXPANSION

Van Buren's presidency was hampered by the Panic of 1837 and tensions with England. Some of Jackson's pet banks were among the many state banks that failed, and by 1840 the government established an Independent Treasury for the deposit of federal funds. The Democrats would not support another Bank of the United States but accepted this compromise measure, which meant the end of pet banks and their speculation with federal funds. While not as effective as a bank would have been, the Independent Treasury provided adequate control over federal finances. The tensions with England centered on the failure to pay debts, issues of copyright, and the Maine boundary. These led to strong anti-English feelings, but war was avoided in spite of strong provocations in Maine.

The Independent Treasury replaces pet banks and provides adequate control of federal finances.

One aspect of the growing democratic spirit (see Chapter VI) of the Age of Jackson was the issue of slavery abolition. It became an issue in Congress, where the leadership avoided the slavery question by agreeing to a "Gag Rule" that effectively blocked petitions to Congress concerning abolition. Slavery would become the major issue in the 1850s after a decade of United States westward expansion under Van Buren's successors.

The Non-Issue Election of 1840

The Whigs in 1840 nominated William Henry Harrison, a war hero with no political experience, and James Tyler, a states rights

Democrat who had turned against Jackson over the issue of nullification in 1832–3. They easily won in a non-issue campaign based on hype and personality—what may be considered a rather typical presidential campaign of the 19th century. The Whigs chanted "Tippecanoe and Tyler too"—General Harrison had defeated Chief Tecumseh at the Battle of Tippecanoe in 1811. The parties held parades complete with slogans, campaign hats, and torches. They eulogized the log cabin background of Harrison. Van Buren could not overcome the effects of the Panic of 1837 and he lost 234–60 in the electoral college, winning only 7 of the 26 states.

General W. H. Harrison, hero of the Battle of Tippecanoe, wins the 1840 presidential election—the first elected member of the Whig Party.

James Tyler Succeeds to the Presidency

President Harrison died of penumonia one month after his inauguration, and James Tyler succeeded, the first Vice President to do so. Since Tyler had been put on the Whig ticket to gain Southern votes, and since his sentiments were with the Democrats, his four years in office were not productive for the Whigs. They wanted to establish a new Bank of the United States but President Tyler twice vetoed bills doing so. As a result, the Whig members of his cabinet resigned. Henry Clay, the most prominent Whig, resigned from the House of Representatives to prepare his campaign for the presidency in 1844. The most important achievement of Tyler's Presidency was the signing of the Webster-Ashburton Treaty with Great Britain, which finally set the United States-Canada border from Maine to Lake of the Woods in Minnesota.

James Tyler, succeeding to the presidency on Harrison's death, frustrates the Whig Party leadership.

Suffrage in Rhode Island

An incident in Rhode Island may be the most interesting development of Tyler's presidency. The Constitution of Rhode Island was the charter that had been issued by King Charles II in 1663. The charter greatly restricted the suffrage[1]. In 1842, those who were disqualified from voting wrote a new charter, or state constitution, and put it into operation. This gave the state two functioning governments, and the new government included the right to universal male suffrage.

Tyler was prepared to use federal troops to support the old government because of Article IV, Section 4 of the Constitution, which upheld the validity of charters. The new government collapsed, but in 1843 a new state constitution was written extending the suffrage as was being done in many states.

After a near revolution, the government of Rhode Island extends the right to vote.

The incident illustrates Tyler's strict construction of the Constitution even if it went against the program, in this case the extension of the suffrage to all males, supported by the Democratic Party.

The First Dark Horse Candidacy

The election of 1844 was a contest between the Whigs, who nominated Henry Clay, and the Democrats, who nominated James

---

[1]*suffrage*   The right to vote.

The Democrat's Dark Horse, James K. Polk, defeats Henry Clay for the Presidency.

K. Polk, the first "Dark Horse"[2] in our political history. A third party, the Liberty Party, carried enough votes in New York to deny the state to Henry Clay, and Polk became president. All three parties used party nominating conventions to pick their candidates, and they thus became an established part of American political life.

The main domestic goal of President Polk and the Democrats was to re-establish the Independent Treasury system, which had been repealed by the Whigs. It was achieved in 1846.

Polk's Foreign Policy

Polk embodies the concept of Manifest Destiny as he settles the Oregon boundary dispute, and fights a war with Mexico.

President Polk's major contribution to history is in the international arena. Under his administration we fought a war with Mexico and we settled a dispute with England over control of the Oregon Territory. These two events completed, except for the small Gadsden Purchase the United States made from Mexico in 1853, the acquisition of the adjacent territories that make up the 48 connected or lower states.

Manifest Destiny

The steps leading to the Oregon settlement and the War with Mexico are complex. They illustrate the concept of Manifest Destiny. The term Manifest Destiny was first used in an editorial stating that foreign nations were blocking the annexation of the Republic of Texas by the United States to stop "the fulfillment of our manifest destiny to overspread the continent allotted by providence for the free development of our...millions (of inhabitants)." This statement provides an illustration of American nationalism and the feeling that the United States was a "chosen" nation with a particular destiny to fulfill. This is the essence of Manifest Destiny.

President Polk in his first message to Congress enlarged the Monroe Doctrine by stating that the people of the Americas had the right to decide their own destiny and European powers could not block the union of the United States with any independent state on the American continent. This was a response to the situation which had developed in Texas in the 1830s.

The United States in Texas

United States citizens settle in Texas and establish an independent state.

United States involvement in Texas began in 1821 when Stephen F. Austin took possession of land grants made to his father by the government of Mexico. In the following years, more Americans settled in Texas. A new Mexican government in 1830 restricted American immigration and outlawed slavery in Texas. Six years of tension, attempted negotiation, and changing government in Mexico, led to war in 1836 between the American settlers and the Mexican government. After losing the Battle of the Alamo in San Antonio, the settlers won a victory and achieved recognition as an

---

[2]*dark horse*   A candidate for political office, particularly the presidency, who was not considered a likely candidate for the office and therefore the nomination is a surprise to many people.

independent, sovereign state. President Jackson finally recognized the independence of Texas. Her formal petition for annexation by the United States was rejected by the Senate in 1837 because antislavery members of Congress objected. Negotiations, which included the threat by Texans that they would ally with England and France, went on for several years.

John C. Calhoun, Secretary of State in President Tyler's cabinet, finally negotiated a treaty of annexation with the Republic of Texas but the Senate rejected it also. Northern abolitionists[3] saw the possible annexation of Texas as a plot to extend slavery. Southerners saw it as an area of economic opportunity, and feared English influence on an independent Texas.

In signing the treaty, Tyler had promised to send federal troops to defend Texas from a possible attack from Mexico. In spite of the Senate's rejection of the treaty, troops and ships were moved to defend Texas from possible attack by Mexico. This issue of the annexation of Texas as well as the Oregon boundary dispute became major issues in the election of 1844.

After the election of Polk in 1844, Tyler asked Congress to accept the Texas treaty by a joint resolution of both houses. This would require only a majority, and not the two-thirds vote required by the Constitution, for the ratification of treaties. This ploy to get around the Constitution was successful. By this treaty, Texas became a state without going through a period as a territory. The slavery issue was addressed by extending the Missouri Compromise line of 36°30' through the Texas territory and so allowing slavery in Texas.

Congress accepts Texas as a State, and this leads to war with Mexico.

Polk in his inaugural address said the issue of the annexation of Texas was between Texas and the United States alone, and did not involve other nations. Mexico disagreed and broke off diplomatic relations, claiming Texas was Mexican territory. There were other issues of dispute with Mexico, such as Mexico's desire to stop United States' immigration into their territory of California. President Polk sent John Slidell to Mexico to negotiate, but negotiations stalled and the Mexican government was overthrown in a coup d'etat[4]. Troops were moved into disputed territory on the Mexican-Texas border. President Polk asked for a declaration of war, which Congress voted on May 13, 1846, but many voted against this war, which lasted for two years.

The Mexican War

The Mexican War (1846–1848) was fought in several areas: first, in California, where United States settlers gained control of the area with aid from Captain John Charles Fremont of the United States Army and Commodore Robert Stockton of the United States Navy; second, in the New Mexico territory, where a United States expedition occupied Las Vegas, Taos, and Santa Fe, securing this large

The United States defeats the Mexicans in California and New Mexico and captures Mexico City, providing training for future Civil War generals.

---

[3]*abolitionists* Before the American Civil War, one who believed in the abolition or ending of slavery.

[4]*coup d'etat* A sudden forceful overthrow of a government.

area for the United States; third, in Mexico, which United States' forces invaded, capturing Monterrey, seizing the port of Vera Cruz, and finally capturing the capital, Mexico City, in September 1847. The war was then quickly brought to a successful military conclusion. Several famous generals of the Civil War, including Robert E. Lee, gained experience in these various campaigns.

While the fighting was progressing, Congress fought over war aims. The Wilmot Proviso, an attempt by Whigs to exclude slavery from the conquered territory, was defeated but focused attention on the issue of the expansion of slavery to new territories. John C. Calhoun led the Southern opposition to any restriction on slavery in the territory.

The United States expands its territory in the Treaty of Guadalupe Hidalgo.

Polk began secret negotiations to end the war, which led to the Treaty of Guadalupe Hidalgo. By its terms the United States acquired Texas as far South as the Rio Grande River, the territory of California, and the New Mexico territory, which included present New Mexico and parts of Arizona, Utah, Colorado, and Nevada. The United States agreed to pay Mexico $15,000,000 and to pay the claims of all United States' citizens against the government. Some opposed the treaty because they wished to annex all of Mexico; others opposed it on the slavery issue. However, the treaty was accepted by the Senate in March 1848, adding the last great block of territory to the continental United States, thus achieving—in some people's eyes—our manifest destiny.

Settlement of the Oregon Boundary

A compromise divides the Oregon Territory between England and the United States.

While the Mexican War was starting, a peaceful solution to the Oregon boundary dispute was achieved through negotiation with England. While the compromise did not satisfy the expansionists and forced Polk to reject his party's campaign slogan of "54°40' or fight," it avoided war with Britain. The Oregon Territory was divided at the 49th parallel, which was the border between the United States and Canada from Lake of the Woods to the Oregon border. England got all of Vancouver Island. With the Senate's approval the territory, later divided into the states of Washington, Oregon, and Idaho, was added to the United States, which now stretched from coast to coast. According to American nationalists, the manifest destiny of the United States had been achieved.

The agreement helped persuade England to remain on the sidelines during the Mexican War in spite of her earlier support for an independent Texas. It also illustrates the benefits from negotiation and treaty making in international affairs, as one can thus gain the support of nations in time of need. England's action was also a sign of the importance to both nations of the United States-English trade relationship, which had been growing since independence.

Slavery in the Territories

With the acquisition of new territory, the question of slavery in the territories became a crucial issue for the nation. The question was very complex. At its core was disagreement over whether Congress could outlaw slavery in the territories or whether the inhabitants should have control of the matter. This latter view was dubbed popular sovereignty or "squatter" sovereignty.

The question of slavery had been a potentially divisive issue from the time of the Constitutional Convention. After much debate the Oregon Territory was organized and slavery was outlawed. President Polk signed this bill, stating it upheld the Missouri Compromise line of 36°30' since Oregon was north of that line. After the Treaty of Guadalupe Hidalgo was signed, President Polk tried to get both California and New Mexico organized as territories, but his proposals failed because of the slavery issue.

The question is raised of the expansion of slavery into the territories acquired from Mexico.

President Polk had said he would serve a single term. In the election of 1848 the Whig candidates, General Zachary Taylor, hero of the Battle of Buena Vista in the Mexican War for president, and Millard Fillmore of New York for vice president, defeated the Democratic candidates. Slavery was a major issue of the campaign. A new third party, the Free Soil Party, which opposed popular sovereignty on the slavery issue, was the deciding factor because it took votes away from the Democrats.

The Compromise of 1850

Congress was badly split on the issue of slavery in the territories. In 1849 when California applied for admission as a state, there were fifteen slave and fifteen free states in the union. The population of California had grown rapidly as a result of the discovery of gold, and the territory moved quickly towards statehood. Californians organized a state government and wrote a constitution outlawing slavery.

The growing controversy over slavery alarmed both moderates and conservatives in Congress. Henry Clay again stepped forward with a compromise solution, which quieted matters briefly but proved to be the last compromise before the slavery issue tore the nation apart in the Civil War. Clay's compromise included five acts, and the five together are known as the Compromise of 1850. The Compromise had something for each sectional interest:

The Compromise of 1850 provides something for each sectional interest.

1. California entered as a free state.
2. New Mexico was organized as a territory with no mention of whether it would be slave or free. But it was understood that popular sovereignty would prevail when the territory applied for admission.
3. The organization of Utah as a territory was approved, and it would enter free or slave as determined by its written constitution.
4. The prohibition of the slave trade in Washington, D.C. and the non-interference by Congress with slavery in Washington, D.C. was established.
5. A strong Fugitive Slave Law, which called for the return of slaves to their owners at federal government expense, was passed.

The union was saved, but many Northerners were prepared to hinder the enforcement of the Fugitive Slave Law. It was a compromise all could accept for the moment because it had something for each interest.

Summary

National and sectional issues maintained an uneasy balance between 1801 and 1850. While there were many sectional issues dividing the nation, there were always compromises that preserved the union, and the nation grew in strength and national spirit. Many saw the expansion of the nation to the Pacific Ocean as the working out of the nation's Manifest Destiny as planned by a "Providence" that had chosen the United States to be great. This spirit of Manifest Destiny allowed the nation to prosper and avoid being torn apart by its sectional interests.

KEY POINT TO REMEMBER

The Oregon settlement and the Mexican War illustrate the concept of Manifest Destiny or the idea that "Providence" or God has "chosen" your nation to fulfill a particular role in history.

LINKS FROM THE PAST TO THE PRESENT

1. Whole political campaigns, from local to presidential, have been based on hype and personality, though this is regularly deplored by historians and the press.
2. The benefits of compromise and negotiation in international affairs can be found in our history from the Oregon dispute to disarmament treaties.

PEOPLE TO REMEMBER

Henry Clay Senator from Kentucky; co-leader of the "War Hawks" in 1812; became known as the Great Compromiser because of his work on the Compromises of 1820 and 1850 and the Compromise Tariff of 1833; ran unsuccessfully for President in 1824, 1832, and 1844.

John C. Calhoun Senator from South Carolina; co-leader of the "War Hawks" in 1812; Vice President under John Quincy Adams and Andrew Jackson until he resigned in 1832; author of *South Carolina Exposition* explaining nullification and states rights, and a strong supporter of Southern rights in his later years.

QUESTIONS

Identify each of the following:

"54°40' or fight"	James K. Polk
The Battle of the Alamo	Martin Van Buren
Treaty of Guadalupe Hidalgo	James Tyler
The Gag Rule	

True or False:

1. The Democrats under Van Buren accepted the establishment of an Independent Treasury.
2. James Tyler, elected as a Whig, was the first vice president to step into the presidency and had a difficult time leading his party since his sentiments were with the Democratic Party more than with the Whigs.

3. People in Rhode Island who were not allowed to vote according to the state charter or constitution organized a successful new government for the state.
4. James K. Polk was a dark horse candidate of the Democratic Party.
5. According to the idea of manifest destiny, the United States was chosen to be a great nation.
6. The United States annexation of Texas was supported by England, France, and Northern abolitionists.
7. The United States captured California and the New Mexico territory during the Mexican War.
8. General Zachary Taylor, who won the presidency in 1848, was a hero of the Mexican War.
9. 50°40' became the northern border of the United States because we were ready to fight for it.
10. Millard Fillmore was the first vice president to step into office on the death of a President.

Multiple Choice:

1. Popular or "squatter" sovereignty meant
   a. the people in a territory had to follow the Missouri Compromise
   b. squatters who just arrived could decide what were the most popular political issues
   c. those living in a territory could vote on whether to have slaves when the territory became a state
2. "Tippecanoe and Tyler Too" and "54°40' or fight" were
   a. political campaign slogans
   b. war slogans in the Mexican War
   c. arguments used to support the Treaty of Guadalupe Hidalgo
3. The Compromise of 1850 consisted of five bills that included the provision that
   a. California entered the Union as a slave state
   b. a strong fugitive slave law
   c. New Mexico and Utah were organized as free territories to enter the union later as free states
4. The Webster-Ashburton Treaty finally set the United States-Canada border
   a. from Maine to Lake of the Woods in Minnesota
   b in Oregon and Washington
   c. in Idaho

ANSWERS
True or False: 1. T, 2. T, 3. F, 4. T, 5. T, 6. F, 7. T, 8. T, 9. F, 10. F.
Multiple Choice: 1. c, 2. a, 3. b, 4. a.

CHAPTER 6

A Growing Nation

APPROACHES TO HISTORY

Law and Society

All people need rules guiding behavior in order to function effectively. Without such rules even rebellious individuals cannot function effectively since they cannot know what to rebel against. Even in our home life we are given certain rules—when we must be home at night, what we can eat in the refrigerator, what TV we may watch. Sometimes we don't like the rules and don't obey. Then judgements are made and decisions, including punishment, are handed out.

A nation operates the same way. So far in the text we have mentioned several laws—which are the same as rules—that were passed by Congress. In regard to the tariffs of 1828 and 1832 passed by Congress, one state, South Carolina objected and announced it would disobey the law by nullifying it. The federal government judged the situation and forced South Carolina to obey the tariff laws.

In the United States during the years from 1800 to 1850, just as today, there were many laws and situations to which people objected. Their recourse was to go to the courts and ultimately to the Supreme Court for judgement and decision on the meaning of the law. If they did not use this process, they were breaking the law and would be subject to punishment including jail.

The decisions of the Supreme Court in these cases shaped the future of the United States. It is important to understand what the Supreme Court said in several crucial cases during these years because those decisions have provided the rules by which the nation has been run since then.

I.   EARLY SUPREME COURT DECISIONS

As one of his last acts as President, John Adams appointed, and the Senate confirmed John Marshall as Chief Justice of the United States Supreme Court. John Marshall was a Virginia Federalist, a wise lawyer and politician who followed the Hamiltonian view of government. As Chief Justice between 1800 and 1835, he handed down decisions that strengthened the federal government and the business community. The latter decisions helped develop the American economy and supported the capitalist system.

Chief Justice John Marshall upholds the federalist viewpoint.

Even when the presidents were Jeffersonian Republicans or Jacksonian Democrats, the Court supported the Federalist position under Marshall's strong leadership. This fact clearly illustrates the power of the Supreme Court and explains why there has been such controversy over the appointment of judges to the Supreme Court in the latter half of the 20th century.

"The Supreme Law of the Land" — Marbury v. Madison

The Constitution stated it would be "the supreme law of the land," but it did not clarify just how this would be enforced if a law passed by Congress or a state was contrary to the Constitution. There had developed a tradition in the Colonies and in England of courts making such determinations, but this concept of judicial review was not written into the Constitution. Marshall, in the case of *Marbury v. Madison* in 1803, decided the case in a way that gave the Supreme Court the power to review and declare unconstitutional laws passed by Congress.

The Marbury v. Madison decision establishes the concept of judicial review.

The case involved Marbury, who had been appointed Justice of the Peace by President Adams just before Adams left office. President Madison refused to give Marbury his commission, and Marbury asked the Supreme Court to issue a Writ of Mandamus that would force Madison to give Marbury the commission.

While Marshall's sympathies may have been with the Federalist Marbury, as a wise politician he realized that the court could not force Madison to act. He therefore looked at the Judiciary Act of 1789, which gave the Supreme Court the power to issue writs, and at the Constitution, which in no place gave the court that power. He and the Supreme Court decided the Judiciary Act of 1789 contradicted the Constitution, the "supreme law of the land," when it gave the Supreme Court the power to issue Writs of Mandamus. The Supreme Court decided, therefore, it could not issue the writ requested by Marbury.

Thus Marbury lost his case and did not become a Justice of the Peace, but John Marshall took upon the court the power of judicial review[1] over laws passed by Congress — a great power for the court

---

[1]*judicial review*   The power of a court to accept appeals concerning laws passed by the legislature, actions of the executive or decisions by lower judicial courts with the possibility of modifying or nullifying such laws, actions, or decisions because they are unconstitutional.

and a great tool for supporting national unity. There were many objections to the decision, but it has stood throughout our history to give the court this power of judicial review.

Obligation of Contract

The Supreme Court in Fletcher v. Peck declares a state law unconstitutional.

In 1810 in the case of *Fletcher v. Peck*, the court invalidated a Georgia state law as contrary to the United States Constitution. The Georgia legislature in 1795 had been bribed into granting a contract to land speculators. At a later session of the state legislature, the contract was revoked. The Supreme Court held this was a violation of the Constitution's clause upholding the "obligation of contract" (Article 1 Section 10). Even though the original contract had been obtained by bribes, it was valid as law. The Supreme Court declared it could not investigate the motives or methods of the legislature in passing the law. It only could read what the law said. The *Fletcher v. Peck* decision was the first in which the Supreme Court declared a state law unconstitutional. It also gave the business community support by assuring them the court would uphold contracts made with state governments.

The Dartmouth College case decision states private contracts are protected by the Constitution.

In the Dartmouth College case in 1819, the court extended the *Fletcher v. Peck* concept to private contracts. Dartmouth College had been established by a royal charter (contract) by King George III. The New Hampshire legislature passed a law making Dartmouth a state institution with a new charter and a new Board of Trustees. The original trustees sued the state, whose Supreme Court upheld the state law. The trustees then appealed[2] to the United States Supreme Court. Marshall and the court held that the state law violated the original contract and was invalid. The original charter was honored.

Private contracts thus were understood to be under the protection of the constitution and outside the control of the states. This encouraged business growth since businesses could count on the court to uphold contracts they made.

The Supreme Court upholds the concept that the State represents the public's interest in business contracts.

In 1837 the new Chief Justice, Roger B. Taney, modified this position slightly in the *Charles River Bridge v. Warren Bridge* case. The Charles River Bridge Company chartered by Massachusetts sued the Warren Bridge Company, claiming the latter broke the Charles River Bridge Company's right to exclusive bridge building over the Charles River in Boston. This point was not specifically in the contract, and Taney held that ambiguous clauses in the contract must be interpreted to benefit the people of the state. This idea of the state representing the public's interest in business contracts made possible later legislation controlling business in the public interest.

The Commerce Clause: *Gibbons v. Ogden*

Another decision of Chief Justice Marshall interpreted the commerce clause of the Constitution very broadly. New York had given a monopoly to Robert Fulton to operate steamboats on New

[2]*appeal* A process in which a case is moved from a lower to a higher court for reexamination or review.

York waters. Thomas Gibbons had received a federal license to operate a boat from New York to New Jersey across the Hudson River. Fulton's successor, Aaron Ogden, sued Gibbons for violating his monopoly of transport on New York waters. In his decision in the *Gibbons v. Ogden* case, Marshall defined commerce as including "every species (type) of commercial intercourse" including navigation. He declared the federal government's power over interstate and foreign commerce did not stop at state borders and took precedence over state control of commerce within their borders. States could control intra-state commerce, that is, commerce strictly within the state, but Congress had an overarching control so Gibbon's federal license prevailed over the state monopoly.

In Gibbons v. Ogden Congress' power over commerce is clarified.

The case thus strengthened Congress' power over commerce and added to the power of the federal government. At the time of the *Gibbons v. Ogden* decision in 1824, internal improvements in transportation were a major political issue. While the President vetoed national transportation measures, Marshall held the states could not monopolize the building of the system.

Loose Construction: *McCulloch v. Maryland*

Marshall's strongest statement of the Federalist position came in the 1819 case of *McCulloch v. Maryland*. He used Hamilton's "loose construction" argument to uphold the constitutionality of the Second Bank of the United States, claiming that while limited in its powers by the Constitution, the federal government is supreme in its designated areas and must have the powers needed to carry out its work. The decision said, "Let the end be legitimate, let it be within the scope of the Constitution, and all means [are constitutional which] are appropriate, [and] which are plainly adapted to that end and which are not prohibited...." The case involved a Maryland law taxing the Bank of the United States. The Bank refused to pay the tax, and the state sued McCulloch, a branch cashier.

Marshall supports Hamilton's idea of loose construction in McCulloch v. Maryland.

The issues of the case as Marshall saw them were, "Was the bank constitutional?" "Was the tax legal?" Having declared the bank constitutional in the argument quoted above, Marshall declared the tax illegal since "taxing involves the power to destroy" and no state had the right to destroy a legitimate federal institution. This strong statement of the loose construction theory antagonized many people and controversy followed.

Throughout its history the court has not always followed Marshall's position, but the case of *McCulloch v. Maryland* stands as a precedent for those who wish to expand the power of the federal government. The Marshall court by 1835 had established rules which still guide our nation. Many people objected at the time and some still object to the exercise of judicial review by the court and to its power over commerce and contracts. However, the interpretation of the constitution made by the Marshall court gave a strong foundation to the nation. Later Supreme Court decisions also greatly affected our nation, and they will be included later in this text.

KEY POINT TO REMEMBER
Supreme Court decisions under Chief Justice John Marshall strengthened the power of the federal government and supported the growth of American business.

PEOPLE TO REMEMBER
John Marshall   Virginia lawyer, member of the Virginia Assembly, Federalist Congressman, Secretary of State under President Adams and Chief Justice of the Supreme Court for 34 years. He wrote most of the Court's decisions, many of which gave greater power to the federal government, especially the Supreme Court, and to business.

LINKS FROM THE PAST TO THE PRESENT
1. Supreme Court decisions interpret the Constitution and thus are of crucial importance to Americans.
2. The Supreme Court's power of judicial review has been exercised to limit the power of federal, state, and local governments.

QUESTIONS

Identify each of the following:

Judicial review	Marbury v. Madison
Supreme Law of the Land	Fletcher v. Peck
McCulloch v. Maryland	Dartmouth College Case

True or False:
1. John Marshall was a Federalist appointed Chief Justice by John Adams.
2. A nation and an individual must have rules to provide guidelines for conduct.
3. In *McCulloch v. Maryland*, by denying the power of the Supreme Court to issue a Writ of Mandamus, Marshall provided the court with greater power, the power of judicial review.
4. The decisions in *Fletcher v. Peck* and the *Dartmouth College Case* both dealt with contracts, but one strengthened business contracts and the other weakened them.
5. The decision in *Gibbons v. Ogden* strengthened the federal government's power over commerce.

Multiple Choice:
1. Although there was a tradition of judicial review in the colonies and in England,
   a. it was not accepted by Congress
   b. it was not written into the Constitution
   c. Chief Justice Marshall did not support the idea
2. The case of *Marbury v. Madison* illustrates that a new interpretation of the law can be established even if the defendant
   a. loses the case
   b. is found guilty but not punished
   c. has no valid argument

3. In the *Gibbons v. Ogden* case, Chief Justice Marshall defined commerce as
   a. only trade done between states
   b. every type of commercial intercourse including navigation
   c. transportation
4. *McCulloch v. Maryland* stands as a precedent for those who support
   a. strict construction
   b. no judicial review
   c. expansion of the power of the Federal government

ANSWERS

True or False: 1. T, 2. T, 3. T, 4. F, 5. T.
Multiple Choice: 1. b, 2. a, 3. b, 4. c.

II. RELIGION AND REFORM: 1800–1850

Religion, like laws and judges, provides individuals with rules or guidelines for behavior. Religion has played an important role in this country since the arrival of the Puritans in New England. Although the First Amendment of the Bill of Rights required the separation of church and state, religion has, in both our personal and public lives, continued to provide guidelines for conduct.

In spite of the first Amendment, religion plays an important role in the United States.

Often these have provided the stimulus for very positive, creative, and beneficial acts. At other times, when one religious denomination or group has tried to enforce its viewpoint on others or when a group of Americans have reacted with intolerance to the views of a religious group, the result has been very negative, creating dissension and division. We see such a division in the United States today in the controversy over abortion, which is partly rooted in different religious viewpoints. Both the positive and negative influence of religious attitudes are reflected in United States history.

The First Great Awakening

We have mentioned 17th century Puritanism and its continued importance in New England. In the 1740s there was a major revival of religious concerns in New Jersey and Pennsylvania, which spread throughout the Colonies and is known as the Great Awakening. Stimulated by preachers from England, ministers emphasized personal revelation and the reading of the Bible. The Methodist church, founded in England, was brought to America as part of this first Great Awakening. One of the longest lasting results of the Great Awakening was the founding of several colleges such as Princeton, the University of Pennsylvania, Columbia, Brown, and Rutgers—all for the training of ministers.

The Great Awakening of the 1740's was the first of many such religious revivals which emphasize one's ability to be "born again" to God's way.

This Great Awakening was only the first of several periods of revivals in American history, all of which had major impact on the nation. Each period of revival has emphasized the individual's personal relationship to God, thus reinforcing American individualism. Revival religion has emphasized that no one's fate is predetermined, as some religious teachings suggest, but instead, that by changing yourself or being "born again" to God's ways, you can determine your own fate and be saved. This has give a great sense of security and of mission to those who have been "saved" or "born again" as Christians.

This sense of mission played a very important role in United States' history in the 1820s and 1830s, leading to many reform movements. Revival religion also had an element of fundamentalism, holding that the Bible contains the specific words of God and must be followed. This in turn has put an emphasis on education and the ability to read the Bible.

John Atwood family
This painting of the Reverend John Atwood and His Family was painted in 1845 by the artist Henry F. Darby. It illustrates many aspects of life in America in the middle of the 19th century. Look at the clothing. Would you like to wear it? Whose style of clothing—wife, husband, children—has changed the most since then? Notice the wallpaper, rug, and spinet piano. The family appears comfortably well off which suggests the importance of the clergy in America.

The Second Great Awakening

A second Great Awakening began in western New York state in 1821 when Charles G. Finney had a religious conversion. His preaching emphasized revival religion and that Christians by making the right choices could find salvation.

His preachings and those of his followers had particular appeal to women on the frontier and in urban centers where women's lives were often isolated. They enjoyed the community activity of meetings with visiting preachers, going to church, and participating in church-sponsored activities out of the home. They appreciated the message of individualism and redemption.

The Great Awakening's impact, however, was not just on women. New religious groups such as the Latter Day Saints, commonly called the Mormons, founded in 1830, grew out of the atmosphere created by the Second Great Awakening. The message of revival religion—individualism, a community of chosen people, the potential worth of each individual in God's eyes—reinforced the growing democratic attitudes of Americans. It gave support to and provided a base for many of the reform movements that developed in the 1830s and 1840s. These reforms are often lumped together under the phrase "Jacksonian Democracy."

Revival religion of the Second Great Awakening provides impetus to many reform movements.

Reforms in Education

The reform aspects of Jacksonian Democracy that probably most affect you, the student, are those that took place in education. These reforms are often linked to Horace Mann, who served as Secretary of the newly created Massachusetts Board of Education from 1837 to 1848. He established the first minimum school year requirement: six months of school. He saw the first training college for teachers established and fifty new high schools built in the state. Curriculum changes instituted by Horace Mann included less emphasis on religion and more on "useful skills" and on making the students into good citizens. This latter included the teaching of American history and you, as you read this work, are following in that line.

Education is seen as a way to attack problems of poverty and crime.

Mann and his fellow education reformers of the pre-Civil War era were convinced that education was the best way to attack problems of poverty and crime. It was an optimistic message, reflecting the optimism of revival religion. Connecticut soon followed Massachusetts in instituting educational reforms and in the years following these reforms spread around the nation.

Some of these reforms were directed at the education of women. In 1821, the first women's high school in the nation was opened in Troy, New York, by Emma Willard. Oberlin College in Ohio became the first co-ed college in the country in 1833, and Mount Holyoke, the first women's college, was established in Mount Holyoke, Massachusetts in 1836.

The Women's Movement

Another reform that may seem very contemporary centered on feminism. Its roots were complex and include women's involvement in the Second Great Awakening. Women's leadership roles in reform efforts such as temperance and abolition and their growing role in the workforce helped train leaders for these reform efforts. A growing realization that the legal status of women was demeaning, since many state laws gave wives no individual rights over

While the Women's Movement was comparatively unsuccessful, the Seneca Falls convention listed women's grievances and provided a program for future action.

money or property and denied them the vote, provided a catalyst for the pre-Civil War feminist movement.

Among the early organizers of the movement were two sisters, Angelina and Sarah Grimke, who began lecturing against slavery but came to realize the status of women was not greatly different from that of slaves. The movement was not as successful as other reforms of the Jacksonian period. Few men joined or supported the women's movement.

An important meeting at Seneca Falls, New York, in 1848, issued a proclamation modeled on the Declaration of Independence listing women's grievances and calling for action. The Seneca Falls convention was led by Elizabeth Cady Stanton and Lucretia Mott, who became the leaders of the movement for women's rights. In the years after 1850, the women's movement focused more and more on gaining the vote for women, believing this to be the first step towards gaining equal rights. However, after 1850, the nation as a whole became more and more focused on another reform movement: abolition.

Abolition

While throughout United States history some individuals and groups such as Quakers had expressed opposition to slavery and the first state, Pennsylvania, to abolish slavery did so in 1780, the movement for total abolition of slavery in the United States did not gain momentum until the 1830s. The American Colonization Society, formed in 1816, had as its goal the resettlement of freed slaves in Africa. Free African-Americans in the North worked for immediate abolition. A few whites worked for gradual abolition.

The abolitionist movement steadily gains in importance in the period from 1831–1860.

Then, in 1831, matters changed with the publication of the *Liberator* by William Lloyd Garrison. He had been a gradualist, but in the *Liberator* called for "immediate and complete emancipation" of slaves. Garrison's leadership, the moral and ethical climate established by the Second Great Awakening, and the political and economic ramifications of the possible spread of slavery into the western territories, such as Louisiana, and later, Texas, California, and the New Mexico territory, combined to create strong support for the abolitionists. Harriet Tubman, known for her efforts on the Underground Railway[1], and Frederick Douglass, a self-educated, articulate former slave, were outstanding African-American leaders of the abolition movement.

Feeling threatened by abolitionist publications, Southern states seized the literature and attacked abolitionists, actions many northerners saw as a threat to individual civil rights. In Congress, the Gag Rule was passed in 1837. It blocked the petitions of abolitionists to Congress and cut out debate in Congress on the issue of slavery.

At first, the abolitionists were not united in their programs, but the activities of the pro-slavery forces particularly in calling for the return of escaped slaves slowly brought them together. The

---

[1]*Underground Railway* An escape route for slaves organized by abolitionists so slaves could travel North, often to Canada, by night and be hidden by day.

Compromise of 1850 attempted to reconcile the political differences between pro- and anti-slavery forces. It could not last, as the abolitionist forces became more united in the 1850s. They saw the political developments of the decade (see next chapter) as a threat to individual rights and a move to force on the nation the extension of slavery. Their attacks, based on moral and ethical objections, made the abolition of slavery a major political issue of the 1850s.

Temperance

Temperance, the reform movement aimed at the banning of alcohol, also had a strong moral and ethical base. The consumption of alcohol was widespread in America. Frontiersmen drank in saloons, city dwellers in public houses, and "respectable" women drank patent medicine at home. Drinking crossed class lines. Revivalist preachers and their followers viewed it as the destroyer of family life. Factory owners saw it as the destroyer of good work habits. Christians saw it as an attack on the holy Sabbath as bars and taverns were open for business on the working man's one day off.

These elements combined to create a movement against alcohol consumption. At first, workers for temperance urged individuals to abstain, but as the movement grew, prohibition of both the sale and manufacture of alcohol became their goal. Under the pressure of temperance groups, alcoholic use dropped dramatically, and in 1846 Maine passed the first state prohibition law.

The Temperance Movement gains support from different groups and achieves success when Maine passes a prohibition law.

Temperance was one of the more successful reform movements of the period of Jacksonian Democracy. The temperance movement remained an important fact in American life throughout the 19th century and had strong political impact. The Anti-Saloon League, formed in 1895, finally achieved the temperance movement's goal of prohibition nationally in 1919 with the ratification of the 18th Amendment to the Constitution. That amendment was repealed in 1933. The concept of prohibition and temperance continues to be a force in America, where its utopian dream of an alcohol-free society appeals to many.

Utopian Communities

Another result of the Second Great Awakening on American life was the growth of utopian[2] thinking. The idea that life on Earth can be improved, that it can, by human efforts, approximate a perfect situation, has many roots but a particularly strong one is its religious root. Revival religion emphasized that by human action one's life can be made better and that one can be saved. If one believes that, then by extension, one can design a community with rules that will make life better or lead to perfection on Earth.

Utopians believed that with rules, humans can design a community that will make life better and lead to perfection on earth.

Utopianism had appeared in America prior to the Second Great Awakening. One example is the religious communities of the Shakers whose founder, the Englishwoman Ann Lee, taught that

---

[2]*Utopian* A visionary who believes in the perfectability of human society.

sin entered the world through sexual intercourse. Shakers established several communities in New England and New York where they lead celibate lives, hoping to improve the world through human action.

Several utopian communities in United States history have focused on ways to improve the lot of the factory worker. The first was organized at New Harmony, Indiana, by Robert Owen in 1825. Unfortunately, when the workers attempted to run the textile mill, it failed and New Harmony collapsed. Later in the century, George M. Pullman created a supposedly ideal community where Pullman railroad cars were manufactured. It too collapsed over economic disagreements between workers and Mr. Pullman. In spite of such failures, utopian communities have continued to be established throughout our history. A large number were established during the Vietnam era of the 1960s and early 1970s.

Utopians attempt to improve life for workers.

Brook Farm and Transcendentalism

The most interesting utopian community of this era was Brook Farm, founded in West Roxbury, Massachusetts. Its founders were Unitarians and Transcendentalists. The teachings of Unitarianism were introduced in Boston by W. E. Channing in 1819. Unitarian faith emphasized both individualism and brotherhood. Transcendentalism was not a systematic philosophy, but Transcendentalists held that each person's individual understanding of experience was unique and sacred, that humans had a divine spark, and in a mystic relation to nature could discover truth. Brook Farm brought together in a community of shared work the greatest literary figures of the first sixty years of United States history. Sharing a belief in Transcendentalism, these authors—Nathaniel Hawthorne, Ralph Waldo Emerson, Henry David Thoreau, James Fenimore Cooper, Herman Melville, Margaret Fuller (the editor of the *Dial*, the journal of Transcendentalism)—shared their ideas and farmed together. The farm experiment proved unsuccessful, but the sharing of ideas helped establish an American literary tradition. The writers emphasized nature, self-reliance, and the individual. These factors formed the basis of the Romantics' view of life. Romanticism[3] has been an important element in the arts in America throughout our history and can be seen especially in painting and literature.

Transcendentalist authors found the utopian community of Brook Farm

While few people read these early American authors today, their works had important impact on succeeding generations. Ralph Waldo Emerson's essays reflect many of the values associated with Jacksonian Democracy. Henry David Thoreau in *Walden* described his voluntary existence in a cabin beside Walden Pond. He emphasized the individual and nature. His comment about each man marching "to his own drummer" was widely quoted during the

Emerson, Thoreau, and Melville help establish an American literary tradition.

---

[3]*Romanticism* A literary movement, but one also seen in the fine arts; the Romantic movement of the 19th century emphasized the importance of imagination and sentiment against the rules and formality of classicism. There was strong emphasis on individualism in both thought and expression.

Vietnam protests. It is a strong statement for individualism and civil disobedience. Herman Melville's major work, *Moby Dick*, relates a struggle of power, of good versus evil, in the story of the obsessed sea captain, Captain Ahab, and his battle with the white whale, Moby Dick.

The Willey House, 1838
In this 1838 print by E. Benjamin and W. H. Bartlett of The Willey House *the American interest in nature and the romantic is seen. It can be found in many of the art works of the pre-Civil War period. The Willey House was located in a notch in the White Mountains of New Hampshire. The area was soon to be a center for vacationing wealthy Americans, and it was works such as this that made these resorts famous. Would you like to spend a vacation at the Willey House?*

Published for the Proprietors by George Virtue, London, 1838.

These three authors, as well as others, reflect the society of which they were a part. By reading these works, the historian can gain important insights into the thought patterns of an age and learn what were the expected rules and guidelines for behavior. The works of these early American writers all suggest the importance of the individual and the choices he or she must make. The writers accept rules of conduct that are grounded in religious understanding—Christian, Unitarian, or Transcendental.

They and the leaders of the various reform movements—education, feminism, temperance, utopian communities—all reflect the good side of revival religion. Unfortunately, there were other movements in the 1830s–1850s also grounded in religious conviction that were negative and reflect a less positive aspect of commitment to a particular viewpoint.

KEY POINT TO REMEMBER

The Second Great Awakening reinforced a growing interest in democracy and reform in the nation, and under the name of Jacksonian democracy many leaders pursued reform especially in education, women's rights, and temperance.

PEOPLE TO REMEMBER

Frederick Douglass   Black abolitionist, writer and orator; born a slave of a white father, he escaped and became a spokesperson for the Massachusetts Anti-Slavery Society; wrote *Narrative of the Life of Frederick Douglass*, edited an abolitionist newspaper, lectured on abolition, and served as United States Consul General to Haiti.

Harriet Tubman   Abolitionist leader; born a slave, escaped, and worked on the Underground Railway leading slaves north to freedom; was known as "Moses" to the movement members.

LINKS FROM THE PAST TO THE PRESENT

1. Temperance, education, and women's reform movements are still important issues today.
2. The influence of revival religion and "born again" Christians is seen in reform movements and government policy, from the first Great Awakening to TV evangelists like Jerry Falwell.
3. Concern for equality, freedom, and the individual has been expressed in many ways throughout our history from the abolition movement to federal laws to Supreme Court decisions to anti-war movements.

QUESTIONS

Identify each of the following:

Great Awakening	Horace Mann
Second Great Awakening	Angelina and Sarah Grimke
Revival religion	Harriet Tubman
Seneca Falls convention	Ralph Waldo Emerson
The *Liberator*	Henry David Thoreau
New Harmony, Indiana	Herman Melville
Brook Farm	Transcendentalism

True or False:

1. The first Great Awakening had no effect on American education.
2. The Second Great Awakening had a particular appeal to women, who in the early 19th century often led lives isolated from community activities.
3. The Massachusetts Board of Education in the 1830s established a six-month requirement for school attendance.
4. The legal status of women and opportunities open to them in the workplace were equal to those of men in the first half of the 19th century.
5. The abolitionists were concerned about the spread of slavery to new territory.

6. The temperance movement never achieved success at the national level.
7. The Shakers lived celibate lives, as they believed there were already too many orphans in the world.
8. Brook Farm was a highly successful and productive utopian agricultural community.

Multiple Choice:

1. In *Walden*, Henry David Thoreau described
   a. his experiences fighting Walden, a white whale
   b. Walden, the ideal community combining intellectual and physical labor
   c. his solitary existence in a cabin beside Walden Pond
2. The Second Great Awakening inspired
   a. the building of Princeton, Brown, and Columbia Universities
   b. many of the reforms of the Jacksonian period
   c. a negative response to religious teaching
3. Abolition became an important issue in American life because of the
   a. ending of the slave trade
   b. concern over the spread of slavery as an accepted institution in the territories
   c. breakdown of the Underground Railway
4. Temperance became an important issue because
   a. factory owners saw it as the destroyer of good work habits
   b. revivalist preachers saw it as a destroyer of family life
   c. both of the above

ANSWERS

True or False: 1. F, 2. T, 3. T, 4. F, 5. T, 6. F, 7. F, 8. F.
Multiple Choice: 1. c, 2. b, 3. b, 4. c.

III SOCIAL CHANGES IN AMERICA

American Nativism

One movement grounded in both religious conviction and a sense of nationalism and uniqueness was the Native American Association formed in Washington, D.C. in 1837. The name is very interesting, since with our current use of the term Native American, we might think it was an Indian tribal organization but it was not. The members of the Native American Association were white Europeans, most of whose ancestors had immigrated to America before the American Revolution. They believed they were the native Americans and resented and feared the new immigrants.

In the 1830s there was increased Irish immigration and many of the new immigrants were Catholic. The focus of the association became, therefore, anti-Catholic and anti-Irish immigration. The Native American Association entered the political arena in 1845, creating the Native American Party. Its program called for changes

The Native American Party is formed to oppose Irish immigration and Roman Catholicism.

in the naturalization laws and restricting the voting rights and office-holding privileges of Catholics. Violent conflict between Catholics and Protestants occurred in Philadelphia in 1844, and twenty people were killed.

The intensity of commitment to one's own religious faith and fear and hatred of others is a reflection of the negative aspect of revivalist religion. Strong feelings of belief are important but can become intolerant of other's beliefs.

The Native American Party was unsuccessful. A new party, the Know-Nothing Party, was organized in the 1850s and had as its major purpose agitation against Catholics. The intolerance of these two political parties, with their strong sense of righteousness rooted in their own religious beliefs, has returned at other times in our history. This intolerance is one example of the negative side of American Nationalism and Jacksonian democracy. As we have seen, Jacksonian democracy itself was a very diversified movement reflecting the great diversity that had developed in American life by the 1830s.

Intolerance is a negative aspect of Nationalism.

Diversity in Wealth and Labor

The diversity in America can be illustrated in several areas.

Some of the more interesting examples of this diversity can be found in the division of wealth and labor, the contrast between urban and farm life, the changes in American economic life, and the increasing number of immigrants in the period between 1830 and 1850. Many families became wealthy during the Colonial period, and many continued wealthy by carefully investing in new enterprises ranging from canals to mills. A few Americans, such as John Jacob Astor in the western fur trade, made fortunes in the early 19th century. It is estimated that by 1860 the wealthiest ten percent in the United States owned seventy percent of its wealth. Such figures for the distribution of wealth continue to the present in the United States.

At the other extreme from this ten percent were the urban poor who lived in slum areas of the cities, as do our poorest citizens today. There was a growing middle class of working men and housewives whose economic position was precarious and who were threatened by every economic crisis, such as the panics of 1819 and 1837.

Industrialization redefines the role of men and women, and reinforces class divisions.

In the Age of Jackson, which was an age of growing democracy, the country had a distinctive class division of slaves, poor, middle class, and wealthy. As industrial growth developed and cities grew, the work done by men and women diverged from the old agricultural life where couples worked the farm together. Men tended to leave the home to work in businesses or factories; women tended to stay home to care for children and do the household chores. There were exceptions, and some women were employed in factories and retail shops, but the majority of employed single women held positions related to the home—cooks, servants, or boarding house managers. As public schools increased, some women found employment there as they do today. The pattern of the distribution of wealth continues today but the distribution of jobs changed drastically during and after World War II.

The Lowell factory girls provide a precursor of the role women were to play in factories during and after World War II. The Lowell system was first established in Waltham, Massachusetts. Large factories were built along the river after the development of water-driven power looms for weaving textiles. Workers, largely young girls from local farms, were employed by Francis Cabot Lowell. The hours were long and the pay low, but the factories were clean and the girls lived under careful supervision in boarding houses designed and controlled by Mr. Lowell. Their parents were thus much happier letting their young daughters go to the growing city.

The Lowell system brought some women into the work force, encouraged the manufacture of textiles in New England, and reflected the moral and ethical attitudes of revival religion, which taught concern for the individual poor. The paternalistic approach to their workers by Lowell and other factory owners in the era reflects both concern for their well-being and a way to make good profits. The girls could be employed at low wages. However, when immigrant labor could be employed at even lower pay in the early 1850s, it was no longer necessary to maintain the expenses of the boarding houses, and profits could be increased.

The Lowell system brings women into the work force.

Diversity in Urban and Farm Life

Cities grew rapidly in the first half of the 19th century, and business patterns and lifestyle changed dramatically as a result. Retail shops became specialized, as did business functions; factories needed workers, and farmers and immigrants came to fill the jobs. Slum areas developed where the poor lived; pleasant areas were planned and inhabited by wealthy citizens. Smells—there were few sewers and little garbage collection—were everywhere; crime flourished. Boston, in 1837, organized the first city police force in the country. As today, there were many opportunities in the city. The cities teemed with life. Entertainment became business. By contrast, life on the farm was more traditional and often isolated and lonely. Entertainment had to be created and often took the form of a trip to the nearest village, where men could gather at the local tavern and women could visit. Barn raisings, a community effort to help a fellow farmer improve his land, quilting bees, or similar events also supplied social life for the farmer.

Cities offer many opportunities but also many problems, while farms are often isolated.

Changes, however, were taking place in farm life as new machines such as the McCormack reaper were invented. The Eastern farms, particularly those small rock stream farms in New England, were not suited to the use of the new machinery. Many New Englanders went west or to the city. Those that remained adapted to dairy and vegetable farming. The farms in the old Northwest prospered using the machinery and with the canal and later railroad lines they were able to ship their produce to ever larger markets.

Today, with TV, telephones, and automobiles, the contrast between farm and urban life may not be as great, but there still exists a sharp contrast between these two lifestyles. It was particularly obvious in the pre-Civil War period.

Rustic Dance after a Sleigh Ride, by Mount
This painting of a Rustic Dance after a Sleigh Ride *by William S. Mount done in 1830 is typical of Mount's work in which he portrayed the daily life of Americans before the Civil War. Note his portrayal of the African-Americans and the place they have in the scene. How has clothing changed from that worn by the Isaac Winslow family? Does this look like a dance scene today? What similarities are there? Do young men still gather together? What is the relationship between the partners?*

Diversity of Peoples: Irish and German Immigrants

As we learned in Chapter 1, all inhabitants of the Americas arrived as immigrants. In the United States in 1800 the majority of European immigrants were English, Scotch-Irish, Scottish or Welsh, from the British Isles. There were settlers from other countries, but after the English victories in the 18th century wars, the future territory of the United States became effectively English and Protestant although there was usually toleration of other faiths. After 1800 the United States expanded both geographically and industrially, and more people were needed. Immigration increased. Some states that were building railroads or canals in the pre-Civil War period even advertised for immigrants to come to take jobs. The first non-English, non-Protestant group to arrive in large numbers were the Irish. They settled largely in New York and

Immigration increases as the United States expands.

114

Boston, whose population reached 35 percent foreign born. The Irish who arrived were Catholic and largely from rural areas. As was true of most 19th century immigrants, at first they found the adjustment difficult. It was made harder by the rise of American nationalism and intolerance described earlier, which was spurred on by the differences, particularly religious, between the Irish immigrants and the majority of Americans. Irish immigration reached its peak around 1850 when over a million Irish arrived in a period of five years.

Germans also came. They too found the adjustment difficult. Many continued to speak German and were Catholic, which separated them from the majority of the American population. Their celebration on Sundays, with dancing and beer drinking, drew the wrath of Protestants, who saw the Germans as profaning God's day, and of the termperance leaders who opposed beer drinking. No immigrant group has found adjustment easy, but they all brought diversity and made great contributions to American life. Gradually the Irish and Germans were integrated into mainstream American life. Antagonism was directed at other immigrant groups who arrived in large numbers between the Civil War and World War I.

While not accepted at first, gradually the Irish and German immigrants were accepted as Americans and antagonism was directed toward other immigrant groups.

In the years between 1800 and 1850 many changes in American economic life increased the diversity of opportunities available to all people. As people moved west, transportation was needed and this led to improvements and new inventions that in turn speeded the westward movement of the frontier. The frontier ran from Ohio through Kentucky and Tennessee to western Georgia in 1800, but by 1850 it was the area between the Mississippi and the Rockies with areas of settlement in Texas, California, and Oregon.

The first of many inventions that changed transportation was the steamboat, patented in 1791. By 1807 Robert Fulton had a truly successful model, and he was given the monopoly for transportation on the Hudson River mentioned earlier. By 1848 the English Cunard company began regularly scheduled steamboat travel between New York and Liverpool, England. The time of passage was approximately two weeks. Transatlantic travel by steamboat made immigrant travel to the United States much easier.

Inventions make transportation easier, which realigns political commitments.

The first railroad opened in 1830, and by 1850 railroads were the chief means of heavy transport between the old Northwest Territory and the East, replacing the Erie Canal. The Erie Canal, an example of an internal improvement built by a state, had opened in 1825 to connect the Hudson River with the Great Lakes. It helped tie the Northwest to the East economically and provided a route west for many New England farmers. The canal and the railroads realigned the political commitments as the Westerners could send their produce to the large urban markets of the East and were no longer dependent on the river traffic down the Ohio and Mississippi rivers.

The telegraph, invented by Samuel F. B. Morse, made almost instant communication possible and tied the nation even closer together. The invention in 1793 of the cotton gin by Eli Whitney set a pattern for American manufacturing. The development of

The concept of standardized or interchangeable parts revolutionizes American manufacturing.

standardized or interchangeable parts made possible the manufacture of many identical items. Colt revolvers used on the frontier to help conquer the West and McCormack's reapers used in the expanding farmlands of the Midwest used this concept making many machines all the same, with parts that could be exchanged or replaced. Later Henry Ford used this concept in manufacturing the Model T Ford.

Specialization, standardization, and interchangeable parts made possible the rapid growth of American industry in the period before 1850. These developments in transportation, communication, and manufacturing increased the diversity of opportunities available to Americans and changed America's way of living. In the first half of the 19th century America grew dramatically.

Pittsburgh Post Office, by Blythe
This painting of the Pittsburgh Post Office by David Gilmore Blythe illustrates the importance of the post office as a place for news and information when only the telegraph competed with the mail as a way of sending news. The place of women in society is illustrated by the "Gentlemens Only" sign above the window. Women were to be "protected" from the harshness of the male's reaction to news. Would you approve of such separation?

Summary

During the period 1800–1850 America grew as a nation. A strong sense of nationalism was reinforced by the decisions of the Supreme Court under Chief Justice Marshall. The Second Great Awakening laid the foundation for reform movements that affected the American way of life. The increase in the numbers of immigrants with different religions created some urban difficulties. The developments in manufacturing, communication, and transportation also created a greater diversity in the American nation.

KEY POINT TO REMEMBER

Between 1800 and 1850 the United States became much more diverse: large numbers of new immigrants, especially Irish, arrived; the gap between rich and poor and the contrast between urban and rural life grew; inventions aided the growth of manufacturing and provided new opportunities for many; a series of reform movements grouped as Jacksonian democracy changed American life.

LINKS FROM THE PAST TO THE PRESENT

1. Fear of and antagonism towards "foreigners" and immigrants has appeared many times and in many forms, ranging from the Alien and Sedition Acts to anti-Irish political parties to immigration legislation.
2. There has been a continuing struggle to provide jobs and other opportunities for women since the 1830s.
3. Changes in manufacturing and transportation transformed the country in the 19th century and changes continue.

QUESTIONS

Identify each of the following:

Native American Association	Standardization and
Lowell factory girls	interchangeable parts
McCormack reaper	Cunard Company

True or False:

1. Tensions between Protestants and Irish Catholic immigrants led to violent conflict in Philadelphia.
2. John Jacob Astor made a fortune in the steamship business.
3. Women who found employment outside the home in the period 1820–1850 usually worked as cooks or servants and sometimes as retail clerks or teachers.
4. Francis Cabot Lowell designed a paternalistic system of care for his factory girls.
5. There were no police departments in any city before the Civil War began in 1861.
6. New England farmers successfully adapted the use of new farm machinery to their rock-strewn fields.
7. Over a million Irish immigrants came to America within a period of five years around 1850.

8. The Erie Canal made easier the transport of Western agricultural produce to the East Coast.
9. Eli Whitney invented the cotton gin and telegraph — two inventions that changed American life.
10. Slums, smells, and crime were all part of urban life prior to 1850.

Multiple Choice:
1. The Native American and the Know Nothing parties
   a. had a strong sense of righteousness rooted in religious beliefs
   b. encouraged immigration of Irish Catholics
   c. were successful third parties
2. As manufacturing grew, most men left the home to work during the day and most women
   a. found jobs in retail shops
   b. stayed home to care for the children and do the household chores
   c. became school teachers
3. The contrast between farm and urban life widened as farms continued to be
   a. centers of entertainment and intellectual stimulation
   b. places where new machinery was never used
   c. isolated and lonely places
4. Among the many changes in American life before the Civil War were the introduction of
   a. railroads and automobiles
   b. the steamboat and telegraph
   c. the McCormack reaper and telephone

ANSWERS

True or False: 1. T, 2. F, 3. T, 4. T, 5. F, 6. F, 7. T, 8. T, 9. F, 10. T.
Multiple Choice: 1. a, 2. b, 3. c, 4. b.

CHAPTER 7

Slavery and
The Civil War

APPROACHES TO HISTORY
Economics and History

There is one group of historians who believe all human actions are the result of economic conditions. They believe that all social standing and political power is based on one's level of prosperity, that economic forces drive us to be who we are and what we are. These historians believe that the desire for material goods and well-being drives all people and determines history.

Historians who believe in economic determinism look for the economic motives that they believe underlie all political and social developments. It is certainly clear that having money and material goods is important in American society. You must realize this whether you have, or do not have, much material wealth. Money allows you to enjoy things you cannot otherwise have, such as new CDs, a shopping trip to the mall, or a new videotape. You may also realize how hard it is to work and save enough money for a major purchase such as a car.

If you do not have money or material goods to begin with, you can easily believe your future is determined. This is what drives economic determinists to see economics as the driving force of history. Karl Marx[1], the German philosopher, first expressed the theory of economic determinism and the historians who follow his interpretation of history are called Marxist historians. As we study the history from 1850 to 1876, it may be easier to understand if we think in terms of the economic needs and motivations of the leaders and people of that time. To what extent were they driven by economics?

---

[1]*Karl Marx* A German philosopher and economist who believed that the forces driving history are material, i.e. economic. We refer to historians who follow this theory as economic determinists or Marxist historians.

I. THE FAILURE OF COMPROMISE

The Institution of Slavery

The Southern way of life in the years before the start of the Civil War in 1861 was rooted in the institution of slavery. While over two-thirds of the homes in the South had no slaves, the social and political leaders of the South did. Slaves worked the larger, wealthier plantations and even a few yeoman farmers had a slave or two to help on their small farms.

After the invention of the cotton gin in 1793, cotton became the great cash crop of the South. Growing it required heavy labor, which was supplied by slaves. Southern spokesmen believed that without the slaves they could not grow cotton and their economic prosperity would collapse. While there were many yeoman farmers on the Southern frontier who lived independent and sufficient lives without slaves and there were a number of free blacks and mulattoes, their economic impact on the South was negligible. These groups, except for the free African-Americans, endorsed the wealthy leaders who set the political and social goals for the South.

Thus at the root of any discussion of slavery, its merits or its horrors, its expansion into new territory or its abolition, was its economic necessity for the South as seen by the Southern leadership.

Unfortunately, this issue was never directly confronted nor solutions offered to make an economic shift in Southern lifestyle possible. Instead, slavery became an issue in political arguments over power and territory and in moral arguments over the treatment of slaves and the need for abolition. The true interests and needs of the South were never addressed, and economic solutions were never offered that might have compensated Southerners for their freeing of the slaves.

Political power and the extension of slavery to new territories were important issues for United States history, but the economic determinist would declare all these arguments missed the true point, the economic importance of slavery to the Southerner.

In recent years a lot of study has been done on the institution of Southern slavery. While the number of slaves grew prior to the Civil War, the percentage of Southerners owning slaves dropped. While the image of large plantations with many slaves still persists, just over ten percent of those owning slaves owned more than twenty. The majority of slaves worked on farms with fewer than five fellow slaves. Life was harsh for all slaves, food was monotonous, clothing was scarce, and housing was inadequate. Slaves were viewed paternalistically as inferior beings who needed to be protected.

This attitude permeated Southern thinking and established race rather than economic class as the divider between groups, setting whites against blacks. Yet the racial division was rooted in the economic need for slave labor. The purpose of a plantation was to make money, and slaves were worked by overseers from dawn to

The economic welfare of the South depended on expanding the growth of cotton, the South's major cash crop, which was cultivated by slave labor.

An ecomomic alternative to cotton production and slavery was never seriously explored.

The attitude that viewed African-American slaves as inferior beings established race, not class, as the divider between white and black.

dusk and in all seasons. A few slaves had it easier, doing jobs within the house. Often planters who had children by slave mistresses treated their offspring well and even educated them. Several of the well educated blacks became leaders in the post-Civil War reconstruction.

On the whole, life for the slaves was bleak, but they were able to maintain a sense of identity and build on their African traditions, which are seen in everything from their clothing style to musical instruments. Many slaves adopted Christianity, which for them was a religion of hope and salvation for all, a point missed by many whites. Slaves maintained a sense of family in spite of the fact families could be split by slave auctions.

Slaves were property. The reason for owning them was to make money. Slaves did greatly affect the social and political life of the South, but the reason they did so was because of their economic importance.

Slavery Issues Before 1850

Slavery was a factor in American life since the first colony. African-American slaves were brought to Jamestown in 1619 to help create wealth by working in the tobacco fields. When the English colonies declared independence and proclaimed that "all men are created equal...," a moral dilemma was also created.

The slavery issue periodically became an important matter after independence: the slave trade was abolished in 1807; the Missouri Compromise which banned slavery north of 36°30' was adopted in 1820; the *Liberator* was first published by William Lloyd Garrison in 1831, and as a result the abolition movement gained life; Congress avoided the slave issue by adhering to the Gag Rule in 1837; anti-slavery forces opposed the annexation of Texas and the Mexican War of 1846–8. The Great Compromise of 1850 included a strong anti-fugitive slave law. The political leaders hoped the Compromise of 1850 would satisfy pro- and anti-slavery forces and put the question to rest. It did not.

Slavery becomes more and more a political issue.

Slavery and Territorial Expansion

The slaves did constitute a powerful interest that the South had to defend. As the nation expanded in the 1840s to reach its Manifest Destiny, it became clear that these new territories would someday enter the Union. If they entered as free states, the South, which had a smaller population than the non-slave states and so had a smaller representation in the House of Representatives, would lose its parity[2] or equality with the North in the number of Senators it had. This loss of political power through loss of representation could have grave consequences at a time the Abolitionists were agitating. The South saw the necessity that some of the new territories be slave territories.

The Compromise of 1850 maintained the balance in the Senate and introduced a new concept, popular sovereignty, into the

The South sees a need to expand slavery to new territories in order to maintain the balance of slave and non-slave states.

---

[2]*parity* Equality; often used when comparing the currency of two nations.

organization of the territories. The New Mexico territory was organized without restriction on slavery and with the proviso that when it applied for statehood it would enter free or slave depending on what the state Constitution said at the time. Leaving the decision up to the people in the territory would give more power to the people and give them more control over their future, according to the theory.

Previously, Congress had indicated when organizing territories whether they would be free or slave. Questions had been raised as to whether Congress had this power. Popular sovereignty[3] seemed to its supporters to be a fair and democratic way to determine the future of slavery in the territories. The idea of popular sovereignty was another side of the movement for greater democracy begun under Andrew Jackson. States had been adopting universal male suffrage, and letting the males in the territories vote on slavery furthered this idea.

The Fugitive Slave Law and *Uncle Tom's Cabin*

A good illustration of the complexity and contradictory nature of the conflict over slavery is the Fugitive Slave Law, approved as part of the Compromise of 1850. While Senators voted to let the inhabitants of the territories vote on whether to adopt slavery, they voted to use federal money to help capture and return escaped slaves to their owners. Again we see the economic importance placed on slaves by the South. They demanded their human property be returned to them.

Uncle Tom's Cabin stirs the conscience of the North and crystallizes anti-slavery sentiment.

The Fugitive Slave Law backfired. While few slaves escaped and were captured, those that did received such publicity in the North that Northerners were exposed to a particularly cruel aspect of slavery and were morally repulsed. A book, *Uncle Tom's Cabin*, strengthened this repulsion through its description of slavery and slave conditions. Written by Harriet Beecher Stowe, an abolitionist sympathizer, and published in 1852, *Uncle Tom's Cabin* in its first year sold over a quarter million copies in a nation of just over 21 million people. *Uncle Tom's Cabin* was one of the most influential books in history as it helped to crystallize Northern opinions about slavery. It is an excellent illustration of both the power of a free press and the influence an individual can have on history.

The Kansas-Nebraska Territory and Popular Sovereignty

Popular sovereignty, which includes the idea of universal suffrage, is supported by Congress, which repeals the Missouri Compromise.

In 1854 attention in Congress turned to the organization of the Kansas-Nebraska territory. This area was north of the Missouri Compromise line of 36°30′ and so, according to that law, should have been organized without slavery. Stephen A. Douglas from Illinois, a Democrat with presidential ambitions who needed

---

[3]*popular sovereignty* Sovereignty is the power to rule, and popular means the people. Popular sovereignty put the decison of who was to rule or how ruling was to be done in the hands of the people in the area concerned. In the specific case of slavery extension, popular sovereignty meant the people in the territory would decide the slavery question.

Southern support, introduced a bill, the Kansas-Nebraska Act, to organize the territory incorporating the idea of popular sovereignty. The South, as Douglas hoped, saw this as a chance to spread slavery into an area previously closed to it.

The bill was passed; the Missouri Compromise was specifically abandoned by Congress. The question now became who would control Kansas. There was fighting in Kansas, which was dubbed "bleeding Kansas" as a result. Pro- and anti-slavery governments were established. Manipulations in Congress prevented either government from being accepted as legitimate.

The Kansas-Nebraska Bill backfired, and Stephen Douglas lost the 1856 Democratic nomination for President. Partly in reaction to the Act, a new party, the Republican Party, was formed in 1854 to oppose the extension of slavery. Kansas finally entered the Union as a free state in 1861 after the Southern states had seceded. Popular sovereignty did not prove successful as a way to deal with the slavery issue.

The Republican Party is formed to oppose the extension of slavery.

The Supreme Court on Slavery: *Dred Scott v. Sandford*

The Supreme Court next offered a solution to the slavery issue in the *Dred Scott v. Sandford* case in 1857. The case involved Dred Scott, a slave, who had been taken by his owner to a free state, Illinois, and a free territory, Wisconsin. Scott sued for freedom in the Missouri courts and appealed its decision to the Supreme Court. Hoping to resolve the issue of slavery in the territories, the Court entered the political arena with its decision. Chief Justice Taney and the Court held that Scott was not a citizen of the United States or of Missouri and could not sue in federal courts. Then the Court went

The Supreme Court attempts to settle the slavery issue in its <u>Dred Scott v. Sandford</u> decision.

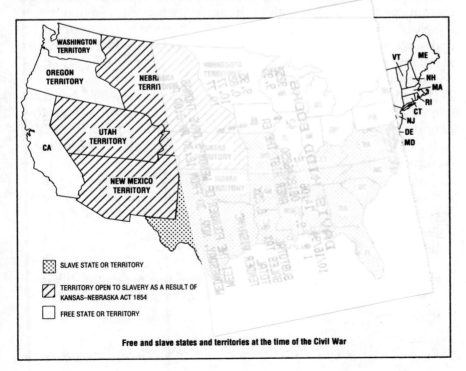

SLAVE STATE OR TERRITORY

TERRITORY OPEN TO SLAVERY AS A RESULT OF KANSAS–NEBRASKA ACT 1854

FREE STATE OR TERRITORY

Free and slave states and territories at the time of the Civil War

on to say that Dred Scott's temporary residence in a free state did not make him free, and the Congress could not outlaw slavery in the territories since it deprived persons of their property, which was unconstitutional under the Vth Amendment.

The Dred Scott decision was a sweeping victory for the South and its institution of slavery. The North and the newly formed Republican Party would not accept it. Instead of healing the nation by its decision, the Supreme Court split the nation more than ever over slavery. In the next three years many Southern leaders, especially in the lower South, insisted the nation respect the Dred Scott decision.

In 1858, the year after the Dred Scott decision, in a famous debate between Abraham Lincoln and Stephen Douglas in their campaign for a United States Senate seat from Illinois, Douglas, the Democrat, repudiated the Dred Scott decision, arguing that a territory could exclude slavery by popular vote. He won the Senate seat but lost Southern support by this step backwards from the Dred Scott decision. Douglas' loss of Southern support was to prove fatal for his Presidential ambitions and for the maintenance of the Union.

The Use of Violence: Harper's Ferry

John Brown attacks the federal arsenal at Harper's Ferry as the first step of a planned slave uprising.

While the events just described may all appear political, behind each was a concern over slavery and the future of this economic institution. However, more and more Northerners were taking a stand against slavery based on ethical standards and moral repulsion. One extreme moralist and abolitionist, John Brown, believed one should fight the evil. John Brown organized a raid on the federal arsenal at Harper's Ferry, Virginia, hoping to seize weapons to arm slaves and start an uprising.

John Brown was captured, tried, and executed, but his action epitomizes the growing split in the nation. He became a martyr in the North, and verses and songs were written about his attempts to end slavery. Meanwhile, Southerners had expanded their rhetoric in defense of the institution of slavery. They used the Bible to justify it just as abolitionists quoted the Bible to condemn it.

The important political events of the decade 1850–1860 were all related to slavery. The events culminated in the war that split the nation. Abraham Lincoln summarized the situation of the 1850s well in this paragraph from his second inaugural[4] address delivered in 1865.

> One-eighth of the whole population were colored slaves, not distributed generally over the Union, but localized in the southern part of it. These slaves constituted a peculiar and powerful interest. All knew that this interest was, somehow, the cause of the war. To strengthen, perpetuate, and extend this interest was the object for which the insurgents would rend the Union, even by war; while the government claimed no right to do more than to restrict the territorial enlargement of it.

---

[4]*inaugural (inauguration):* pertaining to the formal installing into office of an individual.

The Election of Abraham Lincoln

By 1860 the nation was in a severe crisis. Leaders of the lower South had been speaking of secession if their "rights" were not allowed. Virginians still voiced the hope that sectional differences could be settled within the Union. The political parties nominated candidates during the summer, and Abraham Lincoln won the new Republican Party's nomination. Many believed Abraham Lincoln was opposed to slavery. From his public statements it was not clear what his personal views were. However, in 1858, Lincoln delivered a speech that has become famous as the "House Divided" speech. He declared a house divided could not stand and that the nation would have to be all free or all slave.

Southerners are convinced Abraham Lincoln will abolish slavery if elected.

In the election of 1860 Southerners were convinced Lincoln would abolish slavery and establish an all-free Union. It was clear Stephen Douglas controlled the Democratic Convention and that he would only support Congressional non-intervention in the territories. The South wanted a guarantee for slavery in the territories. Douglas won the nomination and eight Southern states withdrew from the Democratic Party Convention and nominated John C. Breckinridge of Kentucky as their candidate. A fourth candidate, John Bell of Tennessee, was nominated by a new party, the Constitutional Union Party, which was ready to compromise to save the Union.

In the election Lincoln won in the electoral college but received a minority of the popular votes. Breckinridge won in the South, Lincoln in the North, but Douglas and Bell combined had more votes than Lincoln or Breckinridge alone, which suggests the majority of voters were still satisfied with the Union. However, the danger that George Washington had warned against of a nation split into political parties along geographic lines had come about. The result was to be disaster for the Union.

In a four-candidate election, Lincoln receives a minority of the popular vote but wins in the electoral college.

KEY POINT TO REMEMBER

In the decade before the Civil War the major issue of political concern was the question of the extension of slavery to the territories. Northerners objected on moral and ethical terms; Southerners saw the extension as an economic necessity and as the only way they would be able to maintain political parity with the North. The slavery issue split the nation and war resulted.

PEOPLE TO REMEMBER

Harriet Beecher Stowe   Author, abolitionist; wrote *Uncle Tom's Cabin* first published in serial form 1851–2; as a book it sold over 300,000 copies the first year and is credited with focusing anti-slavery sentiment in the North.

LINKS FROM THE PAST TO THE PRESENT

1. Social and political issues, whether temperance or homelessness, often have economic roots that must be considered.
2. The Supreme Court has at times tried to settle political issues by handing down a decision such as *Dred Scott v. Sandford*, which did not settle the issue but merely made it worse.

QUESTIONS

Identify each of the following:

Economic determinism   *Dred Scott v. Sandford*
Uncle Tom's Cabin   Harper's Ferry
Kansas-Nebraska Act   Stephen A. Douglas

True or False:

1. Southerners understood that slavery was only an excuse for gaining political power in the new territories.
2. The majority of slaves worked on farms with fewer than five slaves.
3. The Missouri Compromise and the Compromise of 1850 were compromises over issues related to slavery.
4. Popular Sovereignty seemed a fair and democratic way to determine the future of slavery in the territories.
5. *Uncle Tom's Cabin* presented slavery as a benevolent institution and helped Northerners to understand why it was necessary for the South.
6. Stephen A. Douglas had Presidential ambitions, and the Kansas-Nebraska Act was meant to gain him support in the South.
7. "Bleeding Kansas" refers to the situation that developed when farmers shot cattle in order to clear the range for settlement.
8. In the *Dred Scott v. Sandford* case, the Supreme Court attempted to settle the issue of slavery in the territories.
9. Dred Scott was a slave who had lived in free territory and sued his owner for his freedom.
10. John Brown was an example of a moderate abolitionist.

Multiple Choice:

1. In the pre-Civil War period in the South
    a. two-thirds of the homes had no slaves
    b. most slaves lived on large plantations with 20 or more slaves
    c. there were no free African-Americans
2. According to Abraham Lincoln
    a. popular sovereignty was the correct solution to the slavery issue in the Territory
    b. the Fugitive Slave Law should not be enforced
    c. a house divided against itself cannot stand
3. In the election of 1860
    a. John Brown and John Bell were abolition candidates
    b. Stephen Douglas was the Democratic Party candidate
    c. Abraham Lincoln won a majority of the vote

ANSWERS

True or False: 1.F, 2. T, 3. T, 4. T, 5. F, 6. T, 7. F, 8. T, 9. T, 10. F.
Multiple Choice: 1. a, 2. c, 3. b.

II. THE CIVIL WAR

The Confederate States of America

With the election of Lincoln the conflict sharpened. The Lower South insisted on a guarantee of the right to slavery in the territories. Lincoln insisted on holding to the Republican platform, which stood for no extension of slavery to the territories. The average Republican voter may have been willing to compromise, but Lincoln could not afford to compromise. That would antagonize the party congressional leadership, many of whom were strong abolitionists This leadership later became known as the Radical Republicans. This same division in the party later haunted the party's postwar efforts at reconstruction.

There were attempts at compromise in the Senate, but they failed. The days of the Great Compromiser, Henry Clay, were over. South Carolina seceded from the Union in December 1860. Extremists in Mississippi, Florida, Alabama, Georgia, Louisiana, and Texas called conventions, and all six state conventions voted to secede. No Southern state asked the citizens to vote on the issue of secession. The Union was dissolved by the actions of these state conventions.

South Carolina secedes, followed by the states of the Deep South.

By February 1861, the Confederate States of America (CSA) were organized as a new nation. Jefferson Davis was chosen as President, and Montgomery, Alabama as the capital. The Upper South—Virginia, North Carolina, Tennessee, and Arkansas—did not secede until hostilities had begun.

Jefferson Davis is chosen president of the Confederate States of America.

Lincoln was faced with a dilemma: how to restore the Union, his primary goal, without provoking a conflict. Restoration of the Union remained Lincoln's goal throughout the war. Lincoln moved slowly looking for a solution. He determined to hold federal lands in the seceded states, thus maintaining the concept of Union with federal authority operating in all the states. The CSA could not accept this if they were to be a sovereign nation.

The clash came on April 12, 1861, when the Confederate States of America attacked the federal fort, Fort Sumter, in the harbor of Charleston, South Carolina. After two days of shelling, the garrison surrendered and was allowed to leave. War had begun.

The Civil War begins at Fort Sumter, and four more states secede.

The four states of the Upper South seceded to join the Confederacy. The capital was then moved to Richmond, Virginia. Robert E. Lee, graduate of West Point, accepted the command of the army of his home state, Virginia, having turned down command of the Union army. Several states that had been considered Southern did not secede. Kentucky, Maryland, and Delaware remained in the Union, and what is now West Virginia broke off from the state of Virginia during the war to form a new state.

Compromises on the issue of slavery had failed. Slavery was ultimately too important for the South to compromise on, and the Northern Republicans had come to see its extension to new territories as incompatible with the avowed beliefs of a democratic society. As Lincoln had said in 1858, a house divided could not stand. The question in April, 1861, was whether the house could be

Lincoln has no plan for the future of slavery as the war begins.

made whole again. There were no goals at that time on the future of slavery or blacks, there was only a war to be fought and, in the eyes of Lincoln, a Union to be saved, but the origin of the war lay in attitudes toward slavery and the way of life it made possible economically.

The War

The war is very costly.

The Civil War was bloody—one million casualties in a population North and South of approximately 31 million; expensive—the estimated cost of over $20 billion, perhaps a small sum today in terms of governmental expenditure, was five times the total expense of the federal government between 1789 and 1860; and long—it lasted four arduous years. The South's strategy was to hold on and wear the North down. The North's strategy had three parts.
1. Blockade the south in order to starve it into submission.
2. Capture the capital of the Confederate States of America, Richmond.
3. Split the South into two parts along the Mississippi River and then by a thrust through Georgia to the sea to split it further into three units.

The Blockade

The English and French do not recognize or support the confederacy.

The blockade was put into effect immediately. The Confederate States of America hoped for some European support especially from England, who they believed needed Southern cotton for their cotton mills. But England also needed wheat from the Northwest and had long been opposed to slavery. While there was some help from blockade runners and some Confederate ships, such as the *Alabama*, were built in England, the English basically honored the blockade. The French became involved in an attempt to conquer Mexico and stayed out of the conflict.

Splitting the Confederacy

The campaign to split the South was very successful. General Ulysses S. Grant captured Forts Henry and Donelson on the Cumberland and Tennessee Rivers in Tennessee in 1862. This opened a path to the interior of the Confederacy. New Orleans, near the mouth of the Mississippi River, was also captured in 1862.

The capture of Vicksburg splits the confederacy in half.

The campaign continued into 1863 and with the capture of Vicksburg, Mississippi on July 4, the Confederacy was split.

Attacks were then directed at Chattanooga, Tennessee, and after its capture, at Atlanta, Georgia, which fell in September, 1864. General Sherman then led his Union forces on a "march through Georgia," destroying homes and supplies. Sherman captured Savannah, Georgia in December, 1864, splitting the South further.

Sherman wages total war.

The tactics Sherman followed were those of total war. Southerners referred to Sherman as "the brute." The argument in favor of such tactics is that the destruction of supplies meant for soldiers will shorten the war and destruction of homes and families will weaken the will to fight. Sherman's tactics have become familiar in the 20th century and his often quoted comment that "war is hell" proven true too many times.

The Fighting In The East

It took four years to capture Richmond. There were many battles fought in Virginia, beginning with the First Bull Run in 1861 and ending with the seige of Petersburg from June 1864 until its capture April 2, 1865. Richmond was abandoned and fell to the Union forces on the same day. General Robert E. Lee, who had commanded the Army of Northern Virginia for four years, surrendered to General Ulysses S. Grant, who had taken command of the Union Army of the Potomac in 1864. Lee's surrender at Appomattox Court House on April 9, 1865 essentially ended the war although a few skirmishes continued until May.

Lee and Grant fight a long and bloody campaign in Virginia.

The Virginia campaign was the bloodiest of the war. In a few hours on June 3, 1864, Grant lost 12,000 men. In the month of June his losses were equal to the size of Lee's army, but new recruits from the North kept coming and eventually Grant's tactics of pounding away with his overwhelming numbers at Lee's army gained success.

Lee's greatest asset was his ability to outmaneuver the Northern forces. In 1863 he actually invaded Pennsylvania until stopped at Gettysburg, one of the most famous battles of the war. The Battle of Gettysburg not only marked the high point of the Confederacy's attack, it provided Lincoln an opportunity, when dedicating the Union cemetery at Gettysburg, to deliver one of the most memorable and sincere tributes ever given to those who are asked to fight for their country.

In the Gettysburg Address, Lincoln said, "The world will little note nor long remember what we say here...," but he was wrong. The opening and concluding lines of his very short Gettysburg Address set forth the idea Lincoln had come to as the goal of the war. He said:

Lincoln's Gettysburg Address has been long remembered as a statement on war's sacrifice and aims.

> Fourscore and seven years ago our fathers brough forth on this continent a new nation, conceived in liberty, and dedicated to the proposition that all men are created equal. Now we are engaged in a great Civil War, testing whether that nation, or any nation so conceived and so dedicated, can long endure.... We here highly resolve that these dead shall not have died in vain; that this nation, under God, shall have a new birth of freedom; and that government of the people, by the people, for the people, shall not perish from the earth.

Emancipation Proclamation

Previously, in September, 1862, Lincoln had acted on the slavery issue. Lincoln had not wanted to antagonize the border states by abolishing slavery but he finally accepted the views of the Radical Republicans. In the Emancipation[1] Proclamation Lincoln stated

The Emancipation Proclamation frees slaves in those states in rebellion on January 1, 1863.

---

[1]*emancipation* Act or process of setting or making free; freeing, especially applied to slaves.

that as of January 1, 1863, those slaves held in states in rebellion against the United States would be free. It did not free slaves in the border states or in those areas of the South occupied by Northern armies. It was not until Amendment XIII to the Constitution was adopted in 1865 that slavery throughout the United States was abolished.

The Social and Economic Impact of the War

The impact of the war on society in both North and South was enormous. With the loss of the Southern market, Northern industry slumped. The war effort encouraged certain industries—coal, iron, cloth for uniforms—and great profits were made by a few. More machines were introduced into factories as men went off to fight. While many people lived frugally and suffered economic distress as inflation ate up raises, others displayed their new wealth openly. The contrasts were great and these intensified later in the century.

Northern industry grows but prosperity is not evenly distributed.

The Railroad Suspension Bridge near Niagara Falls
This view of The Railroad Suspension Bridge near Niagara Falls *was painted by an anonymous American sometime after 1855. It is an excellent illustration of the changes in forms of transportation in 19th century America. Note the steamboat, the railroad train and the carriages. The bridge illustrates the advances in engineering which were an important part of the growth of manufacturing. Does the painting give you a sense that the artist felt pride in these changes and accomplishments?*

With the South out of the Union, Congress revived Henry Clay's old American System concept and, catering to the manufacturing East, raised the tariff in 1864 to almost twice its pre-war rates. Congress chartered two railway companies, the Union Pacific and Central Pacific, to build a cross-country line from Omaha, Nebraska to Sacramento, California. The railroad would open up the West. The effort was supported by huge government grants of money and land. Another company, the Northern Pacific, was chartered in 1864 to build a line. It had been impossible for the Congress to agree on a location for the transcontinental line until the South had seceded.

A cross-country railroad and free homesteads for settlers open up new territories in the West to settlement.

Aiding Western settlers was the Homestead Act of 1862, which granted settlers 160 acres of surveyed public land if they were citizens or intended to be, were over 21, lived on the land continuously for five years, and paid a registration fee of approximately $30. Until the Homestead Act, public lands had been sold as a source of revenue. Now a new economic policy was introduced, make land cheap so more land would be settled. This would increase the market for goods and provide cargo for railroads. Economics played an important part in determining Northern policy on these three issues—tariffs, railroads, and land.

The war was not universally popular in the North, and there were draft riots in New York in 1863. The impact of the war on the North, however, was not as severe as on the South. The South began from scratch, in 1861, to form a government. An administrative bureaucracy had to be built at a time when men were called upon to fight. Women took over many positions in teaching and in the bureaucracy. The South had been an agricultural economy, heavily dependent on exports, and it suffered from the North's blockade. It lacked the railway system of the North and, while advocating states' rights philosophically, was forced to centralize its efforts in order to run the war machine. This antagonized some of its supporters, and the Confederate States of America resorted to martial[2] law to maintain authority.

The South has to build a government and industrial base from scratch.

Inflation, which was over 7,000 percent by the end of the war, destroyed businesses. Fearing a slave revolt, the Confederate States of America passed a law permitting any male supervising over twenty slaves to avoid serving in the army. Since only the wealthy had this many slaves, it made the war appear a war for the rich's economic advantage but fought by the poor. Economic differences between groups became an important issue in both the North and the South during the Civil War.

KEY POINT TO REMEMBER

The Civil War was a bloody, expensive war that had a great impact on the economic, social, and political life of both the Union and the Confederate States of America.

---

[2]*martial*   Of, or pertaining to, war.

PEOPLE TO REMEMBER

Robert E. Lee Virginian; graduate of West Point; gained military experience in the Mexican War; was offered the command of the Union Army by Abraham Lincoln but rejected the offer and remained loyal to Virginia when it seceded; commanded the Army of Northern Virginia and finally surrendered to General U.S. Grant at Appomattox Court House in April 1865, ending the Civil War.

LINKS FROM THE PAST TO THE PRESENT

1. Both the economic and social cost of war have been greater than the cost in lives and material—a fact often overlooked.
2. Growth of bureaucracy and centralization of power has occurred over and over again during wars from the Civil War to Vietnam.

QUESTIONS

Identify each of the following:

Confederate States of America   Appomattox Court House
Fort Sumter   Battle of Gettysburg
Robert E. Lee   Emancipation Proclamation
Ulysses S. Grant

True or False:

1. North Carolina was the first Southern state to secede.
2. The capital of the Confederacy (CSA) was first Montgomery, Alabama and then Richmond, Virginia.
3. The Alabama was a blockade runner built by the English for the CSA.
4. Lee's greatest asset was his ability to invade Pennsylvania.
5. Congress had chartered two railroad companies—one to build a Southern line and one to build a Northern line—before the South seceded.
6. Ulysses S. Grant was the commander of the Union Army to whom Robert E. Lee surrendered in 1865.
7. The Southern-oriented states of Delaware, Maryland, and Kentucky seceded after the capture of Fort Sumter.
8. The South had a strong agricultural economy and an excellent railroad network, giving it an advantage over the North.

Multiple Choice:

1. The military phase of the Civil War began with
    a. firing on Fort Sumter
    b. the Battle of Bull Run
    c. the fall of Petersburg
2. The Northern strategy for winning the war included a blockade and
    a. the capture of Richmond, Virginia
    b. the splitting of the South into two parts
    c. both of the above

3. In his Gettysburg Address, Lincoln declared the war was testing whether
    a. "government of the people, by the people, for the people" shall perish
    b. Gettysburg was a beautiful site for a cemetery
    c. the South had legitimate reason for seceding
4. Once the South had seceded the Congress passed
    a. the Gettysburg Address
    b. the Homestead Act
    c. the Anti-Inflation Act

Answers
True or False: 1. F, 2. T, 3. T, 4. F, 5. F, 6. T, 7. F, 8. F.
Multiple Choice: 1. a, 2. c, 3. a, 4. b.

The Civil War Amendments to the Constitution

Amendments XIII, XIV and XV are referred to as the Civil War Amendments. The Southern states were forced to adopt them as a condition for their acceptance back into the Union under the Radical Republican plan for reconstruction. The three together were designed to give civil and political rights to the former slaves but they were subject to interpretation by the Supreme Court. By 1896 the Court was very restrictive in its interpretation of the guarantees granted in these three amendments.

Amendment XIII. Prohibition of Slavery   Adopted 1865
1. Neither slavery nor involuntary servitude, except as a punishment for crime whereof the party shall have been duly convicted, shall exist within the United States, or any place subject to their jurisdiction.
2. Congress shall have power to enforce this article by appropriate legislation.

Slavery is declared unconstitutional but jail sentences depriving one of freedom are legal.

Amendment XIV. Civil Rights for Former Slaves   Adopted 1868
1. All persons born or naturalized in the United States, and subject to the jurisdiction thereof, are citizens of the United States and of the State wherein they reside. No State shall make or enforce any law which shall abridge the privileges or immunities of citizens of the United States; nor shall any State deprive any person of life, liberty, or property, without the due process of law; nor deny to any person within its jurisdiction the equal protection of the laws.

Citizenship is defined and the rights of United States citizens are stated—the "due process of law" is meant to guarantee these rights.

2. Representatives shall be apportioned among the several States according to their respective numbers, counting the whole number of persons in each State, excluding Indians not taxed. But when the right to vote at any election for the choice of Electors for President and Vice-President of the United States, Representatives in Congress, the executive and judicial officers of a State, or the members of the legislature thereof, is denied to any of the male inhabitants

Ex-slaves are now to be counted as full citizens in determining Congressional and electoral representation but if an ex-slave is denied the vote, the state's representation will be reduced. This latter clause has never been enforced.

of such State, being twenty-one years of age and citizens of the United States, or in any way abridged, except for participation in rebellion, or other crime, the basis of representation therein shall be reduced in the proportion which the number of such male citizens shall bear to the whole number of male citizens twenty-one years of age in such State.

Confederates who had held office under the U.S. and then served in the Confederacy are denied the right to hold office under the United States unless Congress by a two-thirds vote allows the person to serve again. This was meant to remove from positions of political influence the leaders of the Confederacy.

3. No person shall be a Senator or Representative in Congress, or Elector of President and Vice-President, or hold any office, civil or military, under the United States, or under any State, who, having previously taken an oath, as a member of Congress, or as an officer of the United States, or as a member of any State legislature, or as an executive or judicial officer of any State, to support the Constitution of the United States, shall have engaged in insurrection or rebellion against the same, or given aid or comfort to the enemies thereof. But Congress may, by a vote of two-thirds of each house, remove such disability.

The debt of the Confederacy is repudiated but the southern states must pay their proportional share of the Union debt. If Confederate soldiers were to receive pensions, states had to pay them.

4. The validity of the public debt of the United States, authorized by law, including debts incurred for payment of pensions and bounties for services in suppressing insurrection or rebellion, shall not be questioned. But neither the United States nor any State shall assume or pay any debt or obligation incurred in aid of insurrection or rebellion against the United States, or any claim for the loss or emancipation of any slave; but all such debts, obligations, and claims shall be held illegal and void.

5. The Congress shall have power to enforce, by appropriate legislation, the provisions of this article.

Amendment XV. Voting Rights for Blacks   Adopted 1870

Since the right to vote cannot be denied on the basis of color, all blacks are to have the vote.

1. The right of citizens of the United States to vote shall not be denied or abridged by the United States or by any State on account of race, color, or previous condition of servitude.
2. The Congress shall have power to enforce this article by appropriate legislation.

III.   THE PERIOD OF RECONSTRUCTION

Conflict over Reconstruction Plans

Reconstruction, the name given to the process of reestablishing the Union to again include the seceded states, began during the war and lasted until 1877. Opinions differed as to the process to follow and your opinion depended on your answers to two questions:

Disagreements over how to reconstruct the Union.

1. Were the states in rebellion out of the Union?
2. Who should be in charge of the process of reconstruction?

Abraham Lincoln believed secession was unconstitutional, and so legally, the Southern states were still in the Union. He believed the Executive Branch, particularly the President, should establish the process of reconstruction and the terms should be generous. As the Union army gained control of seceded states such as Tennessee, Lincoln appointed military governors and was prepared to recognize a new state government once 10 percent of the state's 1860 voting population swore allegiance to the Union.

Members of Congress in 1864 presented their own much less generous plan, but Lincoln did not sign the bill, angering the radical or extreme Republicans in Congress. The Radical Republicans, led by Senators Charles Sumner and Thaddeus Stevens, had been a force in Congress since before the war. They were intolerant of slavery, strong abolitionists, and prepared to make the South "pay" for the war. With their plan for reconstruction blocked by the President, the stage was set for confrontation.

Before Lincoln's plan was fully operative, he was shot by John Wilkes Booth, just five days after Lee's surrender at Appomatox. Lincoln died on April 15, 1865, and Andrew Johnson became President. Johnson followed Lincoln's plan welcoming the Southern states into the Union.

Lincoln is assassinated before his Reconstruction plan is fully in operation.

The Senators were not pleased. They resented the growth of executive power during the war. When Alexander Stephens, the Vice-President of the Confederacy, was elected as a Senator from Georgia and Southern states began to adopt "Black Codes" restricting the rights of the freed slaves, Senators Thaddeus Stevens and Charles Sumner believed the situation had become intolerable and offered their own plan for reconstruction.

The Senate Radicals propose a Plan of Reconstruction.

Their plan was embodied in Amendment XIV, which made the ex-slaves citizens. Slavery had been made unconstitutional by Amendment XIII adopted in 1865. Amendment XIV guaranteed all citizens due process in defense of their rights. This was meant to combat the Black Codes. The Amendment also repealed the three-fifths rule of the Constitution so blacks were now counted in determining state representation in Congress. The Amendment provided that if the vote was denied a citizen, the state would lose representation in Congress. This was an attempt by the radicals to assure that blacks would vote in the South, hopefully for the Republican party that had fought the war to free them.

President Johnson could have compromised his views to work with the more moderate Republicans in Congress and thus maintain some of his and Lincoln's more lenient policies. He failed to do so. Amendment XIV was rejected by the South in the election of 1866 in which the Republicans won a large majority in Congress. There had been little progress in Reconstruction in one and a half years. Congress in 1867 focused on the issue.

Impeachment of President Johnson

The entire Senate–President struggle over Reconstruction was tied up in issues of political, not economic, power. Republicans feared the return of the Southern Democrats to Congress. The Congress resented Presidential power, and the President believed Reconstruction was an executive matter. The political power

The Radical Republican Congressional leadership impeaches President Johnson, but he is acquitted.

struggle became intense and culminated in impeachment[1] proceedings against President Johnson.

Behind the impeachment was the belief held by the Radical Republican Congressional leadership that the President was blocking Congressional Reconstruction. The impeachment case centered on Johnson's dismissal of his Secretary of War, Edwin M. Stanton, in 1867. This violated the recently passed Tenure of Office Act, which stated the President could dismiss government appointees who had been confirmed by the Senate only with the consent of the Senate. This law changed the established precedent, followed since George Washington, that the President could dismiss executive appointees at his pleasure even if they had been confirmed in their office by the Senate.

Indictments were brought against Johnson in 1868, and impeachment proceedings began. The impeachment fell one vote short of the two-thirds required under the Constitution. Johnson finished his term in office but was able to exert no power over the radicals in spite of his acquittal.

Ulysses S. Grant, the winning General of the Army of the Potomac, received the Republican nomination in 1868 and was elected President. Military heros continued to have appeal to the voting public even if they had no political experience.

The Congressional Plan for Reconstruction

The Congressional Plan of Reconstruction abandons all that has been done.

After the South rejected Amendment XIV in 1866, Congress adopted a new policy of military reconstruction, which went into effect in 1867. The new plan abandoned all that had been done in the two years since the war. Troops were to stay in the South until states adopted new constitutions, agreed to emancipation, and approved Amendment XIV. The states slowly complied and reentered the Union, but the last military forces were not withdrawn until 1877.

Many of the Southern states' new constitutions incorporated quite liberal ideas and eliminated property qualifications for voting, made more offices elective, gave more property rights to women (but not the vote), and required the building of schools and special institutions for the deaf, the blind, and orphans.

African-Americans served in the state legislatures under these new constitutions until disenfranchised after the end of military reconstruction. Many of them that served had been well educated. Some were relatives of the white representatives—a point rarely discussed.

The Freedman's Bureau is established to aid the freed slaves, but essentially they are given no economic support.

In 1865 Congress established the Freedman's Bureau. This temporary bureau was to help defend the rights of the freedmen and to look after the abandoned lands in the South. It was authorized to distribute up to 40 acres of abandoned land and to provide food,

---

[1]*impeach* To indict a public official for misbehavior. The case is then tried before a jury assigned to the case, and the indicted official is found guilty or not guilty. In impeachment proceedings against the President of the United States, the Senate serves as the jury and the House of Representatives must prepare the charges against the President.

clothing, and education to white refugees and to freedmen. The Freedman's Bureau built schools and churches and arranged for the teaching of reading to many African-Americans.

While there was discussion of economic support to help the ex-slaves buy farms, essentially nothing was done. Reconstruction ignored the economic problems inherent in emancipation, and this led to problems that are still with us today.

The military reconstruction plan of the Radical Republicans provided the African-Americans with access to the political process. This worked while the military occupation forces remained in the South, but when they were withdrawn, African-Americans were slowly eliminated from the political process by disen-franchisement.

Life For The Freed Man

Reconstruction had also ignored the traditional power structure and social structure of the South while concentrating on political reform. While Southern economic life had been disrupted, many families were able to rebuild their wealth. The land was still held by the former owners, and few of them had changed their opinion of African-Americans. Without land of their own, many African-Americans worked as sharecroppers[2], and this made them still dependent on the whites. Neither their social status nor economic power had been changed by the war or Reconstruction.

The former slaves gain neither economic power nor social status as a result of Reconstruction.

In fact, not only did Southern states turn to Black Codes during Reconstruction to keep the freedmen "in their place," but the Ku Klux Klan was organized in 1867. The Klan used terror and violence and was denounced in the North. The KKK was officially disbanded in 1869, but its policies continued to be used and the Klan was reorganized later in the century. The KKK Acts passed by Congress in 1870 and 1871 attempted to curtail the use of violence and to enforce Amendments XIV and XV. In spite of the KKK Acts, the Ku Klux Klan has emerged at several times in United States' history as an organization of intimidation.

Black Codes and the KKK are used to keep the freedmen "in their place."

Civil Rights Act of 1876

As one of its last acts during the Reconstruction era, Congress passed a Civil Rights Act in 1876 to provide equal accommodation in public places like hotels. No enforcement provisions were included, however, and without federal enforcement provisions, the Act was a failure. This failure discouraged Congress from making further attempts to secure civil rights by legislation. When the Civil Rights Movement[3] got Congress to act in the 1960s, enforcement measures were included in the Civil Rights Act.

The Civil Rights Act of 1876 is a failure because it contains no provisions for enforcement.

---

[2]*sharecropper*   One who shares the crops he/she raises with the owner of the land in return for the right to farm the land. It provides a tenant relationship without exchange of cash, as crops are used instead.

[3]*Civil Rights Movement*   A movement in the 1950s and 1960s which, through the use of civil disobedience, obtained civil rights—the right of equal access to lunch counters, hotels, education, etc.—legislation by the federal government. Among many leaders, Martin Luther King, Jr. is the most prominent.

For those who lived through Reconstruction, it was a hard time. Change is never easy to accept, and the members of the federal government were so involved in their own power struggles that they failed to provide direction for the creation of a new South. In the 20th century a new social and political power relationship finally emerged after the struggles of the Civil Rights Movement.

Southern states move to deny the vote to former slaves after the Supreme Court decisions in the Civil Rights cases.

The final blow to Congressional Reconstruction and the effort to provide blacks with access to the political process came in the Supreme Court decision in the Civil Rights cases. The Court interpreted Amendment XV as a statement of how the right to vote could not be denied and not as a guarantee of voting under all conditions. Southern states soon found ways to deny the vote to ex-slaves, such as a Grandfather Clause that simply said if your grandfather had not voted, you could not. Obviously, no slaves had grandfathers who had voted. By the end of the century, most blacks were disenfranchised[4] in the South. Reconstruction had even failed to provide the freedmen with access to the political process.

Economic Exploitation and Development

Economic recovery comes slowly to the South.

The South was split politically during Reconstruction, but economic issues tended to unite different elements. Carpetbaggers[5], Northerners who came South, exploited economic situations and worked to keep the Republican party in power by not allowing ex-Confederates to vote and by supporting the voting rights of blacks. Scallywags[6], white Southerners who cooperated with the Republicans, worked with the yeoman farmers who had not been slave owners to reestablish the farm lands and to stimulate industry. These two groups profited economically from the post-war conditions. Also, the new Southern state governments encouraged economic growth by loans and by providing tax exemptions in certain cases. These again benefited certain groups within the South, but not the ex-Confederates.

There was some corruption in the new state and local governments, but overall they ran well. Corruption was a national problem in the 1870s. There had been a breakdown in the values and ethics of society during the war, and the corruption was as much a result of this breakdown as it was a result of incompetency on the part of Southern leaders of the new governments.

---

[4]*disenfranchise* To remove the right of one to vote. Franchise is used in political science and history to refer to the right to vote.

[5]*carpetbagger* A Northerner who traveled to the former Confederacy during the reconstruction period to participate in the political and economic reorganization of the South with the goal of profiting from the situation. The name originated among Southerners who claimed the carpetbaggers arrived with all their possessions in a carpetbag. In the mid-19th century many suitcases were made from carpet.

[6]*scallywag* A contemptuous name for a Southern white who cooperated with Northerners and blacks during reconstruction.

The Election of General Ulysses S. Grant

Grant easily won the election of 1868, but when he ran for reelection in 1872, liberal Republicans, who favored a more lenient reconstruction policy, lower tariffs to help the South, and civil service[7] reform, banded together. They were opposed to the widespread corruption in government, broke from the party, and nominated Horace Greeley, editor of the *New York Tribune*, as candidate for President. The Democratic party, still attempting to reestablish itself as a national party and not just a party of the South, also nominated Horace Greeley. Grant easily won reelection, however, and the Congressional reconstruction continued.

During Grant's second term, corruption in the federal government was exposed in two scandals—the Credit Mobilier and the Whiskey Ring. In the former, Congressmen were accused of profiting from and giving political influence to the promoters of the Union Pacific Railway Company. In the latter, members of Grant's administration, including his private secretary, were involved in defrauding the government of tax money.

Corruption appeared widespread in the era and reflects the breakdown of ethics and morality that so often follow a war. There was corruption in city government, as in New York City, where the Tweed Ring—the associates of the city's political boss, William M. Tweed—milked money from the city to make themselves rich. Behind this corruption was the desire to get rich without work. Marxist historians see this as another example of economics as the driving force of all history.

Can you relate to this concept of economics being the driving force for these illegal actions?

General Grant is elected President.

Corruption becomes widespread in government.

Election of 1876: The End of Reconstruction

The national political balance began to shift, and in 1874 the Democrats gained control of the House of Representatives. In the Presidential election of 1876, they nominated Samual J. Tilden of New York. The Republicans nominated Rutherford B. Hayes of Ohio. Neither man won a majority in the Electoral College. Tilden had a majority of the popular vote with 51 percent, but he needed one more electoral vote to win a majority. Nineteen electoral votes from Florida, Louisiana, and South Carolina were disputed, and one from Oregon was undecided. A Congressional commission was created to resolve the issue of who won the election by determining the validity of the contested votes. The fifteen-member commission, with eight Republicans, voted 8–7 in favor of Hayes on each of the nineteen contested votes. Tilden had needed only one of them to be elected President, so the final electoral vote was 185–184 for Hayes. The Democrats, quite unhappy, decided to accept the result rather than threaten another war or more uncertainty about the future.

The era of Reconstruction ends after Rutherford B. Hayes is named President by a congressional commission following the disputed election of 1876.

---

[7]*civil service*   The administrative side of government which includes bureaucrats, except those connected with or members of the armed forces, the legislative and the judicial branches. Those who run the executive branch of government are members of the Civil Service.

After his inauguration, Rutherford B. Hayes ordered the withdrawal of troops from the South, ending Reconstruction. For years it was suspected a "deal" had been arranged to pay for this "stolen election," but recent research has found no clear evidence for such a deal. The nation was again united twelve years after the end of the Civil War. Reconstruction had finally recreated the Union, but beyond that, what had been achieved? This is a question we each need to answer for ourselves.

KEY POINT TO REMEMBER

The Radical Republicans in Congress and Presidents Lincoln and Johnson each had plans for reconstruction and the former plan was implemented from 1866–1877 with the result the ex-slaves achieved temporary access to the political process but little social or economic power.

PEOPLE TO REMEMBER

Ulysses S. Grant Ohioan; West Point graduate; served with distinction in the Mexican War; resigned to farm and work in real estate; returned to service as a Colonel of Illinois volunteers in 1861; won victories at Forts Henry and Donelson, Shiloh, Vicksburg and Chattanooga; appointed Lt. General in command of Union forces; defeated Robert E. Lee; elected 18th President; Presidency tarnished by Credit Mobilier and Whiskey Ring scandals and Panic of 1873.

LINKS FROM THE PAST TO THE PRESENT

1. Since the Civil War the United States has been subjected to the periodic recurrence of corruption in the federal government.
2. War has an impact on the ethics and values of members of society, as can be seen in both public and private actions, ranging from the scandals of Grant's administration to the widespread flaunting of the prohibition laws in the 1920s.

QUESTIONS

Identify each of the following:

Black Codes	Radical Republicans
Tenure of Office Act	Tweed Ring
Freedman's Bureau	Election of 1876

True or False:

1. John Wilkes Booth assassinated President Abraham Lincoln in April 1865, just five days after General Lee had surrendered.
2. Lincoln's plan of reconstruction was considered overly generous by the Radical Republicans.
3. Congress brought impeachment proceedings against President Johnson, but he was not found guilty by the Senate.
4. The XIV Amendment declared slavery (involuntary servitude) unconstitutional.
5. Reconstruction dealt effectively with the issues of social and economic reform through the Freedman's Bureau.

6. The KKK lasted two years, and then Americans became disgusted with its use of violence and the organization died.
7. Corruption in the post-Civil War period was confined to governments in the former Confederate States.
8. The Democratic and Republican members of the Congressional Commission, which reviewed the contested electoral votes in the Hayes-Tilden election, did not vote on party lines.

Multiple Choice:

1. Amendment XIV
   a. was gladly accepted by the former Confederate States of America
   b. granted citizenship to ex-slaves
   c. was designed to aid the growth of American corporations
2. The Freedman's Bureau was
   a. a temporary bureau designed to help the former slave in education and economic matters
   b. a social club where former slaves were able to get an education
   c. the cornerstone of Radical Reconstruction
3. Southern whites had not changed their basic view of African-Americans as inferior by 1870 as can be seen by their setting up the
   a. Black Codes
   b. Civil Rights cases
   c. Congressional Commission on Election Fraud
4. During Reconstruction many Northerners came South to profit from the changing economic and political condition and were referred to by Southerners as
   a. Sharecroppers
   b. Scallywags
   c. Carpetbaggers

ANSWERS
True or False: 1. T, 2. T, 3. T, 4. F, 5. F, 6. F, 7. F, 8. F.
Multiple Choice: 1. b, 2. a, 3. a, 4. c.

IV. FOREIGN POLICY ISSUES

United States and Latin America

While the attention of the nation focused on the domestic issues of slavery, Civil War, and Reconstruction in the period 1850–1877, there were several foreign policy decisions that have had long term effects on the United States. All of these had important economic consequences. The first was the Clayton-Bulwer Treaty with England, signed in 1850. There was interest in a canal between the Atlantic and Pacific Oceans, and this treaty guaranteed that if one were built through Nicaragua, there would be equal access to the canal for both England and the United States. It guaranteed the United States would enjoy a canal if the British built one, but meant

England and the United States agree to cooperate in canal building in Central America.

we could not build one we controlled. Later negotiations with England nullified the treaty before the United States built the Panama Canal.

In the 1840s and '50s there was interest in annexing Cuba or other areas in Latin America. Americans led expeditions south and there was talk of our Manifest Destiny to control the Caribbean. Such plans were frustrated by anti-slavery groups, who believed any annexation of territory in the Caribbean or Latin America would provide more territory for slavery.

The Gadsden purchase in 1853 completes the territory of the lower 48 United States.

In 1853 the United States bought a small piece of territory from Mexico, the Gadsden Purchase. Congress had been debating the transcontinental railway line and one route, the far southern route, would have benefited from going through this small piece of Mexican territory. The land was purchased, but Congress could not agree on what route to use until the South seceded, and then the route went through the center of the country. Whatever route was taken, south, north or central, that area would greatly benefit economically from the railroad.

Perry Opens Japan

One of the more interesting foreign policy events of the 1850s was Admiral Matthew C. Perry's trip to Japan in 1853 and the treaty he signed the next year. The Treaty of Kanagawa opened Japan to Western trade and influences. Since then United States relations with Japan have gone through many phases, all of which have had important economic implications. If Perry had not gone to Japan, some other individual or nation no doubt would have. It would have been impossible for Japan to remain isolated from the rest of the world throughout the 19th and 20th centuries. Yet that is what Japan, the Island Kingdom, had been able to do for over 200 years. With the opening of Japan and the market in China, with which the U.S. had been trading for years, there were many economic opportunities available to American citizens in Asia. These became more and more important and helped determine our Asian policy over the next 150 years.

Trading contacts are established with Japan.

Maximillian in Mexico

During the Civil War the French intervene in Mexico but leave when the United States applies pressure after the war.

During the Civil War the Monroe Doctrine was put to a test when Emperor Napoleon III of France attempted to establish Maximillian, Archduke of Austria, as Emperor of Mexico. There was little the United States could do while the war was on, but in 1866 the United States delivered an ultimatum[1] demanding the withdrawal of France and sent troops to the United States-Mexican border. Napoleon III withdrew his troops, and in 1867 Maximillian was shot by Mexican forces. The United States was prepared to keep European powers out of the Americas.

---

[1]*ultimatum* A final proposition, conditions or terms offered by either side in a negotiation between two nations or states; an ultimatum is the final offer, and, in disputes between nations, suggests that if it is not accepted, the next step will involve military force.

Also during the war, England permitted the building of several Confederate ships in English shipyards. These ships raided Northern shipping. After the war the United States and England submitted to arbitration[2] claims for damages. The settlement of these Alabama Claims—one Confederate raider was named the *Alabama*—was one step in the development of closer ties between England and the United States.

The United States Grows Beyond Its Borders

Lincoln and Johnson's Secretary of State, William H. Seward, had dreamed of a United States empire that stretched from Canada to Panama. While his dreams were not realized, he did make two territorial acquisitions that have proven of great importance to the United States. In 1867 the island of Midway in the Pacific was occupied by the United States. It had been discovered in 1859 by the United States and became an important naval and shipping base as our economic interests in Asia increased in the later 19th century. Also in 1867 Seward arranged for the purchase of Alaska from Russia for $7,200,000, and after a progaganda campaign the Senate approved the purchase. Alaska was referred to as "Seward's Folly," but it has proven a great bargain. The economic and strategic importance of Alaska today is testimony to how one man's vision can affect history.

Midway Island and Alaska are acquired.

Summary

Foreign policy issues were of minor importance during the period 1850–1877 though several events occurred that have had important effects on our history. The issue of slavery and its extension to new territories dominated the 1850s. When no compromise could be reached, the nation split into two nations—the Northern Union and the Southern Confederate States of America. After four years of intensive fighting, the Union won and faced the issue of how to bring the seceded states back into the Union. There were several plans for this reconstruction of the Union and the Congressional, Radical Republican plan was adopted. It failed to deal with economic and social problems but did provide the ex-slaves, for a short time, with access to the political process. With the withdrawal of Northern troops from the South after the disputed election of 1876, Southern whites slowly reestablished their control over the political, as well as the social and economic, life of the South.

KEY POINT TO REMEMBER

During the period 1850–1877 while foreign policy issues did not dominate, the United States was involved in creating new markets in Asia, in enforcing the Monroe Doctrine and in adding to the United States the first territory which did not border on the previous states, thus setting a precedent for overseas expansion.

---

[2]*arbitration* Settlement of a dispute by means of an impartial hearing before one or more persons chosen by the parties in conflict.

LINKS FROM THE PAST TO THE PRESENT

1. Economic relations between Japan and the United States have been important from the signing of the Treaty of Kanagawa in 1854 to present tensions over imports and exports.
2. United States involvement in the Caribbean and Central America began before the Monroe Doctrine and continue, as illustrated by our concern over situations in Nicaragua and El Salvador.

QUESTIONS

Identify each of the following:

Clayton-Bulwer Treaty   Alaska
Gadsden Purchase   Commodore Matthew C. Perry
Midway Island

True or False:

1. The United States and England agreed that both nations would have equal access to any canal built across Nicaragua.
2. The Gadsden Purchase was made to round out the southern United States' border and supply access to a water route into the Gulf of Mexico.
3. The Treaty of Kanagawa in 1854 opened up Japan to foreign trade.
4. Napoleon III was established as Emperor of Mexico by Archduke Maximillian of Austria.
5. Midway Island was discovered by the United States and annexed as a potential naval base.
6. Secretary of State Seward had no dreams of empire for America and simply bought Alaska because it was for sale.
7. The settlement of the *Alabama* claims strained relations between England and the United States.
8. Some Americans believed it was the Manifest Destiny of the United States to rule the Caribbean and Central America.

Multiple Choice:

1. The Clayton-Bulwer Treaty guaranteed that
    a. there would be equal access to a canal for England and the United States
    b. no canal should be built through Nicaragua
    c. there would be no later negotiations
2. France supported Maximillian's attempt to become Emperor of Mexico until
    a. the Mexicans captured him
    b. the English threatened to declare war
    c. the United States delivered an ultimatum demanding troop withdrawal
3. Alaska was referred to as Seward's Folly but
    a. it has proven to be a great bargain
    b. it shows how one man's vision can affect history
    c. both of the above

ANSWERS

True or False: 1. T, 2. F, 3. T, 4. F, 5. T, 6. F, 7. F, 8. T.
Multiple Choice: 1. a, 2. c, 3. c.

CHAPTER 8

Changing Lifestyles: 1865–1914

APPROACHES TO HISTORY

The Effect of the Frontier on American Character

In the 1890s a famous American historian, Frederick Jackson Turner, argued that the American character was formed on the frontier. He believed that the ideas and traditions brought to America by the Europeans were changed by the frontier experience, and the "striking characteristics" of the American intellect were the products of the frontier. These characteristics were "that coarseness and strength combined with acuteness and inquisitiveness: that practical inventive turn of mind...; that masterful grasp of material things lacking in the artistic but powerful to affect great ends; that restless, nervous energy; that dominant individualism, working for good and for evil...with exuberance that comes from freedom." Turner wrote *The Significance of the Frontier in American History* in 1893, three years after the census bureau announced that a frontier line no longer existed in the United States. If the frontier had formed the American character and the frontier no longer existed, then Turner wondered, what would happen to the American character, how would it change? While many historians have not accepted Turner's thesis, the frontier certainly played an important part in American life from the time the first settlers arrived on the Atlantic coast.

The frontier experience has been written about at length in novels and short stories, varying from Mark Twain's *Adventures of Huckleberry Finn* to Owen Wister's *The Virginian,* which established the image of the Western cowboy. Television programs and movies have used the theme of the West. In many of these presentations the story involves challenge and conflict. This is what Turner saw in the frontier experience, a challenge to the easier, accepted way of life of Europe or the settled areas of the United States. The individual had to struggle against the unexpected on the frontier—unexpected challenges of weather, geography, and native inhabitants. Most individuals have met and overcome challenges in their lives. It is often these challenges and the way we meet them that helps to form our character. In essence, this is what Turner's thesis says about Americans. Our character was formed by challenges. While we have already considered a number of different challenges to Americans, in the fifty years after the Civil War, the frontier, the growing urbanization of life, industrialization, new waves of immigration, and overseas growth gave special challenges to Americans.

What does the frontier mean to you? Have you had challenges from natural conditions or from other people in your life?

I.   THE FRONTIER AND AMERICAN HISTORY

Changing Frontiers

The westward movement of the frontier is quickened by the discovery of gold and silver.

In the 250 years between the first English settlements and the end of the Civil War the frontier line gradually moved westward, first to the Appalachian Mountains and then slowly on across the country. We have discussed the significance of Manifest Destiny and the march west as it related to the spread of slavery and the Civil War. Before the war the discovery of gold in California in 1849 and of gold and silver in the Rockies brought boom towns and new settlers to these regions. This mining frontier was a rough frontier of great challenges where a few individuals made fortunes but most did not. Companies with Eastern money were more likely to strike it rich, which frustrated the prospectors[1]. Other national resources such as oil and lumber were also exploited on the frontier and presented their own challenges to Americans. After the Civil War, the pace of the westward movement increased.

The cattle frontier leaves a great impression and continues to be an important aspect of American culture.

The cattle frontier provides the material for most of the legends and stories of the West. At first, cattle were raised in the Southwest for their hides. When the transcontinental railroad made it possible to get cattle closer to markets, they were raised for their meat. The proverbial cowboy, an individual alone with his horse on the plains, drove great herds of cattle north on "long drives" to railheads so the cattle could be taken by the railroads to meat processing plants. The cattle frontier, consisting of open range ranching, with no fences marking ownership, turned America into a nation of meat eaters. The cattle frontier gave us a folklore and mythology that is still used today in advertising everything from cigarettes to automobiles. Americans, over 100 years after the end of the cattle frontier, still find the experience appealing and relate to the qualities of character it brought forth.

---

[1]*prospector*   Someone who hunts for gold, silver or other valuable minerals.

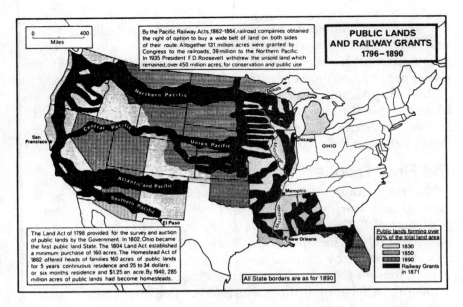

By the Pacific Railway Acts,1862-1864,railroad companies obtained the right of option to buy a wide belt of land on both sides of their route. Altogether 131 million acres were granted by Congress to the railroads, 39 million to the Northern Pacific. In 1935 President F.D.Roosevelt withdrew the unsold land which remained,over 450 million acres, for conservation and public use

PUBLIC LANDS AND RAILWAY GRANTS 1796–1890

The Land Act of 1796 provided for the survey and auction of public lands by the Government. In 1802,Ohio became the first public land State. The 1804 Land Act established a minimum purchase of 160 acres. The Homestead Act of 1862 offered heads of families 160 acres of public lands for 5 years continuous residence and 25 to 34 dollars; or six months residence and $1.25 an acre. By 1940, 285 million acres of public lands had become homesteads.

Public lands forming over 80% of the total land area

- 1830
- 1850
- 1890
- Railway Grants in 1871

All State borders are as for 1890

Native Americans and the Frontier

The white man's frontiers all were developed at the expense of the Native Americans. Treaties were signed and then ignored as lands became valuable because of natural resources or railroad building. Americans tended to think of all natives as the same, but there were great differences between the tribes, which worked to the tribes' disadvantage. There were Indian wars in which the Native Americans were often provoked into action.

The most famous Indian battle in the period after the Civil War took place at the Little Big Horn River in southern Montana in 1876. There, Chiefs Sitting Bull and Crazy Horse of the Sioux Tribe annihilated Colonel Custer's troops. It has gone into history as "Custer's Last Stand." It was more pointedly one of the last stands of the tribes, who were finally overwhelmed by the greater supplies and the persistence of the United States Army.

Until 1887 the United States policy was to gather Indians on reservations. The Dawes Severalty Act reversed the policy, dissolving community-owned tribal lands, giving the land to individual families and citizenship to those who accepted this land. Assimilation into American society rather than separation on reservations became the new policy of the United States' government. The change in policy was in part due to violence between whites and Indians on reservations. In part it was the result of a book, *A Century of Dishonor* by Helen Hunt Jackson, published in 1881. Helen Jackson told a sorry story of broken treaties, massacres, and forced movement to reservations. America's conscience and sensitivity to the needs of others was raised. The Dawes Act was the result.

Unfortunately, the Dawes Act created new problems, and the United States' treatment of the native population continued as a blemish on the American nation and as an example of American intolerance for those who are different. The challenge of and commitment to equality could not be made by the frontiersmen

Westward expansion displaces Native Americans who fight to preserve their lands.

The Dawes Severalty Act attempts to address the needs of Native Americans but fails.

whose material needs and expedient solutions to challenges came first. We still see as part of the American character an intolerance of those different from ourselves, a desire to fill material needs and use expedient solutions to attain them. The nation's treatment of Native Americans improved somewhat with the Civil Rights Movement in the late 20th century, but for most of our history the Native American has not been a full member of the American democratic society.

The Final Frontier

Farmers finally settle on the frontier lands, where life is hard and often lonely.

The final frontier was the farming frontier. Stimulated by the railroad and wartime demand for food and aided by the Homestead Act of 1862, farmers moved westward. Most came from the Eastern states or Europe. Some were enticed westward by promises of a new life by railroad companies, which needed produce to haul to market to make the lines more profitable.

Life on the farming frontier was harsh. With little lumber, homes had to be built of sod. Water was scarce on the Great Plains west of

THE WAIL OF THE MARTYR.

"THERE IS NO GETTING O-ON WITH LO! ALL I DID WAS TO WITHHOLD HIS FOO-FOOD AND BLANKETS, KICK HIM OUT OF HIS RESER-V-VATION, SELL HIM SAND FOR FLOUR, KEEP HIM DRUNK ON CHEAP WHI-HISKEY, AND NOW, JUST BECAUSE HIS PEOPLE ARE STARVING AND THERE IS NO REDRESS, HE GETS MA-MAD AND THER-REATENS TO STRIKE ME!"

Indian Wars continued until 1886. Helen Hunt Jackson's A Century of Dishonor *published in 1881 aroused concern over the treatment of Native Americans. What view is expressed concerning relations between the white men and the Native Americans by the artist, J.A.M., in this cartoon?*

Published in Life, *March 27, 1884.*

100 longitude, where rainfall averaged less than 28" per year, not enough for growing wheat. New machinery aided the farmers and increased productivity, but farmers often cultivated lands which were unsuitable for farming in an attempt to make money to pay for the machinery. The results were disastrous for both the land and for the farmers.

Since farm allotments were 160 acres under the Homestead Act, homes were isolated. Lives were lonely, and church and club meetings provided the few social times available. The Grange (see below) helped to address the issue of loneliness, but the Sears Roebuck and Montgomery Ward mail order catalogues did more as they made the latest fashions and inventions available on the farms. The extension of rural free delivery by the United States Post Office provided another link to the outside world. Wind-up phonographs brought entertainment by the end of the century.

Railroads and the Frontier

The railroads encouraged settlement, but once the roads had a guaranteed source of produce to carry to market, they often raised freight prices and exploited the farmers, who were at their mercy. The anger of farmers at this situation grew when prices fell both domestically and abroad as a result of overproduction and increased competition from other farming nations such as Canada. The Patrons of Husbandry, known as the Grange, which at first was formed as a social and self-help organization, began to organize farmers and apply political pressure. Several states like Illinois passed laws controlling railroads rights to set fares. At first the Supreme Court upheld the laws but later reversed itself, saying the Constitution gave the federal government, and not the states, control over commerce. Federal action followed but the Interstate Commerce Commission of 1887, a first step from the laissez faire[2] business philosophy of the age, proved ineffective.

Railroads exploit farmers who then organize to apply pressure for fair rates.

With the Panic of 1893 farmers turned to a more active role in politics. The resulting People's or Populist Party became the high point of farmer activism to improve farm conditions through political activity. Farmers have not formed another political party since the defeat of the Populist Party. Throughout the 20th century a farm lobby, or bloc, in Congress has labored to protect farmers and the quality of farm life, which Thomas Jefferson viewed as the basis of a democratic society. With the passing of the frontier in 1890, industrial activities as exemplified by railroads, steel, and oil became the focus of most American's lives.

The People's or Populist Party becomes the vehicle for farmers' political protest.

To deal with the farming frontier, people had to have certain traits of character. Were the same traits needed in an industrialized nation, or did American character change after 1893 as business interests came to dominate the nation?

Railroads Change American Life

Railroads transformed American life in the 19th century, just as automobiles have done in the 20th century. By the Civil War the

The railroads transform American life.

---

[2]*laissez-faire*   Non-interference by government in private enterprises; a hands-off policy.

North and West were linked by rails, and the rail network of the North gave it a great advantage over the Confederate States. Before the war no agreement could be reached on an intercontinental rail route, but after the South seceded, the central route from Omaha, Nebraska to Sacramento, California was voted by Congress, with large federal government subsidies in both cash and land given to the builders.

Throughout United States' history the federal government has been prepared to subsidize industries deemed important to the national interest either directly or through tariffs. The railroads in the mid-19th century benefited from such government subsidies.

The building of the railroads brings many challenges.

The building of the road presented many challenges which greatly affected the West. First, labor was needed to lay the rails and blast the route through the Rockies. Chinese immigrants, among the first from Asia, came to work on the roads. As the Asian population grew in California, they met increasing hostility from the white inhabitants. Finally in 1882 Chinese immigration to the United States was banned in spite of the Chinese workers' contribution to the linking of the two coasts.

A second challenge were the herds of buffalo that roamed the Great Plains. The herds interfered with railroad building and operation. They could knock a train off the track. The railroads wanted the herds destroyed, and the army supported their desire for destruction of the herds as a way to starve the Indians into submission. The lifestyle of the nomadic tribes was based on the buffalo.

A third challenge was to make money. The availability of railroads created the long drive in the cattle frontier. Later the railroads encouraged farmers to settle, ending the cattle frontier and replacing it with the farming frontier. The railroads became the target of farmers' anger when the roads abused their power and used rebates and the long and short haul agreements to increase their profits. The railroads made a few men millionaires, such as Leland Stanford and James J. Hill, and provided jobs for hundreds even if at fairly low wages. The building of the railroads stimulated the steel and other industries. Steel rails became the norm, as did a standard gauge[3]. The challenges of transcontinental railroad building were met with ingenuity. The rail lines helped destroy the last frontier and linked America together as a united nation.

Inventions

Inventions, many involving the use of electricity, change America.

The steel industry is just one example of the growth of United States' industry after the Civil War. The war effort in the North also gave impetus to some industries such as cloth- and cannon-making. The population grew rapidly after the war, providing both a market and labor for new industrial developments. Inventions came rapidly and transformed American life.

---

[3]*standard gauge* For railroads, the gauge is the distance between the rails. Once this was the same, railroad cars could move from one line to another, creating a national railroad network.

This page of advertisements from Harper's Weekly *is similar to what one finds in many magazines today. Advertising became a growing business at the end of the 19th century as new products became easily available. One can learn a great deal of history by looking at old ads. What items are advertised? Would you find similar ads today? Do you recognize the items such as the item advertised by H.C. Curtis and Company?*

Answers to these questions will give you a good deal of information about life in the United States at the end of the last century. For instance, there are two bicycle ads and one for the New York Central Railroad in this time before the automobile. There are ads for socks and underwear, furs, tobacco, soft drinks, perfume, olive oil, life insurance and other items most of which would be advertised today. H.C. Curtis and Company advertised stiff collars for men's shirts and illustrates their ad with a drawing of one.

Published in Harper's Weekly, *October 24, 1896.*

Thomas Edison's organized work of invention centered around the use of electricity. It produced both the first light bulb and the phonograph. Think what life for you would be like without them. Singer's sewing machine and Bell's telephone had an equal impact on American lifestyles. The sewing machine speeded clothing manufacture and the phone created a new lifestyle. Together with the typewriter, they provided many opportunities for women in the work force. Advertising, including billboards, entered the American scene. Special incentives to retailers and easy financing for purchasers became part of the way American business was done. By the end of the century people were working on ideas for the automobile, the airplane, and other inventions that drastically affected our life in the 20th century.

Capitalism and Profit

Business needs to make profits and cuts wages to do so.

The guiding principle of business capitalism was to make profits. There were many opportunities to do so as new inventions were made and new machinery became available. New machinery was expensive and needed to be fully used, but increased production meant more produce. In order to sell the added produce, prices had to be reduced and then profits would fall. The cost of running machines and bank payments on loans were both fixed costs. Wages were not. Factory owners would often cut wages to maintain profits. A growing propulation provided new workers in case the old ones quit or went on strike when wages were reduced.

Business Organization

To make profits even more secure, new types of business organizations were adopted. The first organizations used were pools, which were informal arrangements to divide the market among several companies rather than rely on the free market operation. In prosperous times these informal pools worked well, but in times of recession, a more powerful and legally constituted arrangement was needed as companies broke their pooling agreements.

John D. Rockefeller develops a new form of business organization, the trust.

John D. Rockefeller from Cleveland, Ohio had entered the oil industry in 1865, six years after oil was first discovered in Pennsylvania. He and his brother established an oil refining company, the Standard Oil Company. The company absorbed many rivals, and in 1879 John D. Rockefeller turned to the trust arrangement to organize his company. In a trust different companies turn control of their stock, which represents ownership, over to a Board of Trustees who then run all the companies. The trust does not own but merely manages the company for the supposed benefit of all the companies and to obtain higher profits. Trusts worked much more effectively than pools because they were binding agreements.

The holding company becomes a tool for creating monopolies.

A final idea for company organization in order to increase profits and to control the market was the holding company. New Jersey was the first state to allow one company to own or hold stock in other companies and to own property in other states. John D.

Rockefeller again took the lead in trying a new organizational form. He used the New Jersey law to turn the Standard Oil Trust into the Standard Oil Company of New Jersey, a new company that included forty previous companies. It was the first large holding company.

Holding companies could own companies that did various jobs. For instance, an oil holding company could own a drilling company, the pipelines, the refinery, and the distribution centers or gas stations. Such an arrangement is called vertical integration and gave the company great control over the market from the raw material production to retail sale. In other cases a holding company would own all or almost all the companies doing one step in the manufacturing process, and this is called horizontal integration.

Trusts and holding companies became tools of industrialists wishing to create monopolies, that is, to exercise complete control over a particular industry. Such control would allow a company to set prices and thus to make higher profits, very often at the expense of the consumer and worker.

Social Darwinism

Some manufacturers were concerned about the working and living conditions of their employees. George Pullman built a model village for his workers in the Pullman Sleeping Car plant, but he insisted on running the village in his own way, and his plan for a utopian working society collapsed with the Pullman Strike of 1894. Many business and social leaders of the age were less interested in their workers and more concerned about their profits. They followed the tenets of Social Darwinism.

Social Darwinism loosely applied Charles Darwin's Theory of Evolution to economics. Taking Darwin's suggestion of the survival of the fittest as the determinant in evolution, Social Darwinists believed that the state should not interfere in economic life. They believed those on top in the business world were there because they were the fittest. They had survived the battle of the marketplace because they were the best. Any interference in the free market operation would wreck the economy and upset its natural evolution. (This view of economics is known as *laissez-faire*, which means to leave alone.) They believed any person with ability could rise to the top, and laborers were where they were because of natural selection.

This philosophy of Social Darwinism dominated the thinking of many American business leaders in the late 19th and early 20th centuries. The fact the federal government aided businesses through high tariffs and subsidies, such as those for the railroad, was overlooked or ignored.

The Gospel of Wealth

By the end of the century one millionaire, Andrew Carnegie, a brilliant Scots immigrant who created Carnegie Steel and sold it to the banker J. P. Morgan, added a twist to Social Darwinism in a speech on the "Gospel of Wealth" in 1889. Carnegie argued that

While some manufacturers attempt to improve working conditions, others subscribe to the ideas of Social Darwinism.

Andrew Carnegie in the Gospel of Wealth *justifies the accumulation of wealth but endorses philanthropic activity.*

wealth was essential for civilization and by the natural law of competition only a few could achieve it. However, what these few did with their wealth was crucial for society. They could leave their wealth to their children, but this was "injudicious" and undermined the natural law of acquisition since their children began life with an advantage. Secondly, the rich could bequeath their wealth for public purposes after their death, but they would have no control over its use. Carnegie then argued that the rich should administer their wealth through their lifetime to benefit society. Andrew Carnegie did so, spending over $350,000,000 he got from the sale of Carnegie Steel to establish libraries and endow the Carnegie Endowment for International Peace and the Carnegie Foundation for Advancement of Teaching.

Following Carnegie, charitable contributions and philanthropy[4] became the way followed by many of the great entrepreneurs of the age. The railroad builder, Leland Stanford, founded and endowed Stanford University. John D. Rockefeller of Standard Oil Company endowed the University of Chicago and established the Rockefeller Institute of Medical Research and the Rockefeller Foundation. Rockefeller money was used to buy large tracts of land that later became national parks, and his descendants helped purchase the site of the United Nations in New York City. Such philanthropy is a vital part of the American encomic and cultural life today and we all benefit from it in different ways either enjoying museums, libraries, hospitals, schools, orchestras, or special charities supported by philanthropically minded individuals.

While the "Gospel of Wealth" supported philanthropy, Social Darwinism supported an economic system that benefited a few at the expense of many. Wages were kept low and working hours long, which encouraged slum conditions. As a result discontented workers organized but with limited success. By the end of the century "progressive" leaders were calling for reforms in urban government and living conditions as well as in the organization of American business. Some of the qualities of the American character which Turner ascribed to the frontier experience could also be ascribed to competition in the business world—coarseness, acquisitiveness, a grasp of the material, dominant individualism with exuberance of life. The question is, were these qualities born on the frontier and applied to business, or did they arise from economic competition?

There is no agreed on answer. What do you think?

Beginning of Labor Organization

The first attempts at a national labor union fail.

The first unions or organizations of workers came during the era of Jacksonian Democracy and were local. In the post-Civil War period attempts were made to organize workers on a national basis. The National Labor Union was organized in 1866 with the goal of establishing the eight-hour day. In 1868 Congress passed an

---

[4]*philanthropy* The spirit of active goodwill toward one's fellow men as shown in efforts to promote their welfare through gifts or the building of institutions.

eight-hour day for mechanics and laborers who worked for the United States government, but progress elsewhere was slow. Unsuccessfully turning to national politics in 1872, the National Labor Union quickly collapsed. After the Panic of 1873 there was labor unrest, but labor unions were unsuccessful in organizing support. Until the 1930s union strength and influence dropped during times of depression or panic.

Finally, in 1878 the Knights of Labor was organized as a national union of both skilled and unskilled workers. Their platform called for the eight-hour day, boycotts not strikes, a graduated income tax, and consumer cooperatives. The Knights forced some concessions from several railways but collapsed after a general strike for an eight-hour day failed in Chicago and the Haymarket Massacre occurred in 1886 (see below). One inherent weakness of the Knights of Labor was bringing together all workers, skilled and unskilled, in one union. The wage level and concerns of the two groups differed.

The next national union to be founded, the American Federation of Labor (AFL), was formed in 1886. It concentrated on organizing skilled workers. It continues today as the important AFL-CIO. The organizational approach used by the AFL under its first President, Samuel Gompers, was to recognize the autonomy of each specialized trade, such as carpenters or cigar makers. The AFL formed the coordinating group for these separate trades. Membership in the AFL grew. Its program under Samuel Gompers included laws curbing immigration in order to protect jobs, relief from technological unemployment created by the introduction of new machines, and labor legislation to include the eight-hour day and workmen's compensation.

The AFL successfully organizes skilled workers nationally.

Unskilled workers remained largely unorganized after the collapse of the Knights of Labor. The Industrial Workers of the World (IWW) was formed in 1905. It was considered very radical by many Americans and was never very successful as a union. It died after World War I in a period of political and economic reaction.

Strikes: A Tool of Labor Organization

Industrialization created new working conditions and new relationships between the employed and employers. As large textile factories replaced weaving done in homes, workers became just another factor to reckon with in analyzing costs and making profits. The personal relationship of the small shop where the boss knew his employees as individuals was replaced by large impersonal factories where the workers seldom if ever met the owner. As the workers were treated like another machine to be used, they became alienated from their job. Employers in seeking profits often cut wages, and if a worker did not accept the cut, there were others who needed the job. It was a situation in which factory owners, the capitalists, were in control and held the power.

Workers become alienated as they are viewed as just another part in the production machine.

Unions were a way of uniting the workers to give them power equal to the owners. The major tool used by unionized workers to force their program or wishes on the employers was the strike.

Unions give workers power.

How to organize strikes and make them effective was the great challenge. It required as much ingenuity and skill as did organizing business or struggling with the challenges of the frontier.

Strikes sometimes result in violence and lose workers the support of their fellow Americans.

Workers could rarely count on the support of government when on strike. Most city and state governments were under the control of successful businessmen. Also the theory of Social Darwinism worked in favor of the owners who had "made it," they would claim, on their own, overlooking the help of the tariffs. Unionization seemed to be against the individualism that was so highly respected in America. Many workers were recent arrivals in the United States and appeared different from earlier arrivals. Middle class Americans often saw strikes as threats to the stability and security which they had achieved. Some union members did hold radical ideas for reforming American life but they were a tiny minority.

One incident, the Haymarket Massacre in Chicago in 1886, was falsely linked to an anarchists' plot, and it frightened the middle class and destroyed the Knights of Labor, which was seen as the organizer of the incident. In the Haymarket Massacre, just after the Chicago police had broken up an anarchist/communist meeting, a bomb exploded and seven police were killed. The remaining police opened fire on the crowd. Eight anarchists were later arrested, accused of the bombing, and tried. Four were found guilty and hung, yet no one was found guilty of throwing the bomb. When a new governor of Illinois was elected, he released those prisoners still in jail, but the action hurt his political career.

Both political and business leaders were frightened by the incident, and the average American citizen followed their lead in seeing a threat to the traditional standards of society in the actions of the unions. The incident reflects the problems faced by labor protestors and organizers.

Government Intervention in Strikes

President Cleveland uses federal troops to end the strike against the Pullman Company in 1894.

The federal government intervened in the Pullman Strike in 1894. In that strike workers in the Pullman, or sleeper, cars on the railroads went on strike to gain higher wages and better working conditions. Train service was blocked by their work stoppage. The Democratic President, Grover Cleveland, sent in federal troops to end the strike so the United States mail would not be stopped. Both Republicans and Democrats put the delivery of the mail and the operation of the railroads above the needs of workers for pay and improved working conditions.

President T. Roosevelt supports the workers in the Anthracite Coal Strike in 1902.

It was not until the Progressive President Theodore Roosevelt intervened in the Anthracite Coal Strike in 1902 and appointed a commission to set the settlement terms that strikers received any help from the federal government. The coal strikers won a 10 percent pay rise, but the union was not recognized. The incident was unusual in the pre-World War I period, but suggested times would change.

The strike is the final threat used by workers to get employers to hear their demands. It had limited success in the prosperous 1920s but became an effective tool of laborers in the New Deal period. While few industrial workers ever saw the frontier, the traits Turner said developed on the frontier—coarseness and strength, practical, inventive nervous energy, and an ability to effect great ends—were helpful in labor's efforts to organize and improve working conditions.

Immigration

Another matter that hurt the industrial workers and made the establishment of unions difficult was the increasing number of immigrants who came to America after 1880. While most pre-Civil War immigrants came from the British Isles or northern Europe, after 1880 more and more came from southern and eastern Europe. By 1910 almost two-thirds of immigrants came from Russia,

The majority of immigrants come from Southern and Eastern Europe by 1910.

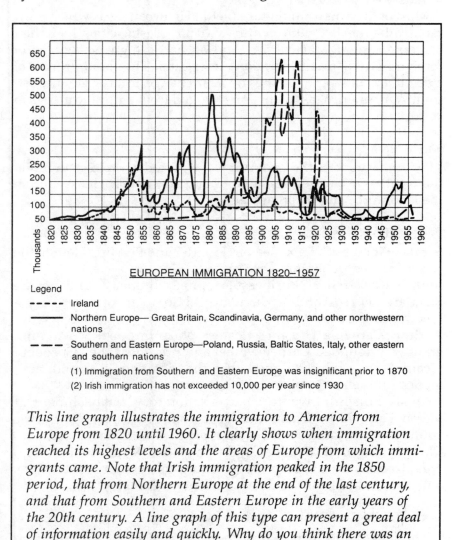

EUROPEAN IMMIGRATION 1820–1957

Legend

- - - - - Ireland

———— Northern Europe— Great Britain, Scandinavia, Germany, and other northwestern nations

— — — Southern and Eastern Europe—Poland, Russia, Baltic States, Italy, other eastern and southern nations

(1) Immigration from Southern and Eastern Europe was insignificant prior to 1870

(2) Irish immigration has not exceeded 10,000 per year since 1930

This line graph illustrates the immigration to America from Europe from 1820 until 1960. It clearly shows when immigration reached its highest levels and the areas of Europe from which immigrants came. Note that Irish immigration peaked in the 1850 period, that from Northern Europe at the end of the last century, and that from Southern and Eastern Europe in the early years of the 20th century. A line graph of this type can present a great deal of information easily and quickly. Why do you think there was an increase of immigration from Northern Europe after 1945?

Source: U.S. Bureau of the Census, Historical Statistics of the U.S., Colonial Times to the Present.

Italy, and the Austro-Hungarian empire. Most were unskilled workers from farms who came seeking a better life. Conditions in the cities were difficult, and they were eager to find work and willing to work for low wages. This hurt the efforts of workers to organize and gain higher wages.

The older immigrants came to resent the new immigrants. There were occasional clashes. There were language, religious, and social differences. As the children of immigrants went to public schools and learned English, they became more American but lost some contact with their own culture, creating tensions within the new immigrant groups. Many of the new immigrants were Roman Catholic, and the difficulties Catholics faced in pre-Civil War America continued for them. Some immigrants were Greek Orthodox and others Jewish, which added both to diversity in America and to tensions.

Most of these new immigrants settled in urban areas which grew rapidly in the late 19th century. Major coastal cities had their centers of immigrant culture, and all had a high percentage of foreign-born or first-generation Americans. The rapid growth of cities illustrates perhaps the greatest change in lifestyle in post-Civil War America, as the nation changed from a rural to an urban culture.

KEY POINT TO REMEMBER

The fifty years after the Civil War was a period of rapid changes on the frontier, in the development of industry and business, and in the labor force and its organization.

PEOPLE TO REMEMBER

Samuel Gompers   Labor leader; founder and first President of the American Federation of Labor (AFL)

John D. Rockefeller   Businessman; philanthropist; founder of the Standard Oil Trust and the Standard Oil Company of New Jersey, a holding company.

Andrew Carnegie   Business leader; philanthropist; Scots immigrant who founded Carnegie Steel and presented the "Gospel of Wealth" idea, which argued that the rich should spend their money on philanthropic enterprises during their lifetime.

Thomas Edison   Inventor; had a laboratory establishment at Menlo Park, N.J., where the light bulb, phonograph, electric voting machine, and sound motion pictures were developed.

Chief Sitting Bull   Native American leader; Sioux chieftan who organized his tribe to stop the westward movement of the whites onto the Great Plains; he defeated General Custer.

LINKS FROM THE PAST TO THE PRESENT

1. The image and legend of frontier is used in everything from political speeches to movies to commercial advertising to gain Americans' support.
2. Large corporations are still important under the capitalist system of the United States.

3. The philosophies of laissez faire and Social Darwinism still have strong support in the United States.
4. Philanthropy has been crucial to the improvement of the quality of life in America.
5. Unions still play a significant role in labor-management relations.
6. New inventions continue to change American lifestyle (VCRs, computers).

QUESTIONS

Identify each of the following:

Frederick Jackson Turner	Social Darwinism
A Century of Dishonor	Gospel of Wealth
Singer sewing machine	Knights of Labor
Standard Oil Trust	American Federation of Labor

True or False:
1. On the long drive, cowboys drove cattle to railheads, where the cattle were slaughtered for food for the railroad workers.
2. The forces of Chief Sitting Bull of the Sioux annihilated Colonel Custer's forces at the Little Big Horn.
3. The Dawes Severalty Act established reservations for Native Americans where the land was held by the tribe.
4. Sears Roebuck and Montgomery Ward catalogues allowed farm families to stay abreast of the latest fashions and inventions.
5. Farmers organized to apply political pressure in an attempt to control railroad fares.
6. Transcontinental railroads received no economic assistance from the federal government.
7. Many of the first Asians to come to the United States worked on the railroads.
8. In spite of industrial growth, advertising did not become a part of American business practices until after World War I.
9. In a trust, different companies give their stock to a Board of Trustees, who run all the companies.
10. A holding company is a company that owns or holds other companies, which do various jobs—for instance, drilling, refining, and distributing oil.
11. Social Darwinists believed government should help the weakest to allow them to compete in the survival of the fittest competition.
12. The "Gospel of Wealth" says people should give their wealth to their children to help them in the struggle for survival.
13. The Knights of Labor organized both skilled and unskilled workers in one union.
14. In the Anthracite Coal Strike President Theodore Roosevelt used the federal government to help the workers' cause.

Multiple Choice:

1. The western frontier developed in this sequence:
    a. first farming, then cattle, finally mining
    b. first mining, then cattle, finally farming
    c. neither of the above
2. Thomas Edison is noted for his work with electricity and for inventing the
    a. sewing machine
    b. telephone
    c. light bulb
3. Social Darwinism is based upon the theory of
    a. laissez faire
    b. management efficiency
    c. evolution
4. The American Federation of Labor organized
    a. unskilled workers
    b. skilled trade workers and unskilled laborers
    c. skilled trade workers such as carpenters and cigar makers
5. Older immigrants resented the new immigrants because
    a. they would accept low wages
    b. they were highly skilled
    c. they could fight better

ANSWERS

True or False: 1. F, 2. T, 3. F, 4. T, 5. T, 6. F, 7. T, 8. F, 9. T, 10. T, 11. F, 12. F, 13. T, 14. T.

Multiple Choice: 1. b, 2. c. 3. c, 4. c, 5. a.

II.   REFORM MOVEMENTS

The Social Gospel

Late 19th century cities had many of the same problems as cities today. There were pockets of poverty, crowded living conditions, rampant crime, and often political corruption. Reared in the tradition of the Puritan work ethic and Social Darwinism, many American leaders and the voting middle class believed poverty to result from a lack of effort and to reflect poor character. While social workers began to realize environment also had an effect on poverty, American voters were not prepared to help the poor.

Preachers of the Social Gospel encourage Americans to help the urban poor.

Help did come from many quarters. After a trip to England where she saw settlement houses having an impact on life in the cities, Jane Addams founded Hull House in Chicago in 1889. This first settlement house in the United States became famous as a model way to improve community and civic pride. Jane Addams was awarded the Nobel Peace Prize in 1931 for her work on behalf of the urban poor.

In churches preachers of the Social Gospel encouraged the establishment of settlement homes and the use of the city churches as centers of learning and recreation. Walter Rauschenbusch in New York and Washington Gladden in Columbus, Ohio were leaders of the Social Gospel movement. They called upon their churches to heed the Sermon on the Mount and act accordingly, giving to the poor and needy. They thought that socialism might be a better way than capitalism if the poor and laborers were not helped by capitalists. Their preaching in the 1880s prepared the way for the reforms of the Progressives early in the 20th century. The Social Gospel helped focus attention on life in the cities.

Life in the Cities

Cities grew rapidly after the Civil War. While the number of buildings increased, the population grew even faster. As wages went up, some were able to purchase homes, and as street cars and trolleys were developed, suburbs became the place to go if you could afford it. Many, particularly immigrants and blacks, could not afford to buy property. They had to rent from landlords. Often the only places they could rent were in tenements[1]. In tenements families of immigrants and the poor often lived in one room and shared kitchens and bathrooms, but many tenements didn't even have indoor plumbing. To make a living, the parents sometimes sewed or rolled cigars in the one room. There were efforts at reforms in different cities but America's commitment to free enterprise prevented the building of public housing.

As cities grow, living conditions similar to those in today's inner cities develop.

Such living conditions encouraged crime, which was often blamed on the immigrants rather than the conditions. Gangs made up of both old and recent city dwellers were a common element of city life. Theft, feuds, and organized vice were the most prevalent crimes. One form of vice was prostitution, which literally enslaved young girls from rural states or from immigrant families. Prostitution, gambling, and other activities were often given police protection in return for a slice of the profits. As more blacks from the South began to move to northern cities after the turn of the century, race riots occurred in many of those cities. Discrimination against Asians and Mexicans increased.

But not everything in cities between the Civil War and World War I was bad. Street lighting was introduced after Edison's invention of the incandescent light bulb in 1879, which made the streets much safer. Fire fighting equipment became a regular part of city life. A clean water supply and sewage disposal made life more bearable and reduced the stench of the city. Streetcars made travel easier. The growth of suburbs allowed escape from the crowded conditions of the inner city, and in the 20th century this opportunity was incorporated in the "American Dream," in which a house of your own in the suburbs became an important element. Cultural offerings—theater, concerts, opera—made urban centers attractive for those who could afford to attend. Free libraries and museums added a welcome diversion for poor and wealthy alike.

Some changes make city life more enjoyable.

---

[1]*tenement*   A dwelling house where separate apartments are rented to families; usually occupied by the lower classes.

The City Political Boss

In many cities where the government was unable to cope with the complexity of problems, political bosses emerged. Bosses controlled political machines[2], which in turn controlled the city. Machine politics were often corrupt and used bribery to stay in power, but they had to have the support of the people who voted. For voting purposes cities were subdivided into wards and the political machine had people working in each ward who knew the residents and could help with their problems. The ward workers would help their constituents[3] find jobs or housing, deal with the police or city administration, and solve many of the problems presented by urban living.

While the boss and his close associates were often driven by greed and power, political machines and their ward workers did make the lives of many immigrants and poor more tolerable. The bosses distributed city business, everything from garbage collection to printing, to those who would help them stay in power. The boss system, while often corrupt, did make the cities function quite efficiently for the poorer residents.

Urban Reform

The corruption and the ever-rising taxes to pay for it and the new city services like sewage and lighting upset many voters, particularly in the middle class. At the end of the century urban reformers emerged in many cities. They formed part of the Progressive Movement (see below). These urban reformers offered plans to reorganize and streamline city government in the same way large American businesses were reorganizing and streamlining. New forms of city government—the city manager and the city commission—were introduced to replace the mayoral system, which was more easily controlled by the political machine. In the mayoral system one person, the mayor, had the executive power and could be bribed. In some cities reformers supported city ownership of electric and gas companies and streetcar lines to prevent bribery. Some worked to provide better jobs and living conditions.

The reformers made government more efficient, but the new efficient governments often lacked the contact with the people that gave bosses their power. Most reform movements were short lived, and machine politics soon returned. Americans wanted their cities to have effective government and to be livable places without crime and poverty, but few reformers or their followers were prepared to work for the city. Therefore, periodic reform became the norm for urban political life.

Many reformers were from the middle and upper classes of the cities. As industrialization continued, a class of very wealthy

---

[2]*political machine*   A group, usually from the same political party, organized to control the political life of a city, or other political unit. Political machines are usually under the control of an individual called the boss.

[3]*constituents*   Those citizens who are qualified to vote for a legislator and to whom the elected legislator is responsible for his or her actions.

people emerged in the United States, and most of them lived in the cities. For instance, in New York City Fifth Avenue was lined with mansions built by the wealthy. These mansions along Fifth Avenue overlooked the new Central Park, an extensive open area in the center of Manhattan that was preserved to provide open space, grass, and trees for all those living in the crowded city. The expenditures of the rich were often extravagant, and the gap between the rich and the poor in the cities steadily widened. Even though wages climbed, industrial profits grew even more rapidly for the few millionaires. Many of the rich did social work, helping the poor as suggested in Carnegie's *Gospel of Wealth*. For instance, Eleanor Roosevelt, born into an upper class family, niece of President Theodore Roosevelt and wife of President Franklin Roosevelt, did social work in New York prior to her marriage, as did many of her class. Other people worked in or contributed monetarily to reform movements or philanthropic organizations.

Entertainment

Middle class America grew in size, and as new types of jobs and the eight-hour day became more prevalent, leisure time increased. This greatly changed the American lifestyle. There were new products to consume and fun to pursue. Entertainment became an industry. Vaudeville shows, in which a series of acts including everything from acrobats to yodellers, were presented on stage were very popular. William (Buffalo Bill) Cody and his Wild West Show was particularly popular. Movies, developed toward the end of the 19th century as slot-machine peep shows, quickly developed into a major mode of entertainment. By World War I, movies were an important form of artistic expression and a new American industry. Movies have had a tremendous impact on American culture and attitudes, providing dreams for the young and homogenizing experiences so we all share certain visions or nightmares.

As some Americans gain leisure time, entertainment becomes a major industry.

Professional sport also emerged as a major industry. The first World Series game was played in 1903. Football, first played between Rutgers and Princeton Universities right after the Civil War, became popular. The mania for winning football games cost eighteen lives in 1905 and was condemned by President Roosevelt. Individuals also participated in sports such as bicycling and croquet. While the latter has faded in popularity, America's interest in sports continues as a major aspect of the American character, perhaps rooted in the need for an active life which was necessary on the frontier.

Literature

After the Civil War, cheaply bound books called dime novels sold in great numbers to an increasingly literate public. Adventure stories laid in the West were replaced by detective stories as the most popular reading as the 20th century dawned. Horatio Alger published 130 books, all on the same "rags to riches" theme of the poor boy who becomes wealthy because of honesty, ambition, and thrift.

Authors reflect the values of society in their works.

Horatio Alger's works were widely popular and reinforced the teachings of the Social Darwinists. These popular books were important in forming the thought patterns of young Americans.

There were also a number of works produced that are considered classics and reveal different sides of American life. The most popular author was Mark Twain, the pen name for Samuel Clemens, whose short stories of the West and great novels, *The Adventures of Tom Sawyer* (1876) and *The Adventures of Huckleberry Finn* (1884), revealed the comic and tragic side of life. Edith Wharton and Henry James wrote about upper class Americans while some, like Theodore Dreiser in *Sister Carrie*, explored realistically the struggles of slum life, sexuality, and violence.

NO LONGER A WELCOME VISITOR.

Paterfamilias: KEEP OUT, SIR! IF MY WIFE AND CHILDREN CAN NOT HAVE THE NEWS OF THE DAY WITHOUT YOUR RECORD OF CRIME AND FILTH THEY SHALL DO WITHOUT IT.

Rogers makes a comment on the newspapers of the late 19th century when the term, "yellow press," first came into use. Papers turned to stories of crime and scandal to attract readers. What does Rogers see as the role of the "Paterfamilias" (father of the family) in dealing with these stories?

Published in Life, *February 7, 1884.*

Newspapers

Newspapers were popular in the post-Civil War period. Analytical, in-depth reporting made good reading, but it could antagonize readers. Such reporting was often replaced by features in order to avoid offending advertisers upon whom the papers depended for their profits. What the reader pays for a newspaper has never covered the cost of publishing. Advertising has been the great source of money in the publishing business.

Joseph Pulitzer, who began with a St. Louis newspaper and moved to New York, introduced the idea of the "yellow" press, which was named for the "yellow kid" in his colored comic page in the *New York World*. Yellow journalism is based on sensationalism and exposures in order to sell papers. Papers battling for more readers and more advertising struggled to outdo each other in reporting scandals. The public bought the papers suggesting an aspect of the American character different from the clean cowboy image of frontier legend. William Randolph Hearst in the *San Francisco Examiner* was another noted practitioner of yellow journalism. Both he and Joseph Pulitzer built large publishing empires.

Yellow journalism is developed to sell more papers.

Editors' competition for readers led to emotional reporting on the international situation in Cuba in the 1890s. The press had a major role in bringing the United States into the Spanish-American War. The press, and more particularly magazines such as *Harper's*, *Scribner's Monthly*, and *The Nation*, published well-researched stories of corruption in cities and business. Influential leaders of business and education read these accounts. The revelations published led to the urban reforms mentioned above and encouraged others who saw the need to reform America in other areas.

The press sensationalizes the situation in Cuba before the Spanish-American War.

How powerful do you think the press or TV news are today in forming our opinions and attitudes?

The Temperance Movement

Among the concerns of reform-minded citizens in the post-Civil War period were several concerns that continued from the era of Jacksonian Democracy. Foremost of these was the temperance, or anti-alcohol, movement. Drinking had increased during the Civil War, and many immigrants came from cultures where drinking was an accepted part of life. A National Prohibition Party was formed in 1869 and ran candidates for office in many elections. Women's Christian Temperance Union (W.C.T.U.) was founded in 1874. Under the leadership of Frances Willard and Carrie Nation, who gained fame for smashing bottles in bars with her hatchet, the organization grew, and in 1893 the Anti-Saloon League was formed.

The Temperance Movement succeeds with the passage of Amendment XVIII.

Agitation for reform by these two groups was widespread. Several states passed prohibition laws. The peak of the temperance movement was reached in 1919, when Amendment XVIII to the Constitution was ratified.

Amendment XVIII prohibited the sale and consumption of alcohol, and Congress was empowered to make laws to enforce it. The acceptance of prohibition by the Congress was tied in with support for World War I since prohibition would save grain for food rather than using it for alcohol. Prohibition became national policy and lasted for fourteen years. Amendment XVIII was repealed in 1933. Prohibition reveals one aspect of American character, the idea of fighting for a good cause.

Women's Suffrage

The fight for women's suffrage began in the era of Jacksonian Democracy and continued after the Civil War. In 1869 the Wyoming Territory granted the vote to women. In some states and territories women were allowed to vote for school board members but not for candidates for political office. In 1890 the National American Woman Suffrage Association was organized. Elizabeth Cady Stanton, who had been a leader of the Seneca Falls Convention in 1848, and Susan B. Anthony were among the leaders. Increased agitation during the Progressive Era at the turn of the century brought some success as several states extended the suffrage to women.

Amendment XIX guarantees women the right to vote in federal elections.

Finally, Congress acted and Amendment XIX was ratified by the states in 1920. Amendment XIX guaranteed women the right to vote in federal elections, but the states controlled who could vote in state elections. The right of women to vote quickly spread to all the states after the XIXth Amendment was adopted. After almost a hundred years of reform agitation, women achieved equality at the ballot box. The good aspects of the American character, fighting for a good cause and support of the individual, overcame negative arguments and the suffrage reform cause was won.

Opportunities for women to work grew greatly after the Civil War. The telephone and typewriter opened many new opportunities for employment, as did the sewing machine. Many poor women had to work to supplement the family's meager income. In World War I women took some positions previously held only by men. Smaller families became the norm in urban centers, and this gave women more opportunities to be out of the home. All of these factors helped create wide-spread support for the granting of the suffrage to women.

The American Red Cross is founded.

There were many other areas where changes and reforms were introduced in the late 19th and early 20th century. One change of particular significance for all of us today occurred in the area of medical and emergency relief. Clara Barton, who had nursed Union soldiers in the Civil War, founded the American Red Cross in 1881. She saw the need for better treatment by and better standards for nurses. Her work has saved hundreds of lives and affects us today.

Civil Service Reform

The spoils system is modified by the Pendleton Civil Service Reform Act.

The reform movement in the cities has already been mentioned. Another political concern of reformers was civil service reform. The spoils system had been an accepted part of United States politics at least since Thomas Jefferson's presidency. It was based on the belief we were all created equal and in a democratic society every citizen could be President or run an office of the government. However, as business turned to greater specialization and efficiency, reformers began to think of ways to apply the same principles to government. While the spoils system was democratic, the rapid turnover of untrained government workers appointed by the winners of elections was inefficient and often led to corruption. The solution reformers offered was to create an effective civil service of trained workers who would run the government bureaucracy as professionals. They could not be replaced by newly elected officials. After a disgruntled office seeker, who expected a reward under the spoils system, assassinated President Garfield in 1881, Congress finally passed the Pendleton Civil Service Act in 1884.

The issue of efficient and noncorrupt people in the government workforce continued to be an issue after the passage of the law, which many thought did not go far enough. Today workers in the government bureaucracy have to pass entrance tests. The bureaucracy has grown greatly, but it is no longer filled solely by the political whims of elected officials. The first civil service laws made government a much more efficient operation.

Summary

All of the reform movements mentioned reflect American values and character, and those characteristics and values are still with us. Whether they were formed on the frontier can be debated, but there is no doubt that working for good with exuberance and working for practical, inventive ways to solve problems, often in materialistic ways, are part of the American approach to problems and reforms. These reforms, as well as the many changes brought on by industrialization, immigration, and the closing of the frontier, drastically changed America's lifestyle between 1877 and 1914.

Many of the qualities and characteristics one identifies with post-Civil War Americans are still seen in America today. Whether they were born on the frontier or simply emerged as responses to the challenges of the era, is a debatable question. What do you think?

KEY POINT TO REMEMBER
Urban changes and growth led to reform movements in several areas, among them voting rights for women, city government, and prohibition.

LINKS FROM THE PAST
1. The needs of the urban poor are still of great concern to many in this country.
2. Leisure-time activities, especially athletics and movies, remain important in American life.
3. Concern over the use of alcohol, as seen in the prohibition movement, and drugs continues in 1990.

PEOPLE TO REMEMBER
Mark Twain Author, newspaper writer; pen name of Samuel Clemens; widely read popular author of stories of the West including *The Adventures of Tom Sawyer* and *The Adventures of Huckleberry Finn*.

Jane Addams Social worker, humanitarian; founder of Hull House, Chicago, the first settlement house in the United States built to improve community and civic life for the poor; winner of the Nobel Peace Prize in 1931 for her work on behalf of the poor.

Susan B. Anthony Reformer, feminist; one of the leaders of the National American Woman Suffrage Association, which finally succeeded in obtaining the vote for women with the passage of Amendment XIX in 1920.

Elizabeth Cady Stanton Reformer, feminist; leader and founder with Lucretia Mott of the 19th century feminist movement; the two organized the Seneca Falls Convention in 1848; Elizabeth Stanton went on to head the National American Woman Suffrage Association and was co-editor of *Revolution*, a publication of the feminist movement.

QUESTIONS

Identify each of the following:

Social Gospel	Amendment XVIII to the Constitution
Political boss	Amendment XIX to the Constitution
Yellow journalism	Pendleton Civil Service Act

True or False:

1. Preachers of the Social Gospel believed the poor were poor because of God's will.
2. Discrimination against Asians and Mexicans increased in the late 19th and early 20th centuries.
3. Ward workers helped their constituents to find jobs and to deal with other problems of urban life.
4. Central Park in New York was designed and built as a playground for the rich who lived on Fifth Avenue.
5. Horatio Alger wrote 130 books, all on the theme of the struggles of slum life, sexuality, and violence, which greatly appealed to the American reading public.
6. Joseph Pulitzer is known for his introduction of Yellow Journalism into the American newspaper business.
7. The temperance movement had its beginning in the age of Jacksonian Democracy and its greatest success in 1919 with the passing of the Prohibition Amendment to the United States Constitution.
8. The American Red Cross is an example of one of the many changes and reforms of American life that came about in the late 19th century.
9. The invention of the typewriter and telephone meant many more women could stay at home.
10. American character in the 1990s reflects none of the qualities one ascribed to the American character in the 1890s.

Multiple Choice:
1. The leadership of Hull House and urban political machines both worked
   a. to help the living conditions of the urban poor
   b. to increase the political power of a political boss
   c. to provide an escape from unsanitary conditions
2. Examples of changes in city living which benefited everyone are
   a. the development of a clean water supply and sewerage disposal system
   b. street lighting and street cars
   c. both of the above
3. Examples of leisure-time activities which were available to all by 1900 were
   a. movies
   b. vaudeville shows
   c. World Series baseball games
4. Civil service reform meant that
   a. the spoils system would be used less
   b. anybody could hold a place in the government bureaucracy since "all men are created equal"
   c. the city manager and the city commission form of government would not be needed

ANSWERS

True or False: 1. F, 2. T, 3. T, 4. F, 5. F, 6. T, 7. T, 8. T, 9. F, 10. F.
Multiple Choice: 1. a, 2. c, 3. b, 4. a.

CHAPTER 9

From Panic to Empire

One way of looking at history is that it follows certain patterns or cycles. Just as season follows season in a never-ending cycle, so some historians see history not as repeating itself but as following a similar pattern, which is repeated over and over. How often in your life do you see patterns repeating? From the daily routine of brushing teeth in the morning to the celebration of holidays—Thanksgiving, Christmas, Yom Kippur, birthdays—we usually repeat the cycle, yet each repetition is different—no two holiday celebrations are the same. So it is with history. There are cycles or patterns, but no two cycles are the same.

The origin of this view goes far back into Greek and Roman history, when philosophers discussed natural laws that guided both nature and human life. This concept of life following laws of nature was reinforced in the 19th century by Charles Darwin's work on evolution. At that time some individuals looked at events and said they were inevitable; they were simply following the natural progression. They concluded that we should not interfere with what was natural.

This viewpoint was used especially to respond to the business cycles of periodic panics or depressions alternating with good economic times. It was also used to describe the movement towards overseas expansion and empire as a natural step in the growth of a nation. According to this cyclical, biological, and evolutionary view, each nation went through the same cycle. Writers described this cycle in human terms and talked about the childhood, adolescence, and young manhood of the United States. In this analogy, growth was natural and not to grow would be to die.

This concept of inevitable, natural growth following messages encoded in your hormones should be familiar to all young students. Do you think the same growth pattern is followed by nations? Many at the end of the 19th century did view history in this way. They saw the United States as a young adolescent emerging from the trauma of the Civil War. They viewed our history as following natural laws. We were going to follow the same cycle of growth and greatness that previous nations had followed.

I. BUSINESS CYCLES

By the time of the Civil War, the United States had already experienced two major economic depressions, the Panics of 1819 and 1837. By 1873 post-war expansion, especially of railroads, a drop in European demand for United States farm produce, speculation and market manipulation by a few individuals, and the failure of the large banking house of J. Cooke brought on a depression that lasted from 1873 to 1878. The government's concern over the debt payment and desire to maintain strong credit rating prolonged the crisis, which began with a fall in security prices, what today we call a "plunge," on Wall Street.

The causes of this depression—overexpansion, speculation, bankruptcy—make a pattern that has repeated itself throughout United States history, but in each case the details are somewhat different. After the New Deal in the 20th century, the federal government has been actively involved in attempts to avoid or control the ups and downs i.e. cyclical movement of the business cycle, but the cycle continues to move up and down. However, the 19th century business philosophy of laissez-faire, supported by the attitudes of the Social Darwinists (see Chapter 8), called for no government interference in the economic cycle, which was considered "natural" and part of the law of nature.

Overexpansion, speculation, and bankruptcy provide the pattern of recurring economic cycles.

The Money Supply

Some people did want help from the federal government in controlling the business cycle. These people suggested the government should increase the money supply either by adding coins of silver to those of gold in order to increase the specie supply or by issuing paper money. Throughout the 19th century and until the United States abandoned gold as the basis of our money supply in 1933, there were many proposals for coining silver and issuing "greenbacks," that is, paper money. At times these requests were accepted. For instance, the Union issued large numbers of greenbacks to help pay for the Civil War. When these greenbacks were recalled, and only specie became correct currency, there was a major impact on the money supply that helped precipitate the depression of 1873.

The money supply has an impact on panics and depressions.

The details of the many acts involving the money supply, and silver and greenbacks need not concern us, but the reasoning behind it does. The arguments for and the groups that support the two policies have been similar throughout the natural cycles of boom and bust. The arguments are still used today as we face recession in the 1990s.

There are two basic economic approaches to, or arguments about, money. One view, the hard money view, believes that the money supply should be restricted or limited. In the 19th century hard money supporters believed the money supply should be linked to something of value—gold—whose availability would naturally limit the supply. The hard money view is a deflationary view, or one that tends to deflate prices. The other view, the cheap money view, believes that the money supply should be flexible and should continually grow. This is an inflationary view, or one that tends to inflate prices. Advocates of hard money are creditors, bankers, those who loan money, and in many cases businessmen who fear inflation. Advocates of cheap money are debtors, farmers, and those who borrow money.

Why would someone want either hard or cheap money? Take this example. You have bought a new bicycle for $300. You borrowed the money at a rate of 10 percent for three years. Your interest payment over the three years will be $30 so you must repay $330. You have a job selling ice-cream that pays $5 per hour. To pay back the money you must work 66 hours. Now if money becomes cheaper, there will be inflation. Prices and wages rise. Your pay goes to $6 per hour, but your loan and the interest rate remain the same at $330 over three years. You now need to work only 55 hours to pay back the loan. As a debtor, cheap money or inflation helps you. Of course, prices are rising and your cost of living rises, which may hurt you, but if your biggest expense is paying debts—mortgages on houses or farms, loans for purchases of major equipment, etc.—then you will be happy with inflation brought about by cheap or easily available money. Too much inflation would make it hard for you to both pay your debts and live decently, but just the right amount would be wonderful.

But what of the banker who loaned you the $300? As you pay it back in cheap money, he can buy less with the money since prices have risen. He has had to increase the wages of his workers just as you got a raise. Although you pay the money back with interest, it still isn't worth as much as when he loaned it. He would prefer a deflationary or hard money situation in which wages and prices dropped. If your pay went to $4, you would need to work 82.5 hours to pay back your loan. The banker would be able to buy more with the money you pay him since prices as well as wages would have dropped. He is happy but you aren't—you must work harder to pay the loan.

This is the essence of the hard money/cheap money, deflationary/inflationary monetary policy that has been argued in the United States through all the business cycles. When farm prices drop, farmers must work harder and sell more produce to pay back loans, just as you would need to work longer to pay back a loan when your wage drops. In the business cycle the same factors occur over and over, but the causes and outcome are different each time. However, the views on hard and cheap money have remained the same through all the cycles.

The Presidency

In the period 1876–1914 the major issues of the day related to business growth and the economic situation of the nation. The Republican Presidents—Hayes, Garfield, Arthur, Harrison, and McKinley—generally supported hard money, a hands-off laissez-faire attitude toward business, and high tariffs. Grover Cleveland, the only Democrat to hold the Presidency between 1860 and 1912, supported the same laissez-faire approach. The Presidents between Grant and William McKinley were elected to single terms. None of the Presidents exercised strong leadership, and until McKinley none were elected to two consecutive terms.

Post-Civil War presidents follow a laissez-faire approach to business.

The Farmer and the Economy

One continual concern in the post-Civil War years was the economic position of the farmer in America. The nation slowly emerged from the 1873 depression only to suffer another cycle of recession in 1884–5. A major factor was declining farm prices. With increased production in other agricultural nations, prices for wheat and other farm products began a decline in 1884 that continued for a dozen years. Hurt further by a bad drought in 1887, discontented farmers organized protest groups that merged into regional bodies—the Southern Alliance and the National Farmer's Alliance of the Northwest. They replaced the Grange as the farmer's spokesman against Eastern bankers, railroads, and the rapidly growing industrial monopolies, all of whom set prices. These latter groups supported hard money and advocated the gold standard, that is, gold as the base of the money supply with no silver coinage or greenbacks.

Farmers suffer as other nations expand their agricultural production.

The ICC

Farmer protests and public anger over railroad abuses finally led the Congress to pass the Interstate Commerce Act in 1887. The Supreme Court's decision in the Wabash case, in which a state law controlling rates of interstate railroads was declared unconstitutional, because only the federal government could control interstate commerce, was the act that finally led Congress to abandon the laissez-faire view toward business.

The Interstate Commerce Act created the Interstate Commerce Commission, the first of many regulatory commissions created by the United States government. Its purpose was to regulate the railroads. The ICC was given power to investigate railroad management, but its orders were not binding. It had to get the federal courts to issue the orders, and the judges were often quite conservative and would not cooperate with the ICC. The Act

The Interstate Commerce Commission is established to regulate the railroads.

prohibited pooling and rebates[1] and made it illegal to charge more for a short haul than for a long haul[2] on the same line, a practice that hurt farmers. Railroads were required to post their rates, which were to be reasonable and just. The act worked quite well at first, but with disagreements over its interpretation and with changing economic conditions in the 1890s, ways were found by many railroad owners to avoid obeying the law.

The Growth of Trusts

The growth of trusts is another example of business growth. The trust issue finally led to another abandonment of laissez-faire. After John D. Rockefeller had established the Standard Oil Trust in 1879, trusts were established in many other industries such as beef (Armour), sugar (E.C. Knight and Co.), and tobacco (American Tobacco Company). Concern and protest over this apparent growth of business monopolies led several states to pass laws controlling trusts, but no state could control a trust engaging in interstate commerce.

As trusts grow in number and power, the Sherman Anti-Trust Act is passed to regulate them.

In 1890 the federal government passed the Sherman Anti-Trust Act to regulate trusts. The act declared illegal any "combination in the form of a trust...in restraint of trade or commerce." By the law the federal government could use the courts to dissolve illegal trusts. Since the act had ambiguous phrasing and terms were not clearly defined, the conservative federal courts interpreted the law to apply to all combinations from labor unions to railroads. The labor unions were brought to court as much as businesses. In the case of the *United States v. E.C. Knight Co.*, the Supreme Court restricted the ICC law, deciding that manufacturing was not commerce and so could not be regulated by Congress, which had power to regulate commerce but not manufacturing. This was considered by many to be a very narrow interpretation of business, but it stuck. Although the E.C. Knight Co. controlled 95 percent of the sugar refining in the United States, according to the Court it was not restraining trade.

Tariffs

The tariff becomes a major political issue for Republicans and Democrats.

Another issue relating to the economic situation in the post-Civil War period was high tariffs. Business wanted them and they were supported by Congress. The tariff issue was addressed by President Cleveland in his annual message to Congress in 1887. He had supported the high tariff but changed his mind and in the annual message called for a lower tariff. Congress failed to pass a tariff,

---

[1]*rebates*   When a bill is paid at the full price, a company can give the payer a rebate after the bill is paid. The rebate is money paid back to the payer.

[2]*short haul and long haul*   When railroads had a monopoly between two locations, they could charge whatever price they wished for the haul between stops along that line. When there was competition between two locations, they would often charge a lower fee even if the distance was longer. Therefore, sometimes farmers needed to pay more for a short haul between two places on a line where there was a monopoly than they would have had to pay for a long haul where there was competition.

and the issue split the parties in the 1888 election, which Cleveland lost to Benjamin Harrison.

In 1890 Congress passed the McKinley Tariff, which raised duties to an average of over 48 percent. It was a boost for manufacturers, and the Republicans hoped to help the distressed farmer by raising some duties on agricultural products. This did not help farmers since the United States imported few agricultural products. Instead, higher import duties added to the cost of manufactured products and hurt the farmers. This has been the essence of the tariff issue throughout American history: high tariffs hurt farmers, help some manufacturers, and force the general public and workers to pay higher prices.

The backlash to the McKinley Tariff was great, and half the Republicans in the House of Representatives lost in the 1890 election. Discontent with established policy was growing.

The Populist Party

The 1892 Presidential campaign included a new party, the People's Party, popularly known as the Populist Party. It was organized by farmers and laborers as a protest against the two established parties' continued adherence to high tariffs and hard money. The Populists' candidate was James B. Weaver of Iowa. Their platform called for the free and unlimited coinage of silver and an increase in the money in circulation, both of which were cheap money policies. Other planks in the platform focused on the concerns of political and economic reformers. The Populist Party platform contained suggestions for changes that became the program for reformers during the next 35 years.

The Populist Party is formed and endorses the free and unlimited coinage of silver, i.e., cheap money.

The Populists were plagued by the issue of race relations. While discontent was widespread in the South, farmers there did not support the Populist cause as was hoped. The white farmers feared losing political power to the African-Americans, many of whom could still vote, if the whites did not vote for the Democratic candidate. After 1892, more restrictions were placed on African-Americans to assure they would not attain political power.

Grover Cleveland, the Democrat who had previously served as President from 1884–1888, was re-elected, defeating the Populist Weaver and the incumbent Republican President, Benjamin Harrison. President Harrison was hurt both by the McKinley Tariff and the brutal way Pinkerton detectives broke a strike at the Carnegie's Homestead Steel Plant in Homestead, Pennsylvania. Seven strikers were killed, and the union was broken. No steel union was formed until the 1930s. Republicans were identified with businesses such as Carnegie Steel, but the Democrat Cleveland was not inclined to pursue the enforcement of the recently passed Interstate Commerce Act and Sherman Act.

Grover Cleveland is elected President in a three-way race.

Soon after Cleveland's election another panic in the apparently inevitable business cycle of boom and bust occurred. The 1893 panic was precipitated by the failure of an English bank. Banks then called in loans, which were payable only in gold, and as businesses and farmers needed gold to pay their loans, the United

The Panic of 1893 appears to help the Populist Party's struggle for power.

States government's gold supply dropped. Panic then hit Wall Street. The result was again a cry for cheap money from those who needed gold to pay back loans. The resulting recession appeared to be a great boost to the program of the Populist Party. And the party looked forward to the election of 1896.

The tariff continues to be a major political issue.

To counteract the Panic of 1893 Cleveland asked Congress to pass a lower tariff in 1894, but when the Senate finished the bill, duties were dropped less than 8 percent. The tariff continued as a major issue between Republicans and Democrats. The Democrats achieved a major reduction in 1913 with the Underwood Tariff, but Republicans raised the duties to their highest level ever in 1930 when they were back in power. With the enactment of the Reciprocal Trade Agreements Act under the New Deal in 1934, duties slowly declined, leveling off at just over 10 percent after World War II. Reciprocal agreements permit negotiation on duties with different countries to the mutual benefit of each.

Tariffs were not a major issue through the latter half of the 20th century, but at the beginning of the 1990s more talk of tariffs is heard in the nation. Today both business and labor see advantages in tariffs: business in order to guarantee the home market for United States' products, and labor as a way to keep prices of foreign made goods high. This, they believe, will keep prices for American manufactured goods high, which in turn will allow the laborers to demand a share of the profits by getting higher wages. The nation has not heard the last of tariffs, which helped to make and break Presidents in the last century. Tariff debates occurred with cyclical regularity; each tariff was different, but the basic arguments were always similar.

The Watershed Election of 1896

The election of 1896 offered the electorate a choice between two very different political views of the future. It was one of the most important elections in United States history.

Republicans nominated William McKinley, author of the high McKinley Tariff. His campaign manager, Mark Hanna, was an Ohio millionaire who followed the Hamiltonian view of government. (See Chapter 3.) He believed government should aid business. The Republican platform praised high, protective tariffs, blamed the hard economic times on the Democrats, and made a gesture toward cheap money by calling for an international gold and silver monetary system, something other nations would not accept.

Most Democrats were disillusioned with Cleveland, who had not vetoed the 1894 tariff. He had broken the Pullman Strike of 1894 by sending in federal troops to keep the United States mail moving, and he had upheld hard money. He made a deal with J.P. Morgan, a New York banker, to avoid a depletion of the government gold supply. Cleveland appeared to many Democrats to be more Republican than many Republicans.

There was, however, no clear choice of a leader to replace Cleveland. Then William Jennings Bryan of Nebraska, a brilliant orator who advocated the unlimited coinage of silver to achieve cheaper money, delivered one of the most momentous speeches in American history. His "Cross of Gold" speech captivated his audience. In the "Cross of Gold" speech Bryan described the conditions in the country and declared cities were dependent on the farm, not vice versa. He argued that prosperity worked its way up from farmers and laborers when they had money to spend; it did not trickle down from the wealthy to the workers as Republican theory implied. Bryan ended his speech with the phrase, "You shall not press down upon the brow of labor this crown of thorns, you shall not crucify mankind upon a cross of gold."

Democrats find a champion of cheap money in William Jennings Bryan.

Bryan's message overwhelmed the Democrats at the convention. They adopted a platform in favor of silver and gave Bryan their nomination for President.

Democratic supporters of hard money nominated their own candidate in 1896. The Populist Party, whose program had been taken over by the silver Democrats under Bryan, also endorsed Bryan as their candidate. Bryan appealed to the debt-laden farmers of the West and the South; McKinley to the business interests of the East. The campaign began well for Bryan, but Mark Hanna's careful spending of large campaign funds and the Republican's attack on cheap money's inflationary impact on prices won the vote of many factory workers to the Republicans.

In the election Bryan carried the South and Plains states, but McKinley carried all the states from North Dakota to Massachusetts plus Oregon and California. The nation voted for business and hard money. The Populist Party died. The call for reform in American economic and political life was taken up at the turn of the century by a new group known collectively as the Progressives.

William McKinley defeats Bryan for the presidency, the Populist Party dies, and the United States is committed to business and hard money.

KEY POINT TO REMEMBER

Business prosperity was cyclical throughout the 19th century with panics occurring regularly; the government between 1877 and 1900 officially maintained a laissez-faire attitude towards business, except for tariffs, the Interstate Commerce Act, and the Sherman Anti-Trust Act.

LINKS FROM THE PAST TO THE PRESENT

1. Alternating economic recession and prosperity have been the pattern of the American economy from the Panic of 1819 to the recession of 1990.
2. Cheap versus hard money arguments have been expressed throughout our history from the time of Shays' Rebellion to today's arguments over interest rates.

QUESTIONS

Identify each of the following:

Greenback	Cross of Gold Speech
Interstate Commerce Act	Election of 1892
Sherman Anti-Trust Act	Cheap money

True or False:

1. Overexpansion, speculation, and bankruptcy have led to many depressions in United States history.
2. The Union issued a large number of paperbacks (greenbacks) during the Civil War.
3. Advocates of cheap money are most likely to be creditors.
4. Too much inflation makes it hard to both pay debts and live decently.
5. The Interstate Commerce Act required railroads to post their fares.
6. The Sherman Anti-Trust Act is an example of the laissez-faire attitude of government toward business.
7. The Supreme Court restricted the Sherman Anti-Trust Act in the *United States v. E.C. Knight Company* case, stating that manufacturing was not commerce.
8. The People's or Populist Party Platform in 1892 called for the free and unlimited coinage of silver.
9. William Jennings Bryan declared to the American people, at the Democratic Party Convention in 1896, that business "shall not crucify mankind upon a cross of gold."
10. The McKinley Tariff of 1890 reduced duties and favored the farmers.
11. President Cleveland lost the support of many Democrats when he broke the Pullman Strike of 1894 and failed to veto the Tariff Bill.
12. The Supreme Court said in the Wabash Case that only the federal government could regulate interstate commerce.

Multiple Choice:

1. The Interstate Commerce Act of 1887
    a. was passed because the Supreme Court ruled states could control interstate commerce
    b. established the Interstate Commerce Commission
    c. made it legal to charge more for a short haul
2. The idea behind the cry for coinage of silver was
    a. the creation of cheap money
    b. the creation of hard money
    c. neither of the above
3. Presidents Hayes, Garfield, and Arthur supported
    a. cheap money and silver coinage
    b. high tariffs and a laissez-faire policy
    c. hard money and low tariffs

ANSWERS

True or False: 1. T, 2. T, 3. F, 4. T, 5. T, 6. F, 7. T, 8. T, 9. T, 10. F, 11. T, 12. T.
Multiple Choice: 1. b, 2. a, 3. b.

II. THE PROGRESSIVE MOVEMENT

The Progressive Program

The Progressives emerge as leaders of reform.

The Progressives of the early decades of the 20th century wanted to clean up and reform government and to use government to advance human welfare. They were opposed to the abuse of power by political machines and monopolies. They wanted to apply scientific management to government just as it was being applied to business and to use it to solve urban problems. Many Progressives had an aversion to party politics. Unlike the Populists whose leadership came from the West and South and whose support came mainly from farmers and some workers, Progressives could be found in all economic groups—laborers, farmers, businessmen, intellectuals—and among all immigrant groups. Progressives were repulsed at the corruption and injustice revealed in the writings of investigative journalists like Lincoln Steffens, who put the spotlight on many urban problems in his book, *The Shame of the Cities*. President Theodore Roosevelt referred to these reporters as muckrakers, a figure in the English poet John Bunyan's *Pilgrim's Progress* who was so busy raking manure he did not see the crown overhead.

In spite of his condemnation of their zeal, Theodore Roosevelt responded as a Progressive would and during his Presidency attacked monopolies and called for reform inspired by the muckrakers. For instance, Upton Sinclair in a novel, *The Jungle*, published in 1906, attacked the meatpacking industry. Horrified by the accusations of Sinclair, Theodore Roosevelt appointed a commission to investigate the meatpacking industry. The commission uncovered clear evidence that rats and rope were included in canned ham. The commission found many other abuses by the industry. President Roosevelt pressed Congress to pass the Meat Inspection Act in 1906. The act established federal inspection from the farm to the finished product of all meat sold in interstate commerce. A government seal of approval assured the public of the quality of meat purchased. We still benefit from this act every time we eat meat. Look on meat you buy for the government seal of approval.

Muckrakers directed their attacks at everything from the Standard Oil Trust to the "white slave" or prostitution trade to the voting allegiance of United States Senators to trusts and railroads. Senators were often supported in their campaigns by the trusts and railroads, and they in turn often voted to help their benefactors rather than the people they were supposed to represent. Progressive reform at the urban level (see chapter VIII) was extensive. Governor Robert LaFollette of Wisconsin made a reputation as a reform governor, introducing the direct primary[1] for the nomination of political candidates rather than party conventions, more equitable taxes, and railroad rate regulation. Other states followed Wisconsin's lead and later as United States Senator, Robert LaFollette supported reforms at the national level.

Theodore Roosevelt

Theodore Roosevelt had become President of the United States on the assassination of William McKinley in 1901, soon after

President T. Roosevelt supports the ideas of the Progressives.

Reforms are instituted by all levels of government.

[1]*direct primary* An election in which voters directly nominate for office members of their own party.

T. Roosevelt brings a variety of experience to the Presidency.

McKinley's election to a second term. Theodore Roosevelt is one of those individuals who have had a great impact on history. A rather weak, asthmatic child, his father sent him West to live and study on the theory that the West would toughen him. A graduate of Harvard, he read law, wrote history, and lived on a ranch in North Dakota before becoming a Civil Service Commissioner and later Police Commissioner in New York City. He served as Assistant Secretary of the Navy from 1897–8 and helped prepare for the Spanish–American War. He organized the first United States Volunteer Cavalry, referred to as the "Rough Riders," and led a charge up San Juan Hill in Cuba during the Spanish–American War. Returning in 1898, he was elected Governor of New York and was put on the Republican ticket as Vice-President in 1900 because his moves toward reform worried the political bosses in his state. When McKinley was assassinated on September 6, 1901, Theodore Roosevelt became President. He used the Presidency as a "bully pulpit" to argue both the cause of reform and expansion.

Roosevelt is an active president and pushes for a Square Deal for all Americans.

One example of reform legislation besides the Meat Inspection Act is the Pure Food and Drug Law, which President Theodore Roosevelt pushed through Congress in 1906. The Pure Food and Drug Law provides each of us with a sense of security when we buy our medicines. He used the presidency to support the labor movement and give it a "square deal"[2] along with business. In the Anthracite Coal Strike of 1902, he forced arbitration on the owners and the miners. While accepting the growth of American business and trusts as an inevitable part of growth, he distinguished between good and bad trusts and had the government use the Sherman Anti-Trust Law to attack the ones he considered bad. In one such case in 1904 the Supreme Court ruled that the Northern Securities Company, a huge holding company created by J.P. Morgan to monopolize the railroads of the northwest, violated the Sherman Anti-Trust Law. It was a shock to big business and a victory for those who felt the government had a role in the economic life of the nation.

Conservation Efforts

Conservation is a major concern of Roosevelt's.

Perhaps Theodore Roosevelt's most memorable efforts from a 1990s perspective were directed at conservation. He set aside 125 million acres of forests in Federal Reserves and did the same for both coal and water resources. The Newlands Act of 1902 authorized the government to use money from the sale of western land for irrigation projects. In 1908 a conference on conservation at the White House helped encourage governors to follow Roosevelt's lead, and forty-one states set up conservation commissions. He appointed Gifford Pinchot, an active conservationist, head of the Federal Division of Forestry. Theodore Roosevelt stimulated interest in our natural resources by such acts as climbing in Yosemite Valley, California with the most famous naturalist-conservationist of the day, John Muir. Theodore Roosevelt was the embodiment of

---

[2]*Square Deal* The slogan used to describe the domestic program of President Theodore Roosevelt.

an active, reform-minded President who would lead the nation. He provided a sharp contrast to the Presidents of the previous thirty years.

Panic of 1907

In 1907 another of the periodic panics hit the United States. It was less severe than the previous ones and hurt businesses more than the average worker, but nevertheless it illustrated the cyclical nature of prosperity. The panic was centered on Wall Street and had as one cause world-wide economic trends. Thus, the first panic of the 20th century illustrated the increasingly world-wide nature of the American economy and the growing position of America in the world.

The panic of 1907 indicates the United States is part of a world economic system.

The Taft Presidency

Roosevelt had antagonized business but was very popular in the nation. He decided not to seek a second term of his own. William Howard Taft of Ohio, Secretary of War in Theodore Roosevelt's Cabinet and a moderate Progressive, won the Republican nomination and the Presidency against William Jennings Bryan, making his third and final try for the Presidency on the Democratic ticket. Theodore Roosevelt went on a trip to Africa.

William Howard Taft is elected President and follows many of Roosevelt's policies.

President Taft has always suffered by comparison to the flamboyant Roosevelt, yet his record of reform is a solid one. In 1912, Congress passed Amendment XVII to the Constitution, establishing the direct election of senators by the people rather than by state legislatures where business interests often manipulated elections. Progressives saw this as a way to make the senators responsive to the people. Taft continued Theodore Roosevelt's trust busting, gaining Supreme Court decisions against Standard Oil Company and the American Tobacco Company. He got legislation through Congress to remove acres of coal lands from exploitation and established a Bureau of Mines to safeguard resources.

However, his Secretary of the Interior, Ballinger, following the law, allowed certain water power sites that Theodore Roosevelt had arbitrarily set aside to be developed by private interests. Gifford Pinchot of the Forestry Department objected. Pinchot was dismissed by Taft, who believed in administrative order and thought Pinchot had been insubordinate. A furor erupted that alienated the Progressives and Roosevelt's followers from President Taft.

Disagreements over conservation issues create a split between Taft and Roosevelt.

A split in the Republican party developed, and a National Progressive Republican League was formed in 1910 under Robert La Follette, who appeared a likely candidate for the Presidency. However, in 1912 Theodore Roosevelt reversed himself on the third term issue. After losing the Republican nomination for President to Taft, Roosevelt accepted the nomination of the Progressive Republican Party, which was nicknamed the "Bull Moose" Party. The Democrats, after a long convention battle, nominated the Progressive Governor of New Jersey, Woodrow Wilson, as their candidate.

Woodrow Wilson

Woodrow Wilson, a progressive Democrat, is elected President in a three-way race.

Woodrow Wilson was an intellectual, an historian, a Virginian, and had served as president of Princeton University before becoming Governor of New Jersey. Son of a Presbyterian minister, he inherited the clergyman's power of expression and commitment to what is right. Raised in the Jeffersonian tradition, he believed in the masses and in government for and by the people. A fine orator, his eloquence could inspire, but he was a private person who appeared cold and reserved in public—a great contrast to the outgoing, jovial Theodore Roosevelt. Wilson had lived in war-ravaged Georgia, and this experience, combined with his Christian training, made him hate war. He was a scholar whose field was government, and he firmly believed in a strong Presidency that led the Congress into action.

THE EMPLOYMENT AGENT.
—Kirby in the New York *World.*

What is Kirby commenting on in this cartoon? In spite of civil service reform, when Wilson was elected President in 1912, the Democrats used the spoils system to reward deserving party members. William Jennings Bryan, the party leader since 1896 and presidential candidate in 1896, 1900 and 1908 was Wilson's Secretary of State. Kirby is commenting that Bryan rewarded Democrats who had supported him since his first Presidential candidacy.

From the New York World *reprinted in* The Literary Digest *of January 30, 1915*

In the three-party race of 1912 Wilson won overwhelmingly in the electoral college, but received less than 42 percent of the popular vote. However, the two Progressive candidates, Roosevelt and Wilson, had won an overwhelming majority of the popular vote. It appeared the nation was committed to reform just as it had been in the era of Jacksonian Democracy. This pattern of recurring periods of reform is another illustration of the cyclical aspect of history. The United States experienced another period of reform in the 1930s and a fourth in the 1960s—each was different, but each had a profound effect on United States history.

Upon the election of Wilson, the second Democrat to occupy the White House since the Civil War, Democrats sought office in spite of civil service reforms. William Jennings Bryan, three times Presidential candidate, a teetotaler and pacifist, was named Secretary of State. As the cartoon suggests, many old Democrats sought government positions through their previous contacts with Bryan, and they got jobs, a blemish on the Democrat's reform record.

Progressive Reforms of Wilson

In other areas Wilson's leadership addressed major issues in need of reform. He first addressed the issue of monetary policy. Congress established the Federal Reserve Banking System in 1913. It was a complicated answer to America's banking and monetary problems. The system was under the control of an appointed Federal Reserve Board in Washington. Under the board were twelve Reserve Banks in different parts of the country. They served as banks for bankers. The Federal Reserve Banks could receive government deposits, could move money to areas in need, and could issue greenbacks, or paper money, called Reserve Notes. Reserve Notes were the Progressive Democrats' answer to the demand for cheap money.

Wilson supports a new banking system and further controls over business.

Wilson next turned to monopolies and, in the Federal Trade Commission Act and the Clayton Anti-Trust Act of 1914, strengthened the government's ability to control monopolies. While neither was perfect, the Trade Commission Act provided for a commission to investigate unfair business practices and stop them before they became a problem. The Clayton Act tightened the Sherman Anti-Trust Act. It forbade business practices that lessened competition, set unfair prices, or created monopolies. It outlawed interlocking directorates, a business device that strengthened monopolies by having directors serve on the Board of Trustees of several companies.

Labor unions were specifically excluded from the provisions of the Clayton Act. The Sherman Anti-Trust Act had been more successful in destroying unions than in destroying business monopolies. The Clayton Act permitted peaceful picketing and strikes and prohibited court injunctions in labor disputes. While there were still many restraints on labor, the Act helped put unions on an equal footing with business. Business leaders accepted the laws; courts punished only the most extreme cases of restraint of trade.

The issue of trusts faded from the public view as World War I drew closer. During the war business production was essential, and anti-trust prosecution was dropped. By then the Progressive movement was over, but these three acts—the Federal Reserve Act, the Clayton Act, the Federal Trade Commission Act—were major contributions to the reform of American business and banking and important steps in addressing the issue of cyclical boom and bust.

Aid to Farmers and Workers

Farmers and workers benefit from Wilson's Progressive attitudes.

In other legislation the Democrats under Woodrow Wilson addressed the needs of American farmers and workers. A Federal Farm Loan Act made low interest loans available to farmers, the Seamens Act required decent food and wages for seamen (which helped the sailors but almost priced American shipping out of business), the Workingmen's Compensation Act gave help to federal civil service employees when they were disabled, and the Adamson Act set an 8-hour day for all employees on interstate trains. The days of laissez-faire appeared to be over. The federal government was acting on behalf of laborers and farmers, and acting to put effective limits on business monopolies.

World War I had begun in 1914 in Europe. In 1916 Wilson was again the Democrat's candidate for President. He won in a very tight race by carrying the state of California. One of Wilson's campaign slogans was, "He kept us out of war." The war was to become the primary concern of America in the next two years, and the movement for reform died as reform movements had died before and have since.

Louis D. Brandeis is appointed to the Supreme Court and supports the liberal view during the conservative 1920s.

One act of Wilson's that won Progressive support and helped maintain a Progressive voice in one branch of government in the post-war years was his appointment of Louis D. Brandeis, the first Jew so appointed, to the Supreme Court in 1916. While usually in dissent, Louis Brandeis provided a liberal view on the Court until his retirement in 1939. Finally, in the next period of reform in the 1930s, Louis Brandeis' voice became that of the majority, but not until after the Supreme Court had declared unconstitutional many of the reform efforts of the New Deal.

Supreme Court Decisions: 1873–1908

The Supreme Court in the post-Civil War years upholds the status quo.

The Supreme Court as an interpreter of the Constitution has played a major role in United States society (see Chapter VI). Through most of its history before the 1930s, the Court upheld a more conservative position than society or the other branches of government would endorse. Occasionally, as in the Dred Scott decision, it attempted to establish social policy and to resolve a political issue, but this approach has been rare. From the Slaughterhouse Cases in 1873 until *Mueller v. Oregon* in 1908, the Court's decisions essentially upheld the status quo.

Several cases in addition to those mentioned earlier were of major significance and illustrate how the Court either blocked what we consider today as reasonable and progressive reform or upheld very conservative legislation. In 1883 the Court declared the Civil

Rights Act of 1875 invalid, since it upheld social not political rights. The Civil Rights Act had forbidden discrimination in hotel accommodations. The decision stopped federal civil rights legislation under Amendment XIV until the 1960s. In the same area of race relations, *Plessy v. Ferguson* in 1896 upheld a Louisiana law segregating railroad facilities. The Court held that if the facilities were separate but equal, the black was not deprived of equal protection of the law under Amendment XIV; separate was not unequal according to the 1896 Court.

Plessy v. Ferguson establishes the doctrine of "separate but equal," which provides a legal basis for segregation.

In *Lochner v. New York* in 1905 the Court upheld a law limiting the hours of labor in a bakery was an unconstitutional interference in the right of free contract. This was a view held by supporters of the free enterprise, laissez-faire system that was being challenged by the Progressive movement. In *Muller v. Oregon* the Court reversed itself and upheld a law limiting the hours of work for one group—women.

The Supreme Court plays a major role in United States history and must always be considered when seeking reforms. Any attempt to change the natural order or cyclical nature of business life had to gain the approval not only of the Congress, especially the Senate, but of the Supreme Court.

KEY POINT TO REMEMBER

Theodore Roosevelt and Woodrow Wilson were Progressive Presidents whose presidencies are noted for reform in the areas of conservation, health, banking, and business.

PEOPLE TO REMEMBER

Theodore Roosevelt   New York lawyer and government worker; as Assistant Secretary of the Navy, he helped prepare for the Spanish–American War and was a hero of the war; 26th President of the United States, worked for reform legislation to benefit the people, won Nobel Prize for making peace at end of Russo-Japanese war, a flamboyant and activist President.

LINKS FROM THE PAST TO THE PRESENT

1. Efforts at getting legislation and other reforms to benefit workers and farmers have been pursued at many different times in our history.
2. Supreme Court decisions on civil rights issues continue to have a major impact on our society.
3. The Meat Inspection and Pure Food and Drug Laws, passed to protect the health of the American people, were only the first of many such laws designed to protect the public.

QUESTIONS

Identify each of the following:

William Howard Taft   Pure Food and Drug Law
Federal Reserve Board   Plessy v. Ferguson

True or False:

1. Vice President Theodore Roosevelt became President when William McKinley was assassinated, and he went on to be elected two more times to the Presidency.
2. Theodore Roosevelt's most memorable efforts from a 1990 perspective were directed toward conservation.
3. The Panic of 1907 again illustrated how isolated the United States economy was from international economic issues.
4. Gifford Pinchot wished to protect United States forests and continue Theodore Roosevelt's conservation efforts.
5. Woodrow Wilson won a large majority in the electoral college but only 42 percent of the popular vote, making him a minority President.
6. The Federal Reserve System can issue money in the form of Reserve Notes to create "cheap money."
7. The Sherman Anti-Trust Act was never used against unions, so the Clayton Anti-Trust Act included the right to use it to eliminate strikes by unions.
8. The Democrats under Woodrow Wilson passed no legislation to benefit workers and farmers specifically.
9. Louis D. Brandeis provided a liberal view on the Supreme Court.
10. Theorore Roosevelt distinguished between good and bad trusts and brought court cases against the bad ones.
11. President Theodore Roosevelt referred to writers like Lincoln Steffens as muckrakers.

Multiple Choice:

1. Among the important legislation passed under Theodore Roosevelt were the
    a. Pure Food and Drug Act, Meat Inspection Act, and Newlands Act
    b. Clayton Anti-Trust Act, and Federal Reserve Act
    c. Meat Inspection Act, Newlands Act, and Adamson Act
2. Among the important legislation passed under Woodrow Wilson were the
    a. Pure Food and Drug Law, Newlands Act, and Clayton Anti-Trust Act
    b. Clayton Anti-Trust Act, Federal Trade Commission Act, and Federal Reserve Act
    c. Sherman Anti-Trust Act, Interstate Commerce Act, and Federal Reserve Act
3. The Supreme Court declared the federal government could not protect social rights under the Constitution
    a. in the Slaughterhouse cases
    b. in *Plessy v. Ferguson*
    c. in the Civil Rights cases

4. In *Muller v. Oregon* the court upheld a law in which the state of Oregon
   a. limited the hours of labor for bakery workers
   b. established separate but equal railroad cars for blacks and whites
   c. limited working hours for women
5. The *Jungle* and *The Shame of the Cities* were
   a. inspirations for Progressive reform legislation
   b. both written by Upton Sinclair
   c. both repudiated by President Theodore Roosevelt

ANSWERS

True or False: 1. F, 2. T, 3. F, 4. T, 5. T, 6. T, 7. F, 8. F, 9. T, 10. T, 11. T.
Multiple Choice: 1. a, 2. b, 3. c, 4. c, 5. a.

III. FOREIGN POLICY

While domestic concerns dominated United States history from 1877–1914, issues of foreign policy were always in the background. They briefly took center stage in the late 1890s and again after 1916. Presidential and Congressional decisions of any type had to take these foreign policy issues into account. America expanded overseas in these years, and just as business cycles were seen as natural, this expansion was seen by many as the natural growth from the "adolescence" of the pre- and immediate post-Civil War period to the era of "young manhood" of the Spanish–American War. Some historians today still find parallels between human growth and the growth of nations.

Foreign policy issues continue to be important.

Imperialism

The last half of the 19th century was a time of great imperial[1] expansion by European powers, who divided Africa among themselves at the Berlin Congress in 1878 and established spheres of interest in China later in the century. Following the teachings of Social Darwinism, the white leaders of Europe and America believed they were chosen to civilize the world. Their nations were the most advanced militarily and commercially, and to them this was the way progress and civilization were to be judged. Competition for overseas possessions was rampant among the European powers, and the United States was not to be left out.

Social Darwinism is applied to foreign policy.

Overseas Involvement: 1875–1898

Between 1875 and 1898 the United States continued to be involved in both the Pacific and Caribbean–Central America area. In the former we acquired rights to a naval base in Pago Pago, Samoa in 1878, keeping the Germans from acquiring full control of the Samoan Islands. Interest in the Hawaiian Islands developed in

The United States expresses interest in Samoa, Hawaii, and the Caribbean.

---

[1]*imperialism* A policy followed by governments in which they annex territory by force or political pressure, thus gaining control of weaker countries.

these years as Americans bought property and became settlers in the islands. In 1893 a revolution planned by these American settlers overthrew the ruler of Hawaii, but President Cleveland blocked annexation by the United States. Five years later Hawaii was annexed to America's growing Pacific empire when we were involved in the Spanish–American War. In the Caribbean area interest in Cuba and Central America pre-dated the Civil War. Under President Garfield, Secretary of State Blaine encouraged United States economic involvement in Latin America and called for the first Pan–American conference in 1881. His successor in office immediately cancelled the invitations. These two actions rather symbolize the United States' attitude toward our neighbors—at one moment friendly and supportive, at the next moment antagonistic or indifferent. A Pan–American conference was finally held in 1889, but the delegates rejected a United States proposal for a customs union and machinery for the arbitration of disputes between the countries. One wonders what United States–Latin American relations would have become if the two proposals had been adopted.

Problems in Cuba

A crisis in Cuba leads to the Spanish–American War.

An insurrection against Spanish rule began in Cuba in the early 1890s. Slowly we became involved. The treatment of the rebels by the Spanish, who confined them in concentration camps, seemed intolerable to the United States. After United States protests, Spain made concessions, but the United States "yellow" press whipped up sentiment against Spain, and with the sinking of the battleship *Maine* in the harbor of Havana in February, 1898, matters reached a crisis. Demand for war seemed to sweep the United States and President McKinley in April, 1898 asked Congress for permission to use "forcible intervention" in Cuba. Congress responded with recognition of Cuban independence, a disclaimer of any desire to annex Cuba, and an authorization to use force to achieve these ends. The United States had embarked on an imperialistic war that was to change the United States and, in the view of some historians, make the United States mature into a young adult.

Spanish–American War

The United States defeats Spain in eight months of fighting with few battle casualties.

The Spanish–American War lasted eight months. Some 5,500 Americans died, but of these only 379 were battle casualties. Theodore Roosevelt, as Assistant Secretary of the Navy, had ordered Commodore George Dewey of the Pacific Fleet in Hong Kong to attack Manila in the Spanish colony of the Philippines in case of war. Dewey did, and Manila fell on August 13, 1898. Cuba was invaded, but it was the defeat of the Spanish fleet outside Santiago that decided the fate of Cuba. United States naval superiority had been assured when the country began building a steel fleet in the 1880s. The United States won the war, and in the process occupied Wake Island and annexed Hawaii, both of which provided good harbors for the fleet.

The Treaty of Paris, 1898

The terms of the Treaty of Paris, which ended the Spanish–American War, stated that Spain would free Cuba and cede Puerto Rico and Guam to the United States. Spain also agreed to cede the Philippines to the United States in return for $20 million. President McKinley had decided to demand the Philippines for economic (a fine market), strategic (a naval base in the Far East), and humanitarian (we could civilize the natives) reasons. The arguments were those of all imperialist nations. The Senate battle over ratification became a forum for expression of ideas that would be echoed over and over again in the 20th century.

As in the election of 1896, the Senate debate was another time when a decision as to the future of the United States had to be made. The debate was between imperialists and anti-imperialists.

Americans argue over the acceptance of an imperialist position.

Uncle S. : WILLIAM, I CAN NEVER DIGEST THAT MESS WITHOUT STRAINING MY CONSTITUTION.

In this cartoon the artist, Attwood, comments on the aftermath of the Spanish–American War and American Imperialism. He makes clever use of the word constitution. "Uncle S.'s" reference to constitution is both to the United States Constitution and to his own personal constitution or digestion. What is the waiter (President McKinley) offering Uncle Sam? Why would it be hard on his Constitution to accept the food (Puerto Rico—the wine; Cuba—under the food cover; the Philippines—on the platter) offered?

Published in Life *November 24, 1898.*

Imperialist arguments focused on economic and strategic advantages, national prestige, and our "civilizing" mission. Imperialists argued that if we did not take the Philippines, another European power would. Anti-imperialists argued that acquisition of the Philippines was contrary to the United States' principles of democratic government and our own arguments in our struggle for independence and contradicted the United States' commitment to isolation from Europe. They argued that the assimilation into United States society of the different population of the Philippines would be impossible. William Jennings Bryan persuaded some Democrats to vote for the treaty in order to end the war. He argued that the future of the Philippines, whether independent or a United States colony, could be decided in the 1900 Presidential race.

The treaty was adopted by two votes more than the necessary two-thirds of the Senate. Bryan ran for President against McKinley in 1900, and Philippine independence was a major issue. Bryan lost and the Philippines became a United States colony for 45 years. The United States had grown up, according to those who see nations following human biological growth patterns. We had joined the European Imperialist Club. We had expanded overseas.

The issues raised in the arguments over the Treaty of Paris get at the heart of imperialism. Are some nations more advanced than others, giving them the right to rule others? How do you measure advanced societies? Are some people inherently less good than others, or are "all men (and women) created equal," as the Declaration of Independence says? The United States as a nation must still wrestle with these questions domestically and in foreign policy.

Some people believe we do have a "God-given right" to rule others. What do you think?

Theodore Roosevelt and Big-Stick Diplomacy

President Theodore Roosevelt based his foreign policy on the assumption that the United States had a special role to fill in world affairs. During the 19th century, the Monroe Doctrine was accepted by Presidents of all parties as United States policy. President Johnson, following the Doctrine, saw to it that the French-supported Archduke Maximillian was forced out of Mexico after the Civil War. In 1895 President Cleveland interjected the United States into a long-standing dispute between Venezuela and England over the boundary between British Guiana and Venezuela. In bringing the dispute to arbitration, Cleveland's Secretary of State said, "Today the United States is practically sovereign on this continent..." and claimed the right under the Monroe Doctrine to force arbitration on the two nations. Theodore Roosevelt in 1904 added a further interpretation, usually called the Roosevelt Corollary, to the Monroe Doctrine:

> Chronic wrongdoing or an impotence which results in a general loosening of the ties of civilized society may in America, as elsewhere, ultimately require intervention by some civilized nation, and in the western hemisphere the adherence of the United States to the Monroe Doctrine may force

Roosevelt expands the original meaning of the Monroe Doctrine.

the United States, however reluctantly, in flagrant cases of such wrongdoing or impotence, to the exercise of an international police power.

In other words, the United States would be the policeman of the Americas. The United States statement came as a reaction to the desire of several European powers to collect debts owed them by the Dominican Republic. The Dominican Republic signed an agreement giving the United States the right to run the customs houses. The Senate rejected it, but Theodore Roosevelt went ahead anyway. The use of the Monroe Doctrine to justify forcing United States views and values on the Americas is another example of imperialism. It is an example of what has been called Theodore Roosevelt's "big stick diplomacy."

Do you believe the United States has the right to be a policeman in the Caribbean?

Another example of Theodore Roosevelt's "big stick" diplomacy can be seen in his dealings with Colombia and the establishment of Panama. For years there had been talk of a canal connecting the Atlantic and Pacific oceans through a Central American country. A French company began such a canal in Colombia's province of Panama. The company failed. United States navy and business interests wanted to build a canal, but the Clayton-Bulwer Treaty signed with England in 1850 stated the United States would not build a canal alone. A new treaty was negotiated with England and ratified in 1900. The United States agreed to keep any canal built neutral. The United States bought the French rights to the canal, and then Colombia balked when the United States demanded perpetual control over the canal zone through which the canal would be dug. President Theodore Roosevelt was not to be blocked. In 1903 the province of Panama revolted from Colombia. Theodore Roosevelt immediately recognized it as a nation; he signed a treaty with the new government leasing the canal zone for 99 years; he ordered United States warships to guarantee Panama's new status. Big stick diplomacy had been exercised again in the Americas.

Panama's independence is assured by the actions of Roosevelt.

Taft's "Dollar Diplomacy"

President Taft was not as flamboyant in his Central American policy, though he maintained the same spirit, sending troops into Nicaragua in 1912 to protect American banking interests. The Nicaraguan government had fallen behind in payments on bank loans. Taft's policies of encouraging economic development in Central America and also in Asia has been called Dollar Diplomacy[2]. As United States investments grew in the Americas, any threat to them would bring in the United States Marines to protect business interests.

In 1912 Senator Henry Cabot Lodge introduced a resolution in the Senate expressing concern over Japanese negotiation with Mexico to lease land for a possible naval base. Senator Lodge's

Taft pursues a policy of Dollar Diplomacy in Central America and Asia.

---

[2]*Dollar Diplomacy* A type of economic imperialism whereby the United States sought to insure its investments abroad.

resolution extended the Monroe Doctrine to include non-European powers and any foreign corporation that had close connections with its government.

The Democrat, Woodrow Wilson, continued the active United States role in Latin America. He sent troops in 1916 to occupy Santo Domingo when that nation was again in financial trouble and continued the Dollar Diplomacy of Taft, using or threatening the use of United States military power to aid and support business.

Revolution in Mexico almost provokes a second war with Mexico.

There was a revolution in Mexico in 1910, which overthrew a dictator. In the succeeding four years, the situation was unstable. An incident with unarmed United States troops in Tampico almost led to war to protect United States interests, but Argentina, Brazil, and Chile mediated the dispute. Further revolutionary activity in Mexico again almost led to war. In 1916 Mexico reluctantly agreed to a United States military expedition into Mexico to stop Pancho Villa, a self-proclaimed leader who opposed the Mexican government we recognized and who had conducted raids across the border. The United States was going to have its way in Mexico even at the expense of Mexican sovereignty.

Party commitment made no difference when the issue was United States influence and control in the Americas. The United States was going to be dominant on this continent. This was United States imperialism. One must understand United States–Latin American relations during this time if one is to have any understanding of United States–Latin American policy in the late 20th century. The cycle of troop intervention and withdrawal to enforce American economic or political interests continues but was suspended during Franklin Roosevelt's Good Neighbor policy.

The United States in Asia

The United States works to maintain open trade and peace in Asia.

The United States had important trade relations with Asia throughout the 19th century. They became more important after the opening of Japan by Commodore Perry in 1854. After the middle of the century, European nations began to establish spheres of influence in China, and by the end of the century, the United States felt such spheres would close areas of China to free and open trade. The United States' solution was for an "open door" into China for all trading nations. This would mean that all nations would have equal access to the China trade.

Not all European nations were pleased with the idea, especially since the acquisition of the Philippines gave the United States a foothold in Asia. However, European nations agreed to the Open Door Policy although the agreement could not be strictly enforced.

Asia at the time was undergoing major political upheavals. War broke out between Russia and Japan in 1905, and President Theodore Roosevelt was concerned that if either side won, it would upset the balance of power in Asia and threaten the Open Door in China. Theodore Roosevelt made several proposals for mediation, and Japan and Russia accepted. A peace treaty was negotiated at Portsmouth, New Hampshire, which ended the war and won the Nobel Peace Prize for Theodore Roosevelt.

United States–Japanese relations after 1906 were strained because of growing opposition over immigration to the United States of Japanese laborers and over the fear of Japanese military strength. A "gentlemen's agreement" with Japan led to restriction of Japanese immigration. To intimidate Japanese military leaders, Theodore Roosevelt sent the United States fleet on a world cruise to emphasize the United States' naval power. Tensions between the United States and Japan were always there, under the surface if not formally stated, until they finally erupted into World War II. It was clear the United States was to be an important player in the affairs of Asia.

The Algeciras Conference

Theodore Roosevelt also helped settle a dispute over the future of Morocco in North Africa. During the last half of the 19th century, through a series of wars Germany became unified and emerged as an important industrial, political, and military power in Europe. By 1904 the traditional European enemies, England and France, felt threatened and concluded an entente or agreement for cooperation and defense. Germany, the newcomer, having been united as a nation only in 1871, felt excluded. At a Congress in Berlin in 1878 agreements between the European powers divided up Africa into spheres of influence. Following the Berlin Congress agreements, France worked to establish a protectorate[3] over Morocco. Germany, angered by the Dual Entente of 1904, declared support for Moroccan independence and asked for an international conference on Morocco's future. Germany asked Roosevelt's support in getting France and England to the conference.

Roosevelt, fearing a war in Europe might grow out of the Morocco crisis, intervened. The conference was held at Algeciras, Morocco. Roosevelt persuaded Germany to accept the settlement, which affirmed Moroccan independence, guaranteed equal commercial opportunities to all nations, yet put the Moroccan police under the control of France and Spain. War was averted.

The Algeciras meeting was a major break in traditional United States foreign policy: We had become involved in a European dispute. The Monroe Doctrine, the cornerstone of our Latin American policy, was ignored. The United States was ready to participate in the affairs of Europe, although we were not actively involved in other European disputes until the outbreak of World War I in 1914.

Peacekeeping

Theodore Roosevelt was an active participant on the world stage as a peacemaker. Besides the Treaty of Portsmouth and the Algeciras conference, he urged the Czar of Russia to call the Second Hague Peace Conference to consider the establishment of a World Court of Justice. Such a court would work to solve international disputes.

A concern for international peacekeeping has been one prong of United States foreign policy since that time. It manifested itself in

Roosevelt interjects the United States into the negotiations of European nations.

---

[3]*protectorate*   A country protected by a more powerful state that shares in its government.

Woodrow Wilson's proposal for a League of Nations and in the United Nations. It illustrates one aspect of the American character, a desire to do good, which has had a great impact on 20th century world history.

Another important prong of United States policy has been a commitment to isolation. However, with the 20th century, United States history has become entwined with world history. Isolation has not been possible even though many Americans have supported the concept, particularly in the 1920s and early 1930s. We hear calls for isolation today, but the United States more often acts as the international peacekeeper.

What policy do you think would be best for the United States?

Summary

Panics and economic crises occurred in regular succession during the 19th and early 20th century. To some they seemed inevitable, and in spite of a few attempts by government to change the economic order, crises continued. Towards the end of the 19th century the United States became more involved with overseas economic investments, and these in turn led to more political and military involvement. Just as a child matures into an adult, so the United States appeared to be maturing into a nation just like other nations. In 1898 we joined the imperialistic nations of the world and annexed Puerto Rico and the Philippines. In the early 20th century, with our large navy and Progressive Presidents, we played an important role on the world stage as befit a strong, powerful, yet young individual.

Some historians have interpreted these developments of 1877–1916 in terms of natural law, inevitable cycles, and biological growth. Do such interpretations help your understanding of this period?

KEY POINT TO REMEMBER

While domestic issues dominated United States history between 1877 and 1914, several foreign policy developments were of great significance, including the Spanish–American War, the annexation of the Philippines, the "policing" of debt-ridden Latin American countries, and business investments in Latin America and Asia.

LINKS FROM THE PAST TO THE PRESENT

1. The Monroe Doctrine and its various interpretations continue to provide the basis for United States policy toward Latin America.
2. Tensions in relations with Japan have surfaced many times and are still a concern as seen in the current discussions about trade.
3. Business investments in Latin America and Asia have been important throughout our history.

QUESTIONS

Identify each of the following:

Imperialists	Dollar Diplomacy
Anti-Imperialists	Treaty of Portsmouth
Open Door Policy	Spanish–American War

True or False:

1. The Berlin Congress of 1878 divided up South America into spheres of economic interest for the United States and Europe.
2. The Spanish–American War lasted only eight months.
3. The Treaty of Paris, which ended the Spanish–American War, provided for no exchange of territory.
4. Philippine independence was an issue in the election of 1900.
5. Both President Cleveland and Theodore Roosevelt added their own interpretation to the Monroe Doctrine.
6. The Clayton-Bulwer Treaty allowed the United States to build a canal across Panama.
7. Theodore Roosevelt was noted for Big Stick Diplomacy and William Howard Taft for Dollar Diplomacy.
8. Woodrow Wilson sent United States troops into Mexico to chase Pancho Villa.
9. Theodore Roosevelt was asked by the Germans to attend the Algeciras Conference but refused since, according to the Monroe Doctrine, the United States would not interfere in the affairs of Europe.
10. The "gentlemen's agreement" with Japan permitted unlimited Japanese immigration to California for five years.

Multiple Choice:

1. President Theodore Roosevelt was not to be blocked in his desire to build a canal across Panama so he
    a. asked Mexico to help persuade Panama to lease the United States the land
    b. signed the Clayton-Bulwer Treaty
    c. ordered United States warships to protect the new Republic of Panama
2. The belief that "the United States is practically sovereign on this continent" is exemplified in President Cleveland's
    a. handling of the British Guiana-Venezuela boundary dispute
    b. forcing Archduke Maximillian out of Mexico
    c. annexation of Hawaii
3. The Anti-Imperialists in the debate over the Treaty of Paris argued that
    a. the United States had a civilizing mission to fulfill in the Philippines
    b. acquisition of the Philippines was contrary to United States principles of democratic government
    c. there was a strategic advantage to holding the Philippines
4. Investments in Dollar Diplomacy were made especially in
    a. Latin America and Asia
    b. Latin America and Africa
    c. Asia and Africa

ANSWERS

True or False: 1. F, 2. T, 3. F, 4. T, 5. T, 6. F, 7. T, 8. T, 9. F, 10. F.
Multiple Choice: 1. c, 2. a, 3. b, 4. a.

CHAPTER 10

Turmoil of War and Depression

Ideology and History

"What do you believe?" is a question one hears often. According to some historians, it is the most important question one can ask about a people or nation. These historians suggest that what a nation believes and what values it cherishes determine a nation's actions. They believe a nation's beliefs or ideology distinguishes it from other nations, and when the ideology is abandoned, the nation fails.

Often there are tensions and conflicts between values a nation holds. Citizens of the United States express belief in both equality and freedom, yet we know that if we try to make all men and women equal, our individual freedom to choose different paths of action will be hampered. The situation is made more complex if we consider the conflicting views of the meaning of equality held by Americans— equality of opportunity as opposed to absolute equality as a final result.

While such tensions exist, the ideology of the United States provides the nation with a sense of national identity and guides the leaders in decisions they make for action. Sometimes the decisions are painful because of the tensions between two good points of view, and then action is delayed, but according to these ideological historians, in order to maintain integrity and attain greatness a nation must follow its ideology.

Individuals also have beliefs or an ideology that guides them. You may not articulate or discuss what you believe very often. Most people do not, but they have certain values varying from "Don't kick a dog" or "Never cheat on a quiz or test" to "All life is sacred." Believing these statements, you will act in certain ways when confronting situations. For instance, if a wet dog jumps on you and you really believe you should not kick a dog, you won't kick the dog down. You will accept getting your legs wet.

We are continually acting upon our beliefs, and so do nations. In the period between 1914 and 1941 the United States confronted three major crises—two World Wars and the greatest economic depression in our history. While slow to act in all three situations, the nation, under strong Presidential leadership, did address each crisis in keeping with avowed American beliefs. Ideological historians believe the only way to understand America's response to these three crises is to look at America's traditional values, such as freedom, individual rights, and democracy.

I. WORLD WAR I

Background

The fighting in the World War[1] began in Europe in August 1914. While many Americans were shocked at the outbreak of war, the crisis precipitated by the assassination on June 28, 1914 of Archduke Francis Ferdinand, heir to the throne of the Austro-Hungarian empire, was only the last in a series of crises among the European nations. Solutions to the other crises had been successfully negotiated. Negotiations also followed the assassination, but this time no solution except military action could be found.

World War I begins in Europe.

In the preceding years the European nations had split into the two alliances which fought World War I. On one side were the Central Powers—Germany and Austria-Hungary and later Turkey and Bulgaria—and on the other side were the Allied Powers—England, France, and Russia and later Japan and Italy (who had originally been allied with Germany). Alliances had been formed by each nation to gain support for its claims to territory in Africa, for markets in Asia, for spheres of influence in China, for security of its borders in Europe, and out of fear.

After the Napoleonic Wars ended in 1815, there were no continent-wide conflicts in Europe during the 19th century, though there was a brief war—the small German states became unified, and they defeated France in 1871—and there was plenty of tension. French fear of Germany and a desire for revenge, German fear of France and England and a desire to be a world power, English fear of losing markets to a growing Germany and a desire to maintain control of her huge empire, Austria-Hungary's fear of breaking into separate nations as a result of nationalism and a desire to remain a power—all these made a compromise impossible in 1914.

At the start of the war Germany invaded neutral Belgium without warning in order to attack France, and this act brought forth great sympathy for the Belgians by the Americans, who believed in fair play. British propaganda made the most of this attack, cate-

---

[1] *The World War* Until the Second World War, the first was referred to as The World War or The Great War.

gorizing the Germans as barbarians. Following United States tradition and the Monroe Doctrine's statement that we would not interfere in European affairs, President Wilson immediately proclaimed United States neutrality, but there was a great deal of support for the Allied cause. Many Americans had English ancestors and had sentimental feelings for the French who had fought with us in 1778. In spite of the many Americans with German background, there was a lot of anti-German feeling in the United States, and when Germany began using submarines to sink merchant ships, this feeling grew.

Copyrighted, 1914, by John T. McCutcheon.

BRITANNIA MUST BE MORE CAREFUL HOW SHE WAVES THE RULES.

—McCutcheon in the Chicago *Tribune.*

John T. McCutcheon uses a clever play on the expression—"Britannia rules the waves"—to illustrate his view of England's use of the Blockade of Germany in 1915. What does he suggest is happening to neutral shipping?

From the Chicago Tribune *reprinted in* The Literary Digest *of January 16, 1915.*

Submarine Warfare

The submarine changes naval warfare.

At the start of the war, the English announced a blockade of German ports and stopped neutral ships to search them. (See cartoon—Britannia waves the rules.) In 1915 the Germans retaliated by declaring the seas around the British Isles a war zone and announcing that any enemy merchant ship within this zone would be sunk on sight without providing for the passengers or crew. Any neutral ship in the war zone waters was there at its own risk.

The Germans used a new weapon, the submarine with underwater torpedoes, to enforce their declaration. Submarines were a dangerous threat to the English since merchant vessels, even if armed, were essentially defenseless against them. Convoys of ships escorted by navy vessels gave limited protection, but even then the submarines could get through and sink ships. President Wilson protested the German submarine warfare and declared the German action "an indefensible violation of neutral rights." We were again defending the rights of neutrals to use the high seas as we had against the Barbary Pirates and the English in 1812.

Wilson protests the German infringement on neutral rights.

On May 7, 1915 a German submarine sank the English passenger ship, *Lusitania,* and 1,198 died, including 128 Americans. Several Americans had been killed in previous torpedoings. President Wilson again protested. The Secretary of State, William Jennings Bryan, resigned, as he was a pacifist and believed Wilson's language was too strong. But Wilson was always a strong spokesman for what he believed was right. The Germans responded by agreeing to stop sinking ships without warnings. The United States' entry into World War I had been delayed.

Wilson Wins Re-Election

Wilson ran for re-election and defeated the Republican candidate, Supreme Court Justice Charles Evans Hughes. The Progressive Party (Bull Moose Party) again nominated the pro-war, pro-English Theodore Roosevelt, but he declined and campaigned as a Republican for Hughes. Until the California vote was counted, it appeared Hughes had won the election, but California went for Wilson and he won. Wilson's support of the eight-hour day and other progressive legislation, combined with the slogan, "He kept us out of war," appeared to be the deciding factors in the election.

Wilson wins re-election as a progressive leader who kept us out of war.

United States Involvement Through Trade

Although we were not in the war, Americans were profiting from it. American munitions companies sold weapons to the Allies, and banks loaned them money. The Germans believed this violated the neutrality position. The United States' response was to welcome purchases of arms from either side, but because of the English blockade, the Central Powers were unable to carry goods from the United States to Germany. Thus, America's commitment to neutrality, equality, and business opportunities for all aided the Allies and upheld our ideology.

There were overtures toward peace from the Germans in late 1916, and Woodrow Wilson made attempts to bring the parties together but was unsuccessful. Wishing to end the war and unable to do so on the battlefield in France, in February, 1917, the Germans announced they would again practice unrestricted submarine warfare.

Wilson articulates United States ideology and attempts to find a way to peace.

On April 2, 1917, Wilson asked Congress to declare war on Germany. German submarine warfare, he declared, was "warfare against mankind," and the United States would fight to make the world "safe for democracy." American ideology or belief in democracy, a common humanity, equality, and individual freedom were all invoked in our move to war. We were fighting for what we believed.

The United States Enters World War I

After Germany renews submarine warfare, the United States enters World War I.

The United States entered the war on April 6, 1917, the month in which English merchant marine losses to the German submarines peaked. 1917 was a bad year for the Allies. The Germans launched a successful attack on Russia; the Bolshevik Revolution in Russia overthrew the Czar; a French attack failed to break the German line in France; the British lost great numbers in an ineffective summer and fall attack; the Italians lost the northern section of their country to the Germans.

Americans fight in Europe.

The United States passed a Selective Service Act (the draft) and immediately began to increase the armed services from about 200,000 to over 4,500,000. An American Expeditionary Force (AEF) was sent to France under command of General John J. Pershing, and by November, 1918 almost 1,500,000 Americans had seen combat in the battles of Belleau Wood and the Marne and in the Somme and Meuse-Argonne offenses. These offenses finally brought an end to the war. The heaviest fighting of the war had been in Europe, but there had also been fighting by the Allies in German colonies in Africa, in the Turkish Empire in the Middle East (modern Jordan, Iraq, Syria), and against German spheres of influence in Asia.

Organizing the United States Government for War

The United States organizes for war.

The war had profound effects on society at home. The nation was highly organized for its war effort. A War Industries Board headed by a millionaire, Bernard Baruch, coordinated the effort to supply the military needs of both the United States and the Allies. Antitrust laws were suspended. Business leaders came to Washington as "dollar-a-year" men to help the war effort, and the power of the government bureaucracy grew. A Food Administration headed by Herbert Hoover, a young engineer who had organized food relief for the Belgians, worked to improve food production and distribution, encouraged "victory gardens" planted in suburban yards and meatless days—all done voluntarily in keeping with America's commitment to the individual.

The Committee on Public Information headed by George Creel was charged with uniting public opinion behind the war effort and did so through everything from news releases to movies. The Committee's charge was to bring Americans together, ignoring differences and individual interests in order to give full support to the war effort. While this seemed to work against American individualism, the Committee emphasized equality based on conformity to a common idea. Other committees added to the government's control over economic life and to the growth of the bureaucracy.

The war created job opportunities, and many African-Americans left the South to find work in steel mills and railway yards. Opportunities for women also increased, but the gains for women faded when the men returned after the war. African-Americans throughout the country continued to meet with discrimination. Segregation was the law even in the armed services, and the Ku Klux Klan was reborn. A movie, *Birth of a Nation*, respected and renowned for its breakthrough in technique had a racist message in its story of the KKK.

The war increases opportunities for women and encourages intolerance.

As hatred of the Germans was encouraged, it helped create intolerance in other areas. An Espionage Act and Sedition Act further limited individual liberty, making it unlawful to obstruct the draft, to use disloyal or abusive language against the armed services, the government, or the flag. The mobilization of the nation was effective in winning the war, but it strained America's ideological commitments to the individual and democracy.

Wilson's Peace Plan

President Wilson led the war effort and mobilized America for victory. He had made a move toward peacemaking in 1916. During 1917 there was talk of a negotiated peace and the need to state war aims. In January, 1918 Wilson addressed Congress and stated fourteen points "as the only possible program" for peace. The Fourteen Points held out the promise of a new world order supervised by the League of Nations. The Fourteen Points appealed to many of the belligerents as promising a peace without victory and the recognition of self determination by peoples so each could create their own nation state.

Wilson introduces The Fourteen Points as a plan for peace.

Although many of the Allies opposed certain points, which would not give them the spoils of victory they wished, by the time Germany signed an armistice on November 11, 1918 and the Kaiser had fled to Holland, the Fourteen Points had been accepted as the basis for a treaty. The English had insisted, however, on reservations[2] on freedom of the seas, and the French had insisted on reparations[3]. The latter created great problems in the 1920s.

Peacemaking: The Treaty of Versailles

World War I was very costly. The United States suffered over 110,000 dead and eventually paid over $75 billion in benefits to veterans but experienced no physical destruction. European nations lost many more soldiers (see chart), and the costs to them were higher, and they also suffered physically. They wanted revenge, yet Wilson's Fourteen Points presented an idealistic, very Wilsonian approach to the peace, based on American ideology.

---

[2]*reservations* Special clauses or qualifications.

[3]*reparations* Payments made by a defeated nation to the victor in a war. Reparations may be in goods, services or money.

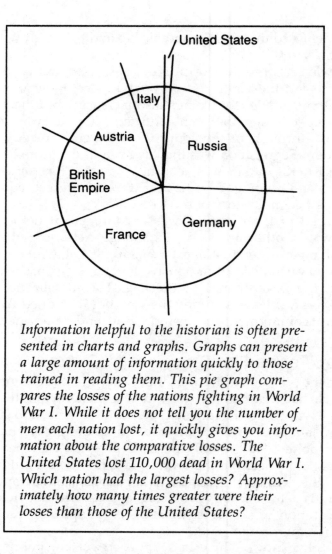

Information helpful to the historian is often presented in charts and graphs. Graphs can present a large amount of information quickly to those trained in reading them. This pie graph compares the losses of the nations fighting in World War I. While it does not tell you the number of men each nation lost, it quickly gives you information about the comparative losses. The United States lost 110,000 dead in World War I. Which nation had the largest losses? Approximately how many times greater were their losses than those of the United States?

Woodrow Wilson had been a college professor before entering politics. He often used scholarly experts for advice. When it came to creating the delegation to attend the peace conference at Versailles, France, he called on experts from various areas to assist him. He decided to go to Europe, the first President to do so while in office, to attend the Versailles Conference. He took with him no member of the United States Senate, which by law would have to ratify the treaty, nor did he take with him any prominent Republican in spite of the fact the Republicans had won a majority in the Congress in the November, 1918 election.

The victorious allies meet at Versailles, France, to write a peace treaty.

When the leaders of the four major powers—Clemenceau of France, Orlando of Italy, Lloyd George of England, and Woodrow Wilson—met at Versailles, Wilson was the only one who did not have the backing of a legislature. The Democratic Party had lost the majority in the Congress, and in a parliamentary democracy modeled on England, this would have meant the resignation of the Prime Minister or leader. It does not work that way within the United States government, but the loss of his party's control of Congress weakened Wilson's position.

During the war the Allies had made a number of secret agreements about the peace terms. Wilson was aware of these but ignored them in pushing for his Fourteen Points. The clash of ideas came at Versailles, when the tradition-minded, imperialistic allies looked for their spoils of victory as Wilson defended his idealistic new vision of a world order. Wilson was a fine spokesperson for America's ideological idealism, but he was not prepared to deal with the realistic views of the Allies.

Secret alliances undermine the Fourteen Points.

At the heart of Wilson's plan was the League of Nations. The purpose of the League was to prevent future wars. After intense debate and intrigue, the Versailles Conference accepted the League of Nations as part of the Treaty of Versailles. It went on to write a treaty in which many of Wilson's points were amended. The Allies were to receive reparations, or payments from Germany for war damage. German colonies were given to the Allies under League of Nations mandates[4], as were Middle Eastern lands formerly within the Ottoman (Turkish) Empire. Imperialism, under a new name, triumphed in these mandates. The Saar Basin, heart of German industrialism, was to be ruled under League of Nations supervision for fifteen years and then it would vote on its future. This was to provide France with security and economic power but was directly against Wilson's ideal of self-determination.

American idealistic ideology was compromised by Wilson at Versailles, but he believed the League of Nations would be able to discuss and resolve any problems growing out of the treaty. President Wilson believed that with the United States in the League of Nations, it would maintain the peace.

The Senate Rejects The Treaty of Versailles and League of Nations

Woodrow Wilson had miscalculated. The Senate, led by Republican Senator Henry Cabot Lodge, rejected the Treaty of Versailles and membership in the League of Nations. There was a personal antagonism between Henry Cabot Lodge and Woodrow Wilson—another example of the role individuals play in history. This disagreement, some say, was the cause of Senator Lodge's strong stand against the League. However, the issues were complex.

A clash of ideology emerged in the debates over the League. Many Americans saw the League as violating George Washington's advice of no permanent alliances and the Monroe Doctrine's commitment to staying out of Europe. These people, known as isolationists, wished to preserve America as a unique nation and to remain isolated from the traditional problem of European politics and international diplomacy. Their ideological commitments stressed traditional American values. They believed in the unique-

After debate, ideological differences cannot be resolved and the Senate rejects the Treaty of Versailles.

---

[4]*mandate*   An order from the League of Nations to a member nation to establish a responsible government over former German colonies or land taken from the defeated Central Powers. Such governments were to be under the review of the League of Nations. The territories so governed were referred to as mandated territories. The idea was that eventually they would become independent nations.

Wilson appeals to the American public, suffers a stroke but remains in office.

ness of America, that it had been called to a special role in world history, and that isolation from Europe was needed to fulfill this role.

Woodrow Wilson and his followers, the Internationalists and League supporters, stressed other American values: the brotherhood of man (all men are created equal), the interdependence of nations, and the need for open trade and freedom of the seas. Wilson represented a new interpretation of Jefferson's belief in the common man. As he had during the war, Woodrow Wilson appealed to the American people to support his program. He traveled by train throughout the country. Unfortunately, the stress of office became too much, and he suffered a stroke and returned partially paralyzed to Washington in September 1919. Although he remained in office, his power to persuade others was at an end.

The United States and the Soviet Union

The United States joins the allies in sending troops into the Soviet Union.

When the United States entered World War I, Russia had just had a democratic revolution. Russia was an ally but after the Bolshevik Revolution of October 1917, the Soviet Union withdrew from the war. In March 1918 the Soviet Union signed the treaty of Brest-Litovsk with Germany. The Soviet Union did not participate in the Versailles Conference, and the new government was ignored by the victors. It was not recognized by the United States as the legitimate government of Russia until 1933. In fact, the United States joined the Allies in sending an army to the Russian port of Archangel in an attempt to keep supplies located there from going to the Germans.

The United States also sent almost 10,000 soldiers to Siberia, ostensibly to keep Japan from taking control of the area and to rescue some Czechoslovakian soldiers. Since Russia was in the throes of a civil war and the Bolsheviks were struggling to control Siberia, they viewed the invasion very differently. For years American textbooks ignored and few Americans knew much about this invasion of the Soviet Union, which was taught to every student in the Soviet Union—a clear indication of differences in viewpoint and ideology. In spite of domestic fear of communism and a growing sense of the Soviet Union as an enemy, the United States withdrew the troops from the Soviet Union after the Bolsheviks established their control of the country. The United States suffered several hundred casualties in this expedition.

Attempts at Disarmament

The United States participates in disarmament conferences endorsed by the League of Nations.

The United States did not join the League of Nations but did participate in many League-sponsored events or meetings endorsed by the League. A disarmament conference, the first of several in the 1920s, was held in Washington and hosted by the United States. At this Washington Disarmament Conference, several disarmament treaties were signed limiting navy building and setting a ratio on the number of large ships. The ratio formula was 5 for the United States and Great Britain, 3 for Japan and 1.75 for Italy and France. The navies of the five powers were to remain in this ratio to each other. Eventually Japan saw the ratio as an insult to her status as a great power. Other treaties defined great power relations, particularly in the Pacific. In 1927 the United States and France sponsored the Kellogg-Briand Pact to outlaw war and eventually 62 nations signed it. Disarmament and the attempt to outlaw war illustrate that America's idealistic ideology and commitment to peace and lasting security continued in the 1920s even if the dominant philosophy of the nation was isolation.

AND SO ON, AND ON—
—Doyle in the Philadelphia *Record*

What is Doyle suggesting about the success of disarmament conferences?
From the Philadelphia Record *reprinted in* The Literary Digest *of November 25, 1933.*

Reparations

In Europe the reparations demanded of Germany proved too much to pay, and the United States took the lead in developing payment plans. The United States was particularly eager that payments continue since the Allies used them to pay their huge war debt to the United States. With the depression of 1929, reparation payments ceased. So did payment on the foreign debt owed to the United States. Throughout the 1920s the United States continued to exercise its power in the Caribbean. Thus the United States was involved internationally in the 1920s in spite of the rejection of the League of Nations and the Treaty of Versailles.

The United States remains active internationally.

KEY POINT TO REMEMBER
The United States' entry into World War I reflected an ideological commitment to human dignity, peace and democracy which, although the nation voted to remain out of the League of Nations, continued in a commitment to disarmament and the outlawing of war in the 1920s.

PEOPLE TO REMEMBER

Woodrow Wilson Virginia-born college professor and progressive, reform-minded Governor of New Jersey; 28th President of the United States; activist in domestic and foreign affairs; reform legislation included the Federal Reserve System and Clayton Anti-Trust Act; his idealism is reflected in the Fourteen Points, which provided the framework for the German surrender and the Treaty of Versailles in 1919; the Treaty including his plan for a peace-keeping League of Nations was rejected by the United States Senate.

LINKS FROM THE PAST TO THE PRESENT

1. Defense of neutral rights on the sea has been United States policy since the issue of impressment in the 1790s.
2. Ideological commitment to peace, democracy, and the equality of peoples has been expressed by Presidents over and over again.
3. Disarmament agreements have been sought throughout the 20th century.

QUESTIONS

Identify each of the following:

Washington Disarmament Conference
League of Nations
Isolationist
Internationalist
Lusitania

Treaty of Versailles
Committee of Public Information
American Expeditionary Force (AEF)

True or False:

1. The fighting in World War I began in Russia immediately after the assassination of Archduke Francis Ferdinand, heir of the Austro-Hungarian Empire.
2. Woodrow Wilson refused to proclaim United States neutrality at the start of World War I since he believed the United States had to make the world safe for democracy.
3. William Jennings Bryan resigned as Secretary of State because he was a pacifist and believed the language Woodrow Wilson used in notes to the Germans was too strong and provocative.
4. In unrestricted submarine warfare the Germans always gave passenger ships a warning before torpedoing them.
5. The American Expeditionary Force was commanded by General John J. Pershing.
6. After the Bolshevik Revolution, the Russians withdrew from World War I and signed the Treaty of Brest-Litovsk with the Germans.
7. Herbert Hoover organized food relief for the Belgians and ran the Food Administration in Washington during World War I.
8. Wilson suggested his Fourteen Points as just one of many possible ways to achieve peace in 1918.

9. Wilson took a very representative delegation to the Versailles Conference including "experts," leading Republicans and Democrats, Senators and Congressmen, and several businessmen.

10. Wilson remained a vigorous President and pushed for the Treaty of Versailles until he was defeated by Warren G. Harding in the 1920 election.

Multiple Choice:

1. United States forces participated in the following battles in World War I:
   a. Belleau Wood, the Marne, and San Juan Hill
   b. The Somme and Meuse-Argonne offensives and Belleau Wood
   c. Belleau Wood and Bunker Hill

2. The major European Allies in World War I were
   a. Germany, Austria-Hungary, Turkey, and Bulgaria
   b. Italy, Russia, England, and Turkey
   c. Italy, Russia, England, and France

3. At the Versailles Conference the "Big Four" victor powers were represented by
   a. Clemenceau of France, Orlando of Italy, Lloyd George of England, and Woodrow Wilson of the United States
   b. Woodrow Wilson of the United States, Churchill of England, DeGaulle of France, Orlando of Italy
   c. Woodrow Wilson of the United States, Clemenceau of France, Lloyd George of England, Francis Ferdinand of Austria-Hungary

4. The Germans stopped unlimited submarine warfare after Woodrow Wilson sent a note protesting the sinking of the
   a. Belleau Wood
   b. Versailles
   c. Lusitania

5. After the Bolshevik Revolution the United States joined the Allies in sending troops to
   a. Siberia and Moscow
   b. Archangel and Siberia
   c. Archangel and Brest-Litovsk

6. Examples of the growth of the bureaucracy and the concentration of power in Washington during World War I are
   a. Dollar-a-year men and the War Industries Board
   b. Food Administration and the Committee on Public Information
   c. both of the above

ANSWERS

True or False: 1. F, 2. F, 3. T, 4. F, 5. T, 6. T, 7. T, 8. F, 9. F, 10. F.
Multiple Choice: 1. b, 2. c, 3. a. 4. c, 5. b, 6. c.

II. THE COMING OF WORLD WAR II

Leaders emerge in Italy, Germany, and Japan who reject the world order established by the Treaty of Versailles and symbolized by the League of Nations.

In 1931 the first aggressive step toward World War II was taken when Japan invaded the Manchuria province of China in violation of the League covenant, the Kellogg-Briand Pact, and numerous other treaties. Manchuria was occupied and made a puppet state under Japan. It was the beginning of a series of military actions against the League of Nations. The World War I Allies proved powerless to halt them.

Salt on the Dragon's Tail

—"The Evening Times" (Glasgow).

Two years after Japan invaded Manchuria, Davidson in this cartoon makes a comment about the League of Nations. The League had been established to preserve the peace and prevent aggression. How effective was it in preventing Japanese aggression in Manchuria according to Davidson?
From the Glasgow Evening Times *reprinted in* The Literary Digest *of February 25, 1933.*

The roots of these actions were deep. The actions of Germany were partly motivated by frustrations created by the Treaty of Versailles; Japan's were rooted in its belief that it should have a major role in the Pacific and China, a belief that had been frustrated by the European powers and the Open Door policy in China. With the coming to power of Benito Mussolini in Italy in 1922 and Adolf Hitler in Germany in 1933 and the growing strength of the military in Japan, leaders were in power in three nations who were prepared to reject the new order of peace through the League of Nations and to revert to the old order of power through military action. Actions taken by Germany, Italy, and Japan during the 1930s led to war in Europe in 1939 and in Asia in 1941.

Hitler's Aggression in Europe

Hitler's steps to war and the appeasement practiced by the European Allies in Europe in response has haunted Americans since the end of World War II. Adolph Hitler in many ways was an opportunist who seized on issues of emotional appeal. He used the Jews as the scapegoat for Germany's ills and killed six million in pursuing his "final solution." The Holocaust illustrates the worst tendencies of human nature. Hitler attacked the Treaty of Versailles, which blamed Germany for the war, demilitarized her, and included some Germans within the borders of the newly created European nations of Austria, Czechoslovakia, and Poland. The latter was in violation of Woodrow Wilson's concept of self-determination expressed in the Fourteen Points.

Hitler rejects the Treaty of Versailles.

Once in power Hitler moved to right these "wrongs." In 1935 he rejected the military restrictions of the Treaty and began building a navy. England accepted this and signed a naval treaty with Germany. In 1936 Hitler occupied the Rhineland, German territory along the Rhine that had been demilitarized and was to serve as a buffer between France and Germany under the League of Nations supervision. England and France did nothing and neither did the League. After a failed attempt in 1934, in March 1938 a coup d'etat in Austria opened the country to German annexation, which Hitler called a reunion of German peoples. It was the third time the Allies ignored Hitler's violation of a clause in the Treaty of Versailles. In September 1938, Hitler was ready to seize the lands in Czechoslovakia along the German border, where over three million Germans lived. After some negotiation, the leaders of France, Italy, Germany, and England met at Munich, Germany, where English Prime Minister Neville Chamberlain agreed to a policy of appeasement of Hitler. Hitler was allowed to seize the Czechoslovakian territory of the Sudetanland where most of the Germans lived. Hitler promised no further aggression, and Chamberlain claimed he had achieved "peace in our time." It was the high point of the appeasement policy, and the word "Munich" has stood for appeasement ever since.

England and France negotiate with Hitler at Munich.

Outbreak of War in Europe

In March 1939 the rest of Czechoslovakia split in two over internal differences. Hitler occupied half of the nation. The Allies did not act in spite of having guaranteed Czechoslovakia's borders at Munich. When Hitler approached Poland in May 1939 concerning his desire to annex the free city[1] of Danzig, England and France assured Poland they would end appeasement and provide aid in case of an invasion.

Hitler invades Poland, and World War II begins in Europe.

Danzig was a free city with a large German population created by the League of Nations to give Poland and Central Europe an outlet on the Baltic Sea. To provide Poland with her own outlet on the sea, a corridor of land was given to Poland separating East Prussia from

---

[1]*free city*   An independent city not ruled by any nation; often there will be special trade agreements set by the city to encourage economic activity.

the main part of Germany. In order for Hitler to seize Danzig, he would have to move across this Polish corridor. To achieve his goal, Hitler next turned to the Soviet Union. Hitler, opportunist that he was, had used the German fear of communism to aid his rise to power. But in August, 1939 he was ready to negotiate a non-aggression treaty with the Soviet Union. The secret terms of the Soviet-Germany Treaty stated that in case of an attack on Poland, the Soviet Union and Germany would divide Poland between them.

On September 1, 1939, having signed the treaty with the Soviet Union, Hitler invaded Poland, and Soviet troops immediately entered to occupy the eastern region of Poland. England and France honored their commitments. World War II had begun.

Americans since then have understood the cause of the war to have been the appeasement of Hitler. On many occasions since then, Presidents have justified foreign policy actions by saying the United States cannot appease a potential aggressor. They often refer to Munich and make comparisons to Hitler and the 1930s as President Bush did in August 1990 after Iraq seized Kuwait. It has become imbedded in our ideology that appeasement is wrong and force must be used to stop any threat of or use of force by an aggressor.

United States Neutrality

The United States pursues neutrality throughout the 1930s.

Other events in Europe in the 1930s had led the United States to pass neutrality acts. In 1935 Benito Mussolini invaded Ethiopia in Africa. King Haile Selassie made a plea for help before the League of Nations, but the League did not act. Ethiopia was conquered and absorbed by Italy in 1936. The United States passed two neutrality acts (1935 and 1936) forbidding loans or credits to belligerents—some believed the United States had entered World War I to protect our loans to the Allies—and prohibiting arms sales or travel by United States citizens on belligerent ships except at their own risk—some believed the United States had entered World War I because of the sale of arms and/or of the loss of Americans killed while sailing on English ships. Civil War broke out in Spain in 1936. Italy and Germany aided the Fascist[2] General Franco, but the Allies and the United States did not support his democratic opponents. Neutrality was the United States' official policy and was confirmed in a new act in 1937.

The United States' reaction to these European wars was the same as it had been to the Napoleonic War and World War I—neutrality. The proclamation of neutrality in European wars had deep ideological roots in United States history. President Franklin Roosevelt himself was not in favor of this stance, but he signed the

---

[2]*Fascism* The political philosophy of dictatorship first developed by Benito Mussolini in Italy. All interest groups—labor, business, etc.—are organized under the control of the central government controlled by a single political party, and all interests are subordinated to the interests of the state.

law. In 1937 he suggested that an international quarantine of aggressors was the only way to preserve the peace. Public opinion was not yet ready for this stand.

Good Neighbor Policy

With his election in 1933, Franklin D. Roosevelt introduced a new policy towards Latin America, called the Good Neighbor Policy. It improved relations, led to less United States economic and military control over Latin America, and created an atmosphere of cooperation that was helpful in World War II. Also, Roosevelt led the United Staes to consider changes in colonial policy. In 1933 independence was voted for the Philippines, to take effect in 1945. Statehood for Hawaii was first considered in 1937. These actions suggested a move away from "Big Stick" and "Dollar Diplomacy" towards a greater respect for other people, more in keeping with the United States' ideological commitment to democracy and equality.

President Franklin Roosevelt wins friends for the United States.

Cooperation with the English: 1939–1941

When war began in 1939 in Europe, Roosevelt moved cautiously to support England and France. In November the arms embargo aspect of the Neutrality Act was replaced with a "cash and carry" policy that allowed nations to buy arms for cash and carry them away in their own ships. The English were able to buy and carry the arms in their large merchant fleet, but the Germans were unable to do so. Negotiations with the English established joint defense measures and finally in 1941 a Lend Lease Act made it possible for nations the President deemed vital to the United States defense to receive arms by sale, lease, or transfer. Roosevelt used the act to aid the English.

Through a cash-and-carry policy and the Lend Lease Act, Roosevelt slowly moves to support the English.

In his annual message to Congress in January, 1941, President Roosevelt described Four Freedoms—freedom of speech and expression, freedom of religion, freedom from want, freedom from fear—the achievement of which should guide United States policy. The Four Freedoms were deeply rooted in America's traditions and ideology. When the United States entered the war, the Four Freedoms became our war goal; they formed the ideology we proclaimed to the world.

In August, 1941 President Roosevelt met with Prime Minister Winston Churchill, the new English prime minister[3], on a cruiser off Newfoundland, and they signed an agreement called the Atlantic Charter. The Atlantic Charter stated the post-war goals of the United States and Great Britain although the United States was not in the war at that time. It indicated how far we had moved from neutrality in the two years since the war in Europe had begun. The Atlantic Charter also showed how deeply committed the United States was to certain values and ideologies.

The Atlantic Charter illustrates how strongly the United States supports the Four Freedoms and other democratic values.

---

[3]*prime minister* The first minister and thus the actual head of government in parliamentary governments.

However, not all Americans agreed with Roosevelt's policies. While Roosevelt made preparations for defense and worked closely with the English and French, others opposed any European involvement.

Opposition to Roosevelt's Policies and the 1940 Election

As Hitler wins victories in Europe, Roosevelt is elected to a third term.

Charles A. Lindberg Jr., a popular American folk hero who had won America's heart when he became the first to fly solo from the United States to France, supported an America-first movement and Hitler's position on a greater Germany. In the spring of 1940 Hitler won a series of victories and France surrendered in June, 1940. Roosevelt then decided to run for a third term, the first President to do so. The Republicans nominated Wendell Wilkie, who had been an anti-New Deal Democrat. Roosevelt promised not to send Americans to war, and he won re-election easily.

The United States Enters the War: Pearl Harbor

Deteriorating relations between the United States and Japan lead to Pearl Harbor.

United States interests in Asia were threatened by Japanese aggression in China. In 1937 an incident near Beijing, China, led to full scale war between China and Japan. The United States remained neutral, but there was great sympathy for China. When France fell to Hitler in June, 1940, Japan signed a treaty with the Vichy government, the German puppet government of France, which gave Japan bases in the French colony of Indo-China. The United States warned Japan not to invade Indo-China. When Japan did so in July, 1941, the United States froze Japanese assets in the United States, which brought United States–Japanese trade to a halt.

During the remainder of the year relations deteriorated in spite of active negotiations. The United States put the Philippine army under command of General Douglas MacArthur, and President Roosevelt appealed to Emperor Hirohito of Japan for peace but on December 7, 1941, Japanese military forces attacked the United States naval base at Pearl Harbor and other installations in Hawaii. On December 8, 1941 President Roosevelt asked Congress to declare war on Japan. They immediately voted for war and the United States entered World War II.

KEY POINT TO REMEMBER

Adolf Hitler of Germany, Benito Mussolini of Italy, and Emperor Hirohito and the military leaders of Japan began a series of aggressive moves in 1931 which led to the outbreak of war in China in 1937 and in Europe in 1939. The League of Nations and the World War I Allies failed to react and this "appeasement of aggressors" has greatly affected the United States' view of foreign relations since that time.

LINKS FROM THE PAST TO THE PRESENT

1. A negative reaction to appeasement of aggression as symbolized by Munich has been an important element of United States policy since then as illustrated by the 1990 Persian Gulf crisis.

2. Commitment to neutrality in affairs of Europe was a goal of early foreign policy, incorporated in the Monroe Doctrine, adhered to in the 1930s, and still supported by some Americans.
3. Values incorporated in the Four Freedoms and the Atlantic Charter have been and still are the basis of the United States ideology.
4. Concern over a major power controlling South East Asia has guided our policy in that region from the turn of the century and is illustrated by our fighting in Vietnam.

QUESTIONS

Identify each of the following:

Emperor Hirohito	Neville Chamberlain
Munich	Ethiopia
Holocaust	Spanish Civil War

True or False:

1. A "cash-and-carry" policy allowed nations to buy arms for cash from the United States.
2. The Lend Lease Act permitted the President of the United States to sell, lease, or transfer arms to nations deemed vital to United States defense.
3. The Atlantic Charter reversed the ideas stated by Franklin Delano Roosevelt in the Four Freedoms speech.
4. Prime Minister Neville Chamberlain proclaimed he had achieved "peace in our time" after the Munich agreement.
5. Japan's first aggressive action in the 1930s was a declaration of war against China.
6. The Holocaust, in which over six million Jews died, was Hitler's final solution to what he saw as the Jewish problem.
7. The Japanese attacked United States military and naval bases in Hawaii on December 7, 1941.

Multiple Choice:

1. Examples of Hitler's breaking of clauses of the Treaty of Versailles are
    a. rejection of military restrictions and the invasion of Manchuria
    b. the occupation of the Rhine Land and the annexation of Austria
    c. seizure of the Sudetenland and the attack on Ethiopia
2. Civil war broke out in Spain in 1936 and
    a. the Allies of World War I immediately sent aid to the democratic forces
    b. General Franco agreed to the Four Freedoms as the goal of the civil war
    c. Hitler and Mussolini aided their fellow Fascist, General Franco

3. After the fall of France to Germany in 1940, the Japanese
  a. signed a treaty with the Vichy government of France for bases in Indo-China
  b. invaded China
  c. began negotiations with the United States for bases in the Philippines

ANSWERS

True or False: 1. T, 2. T, 3. F, 4. T, 5. F. 6. T, 7. T.
Multiple Choice: 1. b, 2. c, 3. a.

III.   DOMESTIC ISSUES: 1918–1932

The Red Scare and Palmer Raids

The Palmer Raids are an illustration of America's fear of Communism.

After the Bolshevik Revolution in Russia, the Soviet Union began an intensive propaganda campaign against the West hoping to precipitate the world revolution predicted by Karl Marx. In a reaction of fear, the Department of Justice undertook a number of raids against political and labor leaders who were suspected of having Communist or leftist sympathies. Over 3,000 people were arrested in raids organized by the Attorney General Mitchell Palmer against what he claimed was a Red or Communist threat. The Palmer Raids in late 1919 and 1921 mark the beginning of 70 years of the use of America's fear of Communism by ambitious politicians to further their personal goals. Palmer had Presidential ambitions but failed to obtain the nomination. At the time of the raids President Wilson had suffered a stroke and was incapacitated. Americans' willingness to accept the Red Scare as real and to prosecute those arrested reveals a continuing aspect of intolerance rooted in American history.

Election of 1920

Warren G. Harding, a Republican, is elected President in 1920.

The war had centralized political and economic power in Washington. Wilson began the decentralization of the wartime concentration of power. Railroads, which had been under government control, were returned to private control on March 1, 1921. In the 1920s government policy became again one of laissez-faire. Warren G. Harding was nominated for President in 1920 and was elected over a Democratic ticket of James Cox and Franklin Delano Roosevelt. Women voted in the 1920 election for the first time. Calvin Coolidge from Vermont became President on Harding's death in 1923 and was nominated by the Republicans in 1924.

The Democrats were in disarray. Torn between Southern Fundamentalists and Northern Internationalists, between urban wets[1] and depressed farmers, they nominated John Davis, a New York conservative on the 102nd ballot at their convention. Calvin Coolidge easily won the election. Nicknamed Silent Cal, he took an inactive role, letting prosperity and the roaring '20s roll along.

---

[1]*Wets*   Those opposed to prohibition.

The Harding Scandals

In 1924 a number of scandals in the government were disclosed. They involved the Departments of Justice, Interior, and the Navy and the Veterans Bureau. They were reminiscent of the post-Civil War scandals under President Grant. The major scandal involved the Teapot Dome Oil Reserve, which had been set aside for the use of the Navy but was leased illegally to oil magnate Harry Sinclair by Secretary of the Interior Albert B. Fall. The Secretary had been "loaned" money by Sinclair. The implication was there had been a private deal. Both Fall and Sinclair served jail terms as a result.

America again experiences post-war scandals in government.

Limiting Immigration

The Red Scare and the Harding scandals were only two examples of intolerance and corruption in the 1920s. The Ku Klux Klan returned in strength, and over 40,000 members marched in Washington in 1925. Lynchings of African-Americans continued in spite of their contributions to the war effort in World War I. Many immigrants had come to America immediately after the war. Having rejected the League of Nations, Americans were ready to turn inward in isolation and to preserve what was theirs. They saw a threat from the immigrants and feared they might be radicals or Communists.

Congress establishes quotas to limit immigration.

Congress passed an Immigration Act, the Emergency Quota Act, in 1921, the first across-the-board restriction on European immigration passed by the United States Congress. In 1924 and again in 1929 laws were passed restricting immigration further. These laws created quotas for the number of immigrants who could come from each country. These quotas were based on the number of United States citizens claiming ancestors from the country according to the 1890 (later the 1910) United States census[2].

The restriction of immigration marked a great shift in American ideology. No longer were we the land of opportunity for all oppressed people. The National Quota System was eliminated in 1965, and many refugees have come to the United States since World War II, but the immigration quotas reflect 1920s isolation, intolerance, and fear. But there was another side to the 1920s.

United States Industry

After a minor post-war economic recession, business boomed. New industries centering on electricity and oil flourished. The automobile industry led the way. Henry Ford had introduced the assembly line for the making of his Model T car in 1913. His Rouge River Plant produced a new car every 10 seconds. The automobile industry stimulated the steel, oil, and rubber industries. Road building and gas stations were needed. As travel and vacations by car became more popular, guest houses and cabins for overnight travelers developed as a business. The automobile provided young people independence and changed dating habits as couples could find privacy away from their home in their cars. A full analysis of the way the car changed American business, values, and lifestyle

United States industry enjoys a post-war boom as the automobile industry leads the way.

---

[2]*census* An official count of the number of people living in a country.

would fill a large volume. Advertising for all the new products stimulated that industry. Prosperity continued for seven years and the stock market reflected this prosperity.

Changes in American Culture

Movies and literature reflect American values and concerns.

Another new invention, the radio, created a complex industry and added a new dimension to entertainment. With the first talking motion picture, Al Jolson's *The Jazz Singer* in 1927, movies experienced a tremendous growth. It is estimated that by 1930 almost four-fifths of the United States population was going to movies weekly. As a result both vaudeville and legitimate stage performances declined.

American authors of the 1920s, and '30s created literature of high quality reflecting American life and values. F. Scott Fitzgerald in *This Side of Paradise* (1920) and *The Great Gatsby* (1925) caught the spirit of the success-oriented generation in which "all gods were seen as dead, all wars fought, all faith in man shaken." Ernest Hemingway wrote brilliantly of the war experience and disillusionment in *The Sun Also Rises* (1926) and *A Farewell to Arms* (1929). William Faulkner created a fictional county in the South and revealed the restricted souls of its inhabitants in *The Sound and Fury* (1929) and *As I Lay Dying* (1930). His reputation has grown, and he now ranks as one of the finest American authors.

African-American culture thrives in the Harlem Renaissance.

In Harlem, New York, there was a great renaissance of African-American culture. The Harlem Renaissance, led by authors Langston Hughes and Claude McKay and jazz musician Louis Armstrong, encouraged African-American artists and produced some of the finest literature of the decade.

Eugene O'Neill emerged as the greatest American playwright. In *Mourning Becomes Electra* (1931), he turned to Greek tragedy for inspiration and wrote a compelling drama of suppression and revenge. He won the Nobel Prize in 1936. O'Neill used ideas from the works of the Austrian psychiatrist, Sigmund Freud, in his plays and helped introduce Freudian principles and understanding of sexuality to Americans. T. S. Eliot, who became an English citizen, was the most noted poet of the period. His *Wasteland* (1922) reflected the futility many saw in contemporary life.

Prohibition changes America's habits and provides a background for the "Roaring '20s."

There were many changes in Americans' attitudes in the years after World War I. The war had disturbed the lives of over 4 million young men, taking them from their homes and exposing over 2 million of them to Europe. Women had gained new places in the workforce. The prohibition amendment, banning the sale of alcoholic beverages, had passed in 1919. America would never be the same again. The distilling of liquor went underground and quickly came under the control of criminal elements in the cities. The era of urban gangsters like Al Capone in Chicago was born. Alcohol could be purchased at speakeasys[3], where men and women drank cocktails and discussed Freud's views on sex.

---

[3]*speakeasys* Illegal bars where liquor could be purchased. They were often controlled by gangsters.

The age of the vamp—a female vampire introduced in the movies—and the flapper—symbol of a devil-may-care, independent young woman—had arrived. The ideal woman of the mid-1920s was the flapper. She smoked cigarettes, wore her hair and skirt short, flattened her breasts, used lipstick, and rouged her face. The flapper replaced the Gibson Girl image of the turn of the century, when the ideal was a slim-waisted, willowy young woman with bouffant hair, long dress, and large hat. Each type reflected an age and to a large extent was created by advertisers.

Since the 1920s, movies and later television have provided us with ideal types for both women and men. Ideal women have ranged from the innocent Mary Pickford of silent movies to Betty Grable, the pin-up girl of World War II, to Marilyn Monroe in the 1950s, to Madonna and Cher in the '80s. For men, the idols have included Rudolf Valentino, the sultry romantic hero of the silent screen, Clark Gable—with his famous line at the end of *Gone With the Wind* (1939), "Frankly, Scarlett, I don't give a damn," the sensitive and rebellious James Dean and the macho John Wayne in the 1950s, and Harrison Ford in the 1980s. Such models from Hollywood and advertising have set the standard not only for the way people want to look but also for the way people think men and women should behave.

Advertisers and the movies create male and female sex symbols.

The Scopes Trial

Flappers and their young beaus danced to jazz bands and explored the new views of sex in darkened movie houses or in parked cars. The sexual revolution had begun, and "petting" and "necking" were added to the American vocabulary. Margaret Sanger, wishing to limit the births of "undesirables," led an organized movement for birth control, which eventually provided women with greater control over their lives. Talk of an equal rights amendment to the Constitution began. But the new ideas were not popular everywhere.

Religious fundamentalists reject the new and support the "traditional American values."

Religious Fundamentalists in Tennessee brought to trial John C. Scopes for breaking a Tennessee state law by teaching evolution in a science class. These Fundamentalists advocated traditional values and condemned Darwin and evolution as against the Bible. They saw a breakdown in the traditional attitudes on sex and morality and believed these had been brought about because Darwinian philosophy made people doubt the truths of the Bible. The Scopes trial (nicknamed the Monkey Trial by the press) attained national prominence. William Jennings Bryan, Fundamentalist and three-times Presidential candidate, testified as an expert on the Bible. Scopes was found guilty, but the trial lawyers made Bryan appear ridiculous and the Fundamentalist cause was temporarily set back nationally.

The 1920s, often referred to as the Roaring '20s, were a time of great change and experimentation for some Americans. There was prosperity for many in urban centers, but the prosperity was not evenly distributed. There were poor in the cities and few blacks shared in the good times.

Photograph of farmhouse in Acworth, N.H. about 1900
The residents of this New England farmhouse paid $75 a year rent
for the house and farm about the turn of the century. The house is
typical of New England farmhouses of an earlier era. The scene
illustrates the starkness, yet dignity, of farm life. What is the main
characteristic of the style of the house?

The Farmers

As agricultural prices fall, farmers do not share in the prosperity of the '20s.

World War I brought prosperity to American farmers. Food was needed to feed the armed forces as well as the Allies, whose food production had been interrupted by the war. The good times for the farmers peaked in 1920 as the rest of the world went back into food production. The demand for United States produce dropped, and prices fell dramatically. Just as in the 19th century, increased demand had led to more land under cultivation, and new machinery had helped to increase production. A surplus resulted.

What to do with farm surplus in order to raise prices and increase farm income became the farm problem of the 1920s and has continued, with few exceptions, as a problem to the present. It can be viewed in two ways. If the problem is overproduction, then the solution is to cut production. However, if it is viewed as a problem of underconsumption, then the solution is to find ways to enable more people at home and abroad to consume the food.

In the 1920s one out of every four farmers abandoned farm work, and a bloc representing farm interests emerged in Congress. The Farm Bloc's solution was based on underconsumption as the cause of surpluses. The Farm Bloc wanted the government to buy surpluses and sell the produce abroad. Congress passed such legislation twice, but President Coolidge vetoed it. In 1929, under President Hoover, Congress passed the Agricultural Marketing Act that established a Farm Board to loan money to cooperatives, which would buy up the surplus and then sell it when prices rose. With the start of the Depression, surpluses grew rapidly, and the Farm Board was overwhelmed.

In an attempt to guarantee themselves a market and higher prices, farmers turned to the tariff. Under President Wilson the Underwood Tariff brought duties down to their lowest level in years. In 1922 they had been raised to roughly 39 percent in the Fordney McCumber Tariff as part of the Republican support for business. While generally designed to help business, tariffs had always included duties on some agricultural products. President Hoover supported some limited changes in the tariffs to help farmers, but when the 1930 Hawley-Smoot Tariff was finally passed, it had made significant changes in the tariff arrangements and had raised duties to an average of just under 60 percent.

The Hawley-Smoot tariff raises duties and, as other nations raise their tariffs, international trade slows.

Disarmament Needed Here, Too

—Cowan in the Boston "Transcript."

In this cartoon Cowan illustrates his view on tariffs. What does he see as the relationship between tariffs, world trade and the depression?
From the Boston Transcript *reprinted in the* The Literary Digest *of May 20, 1933.*

This made it difficult for foreign countries to sell in the United States. Lacking dollars they could not buy farm products. This proved to be a short-sighted move as other nations retaliated by raising their tariffs, and international trade suffered. These artificial trade barriers hurt business world wide at a time when all nations were suffering from the effects of the Depression precipitated by the Wall Street Crash of 1929.

The Stock Market Crash: 1929

The value of stocks drops dramatically, ending the boom of the 1920s.

During the years of business prosperity in the 1920s, the value of stock on the New York stock market climbed steadily. Many people bought "on margin," investing a small amount of cash and borrowing the rest to be paid back when the stock price went up, as everyone came to believe it was bound to do. For example, if a share of stock sold for $100, you the buyer might put up $10 in cash and borrow $90. When the stock rose to, say, $120, you could sell, pay back the borrowed $90 (with interest), and still pocket a comfortable profit on your $10 investment. But what if stock prices dropped? If the share you bought at $100 dropped to $80, you not only lost your $10 investment but could not pay back the full loan. You lost your investment, the person from whom you borrowed lost, and both of you were headed for bankruptcy.

This is what happened in October, 1929. Stock prices dropped. Individuals lost their investments. Then banks began to fail. As banks and businesses went bankrupt, unemployment rose. A recession began and by 1931 had turned into America's worst recession.

A number of factors contribute to the stock market crash.

Why did the stock market crash? A number of factors contributed. They range from the frenzy of speculation and the overpriced nature of stocks to the unevenness of prosperity and the farmers' depressed status. A rise in interest rates in England, designed to attract investment money away from Wall Street and to England, also had an effect as investors moved money from stocks to English bonds to get these higher earnings. Perhaps the most important factor was psychological—a desire to get rich quick, which led to gambling with borrowed money, which is one way of looking at buying "on margin." This psychological factor has always been important in the operation of the stock market.

The United States also suffered from chronic underconsumption of its production both of goods and farm produce. This was another cause of recession. New products were available in abundance. They could not all be purchased because of the unevenness of prosperity. The farmers, suffering from eight years of declining income, were not a good market for manufactured goods. With the great drop in prices on the stock market, margin loans could not be paid. To get cash for their depositors, banks called in other loans. When these loans could not be paid, banks failed. Business activity slowed and layoffs of workers began. With no income, workers could not purchase goods, and this increased inventories of unsold goods. Businesses then had to cut back their production. This meant more lost jobs. The downward spiral of economic depression had begun.

It was not confined to the United States. Europe, to whom the United States had loaned millions of dollars for post-war rebuilding and to help nations pay their reparations, was soon affected as United States banks called in these loans or failed. The depression became world wide and was one of the reasons for Adolf Hitler's rise in Germany and the growing strength of Japanese militarists, who looked outside of Japan to help economic conditions at home.

The depression becomes world wide.

Hoover's Responses to Depression

President Hoover was faced with a deepening recession and had to respond in some way. He was a successful engineer and business man. The American economic system had worked for him, and he was committed to preserving that system as he knew it. He had explained his views on the American system and "rugged individualism" in an article during the 1928 campaign. He had said that the system demanded "economic justice as well as political and social justice" and was "no system of laissez-faire." He also extolled liberalism as "a force truly of the spirit, a force proceeding from the deep realization that economic freedom cannot be sacrified if political freedom is to be preserved."

President Hoover supports the American system of "rugged individualism."

By thus tying economic freedom to political freedom, Hoover firmly believed he could not act to control or infringe the freedom enjoyed by business and business interests. But Hoover also believed that the government was "an umpire instead of a player in the economic game." He believed that the government could have a role in economic activity, but only as an insurer of fair play. With his beliefs, Hoover was torn as to what the government should do in response to the stock market crash.

Hoover's cabinet contained six millionaires, some of whom were much more conservative than the President. Others of his advisers believed they could apply to government the scientific efficiency that had been applied to business in recent years. While Hoover recommended more government involvement than had ever occurred before, he also vetoed several economic measures passed by the Congress because he saw them as infringements on state and individual rights. Farm conditions continued to deteriorate and the Hawley-Smoot Tariff was a response. Instead of helping, it worsened the international economic situation.

By 1930 unemployment had risen, but Hoover was opposed to direct relief (i.e. payments) to the unemployed since he believed such payments would undermine the American ideology of rugged individualism. Instead he proposed a national voluntary effort under federal government leadership. The government could be an umpire. Money was appropriated for public works to be built by the unemployed under state and local supervision. In early 1932 Congress adopted Hoover's proposal for a Reconstruction Finance Corporation (RFC), which would loan money to banks and railroads on the theory that they would supply employment and the benefits of the government loan would "trickle down" to the unemployed workers. When unemployment reached over 10 million in 1932, Hoover accepted the extension of the RFC allowing

Hoover opposes direct aid to the unemployed but proposes a Reconstruction Finance Cooperation.

it to lend money to state and local agencies for funding of public works to provide employment.

Hoover was a compassionate man. He had organized the feeding of Belgians in World War I, but he would or could not abandon his ideology of rugged individualism and lead the government into adopting measures of direct relief for the unemployed. It was up to his successor to do this.

The Election of 1932

Franklin Delano Roosevelt pledges "a new deal for the American people" and defeats Hoover for the presidency in 1932.

The Republicans had lost control of the House of Representatives in the 1930 election. Economic conditions continued to worsen. In the Presidential election of 1932, the Republicans renominated Hoover. Their platform called for no new economic programs. The Democrats nominated Franklin Delano Roosevelt, Governor of New York. Franklin Roosevelt flew to the convention and delivered his acceptance speech before it, the first nominee to do so. It was the type of attention-getting, encouraging move that Roosevelt relied on to instill confidence in the people. In his speech he spoke of reconstructing the economy and pledged "a new deal for the American people." The Democratic Party platform called for unemployment and old age insurance, banking reforms, and regulation of securities and stocks.

Both parties supported changes in Amendment XVIII, the Prohibition Amendment—the Democrats were for repeal, the Republicans for revision. The Amendment had clearly failed to eliminate the consumption of alcohol and had created a whole new criminal element in society.

The 1932 campaign was vigorous. Roosevelt spoke of both reduced expenditures and new programs without addressing the issue of paying for them. He spoke of the forgotten man and of direct relief to the unemployed. Hoover spoke on his old theme of the American system and rugged individualism and said the election was "a contest between two philosophies of government."

The American people voted for a new philosophy. Roosevelt won by over 7 million votes and carried 42 of the 48 states. The Democrats controlled the Senate with 60 seats to 35 and the House of Representatives with 310 to 117. The nation was ready for the New Deal.

The New Deal is rooted in American ideology.

New Deal legislation was extensive and very different from past policies of laissez-faire. The goals of the New Deal, however, were deeply rooted in American ideology. In the 1790s these goals— justice, equality, and a fair deal for all people—were emphasized by Jefferson. An active government aiding a group or groups of citizens was emphasized by Hamilton. Franklin Roosevelt combined these ideas in the New Deal, but whereas Alexander Hamilton advocated government support for business and the wealthy, Roosevelt directed the government's involvement towards the worker and the middle class.

KEY POINT TO REMEMBER

In the Roaring '20s new industries created prosperity for many, but it was not evenly distributed, and this contributed to the severity of the Depression, which began with the stock market crash of 1929.

PEOPLE TO REMEMBER

Herbert Hoover   Engineer, millionaire, and government servant; organized the food relief program for Belgium in 1914, ran the Food Administration under Woodrow Wilson in World War I and served as the 31st President; his belief in the American ideology of rugged individualism made it difficult for him to find new approaches to solving the problems of the Great Depression, which followed the stock market crash in 1929.

LINKS FROM THE PAST TO THE PRESENT

1. Cycles of prosperity and recession have continued since the Panic of 1819.
2. Overproduction and/or underconsumption of farm produce has created problems for farmers ever since the Great Plains were opened to farming.
3. Intolerance and government corruption have occurred with cyclical regularity throughout United States history.
4. Politicians have exploited the American fear of Communism ever since the Bolsheviks seized power in the Soviet Union.

QUESTIONS

Identify each of the following:

Teapot Dome Oil Reserve
Palmer Raids
The Vamp and the Flapper
Rouge River Plant
Reconstruction Finance
   Corporation (RFC)
Emergency Quota Act

True or False:

1. The Palmer Raids marked the beginning of 70 years of the use of America's fear of Communism to advance the ambitions of politicians.
2. The Emergency Quota Act increased the number of immigrants allowed to enter the United States each year.
3. Governor Al Smith of New York was the first Roman Catholic to win a Presidential nomination by a major political party.
4. Henry Ford used the assembly line to produce radios and airplanes.
5. Talking movies and the radio had little impact on the American public.
6. Eugene O'Neill emerged as the greatest American playwright and won the Nobel Prize for literature in 1936.
7. The Harlem Renaissance produced some of the finest literature of the age.
8. The Roaring '20s were a time of change and experimentation for some Americans.

9. The trial of John C. Scopes for the teaching of evolution advanced the cause and ideological view of the Fundamentalists.
10. The Underwood Tariff brought duties down but the Hawley-Smoot Tariff of 1930 brought them down even further.
11. The depression that began in 1929 became world wide.
12. Herbert Hoover believed in "rugged individualism" and in "economic as well as political and social justice."
13. The Democratic and Republican platforms in 1932 both called for protective tariffs, unemployment insurance, and repeal of prohibition.

Multiple Choice:

1. Symbols of the 1920s were
    a. the gangster, the flapper, and the vamp
    b. the gangster, the Gibson Girl, and the automobile
    c. the gangster, the Gibson Girl, and Sigmund Freud
2. The stock market crash of October, 1929 had among its varied causes
    a. the unevenness of prosperity and the depressed status of farmers
    b. the lowering of interest rates in England
    c. the end of buying "on margin"
3. Herbert Hoover used the federal government to combat the recession by having Congress pass
    a. the Reconstruction Finance Corporation Act
    b. the Emergency Quota Act and the Hawley-Smoot Tariff
    c. both of the above
4. Examples of corruption and intolerance in the 1920s include
    a. the return of the Ku Klux Klan and advertisements for X-rated movies
    b. the Teapot Dome Scandal and Red Scare
    c. the restriction of immigration and hate messages on the radio

ANSWERS

True or False: 1. T, 2. F, 3. T, 4. F, 5. F, 6. T, 7. T, 8. T, 9. F, 10. F, 11. T, 12. T, 13. F.
Multiple Choice: 1. a, 2. a, 3. a, 4. b.

IV. THE NEW DEAL

Franklin Delano Roosevelt

Franklin Roosevelt holds a variety of political positions before being elected president.

Franklin Delano Roosevelt was not new to politics. A graduate of Harvard, he had studied at Columbia Law School. He served in the New York State Senate and then as Assistant Secretary of the Navy during World War I under Woodrow Wilson. In 1920 he was stricken by polio and was partially paralyzed in his legs for the remainder of his life. In spite of his handicap, he was elected Governor of New York in 1928 and President in 1932. He went on to be elected again in 1936, 1940, and 1944 — the only President in our history to break with George Washington's tradition and serve more than two terms.

WHAT'S THE NEXT PLAY GOING TO BE?
—Knott in the Dallas *News*

In this cartoon what point is the artist, Knott, making about the reaction of the business community to the NRA?
From the Dallas News *reprinted in* The Literary Digest *of November 11, 1933.*

Roosevelt led the nation as a strong and active President through the later years of the Great Depression and through World War II. In his first inaugural address he set a tone for the nation, balancing optimism with the reality of the harshness of the Depression. In a voice never forgotten once heard, Roosevelt said, "Let me assert my firm belief that the only thing we have to fear is fear itself— needless, unreasoning, unjustified terror which paralyzes needed efforts to convert retreat into advance." He acknowledged Republican attempts to address the Depression but deplored their values based on "monetary profit." Roosevelt called the American people to "apply social values more noble than mere monetary profit." It was a reemphasis on the ideological position of Jefferson and Wilson. He outlined a program that would include first, putting "people to work" and treating the task as we would "the emergency of a war"; second, a "better use of the land";

An optimistic Roosevelt says in his inaugural, "the only thing we have to fear is fear itself."

The Emergency Banking Relief Bill helps restore confidence in the banking system.

third, "strict supervision of all banking"; and fourth, a "good neighbor" policy in world affairs, especially towards Latin America. He called for an immediate special session of Congress.

Since 1929 many banks had failed. There was fear that the Democrats would make matters worse, and there were rushes to get savings out of banks. Many states closed their banks to avoid possible failure due to lack of funds. Roosevelt's first act as President was to declare a four-day national bank holiday, during which all banks were closed. On March 9 Congress passed the Emergency Banking Relief Bill. Its terms provided that all banks connected with the Federal Reserve System would be allowed to open only if licensed by the Treasury Department. This meant that any opened bank had been checked by the government and depositors need not fear that they would lose their deposits since the banks were sound or safe.

On March 12, a Sunday evening, Roosevelt addressed the American people in his first "fireside chat," which became a hallmark of his presidency. Listening on their radios, Americans heard Roosevelt's soothing voice assure them that the banks were safe and the money crisis was over. The people believed. A corner was turned, and although the Depression continued, the mood of the nation began to shift. Roosevelt had addressed the question of fear, and the public responded.

The One Hundred Days

The Emergency Banking Relief Bill was the first of many important measures passed in the three months following Roosevelt's inauguration, a time period that has been referred to as the One Hundred Days. Roosevelt had gathered a Brain Trust to advise him. They were men with many talents, and they decided that bigness was part of American life and business. What was needed was some central planning and regulation by the government. The Brain Trust recommended legislation to address problems in agriculture, business, and banking and to make reforms. Roosevelt and the Democrats were ready to give direct aid to the unemployed in the form of relief and to help business recover from the depths of depression.

Roosevelt, advised by his Brain Trust, introduces many pieces of legislation for relief and reform during the first One Hundred Days of his presidency.

Some historians have grouped all the New Deal measures under these three headings: relief, recovery, and reform. While it is helpful to think of the New Deal as working in these three areas, the measures proposed often overlapped the three divisions. Some measures were tried and abandoned; others were modified and continued; a few are still in effect to the present. Some of the ideas which guided the New Deal legislation were rejected in the 1980s during the presidency of Ronald Reagan, but the lives of all Americans have been affected by the New Deal legislation.

Relief: Supplying Jobs

So much important legislation was passed in the first One Hundred Days it often seems overwhelming. It is not necessary to understand all the details of this legislation, but it is important to understand its purpose and the basic approach of the New Deal to the reforming of American economic life. One goal was to supply jobs for people of different talents.

Relief legislation supplies jobs for the unemployed.

The Civilian Conservation Corps took unemployed young men from the cities and put them to work in rural areas, building roads and working on preventing soil erosion and on reforestation. A reestablishment of the CCC has been discussed in the late 1980s as a response to present environmental concerns. Several agencies, including the Public Works Administration (PWA) and the Works Projects Administration (WPA), were established to supply unemployment relief through work projects that ranged from bridge building to mural painting in post offices.

Reform: Helping Business

The major piece of legislation relating to business was the NIRA. Its premise accepted bigness in industry and asked business and labor to develop fair trade codes of conduct, which would apply self-regulation to the industry. These codes would be administered by the National Recovery Administration (NRA). The government was given power to develop codes for industries that did not do so. Section 7-A stated certain rights that each code had to guarantee to labor. The NRA began well, but the complexity of organizing and regulating all industry became overwhelming. The Supreme Court in 1935 in *U.S. v. Schechter Poultry Corporation* declared the law unconstitutional as it delegated Congressional power to legislate to an agency of the executive branch of government. It was declared in violation of the separation of powers.

Business is to be self-regulated under the administration of the NRA.

Reform: Helping the Farmer

Democrats saw the farm problem as one of overproduction, not underconsumption. In the Agricultural Adjustment Act they introduced the principle of subsidies to cut production. The subsidy principle established by the AAA set cash benefits to be paid to farmers who voluntarily did not grow certain products, thus reducing acreage and production. The cash for the benefits was obtained by a tax on the processors of agricultural goods. The Supreme Court said this was an illegal use of the tax power and declared the first AAA unconstitutional.

The New Deal sees the farm problem as one of overproduction, not underconsumption.

A second AAA was passed in 1938 and continued the subsidy principle but without the taxes on processors of agricultural goods. This Democratic approach to the reduction of farm production is still in use in 1990.

Other Reforms

Other reforms that affect us today include the Federal Deposit Insurance Corporation (FDIC), which insures individual bank deposits so individual depositors will not lose their money if their bank fails, and the Securities Exchange Commission (SEC), created to oversee the stock markets. The Tennessee Valley Authority (TVA) was established to plan the regional development of the

Other New Deal legislation affects us today.

Tennessee River Valley with everything from flood control projects to protect the environment to hydroelectric plants. In the 1940s, the hydroelectric plant built by the TVA supplied the power needed for the building of the first atomic bombs. The New Deal in its first One Hundred Days had addressed many concerns and developed new approaches to old problems. However, many old problems continued.

The Second New Deal

The Social Security Act provides unemployment and old age insurance.

The election of 1934 showed the nation's support for the New Deal. The Democrats won 7 new seats in both the Senate and the House of Representatives, an unusual event since traditionally the party in power can expect to lose seats in Congress in non-presidential election years. With the economy still depressed, Roosevelt launched what has been called the Second New Deal in 1935. The Second New Deal emphasized social security. The industrialized countries of Western Europe had had social security legislation for over 20 years, but the American ideology of individualism and self-help had worked against the adoption of such a program. The major legislation of the Second New Deal was the Social Security Act of 1935, which provided unemployment insurance, old age insurance, and grants to the states for relief for the blind and for homeless children.

Helping the Worker

Workers benefit from the Wagner and Fair Labor Standards Acts.

Two acts greatly helped workers. The National Labor Relations Act, known as the Wagner Act, established workers' rights to join unions and to bargain collectively. The Fair Labor Standards Act established the first minimum wage ($.40) and maximum hours (40 per week) for workers in industries engaged in interstate commerce. These had been the goals of labor unions for many years, and they were finally achieved through New Deal legislation.

The CIO

The CIO organizes unskilled workers in major industries.

At the start of the Depression, unions were ineffective in keeping jobs in companies that were hurting economically. Most major industries—coal, steel, automobile, rubber—were not unionized at all. The AFL was a union of crafts and skilled workers, few of whom worked in major industries. Labor provisions of the NRA encouraged growth in union membership. There were disagreements within the AFL as to whether it should organize unskilled workers in major industries. The AFL decided against it. However, John L. Lewis of the Coal Miners Union and others organized the Committee for Industrial Organization (CIO) within the AFL to organize these unskilled industrial workers. The CIO's goal was to organize unskilled workers on an industry-wide basis. The United Automobile Workers Union of the CIO introduced a new technique, the sit-down strike, when fighting for recognition by General Motors, Chrysler, and Ford. In a sit-down strike workers remain in the plant at their jobs but do not work. General Motors called in the police and obtained a court order to force the evacuation of the plant, but the workers stuck together and finally General Motors recognized the union. By the end of the decade, the CIO, which had been expelled from the AFL, had won recognition from most major industries.

Women and the New Deal

The number of employed women increased in the 1930s although women still suffered from job discrimination. Women were often the only employed member of a family. This antagonized some men, who suggested that if the women stopped working, there would be no unemployment as all the men would have jobs.

What do you think of that type of reasoning? Is it compatible with America's ideology based on equality and individual rights?

Eleanor Roosevelt, wife of the President, worked hard to change attitudes. She was a close advisor to her husband and often traveled where he could not, bringing back reports on conditions. When the Daughters of the American Revolution refused to let the African-American opera star, Marion Anderson, sing in their Washington headquarters auditorium, Eleanor Roosevelt arranged a concert for her at the Lincoln Memorial.

The first woman ever to serve in the Cabinet, Frances Perkins, served as Roosevelt's Secretary of Labor. She had worked with Roosevelt in New York State and was a friend of Eleanor's. Together, Eleanor Roosevelt and Frances Perkins formed the center of a network of women in government—women who supported each other and attempted to make the government more sensitive to women's issues.

Although they laid foundations for future action, they had limited success at the time. For example, federal relief agencies seemed to emphasize finding jobs for men, the Social Security Act did not protect low-income workers (many of whom were women), and the CCC excluded women.

Eleanor Roosevelt and Frances Perkins further the cause of women in government.

African-Americans and the New Deal

Segregation remained the rule, and race relations remained tense throughout the 1930s. There were outbreaks of racial violence in several cities. Roosevelt had African-Americans as advisors and appointed several to positions in government, including Mary McLeod Bethune in the National Youth Administration and Robert C. Weaver in the Department of the Interior, but much New Deal legislation was not color blind. Both the TVA and CCC were segregated, and federal mortgages were not available to African-Americans who purchased homes in white neighborhoods.

As World War II neared and more jobs became available, African-Americans still did not get many of them. A threat of a march on Washington made by A. Phillip Randolph, the African-American President of the Brotherhood of Sleeping Car Porters Union, forced President Roosevelt to issue Executive Order Number 8802, setting up the Fair Employment Practices Committee. The Committee was to address the issue of segregation and discrimination in employment. It was a welcome step, but there was still a long way ahead

African-Americans benefit from Roosevelt's Executive Order Number 8802.

for minorities to achieve recognition and equality in the American workplace.

Critics of the New Deal

Some critics suggest the New Deal has abandoned America's values; others say it has not done enough to reform the nation.

The New Deal won the support of the farmers, the unemployed, the aging, and the workers with its legislative program, but there were also critics. Conservative businessmen who still believed in rugged individualism worried about the government giving direct relief to the unemployed, while some workers thought the NRA was too supportive of business. Other critics deplored the growing bureaucracy needed to run the New Deal programs. Some believed the legislation limited freedom unnecessarily, and others thought the deficit financing[1] used to pay for the programs would require higher taxes in the future and might bankrupt the government. A few critics saw a danger in the increased power of the presidency. Today we hear similar concerns expressed over the size of the deficit and the bureaucracy and the power of the president.

Some reformers believed the New Deal had not gone far enough in helping the people. For instance, Huey Long, United States Senator and former Governor and political boss of Louisiana, presented a simple idea to solve the Depression and help the unemployed. His Share Our Wealth program called for the government to tax all income over $1 million and give each family an income of $2,500 per year with the money. Supposedly close to seven million members joined Long's Share Our Wealth program. Huey Long was a demagogue[2], an astute politician, and ambitious. He was assassinated in 1935. If he had not been shot, he would have been a strong contender in the Presidential race of 1936. As it was, Roosevelt won renomination and the Presidency.

The Supreme Court and the New Deal

The Supreme Court declared two important acts of the New Deal, the AAA and the NIRA, unconstitutional. Roosevelt offered a plan, referred to as "court packing," to increase the size of the Supreme Court. There were strong objections to the plan in Congress, and it was not passed. However, the Supreme Court upheld the Social Security Act of 1937 while the battle over Roosevelt's proposal was still raging in Congress.

Some believe the Court shifted its position under this threat, but most believe the Supreme Court justices were carefully interpreting the Constitution. Because of natural attrition on the Court,

[1]*deficit financing* The concept of deficit financing originates in the economic philosophy of John Maynard Keynes. The theory is that in times of prosperity, governments will raise taxes to slow the inflation, and in times of recession, money will be spent on government programs to "prime the pump" to get business working again. If there is not enough money in the treasury, the programs are financed through borrowing, which creates a deficit. Thus deficit financing means paying for programs when you do not have the funds to do so and must borrow.

[2]*demagogue* One who appeals to the lowest interests of the people, stirring them up to support a program by emotional speeches.

Roosevelt was able to appoint seven justices of his choice by 1941. The change in the Court's view of New Deal legislation made possible a permanent shift in American ideology.

Summary

During the decade of the 1930s Europe was moving towards war. The New Deal program was developed against a background of world depression and growing aggression. American neutrality, proclaimed in 1935, emphasized the public's desire for isolation. Roosevelt, however, was inclined to become involved, and from 1937 on foreign policy issues required more and more of his attention. A slight business downturn in 1937–9 ended as United States industry responded to United States government mobilization efforts and the military needs of those opposing Hitler's Germany and Mussolini's Italy.

When the United States declared war against Japan on December 8, 1941, the New Deal was over. America's war effort finally ended the Depression. By 1944 unemployment was down to roughly 1 percent from its height of over 25 percent in 1932.

Historians agree the New Deal legislation did not end the Depression, but it did provide a more optimistic outlook than the nation had when Roosevelt was first elected, and it avoided a revolution, which might have ended democracy as happened in Germany. The New Deal advanced the rights of labor, improved the income of farmers, provided old age security for the elderly, and unemployment compensation for the unemployed. The New Deal ended a period of laissez faire government and greatly expanded the government bureaucracy and the power of the executive branch, especially the president. It was the most intense and important period of reform and change in American history, a history that has periodically had movements of reform.

Many of the ideas found in the Populist Party Platform in 1892 were incorporated in the New Deal program, suggesting there is a continuity in America's concern for reform to create greater equality and improve the life of the people. This belief in equality and the idealism that believes conditions can be improved runs through America's ideology. It clearly was behind the United States' actions in the New Deal and in World Wars I and II.

KEY POINT TO REMEMBER

The New Deal was a major effort to solve the problems created by the Depression by having the federal government take action and intervene in the business cycle, reversing the laissez-faire policy of the 1920s.

PEOPLE TO REMEMBER

Franklin Delano Roosevelt New York lawyer and politician; State Senator, Assistant Secretary of the Navy, Vice-Presidential candidate, Governor of New York, and 32nd President; although paralyzed in his legs by polio, he provided vigorous presidential leadership through the Depression and World War II. Elected

President four times, he instituted the New Deal to help fight the Depression and bring about relief, recovery, and reform; in spite of neutrality legislation, he provided support to England and France before the United States entered World War II. He died in office just before the war ended. His wartime conferences with the Allies determined the post-war future including the United Nations.

LINKS FROM THE PAST TO THE PRESENT
1. Environmental concerns have been important to some Americans since the time of Theodore Roosevelt and are reflected in the CCC and the environmental legislation since the 1970s.
2. Farm subsidies as a way to solve the farm surplus problem began with the New Deal and are still used.
3. Labor unions in the United States have played an important role since the Civil War, and the CIO in the 1930s is one example.
4. Cycles of reform occur regularly in American history from the 1830s on.

Two Views of Government at the time of the New Deal

Laissez-faire

This view of government intervention in the business cycle is rooted in the classical economic ideas of Adam Smith. Smith believed that economic conditions are regulated by natural forces and people should not attempt to change economic conditions but rather should leave them alone to work their natural course. Intervention only upsets the natural balance and makes the situation worse.

Interventionists

Many who supported government intervention in the business cycle to combat the Great Depression followed the theories of the economist, John Maynard Keynes. Keynes believed government had the responsibility to tax heavily in times of prosperity to provide funds for economic relief and support including unemployment payments in times of recession. These interventionists believed government was responsible for the welfare and economic well being of the people.

QUESTIONS

Identify each of the following:

Emergency Banking Relief Bill
Civilian Conservation Corps (CCC)
Social Security Act
National Recovery Administration (NRA)
Agricultural Adjustment Administration (AAA)
Tennessee Valley Authority (TVA)
Congress of Industrial Organization (CIO)
Executive Order Number 8802
Share Our Wealth Program
Federal Deposit Insurance Corporation (FDIC)

True or False:
1. In his first inaugural President Roosevelt declared "the only thing we have to fear is fear itself."
2. The New Deal built its program around relief and recovery but not reform.
3. The AAA adopted the principle of subsidies to cut farm production.
4. Your money is not insured by the FDIC against bank failures if you have an individual account.
5. The major legislation of the Second New Deal was the Social Security Act of 1935.
6. The Committee of Industrial Organization fought with the AFL because the AFL wanted to organize all unskilled workers and the CIO did not.
7. In Washington during the New Deal there was an important network of women led by Eleanor Roosevelt and Frances Perkins.
8. President Roosevelt issued Executive Order Number 8802, setting up the Fair Employment Practices Committee, because he and the New Deal leaders were committed to wiping out segregation.
9. Most historians agree that the New Deal legislation did not end the Depression.
10. The electric power plants built by the TVA in the 1930s supplied the electric power needed for the building of the first atomic bomb.

Multiple Choice:
1. Franklin Delano Roosevelt before his election to the Presidency had been
    a. Secretary of State under Woodrow Wilson
    b. Vice President of the United States
    c. Governor of New York
2. Over 2 million young men were employed by the New Deal in
    a. reforestation work under the CCC
    b. painting murals in post offices under the PWA
    c. farm rehabilitation under the AAA
3. Some people did not believe the New Deal had gone far enough and offered their own solutions to the recession such as
    a. Huey Long's Share Our Wealth program
    b. John Maynard Keynes' deficit financing
    c. both of the above
4. Among the great periods of reform in American history are
    a. the New Deal, Progressive, and Jacksonian periods
    b. the New Deal, the Populist, and Reconstruction periods
    c. The Jackson, Wilson, and Coolidge presidencies
5. Which of the following New Deal legislation attempted to restructure American business practices?
    a. TVA and AAA
    b. CIO and FDIC
    c. NIRA and SEC

ANSWERS
True or False: 1. T, 2. F, 3. T, 4. F, 5. T, 6. F, 7. T, 8. F, 9. T, 10. T.
Multiple Choice: 1. c, 2. a, 3. a, 4. a, 5. c.

CHAPTER 11

World War II and The Early Years of The Cold War

APPROACHES TO HISTORY
The Significance of War in Human Activity

In the study of history, war has had a major role. Some historians seem to suggest in their writings that peace is merely that brief period of time between wars. They emphasize in their works the causes of war, the strategies employed in fighting, and the results or peace treaties. By the emphasis they place on war, other human activities fade in significance.

After World War II several anthropologists gave support to this perception of war as the primary activity of human history. These anthropologists emphasized the evolutionary connection of humans to animals, whose primary drive after reproduction is for territory and tribal dominance. Animals will fight to defend both territory and tribe. Robert Ardrey identified these drives as the "territorial imperative."

Long before Ardrey's concept became popular, some historians had presented their version of it in the texts they wrote. While many more recent texts place less emphasis on war-centered history, it is still appealing to many authors. It is also interesting to many readers. Certainly war greatly affects the history of nations and the lives of all those involved in it. As warfare has become "total war" over the past 200 years, no one—man, woman, or child—can escape its impact, whether directly as the victim of bombings of a city or indirectly as a sufferer from food shortages or industrial losses. War has an impact on us all, as these war-centered historians emphasize.

War not only affects all citizens of the nations involved, but can also be exciting and stimulating. War is violent, and anyone who views television realizes how much violence is portrayed on the screen. Why? Does it appeal to the basic nature of humans? Is it one way of affirming Ardrey's work? How have you reacted to moments of verbal or physical violence?

Many who have experienced war know that it brings those involved close together and that it leads them to noble acts and sacrifices. War and violence can bring out the best in humans but they also bring out the worst. War creates extraordinary challenges to which the people and the leaders must respond. Both World War II and the Cold War that followed produced such challenges.

I. WORLD WAR II

The Japanese attack on Pearl Harbor presented great challenges to the American nation. A major portion of the Pacific fleet was damaged or destroyed. When Germany and Italy declared war on the United States on December 11, 1941, the war became world wide. Because the Allies' resources were limited, a decision was soon made to concentrate on the war in Europe. While forces in the Pacific were strengthened and attacks launched, the challenge of Hitler and Mussolini received major attention.

The War in Europe is given top priority.

The War in Europe

By the time the United States entered the war, Hitler had conquered France, the Low Countries, Denmark, and Norway. The Atlantic coast of France had been occupied, and England had been subjected to intensive bombing raids in the Battle of Britain. Failing to force England's surrender, Hitler made his greatest mistake. He invaded the Soviet Union, which immediately became England's ally. When the United States entered the war, the Soviet Union became our ally also in spite of our long antagonism to Communism.

Germany had conquered much of Western Europe by December 1941.

The Soviets were hard pressed and desired her allies to open a "second front" to draw German forces away from the Russian front. Churchill feared the loss of life involved in an invasion along the Atlantic coast. He also was worried about the future of Europe and feared Soviet domination of Europe. Churchill wanted American help first in repulsing a German attack on Egypt and the Suez Canal. Then he wanted to invade Europe through the Balkans to be able to contest post-war control of that area with the Soviet Union. Roosevelt agreed on the first point, and in November 1942 as the English launched from Egypt an attack against the German General Rommel, United States forces invaded German-occupied North Africa in the west. The North African campaign was a success, and in July, 1943, Sicily was invaded and captured. In September an invasion of Italy was launched.

Russia stops the German advance at Stalingrad.

In the meantime, the Russians broke the 17-month-old seige of Leningrad and stopped the German advance into Russia at the Battle of Stalingrad. This battle was the turning point of the war in Russia and probably of the entire European war. A German army surrendered at Stalingrad on February 2, 1943, proving the Germans were not invincible. Hitler's challenge had been met by the Soviet Union, and although civilian and military casualties were huge, the Russians went on the attack and crossed into Poland in January 1944.

The American Air Force based in England began massive bombings of German industrial and rail centers in early 1944 in preparation for an invasion. The Germans had failed to defeat England through air attacks. While heavy damage was done, Germany did not capitulate because of air raids either.

The Allies invade France on D-Day.

On June 6, 1944, D-Day[1], United States, British, and Canadian forces under the supreme command of General Dwight David Eisenhower invaded the Normandy peninsula of France. After heavy fighting on the beaches, the United States Third Army under command of the flamboyant General George S. Patton broke out at St. Lo. The French capital, Paris, was captured on August 25. Another Allied army invaded southern France on August 15. By September, American forces entered Germany.

The Germans counter attacked in December, when they attempted to break through the Allied line in Belgium, drive to the coast, and cut the Allied supply line. After Americans gave up a "bulge" of territory, they were able to stop the German advance. In this Battle of the Bulge, fighting was heavy and losses high.

The Allied offensive continued through the winter and spring. Auschwitz and other death camps where Hitler's Nazis had killed millions of Jews and East Europeans were liberated. They revealed to a disbelieving world the worst horrors of the Nazi movement.

Hitler commits suicide and the Germans surrender.

The Russians advanced from the east. On May 1, 1945 Hitler committed suicide in Berlin. On May 8, V-E Day[2], General Eisenhower signed with the new German government a document of unconditional surrender[3].

Headlines from *The New York Times* tell the dramatic story of the last week of World War II in Europe. Italy had surrendered in 1943, only to be occupied by the Germans. Mussolini was killed by Italians in April 1945 as the Allied forces moved quickly northward, having been blocked for a long time south of Rome. The Axis powers in Europe had been defeated. The challenge of war had been met, but at a terrible price.

---

[1]*D-Day* D-Day was the designation for the day allied forces invaded Europe across the English channel.

[2]*V-E Day* V-E Day signified the day victory was won in Europe in World War II.

[3]*unconditional surrender* Unconditional surrender became the terms decided upon for victory in World War II by the Allies. It was applied to Italy, Germany, and Japan.

The War in Asia

While the Allies had determined to concentrate first on the war in Europe, there were campaigns in Asia throughout World War II. The Japanese had attacked China in 1937 and fighting continued on the mainland—with major United States aid after December 7, 1941—until the Japanese surrender. The Japanese attack plan after Pearl Harbor was masterfully executed. Guam, Wake Island, and Hong Kong fell quickly. Malaysia, the Philippines, and, after the fall of Singapore, the Netherlands East Indies (now Indonesia) were all invaded. The Philippines fell after a gallant defense by American and Philippine forces on the Bataan Peninsula, which forms one side of Manila Bay.

Japanese advances after Pearl Harbor.

The only attack on the United States mainland occurred when a submarine shelled an oil refinery near San Francisco. Two great sea battles—Coral Sea in May 1942, the first sea battle fought entirely by aircraft from ships, and Midway in June, considered the turning point of the Pacific war—stopped the Japanese advance and prevented an invasion of Australia.

The United States went on the offensive in August 1942 with the invasion of the island of Guadalcanal. It was the first in a series of island invasions across the Pacific that finally brought United States airpower close enough to bomb Japan. A campaign in Burma opened up a supply route to China. Indonesia was recaptured. After the Battle of Leyte Gulf in October, 1944, which destroyed most of the remaining Japanese naval forces, the Philippines were invaded in January, 1945. They were quickly recaptured and General Douglas MacArthur, the supreme commander of the army forces in the Pacific, returned to the Philippines where he had been commander before the attack on Pearl Harbor, fulfilling the promise he had made when he had fled the Philippines, "I shall return."

The United States goes on the offensive.

The United States mounted a series of air raids on major Japanese cities. In the fire bombing of Tokyo in May, 1945, over 80,000 civilians were killed by the fires set by Napalm bombs. Still the Japanese would not surrender.

Throughout the war the United States worked on improving old and developing new weapons. The most important of these was the atomic bomb. As early as 1942 President Roosevelt created a secret project, called the Manhattan Engineer District, and referred to as the Manhattan Project, to explore the possibility of creating such a weapon. In 1945 a weapon was tested at Alamogordo, New Mexico. The new President, Harry S. Truman, decided to use it against Japan.

The atomic bomb is developed secretly by the United States.

There were many arguments over its use, but the deciding argument then seemed to be that it might save the lives of many Americans if the bomb forced Japan into surrender without an invasion of the islands. On August 6, 1945 a bomb was dropped without clearly informing the Japanese of the potential power of the weapon. The city of Hiroshima was destroyed in a matter of seconds with well over 150,000 people killed or wounded. Two days later a second bomb destroyed Nagasaki. On August 15, V-J Day[4], the Japanese surrendered, and on September 2 aboard the battleship *Missouri* in Tokyo Bay, General Douglas MacArthur, Commander in Chief of the Allied forces, signed a formal document of Japanese surrender. World War II had ended.

Challenges of War

Reading about the military planning and efforts of World War II or seeing movies of the heroism displayed by young men in the war can be exciting. Both clearly illustrate the challenges war presents to humans—challenges that often bring out the finest in individual emotions but that also allow for horrible incidents.

The human and economic costs of the war are staggering.

The cost of World War II in human lives and human suffering was staggering. The United States alone had over 800,000 wounded and over 300,000 dead, and our losses were among the smallest of the participating nations. The economic costs to the world were huge. The United States is still paying some of those costs in veteran's benefits and pensions. While meeting the challenges of war, the Allies began to address the challenge of creating a postwar world.

Wartime Conferences

Even before the United States entered the war, President Roosevelt had met with the English Prime Minister, Winston Churchill, to discuss military plans and postwar possibilities. The resulting Atlantic Charter outlined the war aims. Conferences involving Cabinet level officials continued throughout the war. In two important conferences—Teheran in November, 1943 and Yalta in February, 1945—Winston Churchill, Franklin Roosevelt, and Joseph Stalin, the leader of the Soviet Union, met to make decisions about war policy and the postwar world.

Conferences at Teheran and Yalta establish the pattern for the postwar world.

At Teheran agreements were reached on a second front and on a United Nations organization. At Yalta unconditional surrender was accepted as the condition for ending the war. The Soviet Union in return for several Japanese islands and a sphere of influence in Korea agreed to enter the war against Japan after the war in Europe ended. Free elections were set as the way to reestablish governments in the occupied nations of Europe, but the Western allies, and the Soviet Union, a totalitarian state, later differed as to what this meant and how it should be implemented. This made it possible for the Soviets to control those nations in Eastern Europe that it had conquered or "liberated" as the war ended. Finally, at Yalta the United Nations Security Council voting procedures were agreed upon. In essence they gave the "Big Five"—England, France, China, United States, and the USSR—veto power over Security Council resolutions.

Later some Americans saw the Yalta agreements as a sell-out to Stalin. They believed an ailing President Roosevelt had been duped. At the time the agreement seemed wise. The atomic bomb had not yet been tested, postwar tensions and disagreements had

---

[4]*V-J Day* V-J Day signifies the day Japan was defeated.

not surfaced, and the conference participants were just about to conclude successfully a war in Europe in which they had cooperated. From a later Cold War perspective, the agreements do not appear as wise, yet they did lead to the successful establishment of the United Nations at the San Francisco Conference in the spring of 1945 when 50 nations subscribed to the Charter.

Modeled on the League of Nations, the United Nations was to have a Secretariat, a Security Council of 15 members including the "Big Five" permanent members, and a General Assembly open to all nations, in which each nation regardless of size or economic strength would have one vote. This time the United States joined the international organization. The United Nations has played an important role in the postwar world.

The final wartime conference was held at Potsdam, Germany after Germany surrendered. Stalin still represented the USSR, but Clement Atlee had replaced Winston Churchill as leader of England and Harry Truman had replaced Franklin Roosevelt. It was agreed draft treaties were to be prepared for the defeated enemy, war criminals were to be tried, and no monetary reparations were to be paid. The USSR was given the right to remove factory equipment from Germany.

New western leaders meet at Potsdam with Stalin.

The new Allied leadership was not comfortable together. These wartime conferences set the pattern for summit diplomacy, which has been practiced throughout the Cold War years. While these major wartime conferences set the outline for the postwar world, much of the work was done by lower-level officials of the Allied powers. The leaders provided directions, but the real challenges of war and peace were met by hundreds of hard working staff members.

The War At Home

Long before Pearl Harbor, private industry began slowly turning to production for war. As soon as the United States entered the war, the federal government organized the war effort. A War Production Board (WPB) and many other organizations were established to oversee the transformation of a civilian economy into a full military economy. Anti-trust suits were stopped and cost/payment arrangements were made to benefit war industries. When labor disputes threatened, a National War Labor Board (NWLB) was established to control disputes. It was given broad powers to set 30-day cooling off periods before strikes and to seize and operate plants. Both labor and industry came under strict government supervision.

The War Production Board and other organizations are established to run the war effort.

An Office of Price Administration (OPA) set prices and supervised rationing of goods in short supply. Americans were issued coupon books with coupons that could be turned in for one's share of gas, sugar, and other scarce commodities. New industries, ranging from synthetic rubber to replace the rubber lost when the Japanese occupied Malaysia and South East Asia to the atomic bomb, were developed.

By 1943 full employment had returned to the United States, and the Great Depression had ended. The challenge and stimulation of

Full employment returns to the United States and the Great Depression is considered over.

war had achieved what government legislation could not. With over 12 million in the armed services, there was a shortage of industrial workers. This created many opportunities for minorities, and more African-Americans left the South for the North and West, where industries were growing. Women joined the work force in large numbers, both in offices and factories. "Rosie the Riveter" became a famous wartime symbol—a woman working in heavy industry riveting airplanes or ships needed in the war effort. The armed services all opened their ranks to women in non-combat support services. WACs (Women's Army Corps) and WAVES (Women Accepted for Volunteer Emergency Service) served in many positions on the mainland and overseas.

The armed services are opened to women, but African-Americans are kept in segregated units.

While new opportunitites opened for women in the armed services, African-Americans still served in segregated units. Intolerance still plagued minorities, and there were race riots on several military bases and in several cities where African-Americans had come to take advantage of new jobs. Military service provided African-Americans opportunities to exercise leadership and to gain self-esteem. Many African-Americans who served in the armed services were not willing to accept the segregated conditions of prewar American life. America met the challenges defeating oppression overseas; in the postwar years the United States would need to meet the challenge of ending oppression at home.

Wartime Intolerance

War breeds intolerance as the people are taught to hate the enemy. Intolerance, always a part of American life, intensified during World War II. Besides manifesting itself in race riots, there was intolerance in the actions of the Committee on UnAmerican Activities, first organized to keep communists out of government. This committee of the House of Representatives was chaired by Martin Dies and had as its charge the maintenance of loyalty in government. It recommended over 3,500 government officials be dismissed, of whom, after investigation, only 36 were. These numbers suggest the type of hysteria that was rampant in the country.

Japanese-Americans are placed in camps to protect the nation's security—one example of wartime intolerance.

While the general persecution of those suspected of connections to the enemy was less than during World War I, the government put Japanese-Americans on the West Coast into camps. This clearly was an infringement of the Bill of Rights, but it was done in the name of national security. Panicked by the attack on Pearl Harbor and the fleet losses that seemed to make the West Coast vulnerable to attack and not knowing where the Japanese might attack, the government ordered all Japanese-Americans to leave their West Coast homes. They were settled in relocation centers throughout the West. Almost two-thirds of the resettled Japanese-Americans were American citizens. Not one of them was ever accused of a crime. They were simply identified on the basis of race as a threat to American security. Many lost their property—homes, businesses, furniture, possessions. They were released at the end of the war, and finally in 1982, the government recommended that those interned be compensated for their losses.

The internment of the Japanese-Americans illustrates how easily war can lead people into acts of intolerance and persecution. It is just one illustration of the horror war can bring on the innocent; in modern warfare everyone in a society can become a combatant or a victim.

Franklin Roosevelt's Fourth Election: 1944

In 1944 Roosevelt was elected to an unprecedented fourth term, defeating Republican Governor Thomas E. Dewey of New York. Roosevelt had picked Senator Harry Truman of Missouri as his Vice President. Roosevelt died April 12, 1945 of a massive cerebral hemorrhage. He did not live to see either the end of the war or the establishment of the United Nations, both of which occurred within weeks of his death. While Roosevelt was disliked by many for his attempted solutions to the problems of the Depression, it is generally agreed he was a great President who successfully led the United States through depression and war. He was not as successful in preparing Harry Truman for the presidency.

Roosevelt is elected to a fourth term but dies before the war ends, and Harry S Truman becomes President.

Truman succeeded Roosevelt knowing nothing about the atomic bomb research and several other matters of significance. Truman quickly mastered the intricacies of the government and led the nation through the first postwar years. During these years Allied wartime cooperation gave way to the Cold War between the Communist East led by the Soviet Union and the democratic West led by the United States.

Transition to Peacetime

In 1944 the war effort was proving successful and Congress addressed the issue of demobilization[5] of the armed forces. The Serviceman's Readjustment Act, known as the GI[6] Bill of Rights, passed in 1944 to make the soldiers' transition to civilian life easier. The GI Bill included several provisions: it provided mustering-out pay[7], unemployment pay for up to a year, and low interest loans for homebuilding. There were special advantages offered in the Civil Service, and the bill guaranteed the rehiring by former employers and seniority in those jobs. The GI Bill also made available money for education and apprenticeship training. Using these funds, over a million returning GIs entered college—the greatest single boost to higher education in American history. Within a year of the end of the war, over 9 million servicemen had returned to civilian life.

The nation begins to plan for peace with the passage of the GI Bill.

The country feared the impact demobilization would have on the economy. There was a sharp rise in unemployment in 1946. The

---

[5]*demobilization* Returning to civilian status of those serving in the armed forces at the end of a war.

[6]*GI* GI is the term applied to the soldiers in the American army. It comes from the term General Issue (GI). The uniform and other equipment for the average soldier came under the category of General Issue. Officers often received Special Issue items, which separated them from the common foot soldier.

[7]*mustering-out pay* Pay given to a soldier when he leaves service. Mustering out means returning to civilian life.

Unemployment Act of 1946 set deficit spending as a government policy to combat such unemployment and established the Council of Economic Advisers to help the President determine economic policy. Prices rose dramatically when price controls were ended, and inflation became a concern. Truman acted firmly against labor strikes, seizing the coal mines and threatening to draft into the army any striking workers. The built-up demand for goods such as cars, stoves, refrigerators, and homes stimulated the economy and opened job opportunities for many returning soldiers. Overall the return to a peacetime economy was made successfully presided over by the new President, Harry Truman.

KEY POINT TO REMEMBER

World War II was a very costly world-wide conflict that required great organization and sacrifice to win; the use of atomic bombs brought the end of the war against Japan.

LINKS FROM THE PAST TO THE PRESENT

1. Intolerance and fear of foreigners continued to be seen during World War II and is still seen today.
2. Every war from the French and Indian War to Vietnam has had a high cost in both lives and money.
3. Use and control of nuclear weapons has been a concern since the atomic bomb was used at Hiroshima.

QUESTIONS

Identify each of the following:

Pearl Harbor	Yalta Conference
D-Day	Battle of Midway
Battle of Stalingrad	War Production Board
The Manhattan Project	Battle of the Bulge
Battle of the Coral Sea	GI Bill

True or False:

1. The Soviet Union desired the Allies to open a second front to draw German forces away from the Soviet Union.
2. The Battle of Stalingrad was the turning point of the war in the Soviet Union.
3. On D-Day United States forces invaded North Africa.
4. General Eisenhower signed the document of German unconditional surrender.
5. After Pearl Harbor the Japanese failed to follow up on their advantage and fought only in China.
6. The United States dropped only one atomic bomb on Japan, destroying the city of Hiroshima.
7. The Allied leaders failed to meet during World War II, leading to postwar disagreements.
8. The United States controlled prices and rationed goods during World War II.
9. "Rosy the Riveter" became a symbol of African-Americans in the workplace.

10. The United States placed thousands of Japanese-Americans in relocation centers during the war.

Multiple Choice:

1. Germany and Italy declared war on the United States
   a. which precipitated the attack on Pearl Harbor
   b. after the United States attacked North Africa
   c. after Japan attacked Pearl Harbor
2. Winston Churchill wanted to attack Europe first
   a. through the Balkans
   b. through Italy
   c. through France
3. The Battle of the Bulge was the
   a. most successful attack on Germany by United States forces
   b. the last German counterattack
   c. the final attack on Italy
4. Two great sea battles of the Pacific war were
   a. the battles of St. Lo and the Coral Sea
   b. the battles of Midway and the Coral Sea
   c. the battles of Midway and Guadalcanal
5. The Japanese signed a document of surrender on the battleship *Missouri* with the supreme commander in the Pacific
   a. General Dwight Eisenhower
   b. General George S. Patton
   c. General Douglas MacArthur
6. The United Nations was established by 50 nations meeting in the spring of 1945 at the
   a. San Francisco Conference
   b. Yalta Conference
   c. Potsdam Conference
7. Among the many agencies established to oversee the United States war effort was
   a. the National War Labor Board
   b. the Works Progress Administration
   c. the Civilian Conservation Corps
8. The GI Bill helped make the transition from military service to civilian life easier for millions of service men and women by supplying
   a. unemployment pay and low interest loans for homes
   b. money for education and apprenticeship training and mustering-out pay
   c. both of the above

ANSWERS

True or False: 1. T, 2. T, 3. F, 4. T, 5. F, 6. F, 7. F, 8. T, 9. F, 10. T.
Multiple Choice: 1. c, 2. a, 3. b, 4. b, 5. c, 6. a, 7. a, 8. c.

II.   THE FIRST YEARS OF THE COLD WAR

Background

Differences between the Western allies and Soviets surface after the end of the war.

Throughout the war the Allies had met to plan and reach agreements on the makeup of the postwar world. Like all international agreements, these were all based on certain assumptions about power, security, government, and human behavior. Unfortunately, the assumptions of the Western Allies and the Soviet Union were not always the same, yet the differences were not fully explored under the military pressures of the time. In the immediate postwar period these differences surfaced as attempts were made to put agreements into operation.

In the West, and particularly in the United States, there had always been a great distrust and fear of communism since the establishment of the Soviet Union. The Soviets, following the teachings of Karl Marx, believed capitalism was doomed. During the 1920s and '30s they established international communist organizations to work to speed the downfall of capitalism. While the Soviets claimed to have abandoned such organizations, the fact of their former existence frightened Americans and colored their interpretation of Soviet activities. Likewise the Soviets' assumptions about capitalistic exploitation of workers and the imperialistic ambitions of Western nations colored their views of the Allies' activities.

The Soviet Union and the West have different definitions of democracy and democratic elections.

Also, the Soviets had suffered great losses in the war, and much of European Russia had experienced the presence of occupation armies. The Soviets had suffered invasions from the west under Napoleon and in World War I by the Germans. Their primary goal in Eastern Europe was to prevent another invasion. They wished to be certain the nations on their borders were friendly. Although wartime agreements had called for democratic elections in these countries, the election process and the definition of "democracy" were very different in the Soviet Union and in the West. Since the Russian armies had liberated and occupied the states of Eastern Europe in the last year of the war, the Soviet armies were in a position to enforce their idea on these nations.

Winston Churchill describes an "iron curtain," which separates the Soviet bloc of Eastern Europe from the West.

The result was the split of Europe into two blocks, and the cold war between them lasted forty-five years. In 1946 Winston Churchill in a speech at Fulton, Missouri, said an "iron curtain" had descended on Europe separating East and West. The concept of an Iron Curtain became the symbol of postwar separation between the two blocks.

Peace Conferences and Occupation of Germany

Treaties are finally negotiated.

Peace negotiations were to be conducted by the foreign ministers of England, the United States, and the Soviet Union. At the first conference in September 1945, no agreement could be reached. England insisted on including France in the negotiations. Finally, in 1946 agreement was reached on treaties for Italy, Hungary, Bulgaria, Romania, and Finland, and the treaties were signed in 1947. No agreement was achieved on the future of Japan, Austria, or Germany.

Germany had been split into four separate Occupation Zones administered by England, the United States, France, and the Soviet Union. Berlin, the German capital, was within the Soviet zone, but it was divided into four Occupation Zones also. Determining the future of Germany was one of the great challenges of the Cold War. The Soviets wanted a united Germany that they could control. The West wanted a federal Germany with power shared among the several German states.

Germany and Berlin are divided into Occupation Zones, and the first crisis of the Cold War in Europe centers on Berlin.

Berlin presented the first crisis of the Cold War in Europe when the Soviets rejected a Western proposal for a unified Berlin and the West rejected the Soviet insistence that Soviet Zone money be used throughout Berlin. When the West went ahead and issued its own new currency in Berlin, the Soviets closed all roads and rail lines between the West's three Occupation Zones and their sections of the city of Berlin. The land blockade was successful, but the Allies responded with an airlift that kept western Berlin supplied with food.

A year later the Soviets ended the blockade and treaty negotiations began again but with little success. The western allies then combined their Occupation Zones and established a government, the Federal Republic, usually referred to as West Germany, with its capital in Bonn. The Soviet Union then created the German Democratic Republic from its Occupation Zone with the Soviet Zone of Berlin as its capital. Berlin remained divided.

Another crisis in Berlin in 1961 resulted in the building of the Berlin Wall to further isolate the west from Eastern Europe. This confirmed the iron curtain concept. The Berlin Wall became a sign in concrete of the division of Eastern and Western Europe. When the Berlin Wall fell in November, 1989, it marked the end of the Cold War.

The Berlin Wall is built in 1961.

Containment Policy

The first confrontation of the Cold War involving military deployment occurred in Iran in 1946. Iran occupies a strategic location in the Middle East, bordering the Soviet Union and the Persian Gulf, and Iran has large oil resources. The Soviet army occupied the northern part of the country. Wartime agreements had called for withdrawal of the Soviet forces as well as of the English forces in the South. The Soviets did not withdraw. Iran complained to the United Nations, which considered the matter. An agreement including concessions on the right to oil exploration by the Soviets was signed between Iran and the Soviet Union. The troops were withdrawn. During the next year the United States persuaded the Iranians to cancel the oil exploration agreement. Such actions added to the distrust on both sides.

One of the most significant events illustrating the separation between the Soviet Union and its former allies occurred in Greece. In some analyses, it is noted as the first event of the Cold War. It was precipitated by the economic situation of Western Europe, which was deteriorating rapidly. In 1947, England announced she could no longer support the Greek government the English had been

Crises in Iran and Greece lead to the Truman Doctrine.

subsidizing. A civil war was raging in Greece between the government and Communist forces. President Truman decided Greece and Turkey should be helped. Announcing the Truman Doctrine, he asked Congress for funds to aid Greece and Turkey, replacing the aid from England. The Truman Doctrine declared the United States would aid any free peoples who resisted armed minorities attempting to overthrow an established government. With this support from the United States, the Greek government defeated the Communist guerrillas. Throughout the conflict there was no evidence of Soviet support for the Greek Communists. The acceptance of the Truman Doctrine illustrates the fear of communism, an important factor in Cold War decisions.

The "X" Article presents the concept of containment, which becomes official United States Cold War policy.

Soon after the Truman Doctrine was announced, George F. Kennan, the leading expert on the Soviet Union in the United States Foreign Service and the director of the policy planning staff of the State Department, published in the magazine *Foreign Affairs* an article that has become known as the "X" Article because the author was simply identified as "X." The X Article set forth what became United States policy for the Cold War. The policy is known as "Containment." In the article Kennan said the way to deal with the Soviet Union was to contain it with force—economic or political or military—applied to counter Soviet influence wherever it encroached "upon the interests of a peaceful" world.

For the next forty years the United States applied force in varying degrees to counter Soviet pressure. There were periods of some cooperation and times of dangerous confrontation during these years. To better prepare for the latter, the United States defense establishment was changed and a new Cabinet position, the Department of Defense, was established, replacing the Departments of the Army and Navy. The Central Intelligence Agency (CIA) was established and the National Security Council organized to advise the President and to plan for any international emergency, *i.e.*, to plan how to apply force against any Soviet force.

The CIA became a very controversial body as its role changed from collecting information to carrying out policies. For example, in Guatemala in 1954 the CIA overthrew the elected government, which had confiscated lands of the United Fruit Company, a United States private concern. The United States government claimed a Communist threat existed, but no proof had been uncovered. The new Guatemalan government returned the lands to the United Fruit Company. Later the CIA overthrew the government in Iran and plotted the unsuccessful assassinations of Fidel Castro and several other international leaders. In later Cold War years there were major discussions as to what the role of the CIA should be.

The Marshall Plan and NATO

The Marshall Plan is presented to revitalize the European economy.

Along with the Truman Doctrine, 1947 saw the introduction of the Marshall Plan, designed to aid the recovery of the economies of the Western European nations still suffering from the war. The dollars supplied through the Marshall Plan to the European nations were to be spent in the United States, which helped business at home. The Marshall Plan, named for President Truman's Secretary of State, George C. Marshall, who had served as Chief of Staff of the United States Army during World War II, revitalized the European economy. In doing so it provided one example of a "counter force" to the Soviets since capitalist or socialist prosperity in Western Europe reduced the attractiveness of communism as an economic system. Under George Marshall's original invitation, Eastern European nations could have joined the Marshall Plan, but none did so at the insistence of the Soviet Union. It is now clear that there were weaknesses in the Marshall Plan approach to rebuilding the economy of Western Europe. It did not push European integration, which developed slowly in the following forty years. However, overall it is a fine example both of America's help for others and a response to a Cold War challenge.

Another response following the policy of containment was the establishment of NATO—the North Atlantic Treaty Organization—in 1949 after the ending of the Berlin Blockade. Breaking with the precedent set by George Washington of not signing peacetime alliances, the United States joined NATO. United States troops were to be stationed in Europe, guaranteeing that the United States was prepared to counter a military thrust by the Soviet Union into Western Europe. Concern was expressed that the NATO alliance could involve the United States in war without a declaration of war. That was not to be the case in Europe.

NATO is organized to combat Soviet aggression in Europe.

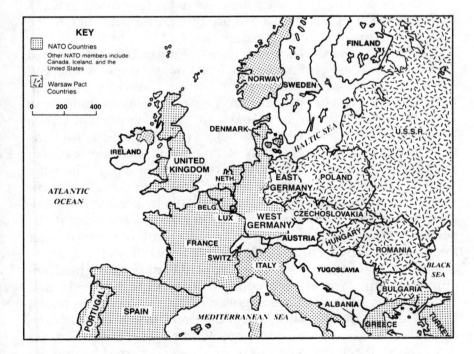

KEY

NATO Countries
Other NATO members include:
Canada. Iceland. and the
United States

Warsaw Pact
Countries

0   200   400

NORWAY SWEDEN FINLAND

DENMARK

IRELAND

UNITED
KINGDOM

NETH.

EAST
GERMANY POLAND

BELG.

LUX

WEST
GERMANY CZECHOSLOVAKIA

FRANCE

AUSTRIA HUNGARY

SWITZ.

ITALY YUGOSLAVIA ROMANIA

PORTUGAL SPAIN

BULGARIA

ALBANIA

GREECE TURKEY

ATLANTIC
OCEAN

BALTIC SEA

U.S.S.R.

BLACK
SEA

MEDITERRANEAN SEA

Nuclear Proliferation

At the end of the war as the only nuclear power, the United States offered to turn its nuclear secrets over to United Nations supervision with no vetos allowed. The Soviets objected to international control and particularly to inspection. The United States' offer was

The Soviet Union rejects international control of nuclear energy and develops its own nuclear weapons.

not accepted. In 1949 the Soviet Union detonated an atomic bomb. The United States and the USSR soon developed hydrogen bombs, and both powers tested their nuclear weapons, polluting the atmosphere. This led to many protests. In 1958 the Russians unilaterally announced no more testing. The United States followed. Tests were resumed in 1961. Finally, a no-testing treaty was accepted by the two powers.

Meanwhile, a non-proliferation[1] treaty was passed by the United Nations General Assembly, but not before England, France, and China had all developed atomic weapons. In spite of the non-proliferation treaty, other nations are believed to have built a limited number of atomic bombs.

The United States and the USSR developed many different nuclear weapons—everything from battlefield artillery shells to ICBMs (Intercontinental Ballistic Missiles). The history of the Cold War unfolded against the background of potential nuclear war. Negotiations over nuclear arms limitations finally led to the first SALT (Strategic Arms Limitation Treaty) in 1972.

Brinkmanship

In 1952 General Eisenhower defeated the Democrat, Adlai Stevenson, for the Presidency. Eisenhower's Secretary of State, John Foster Dulles, added a new dimension, brinkmanship, to containment. Dulles believed in pushing the Communists to the "brink" of nuclear war in order to preserve the free world. It was a frightening concept. Some claim it brought the Soviet Union to the first summit meeting since Potsdam.

Secretary of State Dulles proposes brinkmanship as United States policy, and the Soviets agree to a summit meeting.

In 1955 at Geneva the leaders of France, England, and the United States met the new Soviet leader, Nicolai Bulganin, who emerged as leader of the Soviet Union after the death of Joseph Stalin in 1953. Little was achieved but negotiations began on arms limitations. In 1960 a summit with the new leader of the Soviet Union, Nikita Khrushchev, was set. Two weeks before the meeting the Russians shot down a United States U2 spy plane. Spying was a major part of the Cold War but Khrushchev cancelled the summit when the United States refused to apologize for flying over Soviet airspace.

John Foster Dulles exercised brinkmanship in offering no apologies. It was meant to illustrate American toughness against the perceived Communist threat. It was a policy with potential danger for human survival. However, it was not fully followed.

The Soviets crush the attempt of the Hungarians to establish a non-Communist government.

In 1956 the Hungarian people attempted to overthrow the Communist government of their country. They thought the United States, under the brinkmanship policy, might aid them if the Soviet Union sent in troops. The Soviets did send troops to crush the revolt, but the United States did not intervene. There were limits to brinkmanship and containment when events occurred behind the Iron Curtain.

---

[1]*non-proliferation*   Non-proliferation means not spreading. The non-proliferation treaty was designed to limit the spread of nuclear weapons to other nations.

The United Nations

The policy of brinkmanship was one extreme articulation of Cold War attitudes. Other attitudes manifested during the Cold War are seen in the work of the United Nations. At the end of the war hope had been high that the United Nations would function effectively to maintain the peace. Unfortunately, the divisions between the communist and capitalistic views of the world and the veto power of the Big Five in the Security Council made united action on the international political scene impossible.

However, the United Nations did operate effectively in other spheres, with its agencies helping war refugees, organizing health campaigns, and monitoring labor conditions. It also served as a forum for discussions of opposing views. A major success of the United Nations General Assembly was the agreement reached on a Universal Declaration of Human Rights.

The success of this was largely the result of the work of Eleanor Roosevelt, widow of the President, whom President Truman appointed as a United States delegate to the United Nations. Eleanor Roosevelt had already acquired an international reputation as a spokesperson for the oppressed and downtrodden. As chair of the Committee on Human Rights, Eleanor Roosevelt was able to bring together opposing views and the final declaration contains both individual rights such as free speech, press, and trial, advocated by the capitalistic western nations, and economic rights, such as those to a job, a house, and education, supported by the communist nations.

The Universal Declaration of Human Rights was accepted in 1948. It has served as a guide to new nations as they write constitutions. The United Nations General Secretary, U Thant, called it "the Magna Carta of mankind." The United Nations has no power to enforce the Declaration, but it stands as a hope for humanity and a standard by which to judge the actions of governments. It and the other actions of international cooperation showed there was a place for the United Nations in international affairs. During the late 1980s the United Nations became more effective in settling disputes.

The Middle East

Brinkmanship was not the only international policy of the Eisenhower presidency. In 1955 the USSR and the United States finally agreed on a peace treaty with Austria. In 1956 they cooperated in forcing England, France, and Israel to withdraw from the Suez Canal, which the three powers had seized.

The background to the Suez crisis was involved and reveals the many pressures at work in the Cold War. In 1948 the United Nations had established a Jewish state, Israel, in the Middle East on land claimed by both Arabs and Jews. War broke out and Israel won. A coup in Egypt brought an Arab nationalist, General Nasser, to power. This began the long history of the United States' involvement in the Middle East, caught between the interests of both Arabs and Israelis.

The United States offered to help General Nasser build a dam at Aswan to provide electric power for Egypt's development. When

The establishment of the nation of Israel by the United Nations precipitates war in the Middle East.

Nasser declared neutrality in the Cold War, Secretary of State Dulles withdrew the offer of help in building the dam. General Nasser then seized the English-owned Suez Canal to gain its revenues. Fearing loss of their oil supply, England, France, and Israel attacked. Eisenhower essentially told them to get out and the USSR supported his stand. The three nations withdrew and Egypt gained control of the canal.

It was a rare moment of cooperation between the two great powers. In spite of this cooperation, John Foster Dulles feared the extension of Communist influence into the Middle East. He also believed that no nation could be neutral in the Cold War. It was this viewpoint that led him to withdraw the aid from the building of the Aswan Dam.

Proclaiming the Eisenhower Doctrine, the President sends troops to Lebanon.

Following Secretary of State Dulles' views of brinkmanship in the Cold War, in a Congressional address in 1957, President Eisenhower asked for permission of Congress to use United States armed forces to aid any nation that asked for United States support against aggression by any country under the control of international Communism. This became known as the Eisenhower Doctrine. Soon after, the President of Lebanon sent a request to the President to send United States troops to Lebanon to help crush a rebellion. Troops were sent and the Lebanese rebellion crushed. However, it precipitated a coup d'etat in nearby Iraq, in which the royal family was overthrown and the Baathist Party came to power. Eventually Saddam Hussein emerged as leader of the party and ruler of Iraq. Cold War action by President Eisenhower led to events that came to dominate the Middle East in 1990.

The CIA supports the Shah of Iran.

Before the Eisenhower Doctrine, the CIA had been instrumental in overthrowing a popular government in Iran and establishing the Shah on the throne. Behind these Cold War moves were the West's need to have access to the oil of the Middle East and fear of Communist expansion into the area. To United States policy makers it seemed an appropriate application of containment and a logical reaction to the Cold War challenges. It provides the background for the United States' involvement in the Persian Gulf crisis of 1990 and the Iran-Iraq war in the 1980s. The Cold War reached into all parts of the globe.

The Korean War

How to restore occupied Korea as an independent, united nation was another Cold War challenge. United States forces occupied the south and Soviet forces the north as a result of agreements made at Yalta. With no progress on the issue as a result of the Cold War differences, the United States established the Republic of Korea, usually referred to as South Korea, with Syngman Rhee as President. The Soviets countered, establishing a Communist Peoples Republic, referred to as North Korea. The United Nations tried to resolve the issue but failed.

Soviet-supported North Korea invades South Korea, and the United Nations votes to assist South Korea.

In a speech, Dean Acheson, Secretary of State under Truman, mentioned that Korea was not essential to the defense of Asia from the Communists. Reading this as a statement of no interest in Korea, on June 25, 1950, the North Koreans turned the Cold War hot by invading South Korea.

The United Nations Security Council adopted a resolution asking the United Nations members to "furnish such assistance to the Republic of Korea as may be necessary to repel the armed attack." The Russians were boycotting the Security Council because of its refusal to accept the Communist government of China as the holder of the Security Council seat assigned to China, so they were unable to veto the resolution. President Truman responded and ordered United States troops into action without a declaration of war by Congress—a precedent followed several times throughout the Cold War. The Korean War, under United Nations auspices, had begun. Over 30,000 Americans lost their lives in this undeclared war, which successfully halted the military aggression of a Communist nation. Unlike the League of Nations, the United Nations had stood up to aggression.

The United Nations forces were put under Command of General Douglas MacArthur. The North Koreans swept through the south, occupying almost four-fifths of the country and confining the United Nations troops to the region around the southern port of Pusan. The United Nations mounted an offensive, landed forces at Inchon behind the North Korean battle line, and swept through the north almost to the Yalu River, the border between Manchuria, a province of the People's Republic of China and Korea.

The United Nations forces, commanded by General Douglas MacArthur, approach the Chinese border.

The Chinese, concerned over the motives of the United Nations and fearing the presence of United States forces on its borders, entered the war in October 1950. General Douglas MacArthur threatened China, an ally of the USSR with atomic attack and was removed from his command by President Truman. It was not United States government policy to use atomic weapons. Truman and the United States were not ready to turn the Korean War into another World War by attacking an ally of the USSR. The Chinese Communists forced the United Nations' troops to retreat until a line was finally stabilized along the 38th parallel, the old dividing line between North and South Korea.

The Chinese Communists join the war in support of North Korea.

The war became a stalemate. It was an issue in the Presidential election of 1952, when General Eisenhower promised to "go to Korea" if elected. He was elected and went. Finally, an armistice was negotiated, but United States forces remained in Korea. While the Republic of Korea has prospered economically since the armistice, the nation is still not united and tensions exist. The Korean War confirmed for United States policy makers the aggressive intentions of Communist nations and the value of the containment policy and the use of counter force to block Communist expansion.

The Cold War in Japan

World War II began in Asia with the Japanese attack on China. With the Allied victory, the United States occupied Japan. General Douglas MacArthur headed the occupation forces. Following the Yalta Agreement, the Russians occupied North Korea and half of

The United States signs a separate treaty with Japan.

Japan's Sakhalin Island. The island of Taiwan, called Formosa by the Japanese occupiers, was returned to China. Cold War disagreements between the United States and the USSR delayed a peace treaty with Japan until 1951, when the United States signed a separate treaty establishing Japan as a non-nuclear, non-military, democratic monarchy and ending the occupation. The United States and Japan signed a defense treaty that allowed United States troops to remain in Japan, an agreement still in effect. But peace did not come to China.

The People's Republic of China

Nationalists and Communists fight a civil war for control of China, and Mao Zedong's Communist forces win.

In China throughout the 1920s and '30s there had been conflict between the Nationalist government led by General Jiang Jieshi (Chiang Kai-shek) and Communist forces led by Mao Zedong (Mao Tse Tung). Mao had escaped defeat by leading his forces from the coastal cities on a "long march" inland, where his urban soldiers were transformed into a peasant army. A wartime truce between the two groups proved very shaky but allowed the Nationalists and Communists to fight the Japanese. With the end of World War II, the conflict between the two Chinese factions turned violent. The United States made several attempts at mediation but stopped the efforts in 1947. Both Jiang Jieshi's Nationalists and Mao Zedong's Communists share the blame for atrocities that occurred in the conflict and for the failure of mediation. The United States sent supplies to the Nationalists; the USSR sent supplies to the Communists.

Finally, in December, 1949, Mao Zedong triumphed and Jiang Jieshi and his army fled to the island of Taiwan, where a Nationalist government was established. Mao Zedong ruled the People's Republic on the Asian mainland with its capital in Beijing. There were two Chinese governments each supported by one of the Cold War antagonists.

The China Lobby in the United States claims the Democrats under Truman "lost" China.

There were outcries in the United States that China had been lost. The Republican Conservatives claimed that Mao's victory was a result of the inept foreign policy of the Democrats under Truman. A strong China lobby in Congress supported Jiang Jieshi for years. There had always been a strong sentimental attraction for China in the United States, but this was not transferred to Mao and his Communist forces. After fleeing to Taiwan, Jiang Jieshi continued to control China's permanent United Nations Security Council seat over the protests of the Soviet Union. The Soviets boycotted the Security Council from January to August, 1950 in protest and thus were not present to veto the United Nations resolution calling for force to combat the invasion of South Korea.

Foreign Aid

Former colonies in Asia gain independence.

Monumental changes took place elsewhere in Asia in the early years of the Cold War. In 1947 the English withdrew from India, establishing the new independent nations of India and Pakistan, and in 1948 England withdrew from Burma and Ceylon, making them independent. The Dutch granted independence to the

United States of Indonesia in 1949. The United States met its commitment to the Philippines, and they became independent in 1946. The old world of imperialistic powers was changing. Similar changes were to come about in Africa in the 1960s.

As the Cold War continued, one issue for the United States foreign policy makers was how to gain the support of these newly independent nations or to keep them from joining the Communist side. This created a polarized view of the world made famous by Secretary of State John Foster Dulles' view that if you are not with us, you are against us.

One solution the United States found to the problem was the development of foreign aid as a tool to win support of newly independent nations. It began with President Truman and his "Point Four" Program in 1949. Under the "Point Four" program, Truman offered economic aid to undeveloped areas around the world. By 1960 the United States had spent almost $73 billion in foreign economic and military aid. Some Americans believed it was money well spent; others believed it would have been better spent taking care of domestic concerns. War, cold or hot, was costly and provided challenges and stimulation to those who fought.

Truman introduces the concept of foreign aid with his "Point Four" program.

Summary

A breadth and clarity of view was lost by these people who saw the world in black and white, we and they, terms only. They often failed to understand or appreciate the complexity of issues and forces driving nations and people. It became easy to see Communists behind every action with which Americans disagreed. It was easy to use economic aid to bribe nations to support American views. Later, foreign aid became more heavily military aid. The "with us or against us" approach to foreign policy led the United States to support with economic and military aid many leaders who were anti-Communist but not democratic and did not support American values.

KEY POINT TO REMEMBER

The World War II allies soon fell into disagreement over the structure of the postwar world and the resulting conflicts and tensions between the West, or democracies, and the East, or Communist states, was called the Cold War.

LINKS FROM THE PAST TO THE PRESENT

1. The black and white, we versus they, oversimplified view of complex international issues has been a characteristic of American foreign policy.
2. The division of Korea and tensions in that area continue today.
3. Arab-Israeli tensions and disagreements still prevent the establishment of peace in the Middle East.
4. Issues relating to the unification of Germany and Berlin were an important part of the Cold War and are a concern still since Germany is now the single strongest economic power in Europe.
5. The origins of the Cold War and the split of Europe into East and West are important for understanding Europe today in spite of the end of the Cold War.

QUESTIONS

Identify each of the following:
Berlin Wall   "X" Article
Truman Doctrine   United Nations Universal Declaration
The Iron Curtain   of Human Rights
Brinkmanship

True or False:
1. Peace treaties were signed with Japan, Austria, and Germany in 1947.
2. The Western Allies combined their occupation zones in Germany to create the German Democratic Republic.
3. George F. Kennan, an expert on the Soviet Union, wrote the "X" Article.
4. The Containment policy called for counterforce to meet any force from the Soviet Union.
5. The Marshall Plan was designed to restore the military strength of Western Europe.
6. NATO was the first permanent peace time alliance entered by the United States since the presidency of George Washington.
7. John Foster Dulles believed that brinkmanship was a dangerous policy and should be abandoned.
8. Eleanor Roosevelt chaired the United Nations Committee that wrote the Universal Declaration of Human Rights.
9. In the Suez crisis of 1956 the United States and the USSR cooperated to force the withdrawal of English, French, and Israeli forces from the Suez Canal.
10. The Nationalist government of China led by Jiang Jieshi was defeated by the Communists and forced to flee to Taiwan.
11. In the Korean War, at first the United Nations forces fought under the command of General Douglas MacArthur.
12. The Korean War ended in a victory for North Korea.
13. Truman's Point Four Program offered economic aid to undeveloped countries.
14. The Cold War led people to believe Communists were behind every action with which they disagreed.

Multiple Choice:
1. Among the reasons for the start of the Cold War were
   a. basic ideological differences over capitalism and its future
   b. the fact the Soviets had suffered so little in World War II
   c. Russian desire for revenge on Napoleon
2. The changes made in the United States defense establishment to better conduct the Cold War included
   a. the CIA and the National Security Council
   b. separate Cabinet level posts for the army and navy departments
   c. both of the above

3. Nuclear proliferation in the postwar period included
   a. the United States giving atomic secrets to all United Nations members
   b. the development of hydrogen bombs by NATO
   c. the development of atomic and hydrogen bombs by the USSR
4. The United Nations could respond to the invasion of South Korea with military action and without a Security Council veto because
   a. President Truman was ready to send troops
   b. the USSR was boycotting the Security Council
   c. the USSR and the United States agreed it should be done

ANSWERS

True or False: 1. F, 2. F, 3. T, 4. T, 5. F, 6. T, 7. F, 8. T, 9. T, 10. T, 11. T, 12. F, 13. T, 14. T.
Multiple Choice: 1. a, 2. a, 3. c, 4. b.

III. CHANGES IN AMERICAN SOCIETY: 1945–1960

Domestic Impact of the Cold War

The American people first reacted to the international divisions of the Cold War by looking for possible Communist infiltration into government. The Smith Act of 1940, enacted against the Nazi threat, had made it illegal to advocate the overthrow of the United States government or to belong to any organization that did. President Truman used the act to jail leaders of the Communist party in the United States. He established a Loyalty Review Board in 1947 to review the loyalty of government employees. The House UnAmerican Activities Committee, the Dies Committee, mentioned earlier, also turned its investigations towards possible Communist infiltration into government. The Committee gained extensive publicity for its efforts, which included accusing Truman of being "soft on Communism."

Concern grows over possible Communist connections of government employees.

In 1948, Whittaker Chambers, an editor of *Time* magazine and a former Communist spy, accused Alger Hiss, the President of the Carnegie Endowment for International Peace, of being a Communist agent. The implications for government security were great. Alger Hiss had been a member of the State Department and a close advisor to President Roosevelt. Hiss had been with Roosevelt at the Yalta Conference, which the Republicans were calling a "sellout" of Europe to the Communists. Alger Hiss denied the charges. The case received much publicity and scared many people. They thought that if Chambers was correct, the entire planning for peace by the United States and the USSR could have been controlled by Communists. Since the legal statute of limitations had run out and Hiss could not be convicted on spying charges, charges of perjury[1]

---

[1]*perjury* The deliberate and willful giving of false or misleading information when under oath in a criminal proceeding whether in court or in an affidavit.

were brought against him for his conduct in the preliminary hearings. He was tried on the perjury count and was found guilty. Hiss claimed his innocence until his death. In 1950 Julius and Ethel Rosenberg were found guilty of giving atomic secrets to the Soviets. They were executed for treason in 1953.

Congress responded to the Cold War with the McCarran Internal Security Act of 1950, which required any Communist front[2] organization to register with the government and prevented the organization's members from working in defense companies or from traveling. It was a restriction on individual liberty and reflects the national mood of fear and uncertainty similar to that during the Palmer Raids after World War I.

McCarthyism

Senator Joseph McCarthy claims he has evidence of Communist infiltration into the State Department and army.

In 1950 Republican Senator Joseph McCarthy from Wisconsin used the national mood to project himself onto the national political stage as a major player. In a speech he claimed he had the names of 205 Communists in the State Department. He never produced the names and kept changing the numbers, but he captured national attention. McCarthy and his accusations became a campaign issue. Eisenhower, after his election, did nothing to stop McCarthy, who expanded his accusations to include scholars and the United States Army. His accusations against the Army led to a Senate hearing. It was televised nationally—the first Senate hearing to get such publicity.

McCarthy's tactics at the hearing disgusted many viewers, who responded favorably to the Army's Chief legal counsel, lawyer Joseph Welch. The hearings backfired. No clear proof of misdeeds was produced, so McCarthy's case was destroyed. In 1954 the Senate censored McCarthy for discrediting the Senate. The Senate never condemned McCarthy for the methods he used, which violated the Bill of Rights. McCarthy's activities and their acceptance for four years by the people and the government again illustrate the challenges of the Cold War and the impact they had domestically. It also illustrates that tendency towards intolerance so often seen in American history.

McCarthy and his tactics are discredited.

Joseph McCarthy gave a new word, McCarthyism[3], to the language. Fortunately for the nation, Senator McCarthy lost all credibility after his censure. He died in 1957. However, his actions frightened many government civil servants. some of whom quit government service, and silenced others who remained. McCarthyism made many young scholars decide not to enter government service for fear of being falsely accused, and it reduced the effectiveness of the Foreign Service for a number of years. It

[2]*Communist front*   A front organization is an organization which is designed to hide the activities of its members. Therefore, a Communist front organization is one in which the organization is not stating it is Communist but is working for Communist causes.

[3]*McCarthyism*   "Smearing" people with unsupported accusations, usually of disloyalty.

was an unfortunate period, but in many ways resembles the breakdown of ethics that followed both the Civil War and World War I.

Civil Rights

Segregation policies worked against the United States' position in the Cold War as a champion of free peoples. Foreign diplomats from newly independent Asian and later African nations were subjected to situations that proved embarrassing to the United States. The time had finally come for federal action to change segregation and to guarantee the civil rights of all Americans. It took time and although racist attitudes and discrimination remain in the nation, great changes were made in the 1950s and 1960s

Foreign diplomats encounter segregation in the United States.

During World War II segregation prevailed in military units, but the exposure to leadership positions and the experience of visiting other countries created a cadre of future black civil rights leaders. Also in wartime black workers worked alongside white workers in war industries as members of those CIO industrial unions recognized in the 1930s, and some African-Americans moved into the middle class. These people joined leaders like A. Philip Randolph of the Pullman Porters Union who had been working for civil rights for years.

The cause of civil rights was aided by the changing urban voting pattern created by the migration of African-Americans to urban areas. Their votes were important and made members of the government more responsive to civil rights needs.

The National Association for the Advancement of Colored People (NAACP) had been working through the courts for years to improve the situation for African-Americans. The Supreme Court declared in 1944 that Democratic party primaries, which permitted only whites to vote, were unconstitutional, and in 1946 the Court declared segregation on interstate buses unconstitutional.

The Supreme Court declares all-white Democratic Party primaries unconstitutional in a case brought by the NAACP.

President Truman, a student of American history, had a personal commitment to civil rights. In 1946 Truman appointed a Committee on Civil Rights whose report, *To Secure These Rights*, set the goals of the civil rights movement of the next 30 years. The Committee recommended a civil rights division in the Department of Justice, voting rights legislation, and the end to segregation. In 1948 Truman moved to end racial discrimination in government and ordered the start of desegregation of the military, which Eisenhower completed.

The Supreme Court decision in *Brown v. Board of Education* in 1954 is often considered the start of the postwar Civil Rights Movement, but it had already begun. The case, however, is very important. In *Brown v. Board of Education* the Supreme Court declared "separate but equal," the formula the Court first declared in the *Plessy v. Ferguson* case in 1896, unconstitutional in schools. The Court accepted the arguments of psychological damage done by segregation and ordered its end in schools. In a follow-up decision in 1955 the Court ordered desegregation of educational facilities with "all deliberate speed."

The Brown v. Board of Education decision reverses the "separate but equal" doctrine of Plessy v. Ferguson.

The Little Rock Nine, supported by federal troops, attend a formerly all-white high school in Little Rock, Arkansas, but much of the South resists the integration of schools.

Since education is a local concern in America and controlled by local governments and school boards, each community with segregated schools had to determine how to integrate them. The struggle was fought throughout the South and later in northern cities, where housing patterns created all or nearly all African-American urban schools.

The struggle for integration continues. Several school districts are still run by judges and court orders rather than by elected school boards. School integration has not come easily. An early example of a failed attempt to integrate schools in the South is Little Rock, Arkansas.

Arkansas, on the edge of the South, does not have as large an African-American population or as strong a tradition of segregation as states further south, but when the city school board selected nine outstanding young African-Americans to enter the white high school, rioting occurred. At first Governor Orville Faubus ordered in the Arkansas National Guard to stop the students' entry. When one teenage African-American girl alone tried to enter the school, a mob was ready to lynch her, but a white woman got her away safely.

President Eisenhower was slow to act. His personal stance on civil rights and his style of Presidential leadership opposed strong federal intervention. Finally, however, Eisenhower sent in federal troops; the Little Rock Nine completed the year with the troops protecting them. The public schools, however, were closed for the next two years rather than continue with integration.

Public schools were closed in Virginia and other parts of the South in order to avoid integration. Eventually they were opened as integrated institutions. Many private, often church-sponsored, white schools opened in the South. School desegregation was finally accepted by most Americans, but there are still problem areas in both the South and in northern cities.

Civil Disobedience

In Montgomery, Alabama, in December, 1955 the Civil Rights Movement took a new direction away from the courts and into direct action. Rosa Parks, a tired seamstress who had worked for the NAACP, refused to give up her seat to a white man on the city's segregated private bus line. Local African-American leaders had been waiting for an opportunity to make a case against segregated buses. When Rosa Parks was arrested, they began court proceedings, and at the same time a bus boycott was organized by African-Americans in Montgomery. African-Americans, who far outnumbered whites as riders, stayed off the buses for almost a year. A young minister, Martin Luther King, Jr., emerged as the spokesperson for the boycott and went on to become a leader and hero of the Civil Rights Movement until his assassination in 1968. The United States Supreme Court in 1956 declared segregation on local buses unconstitutional under the Bill of Rights and Amendment XIV. The Montgomery bus boycott was ended and the buses integrated.

In the Montgomery boycott the idea of civil disobedience was first used by the Civil Rights Movement. Articulated by Martin

Luther King, Jr. and the other African-Americans ministers who led the boycott in Montgomery, civil disobedience combined the teachings of Jesus and other religious leaders, the teachings and practices of the American Transcendentalist thinker Henry David Thoreau, the practices of Gandhi's civil disobedience movement (which led to India's independence from England), and the experiences of African-Americans.

Civil disobedience was used to draw attention to legal injustices by breaking the law and going to jail. No violence was used against the forces of the law. Those breaking the law appealed to a higher moral and ethical code than that supported by the local law. By making this appeal, attention was drawn to injustices. It was hoped that correction of these injustices would follow.

Civil disobedience required the support of the people who were oppressed. It required leaders to organize the protests, and the charismatic Martin Luther King Jr. and other religious leaders founded the Southern Christian Leadership Conference (SCLC) to provide this leadership. Another organization, the Student Non-Violent Coordinating Committee (SNCC) was organized in 1960. SNCC provided more grass-roots leadership for the movement, not relying on nationally known figures. It was people, young and old, African-American and later their white supporters, and not the leaders who made civil disobedience work.

In 1960 four African-American students from North Carolina Agricultural and Technical College sat down at a white lunch counter in Greensborough, North Carolina, and refused to leave until served. The sit-in technique of civil disobedience was born. The sit-in technique was applied to bring about desegregation of buses, lunch counters, and other facilities in the South.

Martin Luther King, Jr. introduces civil disobedience into the struggle for integration in the Montgomery Bus Boycott.

The sit-in technique is used to integrate lunch counters.

Presidential Elections: 1948–1956

In 1946 in the first postwar election, the Republicans made large gains and took control of Congress for the first time since the start of the Depression. It appeared the nation was ready to toss out the Democrats and perhaps return to a period similar to that of the Harding post-World War I years. In 1948 Southern Democrats, concerned over maintaining segregation and upset by the Democratic Party's platform plank on civil rights, formed their own party, the States' Rights Democratic Party (Dixiecrats). The Dixiecrats ran Senator Strom Thurmond of South Carolina for President. However, in spite of this third party and the nation's concerns over postwar inflation and other domestic issues, in 1948 Harry Truman won a term of his own as President by narrowly defeating Republican Thomas Dewey of New York.

In 1952, Senator Robert Taft of Ohio, son of President William Howard Taft was the leading Republican contender for the nomination. After some uncertainties it became clear that General Dwight Eisenhower, World War II leader of Allied forces in Europe, postwar head of NATO, and president of Columbia University, would run as a Republican if nominated. He received the Republican nomination and Richard M. Nixon, a young Congressman from

In a three-way race Truman narrowly wins the presidency in 1948.

General Eisenhower defeats the Democratic candidate, Adlai Stevenson, in 1952 and 1956.

California who had made a reputation as both a conservative and a strong anti-Communist, was named his Vice-Presidential candidate. At the start of the campaign a question was raised over Nixon's campaign financing in California. In a memorable television speech Nixon appealed to the people using his dog Checkers as a prop and won Eisenhower's strong endorsement.

The Democrat candidate, the scholarly, clever, and witty Governor Adlai Stevenson of Illinois, was overwhelmingly defeated by the popular "Ike." Eisenhower's campaign slogan, "I like Ike," his aura as a military hero while the Cold War raged, and his promoise, if elected, to "go to Korea" and speed an end to the fighting made him unbeatable. He and Nixon again defeated Stevenson in 1956.

Kennedy-Nixon Election

John F. Kennedy, gaining national recognition in televised debates with his Republican opponent, Richard Nixon, wins the 1960 election.

The 1960 election proved to be extremely close. It illustrates the importance of voting, since a shift of one vote in a number of wards in large states such as Illinois could have changed the result. The Republicans had nominated Richard Nixon; the Democrats nominated John F. Kennedy. Kennedy chose as his Vice-President Lyndon B. Johnson of Texas, the Senate Majority Leader, who had been his leading opponent for the nomination. Kennedy was young, good looking, a naval hero of World War II, a Senator, and the son of a millionaire who had supported Franklin Roosevelt and had served as ambassador to Great Britain during the War. Kennedy was an Irish Catholic from Boston—the only Catholic except Al Smith in 1928 to win a Presidential nomination.

The campaign is remembered for the first televised debates between Presidential candidates. In the first debate, John F. Kennedy's looks and charisma overshadowed Nixon. The debate gave John F. Kennedy the national recognition he needed. Kennedy attacked the military preparedness of the United States and appealed to Cold War fears. He spoke of a "new frontier" for America. Although the campaign lacked real substance, the young Kennedy and his attractive wife, "Jackie," inspired enough Americans for him to win a narrow victory and bring the Democrats back to the White House.

Domestic Legislation in Response to the Cold War

The Atomic Energy Act and the National Defense Education Act are passed in response to Cold War tensions.

Several pieces of important domestic legislation came as responses to Cold War events. In 1946 when the United Nations failed to agree on international control of atomic energy, the Atomic Energy Commission was established to control domestic nuclear developments. The legislation gave the President sole power over the use of the atomic bomb. In 1954 the Atomic Energy Act authorized the building of private nuclear power plants under supervision of the Commission. The military reorganization and the McCarren Act mentioned earlier were passed in response to the Cold War.

In 1957 the Soviet Union launched into space the first satellite, known as Sputnik, the Russian word for satellite. After the launch of Sputnik, there was fear the American educational system was not preparing students for the challenges of the Cold War. There was fear American engineering and science were inadequate. In reaction, Congress passed the National Defense Education Act to improve American education in foreign languages, mathematics, and science.

The Taft-Hartley Act and the Fair Deal

In 1947 the Republican Congress passed the Taft-Hartley Labor Act over President Truman's veto. The Taft-Hartley Act put certain limits on unions which had benefited greatly from the New Deal legislation. The Act made illegal a closed shop[4] and required, under specified conditions, an 80-day "cooling-off" period[5] before a union could call a strike. Truman was a supporter of the New Deal and wanted to continue similar legislation to create a "fair deal" for every American. Congress failed to act on his request, but it did not abandon any major New Deal concepts except those repealed by the Taft-Hartley Act. Truman did achieve passage of a Government Reorganization Act, which he used to make government operations more efficient.

The Taft-Hartley Labor Act puts some limits on the power of labor unions.

Dynamic Conservatism of Eisenhower

President Eisenhower, although a Republican, also supported the New Deal legislation. He claimed he was a conservative in economics, but a liberal in human affairs. His approach to government has been dubbed "dynamic conservatism." There was little social legislation passed, but Congress did pass a Civil Rights Act in 1957, which established a Civil Rights Divison in the Department of Justice and a permanent Civil Rights Commission. These two agencies gave the federal government a way to investigate infringements of civil rights and to enforce adherence to them. During Eisenhower's presidency social security coverage was extended to 10 million more people.

Eisenhower's "dynamic conservatism" supports civil rights and a new plan for highway construction.

President Eisenhower deserves the title "Transportation President" for two measures. The first, the building of the St. Lawrence Seaway, opened the Great Lakes to ocean-going ships through a series of canals and the development of the St. Lawrence River. The second, the Federal Aid Highway Act, called for a massive interstate highway system, with the federal government paying 90 percent of the cost. The act was a great boon to the automobile industry but helped make the United States dependent on autos and oil. It hurt the railroads. The Federal Aid Highway Act had a major impact on American industry and on the infrastructure[6] of the nation.

---

[4]*closed shop*   A plant or manufacturing shop in which newly hired workers are forced to join a union as a condition of employment.

[5]*cooling-off period*   A set period of time in which an action may not take place while a resolution to the situation is pursued by the parties involved.

[6]*infrastructure*   Those parts of the economy such as roads and highways upon which other industries depend. These are normally paid for by the government.

New Industries and Affluence

A postwar baby boom increases the population and creates a great demand for products.

Between the end of World War II and the election of John F. Kennedy, the United States economy grew rapidly. Military spending in response to the Cold War stimulated old industries, and military research created new ones, especially in electronics, chemicals, and aviation. A postwar baby boom helped increase the population by almost 30 percent and created great demands for products. The automobile industry produced 8 million cars in the mid-1950s, up from 3 million only five years before. Television broadcasting and manufacturing became major new industries. Business organization and consumption habits changed. Industry turned to conglomerates[7] as a new organizational form. Teenagers became an important consumer group, and advertisers learned to use television to appeal to them. In spite of several mild recessions in the Eisenhower years, the economy essentially boomed. The low inflation rate of roughly 2 percent and the steady growth in the gross national product (GNP)[8] of over 3 percent, made it a time of affluence for many.

The United States becomes the "affluent society."

In 1958 John Kenneth Galbraith, one of the leading economists of the time, wrote a book, *The Affluent Society*, describing this postwar phenomenon of affluence. He claimed that there was overexpenditure on private consumption and underexpenditure on the public sector, *i.e.*, schools, state hospitals, transportation. He believed the public sector was under-funded because Americans pursued the good life for themselves in the suburbs.

This was seen in the boom in personal house building. What had been open country around cities became endless acres of similar suburban housing. Ranches, Garrisons, and Capes as well as shopping centers and acres of asphalt for parking and roads dominated the landscape outside cities while little money was spent on improving public services or transportation in the cities. Work for many individuals was still in the city centers and commuting, usually by car and often for an hour or more, became a way of life for many individuals. Many women, "moms" in the terminology of the day, ran the home and chauffered children to activities. After the progress in job opportunities for women during the war, a reaction set in, and the ideal woman portrayed in many articles and ads was the good mother or "mom."

The growth of population in Florida, California, and the Southwest (called the Sun Belt) made those areas important both economically and politically.

The United States emerged as the great consumer society using much greater amounts of resources and goods per capita than any

---

[7]*conglomerate*   A form of business organization in which one company owns many companies involved in a diversity of activities. The concept is that if you own companies doing different things, a recession will not hurt the larger corporation because some company will still be prospering.

[8]*gross national product (GNP)*   The total production of goods and services in a nation. It has become the major measurement of the economic growth of a country.

other nation. Consumer credit grew and savings dropped in the 1950s, all of which added stimulation to the growth of the affluent society.

Poverty in Postwar America

In the postwar period, as the population grew, so did the numbers in the middle class, giving the impression that prosperity was universal. In actuality there were many who did not share in the affluent society. As a group, the Native Americans benefited less from postwar prosperity than any other group in American society. Under Eisenhower an attempt was made to close the Indian reservations and integrate those living there into the mainstream of American rural and urban life. It was unsuccessful and more Native Americans entered the ranks of the poverty stricken. The economic problems were compounded by problems with alcoholism. Many white Americans held stereotypes of the alcoholic, non-working, poverty-stricken Native American, a stereotype that allowed the white American to ignore the situation or blame the Native Americans themselves for their condition. After the success of the Civil Rights Movement, a few Native American leaders began to organize their people to create an awareness of their problems and to gain a better place for them in American life. For many reasons progress has been very slow.

Native Americans do not share in the prosperity.

Urban and Rural Poverty

Few people living in the inner city slum areas benefited from the affluent society. In fact, since the postwar era was one of slow but steady inflation of approximately 2 percent per year and since the wealth of a few in the cities grew rapidly, the gap between the urban poor and the rich widened. The general affluence and the Civil Rights Movement raised the expectations for those African-Americans in the cities, but the expectations were not realized. Conditions actually worsened. Under President Lyndon Johnson these expectations were addressed in the War on Poverty (see page 00) but with limited success due to the escalation of the war in Vietnam.

The gap between urban poor and the rich widens.

Not only did the African-Americans in the inner cities not enjoy the affluent society, neither did many of the Mexican Americans in the population. In the postwar era the Mexican American population in the Southwest and in California began to increase, and many of them found homes in the inner cities. Most of those who were recent immigrants from Mexico had left impoverished conditions to find a better life in the United States. Instead they met with racist attitudes and lived in urban poverty. Some Mexican Americans found work as itinerant farm laborers. While they had jobs and food, the conditions were as bad as those in the cities.

Rural poverty was widespread in the postwar period. Because it was not as concentrated, rural poverty was not as obvious. Yet in absolute numbers there were more poor in the country than in the cities. Farm lands in the postwar period were being consolidated throughout the nation to make large, efficient, business-like operations. They produced surpluses that created a problem for the

Rural poverty persists throughout the nation.

government and for those farmers who remained on small farms. The small farms were comparatively inefficient, and farmers' incomes were low. The small farm economy was in depression as it has been so often in American history.

Areas of rural poverty could be found throughout the nation, particularly in the tenant farms of the South and the few remaining small farms of the Midwest and West, in New England, and in the Appalachian Mountains of the South. Later Appalachia became a synonym for rural poverty in America. In these same regions there were poor in small towns. Often in these towns neighbors helped neighbors and on the farms there was often some food, but living was bleak and opportunities for change almost non-existent without some government assistance. It was these conditions of poverty that President Johnson was to address in the 1960s.

Home and Family Patterns

The middle class grows dramatically.

As after every war, the immediate post World War II years saw changes in American life styles. Several of these changes have been mentioned, including the role of television in keeping families at home for entertainment and the growth of the suburbs. The number of families classified in government statistics as middle class grew from roughly 5.5 million to over 12 million during the Truman and Eisenhower presidencies. The Eisenhower years have been considered years of conformity, in part because of those attitudes summarized in the word "McCarthyism."

In those years the road to economic success was the business road and the "man in the grey flannel suit" became the symbol of success of the age. Sloan Wilson in his novel of that title described the conformity needed in the business world.

Critics suggest everything is not fine in America.

There were critics of the postwar society. John Keat's *The Crack in the Picture Window* criticized the suburban mass-produced communities where all houses were the same, stores sold the same goods, and members of the middle class lived lives of smugness, indifferent to or unaware of how homogeneous their suburban life was. Another type of critic was Dr. Albert Kinsey, founder of the Kinsey Institute for the Study of Behavior of American Sexuality. In 1948 Dr. Kinsey published his first study, *Sexual Behavior of the American Male*. Using the statistical methods of sociology, he interviewed American males about their sexual habits. Almost all reported some experimentation or practices—pre-marital or extra-marital affairs, homosexual encounters, masturbation—that went against the traditional moral and ethical teachings of the society. A later publication described similar but not as widespread behavior among American females. Kinsey's work suggested that the conformity of the 1950s did not mean personal conformity to the established teachings of sexual morality.

Although Kinsey's research methods have been criticized, his reports were widely read and discussed. In spite of Kinsey's reports, or perhaps in reaction to them, the values of family and home were given publicity, and society's expectations reflected traditional values. The nuclear family of parents and two or three children, a home in the suburbs, a job for father in the city, and a wife at home became the "American dream" in this period. A revolution against these traditional attitudes burst forth in the 1960s.

The American Youth Culture

The postwar baby boom affected not only the economy but also the culture. One of the most popular books of the period was Dr. Benjamin Spock's *Baby and Child Care*, published in 1946. A whole generation was raised according to Dr. Spock's principle that the child was to be the center of a mother's life. Fathers were essentially ignored in Dr. Spock's book which called on the mother to meet the child's needs. Prospective parents studied Dr. Spock's works and referred to it often as their children grew. Whether it was Dr. Spock's teachings or a combination of factors including the sheer numbers of children, by the 1950s a youth culture dominated America, and many aspects of it are still present. Youth presented a huge market, and fads swept the nation as they still do. Everything from coonskin caps made popular by a TV program on Davy Crockett to hoola hoops and frisbees had to be had by young people if they were to be an accepted member of their 1950s group. Expenditures by the young as well as money spent by their parents on them became an important part of the American economy.

The baby boomers begin to have an impact on American life.

Elvis Presley and American Music

Perhaps the greatest manifestation of the impact of youth on American culture was in music. With the introduction of inexpensive phonographs and the 45 rpm record, the recording industry boomed. Rock 'n' roll with its roots in black rhythm and blues swept the country. Its new sound and approach is best personified by Elvis Presley, who sang and gyrated through many movies in the 1950s and became the first rock 'n' roll superstar. His records sold in huge numbers. Although he did not originate rock 'n' roll, Elvis Presley made it the new music of America. Youth responded and rock 'n' roll became the music of the young.

Elvis Presley popularizes rock 'n' roll, and American popular music is transformed.

Dancing to rock 'n' roll required an entirely new approach with loose joints and individual actions. It was a perfect style for a generation raised on Dr. Spock's theory that the individual child was the center of attention. Many parents were shocked by Elvis Presley's gyrations, which were considered lewd, but they became incorporated in American dancing and in performances of American musicians. They have been exported around the world. Jazz in the form of bebop was popular among black musicians in the 1950s and had an impact on the development of American popular music. The music of the black cultural tradition has been a very important part of the American musical scene throughout the 20th century.

Television

Perhaps the greatest change in American culture in the postwar years was the growth of the television industry. Everyone has heard statistics of how many hours of television the average high

Television becomes a major factor in the daily lives of the American public.

265

school graduate has seen or a child has viewed before entering kindergarten. Specific numbers vary but they are always staggering and in the thousands of hours. Yet in 1945 there were only 7,000 TV sets in the nation, illustrating how different were the experiences of childhood and adolescence of those born before World War II and those born after. By 1960 there were 50 million television sets in America. As a result, movie attendance dropped dramatically as people stayed home to watch sit-coms. TV provided shared experiences for Americans. It reinforced and confirmed the conformity that was a hallmark of the Eisenhower years.

There are several explanations as to why this conformity prevailed. One is the influence of television. Another is the fear of the Communist enemy, which created a need to be like others at home. A third is the tendency of young people to band together in cliques to give themselves a sense of identity.

Whatever the explanation, certainly television provided standardized entertainment for the American people. It also provided shared experiences in such matters as McCarthy army hearings and the Presidential debates between John F. Kennedy and Richard Nixon in 1960. Newspaper and magazine reading declined, as did the appeal of radio as television became ever more popular. However, cheap paperback books, widely available in the 1950s, meant more books were bought than in the past.

Television is now available world wide, and as with American music, American shows dominate. The culture and values presented in these shows are what most people identify as American. It is interesting to consider what impressions of American life and values foreigners got as a result of seeing American television shows.

Movies, Books, and Art

Movies provide popular entertainment.

American culture, however, was not confined to popular music and television shows. The movie industry, in spite of a drop in attendance in the 1950s, continued to provide popular entertainment. After her very successful performance in *Gentlemen Prefer Blondes* (1953), Marilyn Monroe emerged as the female sex symbol of the '50s. Cary Grant and John Wayne provided the male symbols. Alfred Hitchcock directed a series of mystery films such as *To Catch a Thief* (1955) starring Grace Kelly and Cary Grant that still rank among Hollywood's best. Katherine Hepburn gave several memorable performances including *The African Queen* (1951) with Humphrey Bogart and *State of the Union* (1948) with Spencer Tracy. *Casablanca* (1944) with Humphrey Bogart and Ingrid Bergman confirmed the two leads as top box office stars. It became one of the most popular films for the baby boomers in the 1950s and established itself as one of the first "cult" films—films that have a particular audience who like to see the film over and over again. A few movies revealed memorable developments in technique such as Orson Welles' *Citizen Kane* (1940) and Walt Disney's *Fantasia* (1940), a full-length animated cartoon illustrating the artists' responses to several classical music scores.

American authors produced several books of major significance in the period. Among them are Jack Kerouac's *On the Road* (1955), Joseph Heller's *Catch 22* (1961), and Ralph Ellison's *Invisible Man* (1952). The latter is autobiographical and tells of the experience of being black in America. Heller's *Catch 22* is a vivid anti-war novel. Kerouac is a member of a group of authors, the Beat Generation, who rebeled at the middle class values and conformity of the Eisenhower years. The Beat Generation experimented with and wrote about drugs and their own sexual experiences. They, as did Elvis Presley, appealed to the younger generation of Americans. These works are still widely read in the United States by those wishing to understand the post-World War II era. One of the most popular works of the decade for younger readers and one still widely read in schools was J. D. Salinger's *Catcher in the Rye* (1951), which told the story of an affluent yet alienated adolescent.

Authors reflect different aspects of the American experience.

American artists of the 1950s painted in many styles, reflecting the diversity of American culture and views. Jackson Pollack worked in an abstract style in which he dropped paint onto canvasses, while Andrew Wyeth painted in minute detail realistic and personal scenes of individuals in the farmland country southwest of Philadelphia and in Maine. Other artists painted in every style between these two extremes. While some critics deplored the quality of popular culture as seen in television, movies, and music, fine contributions were being made by Americans in these areas of the arts. The 1950s were not devoid of cultural contributions by Americans.

In spite of criticisms of popular culture, Americans make important contributions to the arts.

KEY POINT TO REMEMBER
The Cold War had an impact on domestic legislation and attitudes and a postwar "baby boom" affected both American culture and industry.

LINKS FROM THE PAST TO THE PRESENT
1. Since Elvis Presley, music, its form and lyrics, has been a major part of the culture of America's young people.
2. Television plays an important part in American life.
3. Rural and urban poverty continue in American society.
4. The importance of the automobile for American industry and prosperity can be seen in the relationship between car sales and recessions and the impact the automobile industry has on so many others from steel to drive-in fast-food stores.

QUESTIONS

Identify each of the following:

Alger Hiss
Montgomery bus boycott
McCarthyism
Sputnik

To Secure These Rights
Appalachia
Brown v. Board of Education
Elvis Presley

True or False:

1. The McCarren Internal Security Act encouraged Communist-front organizations to spy on the Communist Party.
2. Senator Joseph McCarthy identified and proved there were Communists in the United States Army.
3. The NAACP worked through the courts to improve the situation for African-Americans in America.
4. Nine African-American students enrolled in the Little Rock, Arkansas high school in an attempt to integrate the school following the *Brown v. Board of Education* decision of the Supreme Court.
5. Rosa Parks' refusal to give up her seat on a bus precipitated the Montgomery bus boycott.
6. Martin Luther King Jr. was an outstanding civil rights leader who singlehandedly made the Civil Rights Movement a success.
7. The National Defense Education Act was passed to improve education in foreign languages, math and science.
8. General Eisenhower was World War II Allied Commander in Europe, head of NATO, and President of Columbia University before being elected President of the United States.
9. The postwar baby boom had little impact on the economy.
10. The Sun Belt grew very little in the postwar period.
11. In spite of the affluent society, many on farms and in urban centers lived in poverty.
12. The Kinsey Institute studied the sexual patterns of Americans and declared they had not changed in the post-war period.
13. Dr. Benjamin Spock advocated that the child be the center of a mother's life.
14. The Beat Generation rebelled against middle class values.

Multiple Choice:

1. Civil disobedience was rooted in the teachings of
    a. Rosa Parks and the Little Rock nine
    b. Henry David Thoreau and Gandhi
    c. Martin Luther King Jr. and Joseph McCarthy
2. Among the important legislation of the 1945–1960 period were:
    a. the National Defense Education Act and the Sputnik Act
    b. the Taft-Hartley Labor Act and the Federal Aid Highway Act
    c. the St. Lawrence Seaway Act and the Civil Disobedience Act
3. Examples of the youth culture of the postwar period are:
    a. the appeal of Elvis Presley and rock 'n' roll
    b. sitcoms on TV
    c. the popularity of movies
4. Among the important books of the post-war period were:
    a. Ralph Ellison's *Catch 22*
    b. Orson Welles' *Citizen Kane*
    c. John Kenneth Galbraith's *Affluent Society*

ANSWERS

True or False: 1. F, 2. F, 3. T, 4. T, 5. T, 6. F, 7. T, 8. T, 9. F, 10. F, 11. T, 12. F, 13. T, 14. T.
Multiple Choice: 1. b, 2. b, 3. a, 4. c.

CHAPTER 12

Civil Rights, Vietnam, the Cold War, and Watergate: 1960–1976

APPROACHES TO HISTORY
Defining Who You Are

One analysis of human behavior suggests that humans often define who they are by who they are not. As an American, you are not some other nationality. This provides a sense of who you are. The analysis can be applied at many different levels. If you are white, you are not black. If you are a father, you are not a mother. The divisions can go on and on.

This analysis presents a clear but simplistic view of human behavior since we know that all humans share many characteristics and many characteristics are blurred. For instance, at the start of this book it was pointed out that all Americans are immigrants, so all Americans have their origins somewhere other than in America. Therefore, to say that as an American you are not another nationality is not completely true—it is blurred. Likewise, mothers and fathers share many qualities and responsibilities, but mothers and fathers are taught or learn from society what qualities should be emphasized to make, for instance, an American male a "typical American father."

Even though individuals know the divisions are blurred, humans find it easy to define themselves and others—both friends and enemies—in terms of how they differ from us. This way of thinking leads us to identify others by the fact that they are not "like us." These others are then often seen as a threat or inferior. They are often attacked and become "the enemy."

Can you think of situations in your life where you verbally abused or turned against someone or some group simply because they were not like you?

A simple example is provided by sports contests where fans scream for their team to "kill" the opponent. Fans don't truly mean what they yell, but it allows them to define themselves as different from the opponent. Their opponent is not like them.

Historians often describe situations in history in terms of this concept of enemies, based on those who are not like themselves. Several psychologists have discussed the need to have a devil, someone to hate, in order to identify yourself or your cause. In American history the concept of an enemy or devil can be illustrated by many examples of intolerance or fear of others. The Civil Rights Movement, Vietnam, the Cold War, and Watergate all provide illustrations of this concept of human behavior. In each situation there was a division between us and them, black and white, "gooks"[1] and good Americans, "commies" and freedom lovers, hippies[2] and the "silent majority[3]."

I. THE PRESIDENCIES OF JOHN F. KENNEDY AND LYNDON B. JOHNSON

Camelot

John F. Kennedy brought to the White House an aura of youthful idealism. He surrounded himself with bright young advisors and Cabinet members such as his brother, Attorney General Robert Kennedy, Secretary of Defense Robert McNamara, and Special Assistant for National Security McGeorge Bundy. Kennedy and his wife, Jackie, exuded charisma, which inspired people and created a surge of purpose and confidence in the nation.

Kennedy brings a new spirit to the White House but has little success in getting legislation passed for his New Frontier program.

In spite of the new spirit in the White House, Kennedy had little success in getting Congress to pass major domestic legislation that he suggested as part of his "New Frontier," including a number of reforms in housing and medical care. Before his assassination in 1963, Kennedy sent to Congress plans for a major tax reduction and an extensive Civil Rights Act but these, too, were not accepted.

Kennedy's idealism and goals for America are illustrated in his inaugural address and in his establishment of the Peace

---

[1]*gook*   Derogatory term used by Americans for the Vietnamese.

[2]*hippies*   Members of the counterculture of the 1960s and 1970s who, alienated by bureaucracy and materialism, pursued a different life style based on love, drugs, and rock n' roll.

[3]*silent majority*   Term used by President Nixon to describe those whom he believed supported his conservative views on law and order and did not approve of the hippies and other protest groups.

Corps, in which young Americans worked as volunteers on projects in undeveloped countries to aid the people, not the government, of those countries. Kennedy provided a national purpose when, responding to the Soviet challenge in space, he called on the nation to place a man on the moon by the end of the decade. This goal was achieved when Neil Armstrong took "one long step for mankind" on the moon's surface on July 20, 1969.

In his presidential campaign Kennedy had suggested United States defenses had been weakened under Eisenhower. He was prepared to stand up to the Russians. Under John Foster Dulles' concept of brinkmanship, massive nuclear retaliation was to be the response to Soviet international pressure. Of course, it was not applied since it would have meant nuclear disaster for the world. Kennedy substituted for nuclear retaliation a concept of "flexible response" under which the United States would use different degrees and kinds of force in response to Soviet pressure. Kennedy was a true Cold War warrior who was out to win the war and who saw the Soviets as different, as the enemy. Using the flexible response principle, Kennedy threatened nuclear retaliation in confronting the Soviet Union in Berlin and Cuba and applied a more limited response in Vietnam. The Kennedy policy was still one of containment of the Communists, who were the enemy, who were different from us.

Kennedy adopts a policy of flexible response in responding to Soviet pressure.

Assassination of Kennedy

On a political campaign trip to Dallas, Texas, Kennedy was assassinated on November 22, 1963. Lee Harvey Oswald was arrested as the suspect but was shot and killed by Jack Ruby while being transferred from jail. TV cameras recorded the shooting of Oswald, and it was shown on national TV as was Kennedy's funeral. The events of the assassination traumatized the nation and plunged it into a period of grief and mourning. At the time it was not clear if the assassination was part of a major plot or the act of one individual. While most accept that Oswald acted alone, there are still a few scholars who continue to pursue other possibilities.

Kennedy is assassinated in Dallas, Texas on November 22, 1963.

The 1,000 days of the Kennedy presidency have been referred to as "Camelot," the legendary castle of King Arthur of Britain where the king and his Knights of the Round Table fought for good and justice. This Camelot version of the Kennedy years is appealing, but is too idealistic a view. Kennedy supplied the nation with a new national mood of optimism, signified in his call for the nation to move to the "New Frontier," but his presidency also included the brashness and harshness of the frontier as seen in his foreign policy confrontations and his forcing the steel companies and steel union to settle a strike over profits and wages in 1961 simply by "jawboning"[4] the two antagonists. Camelot suggests a mystical world of ideals and good. If the Kennedy presidency had that, it was only one side of those years.

The image of Camelot is only one side of the Kennedy presidency.

---

[4]*jawboning* To influence or pressure through persuasion, especially to pressure for voluntary compliance with official policy or guidelines.

Lyndon Baines Johnson

Lyndon B. Johnson became President on Kennedy's assassination. Johnson had been a Senator from Texas and had served as the Senate Majority Leader. He knew the intricacies of Capital Hill. He knew the members of Congress and the way they worked. As President he used this knowledge to get legislation passed. Johnson had great sympathy for people, especially the common people, but was not experienced in foreign affairs. He viewed the world strictly from a Texan, a Southern, and an American perspective. His presidency has a tragic quality, in which this man of compassion for and understanding of the average American was forced to devote much of his time as President to the situation in Vietnam.

Johnson was sworn in as President in a dramatic ceremony aboard Air Force One, the President's plane, which took Kennedy's body back to Washington. Kennedy's funeral, viewed on TV by millions, was a time of shared grief. The new President immediately addressed a joint session of Congress and said the best eulogy for the slain President would be to pass his domestic legislative program. Congress soon passed the tax reduction plan and the Civil Rights Act Kennedy had proposed.

Johnson had his own program for domestic legislation, the War on Poverty, the first part of which he introduced in January, 1964. The War on Poverty had close links to the major domestic issue of the Kennedy and early Johnson years, the Civil Rights Movement.

University of Mississippi and Birmingham, Alabama

The Civil Rights Movement begun after World War II (see pages 257–259) continued. In 1961 the Council on Racial Equality (CORE) organized the Freedom Riders, who forced the integration of interstate buses. In 1962 Kennedy, who had been slow to act, ordered the Mississippi National Guard into federal service in order to support the federal marshalls who were ordered to enroll James Meredith, an African-American student, at the University of Mississippi. James Meredith's enrollment forced the integration of the University.

In the spring of 1963 SCLC organized sit-ins[5] to protest segregation in Birmingham, Alabama. The Chief of Police, "Bull" Connor, used dogs and firehoses on demonstrators, including children. These actions, seen on national TV, gained support for the African-American protestors. Martin Luther King, Jr. was arrested and while in jail wrote *Letter from a Birmingham Jail*, one of the most eloquent statements of the movement's philosophy, explaining why the African-Americans could no longer "wait" for integration and their full civil rights. A settlement was reached between King

---

[5]*sit-ins* Demonstrations in which protesters occupy seats and refuse to move until they are recognized and/or their demands are met. Used by the Civil Rights Movement to break down segregation in public places.

and the Birmingham city government, which integrated the lunch counters. The TV coverage of the event aroused the public and Kennedy responded.

March on Washington

It was then Kennedy called for Congress to pass a Civil Rights Act guaranteeing equal access for all races to public accommodation and withholding federal funds from state-run progams that were segregated. A filibuster in Congress delayed action. Civil rights leaders from SNCC, CORE, SCLC, and other groups organized a March on Washington in support of the Kennedy Civil Rights Bill. A. Philip Randolph of the Pullman Porters Union had suggested such a march in 1940 to call attention to segregation in government. It did not happen then and it took 23 years before his idea was fulfilled.

Over 250,000 people from all races and all walks of life gathered before the Lincoln Memorial on August 28, 1963 in one of the largest demonstrations held in the Capital. The peaceful demonstrators were thrilled by King's memorable "I Have a Dream" speech, which includes the repeated phrase, "Let freedom ring." It was a masterful appeal to all that was best in America for fairness, for equality, for understanding. It was the high point of the civil disobedience movement led by King.

Unfortunately, the mood of optimism and hope generated by the March on Washington did not last. In September in Birmingham, Alabama, four African-American girls were killed while at Sunday school by a bomb thrown at their church by white extremists. 1964 was to be a year of confrontations.

King delivers his "I Have a Dream" speech as the climax of the March on Washington.

The Civil Rights Movement Explodes

In 1964 CORE and SNCC organized the Mississippi Summer Project to register African-Americans to vote. Three civil rights workers were murdered by a group of whites that included deputy sheriffs who were supposed to be protecting the civil rights workers. It was reported that the Federal Bureau of Investigation (FBI) investigators were aiding white extremists. The longtime head of the FBI, J. Edgar Hoover, ordered King's telephones tapped, and he leaked uncomplimentary stories about King. Some accused Hoover of being a racist. By keeping African-Americans "in their place," Hoover helped define his own place and identity. Hoover did not use the FBI to support the Civil Rights Movement— a clear demonstration of the power and influence one man can have on history.

Opposition to integration becomes violent as civil rights workers are murdered and the FBI head fails to support the movement.

Black Muslims

In the meantime, new leaders were emerging in the ghettos of the North, where almost three-quarters of African-Americans lived. The most prominent was Malcolm X, a leader of the Black Muslims. Malcolm X and other Black Muslim leaders were preaching a new approach to gaining equality. They called on African-Americans to be sober and thrifty and to seize freedom by any

Malcolm X presents a new approach to gaining equality for African-Americans.

means including violence. They inspired and encouraged self-awareness and a sense of self-respect and power for people in the ghettos. There was much that was good in their message. However, there was a negative side as they spoke of using violence rather than civil disobedience.

Violence did erupt in the Harlem ghetto of New York City and in Rochester, New York, in the summer of 1964—violence directed at a society that appeared insensitive to African-American needs. A government commission that investigated the riots said they were the result of a social system that provided little opportunity and few jobs for African-Americans. Other city ghettos erupted in riots in the 1960s, yet the same problem of a lack of opportunity in ghettos persists today.

Mississippi Freedom Democratic Party

The Civil Rights Movement puts pressure on the Democratic Party.

Meanwhile, the Mississippi voter registration drive resulted in the formation of the Mississippi Freedom Democratic Party (MFDP), which elected representatives to the Democratic Party Convention of 1964 in Atlantic City. Denied the vote in the Democratic Party all-white primary in Mississippi, the MFDP claimed that they were the true representatives of the state's Democrats since their primary was open to all. President Johnson, who was assured of his party's nomination, was in a political squeeze. Although he advocated civil rights legislation, he dared not lose the support of the South in the 1964 election. Following the rules of political life, a compromise was offered, but the MFDP through its spokesperson, Fannie Lou Hamer, refused the compromise. The Democratic Party did, as a result of the MFDP, change the rules for representation at the 1968 convention. It made that convention much more representative of the American people, with quotas for women and minorities established. Still, the lack of support for the MFDP by the Democratic Convention was a blow to the leaders of non-violent civil disobedience.

Selma, Alabama

Violence in Selma leads to the Voting Rights Act.

In the spring of 1964 SNCC began a campaign to register voters in Selma, Alabama. It was not going well, and they asked King and SCLC for support. The city's white mayor was inexperienced. The city sheriff, Jim Clark, blocked the registration attempts. In early 1965, a white minister supporting King was killed by whites in Selma. The African-Americans refrained from violence but organized a march of protest from Selma to the state capital at Montgomery. The march was blocked by Sheriff Clark and the state National Guard under orders of George Wallace, recently elected Governor of Alabama and at that time an intense segregationist. Again, national television recorded the incident on the Pettus Bridge during which police on horseback attacked the marchers and threw tear gas at them. Again, national reaction was strong.

Soon thereafter the Congress passed the Voting Rights Act of 1965, which gave authority to the United States Attorney General to appoint officials to register voters in states where only a small percentage of minorities were registered. In the next few years voter registration increased dramatically, providing African-Americans with the power of the ballot box as a way to implement change.

The Voting Rights Act was a great achievement of the movement brought about by civil disobedience. Unfortunately, it was the last major achievement. The movement dissipated and the leadership went in different directions as the nation focused more and more on the Vietnam war.

Emergence of Black Power

In 1964 SNCC's Stokeley Carmichael declared that SNCC should not include whites. The next year he spoke of the need to achieve black power. While achieving successes through the political process, the Civil Rights Movement had not achieved many economic changes. The goals and organizing methods of the movement's leaders became fragmented as they sought ways to gain more economic power for the African-American community. CORE and SNCC demanded black studies in schools and colleges. Adding to the mood of violence was the assassination of Malcolm X in 1965. He was assassinated by fellow Black Muslims who disagreed with his positions. In 1965 the ghetto of Watts in Los Angeles erupted in a riot in which 34 were killed and 810 wounded. In 1966 there were riots in New York and Chicago and in 1967 in Newark and Detroit.

The Black Panthers, a revolutionary group, are organized and preach the use of violence to achieve their economic and political goals.

The Black Panthers were organized in 1966 to patrol the streets in the ghettos. They quickly became urban revolutionaries and used violence to call attention to the conditions in the ghetto. In 1968 Stokeley Carmichael joined the Black Panthers organization as the Prime Minister.

Martin Luther King, Jr. was still advocating peaceful confrontation, but the level of frustration in the ghettos could not be held in check. King and the SCLC saw the Vietnam war taking the money and attention needed to address the poverty of the African-Americans. King protested the United States involvement in Vietnam, not yet a popular stand, and he began to organize a poor people's march on Washington. In 1968, while in Memphis to support garbage workers who were striking for higher wages, Martin Luther King, Jr. was assassinated. King's assassination touched off rioting in over 150 cities—not the memorial celebration this great leader of peaceful change through civil disobedience should have had, but a clear indication of the anger of the African-American urban population. The turn to violence and confrontation to achieve goals was not confined to African-Americans in the mid-1960s.

Martin Luther King, Jr. is assassinated and riots erupt in over 150 cities.

The Student Protest Movement

In 1964 white, middle-class students who had participated in Mississippi Summer began the Free Speech Movement at the University of California at Berkeley. As the baby boomers headed to college, universities grew rapidly. Clark Kerr, chancellor of the University of California, compared the university to a business. Students at the university were concerned by the school's bigness

University students organize to protest limitations on freedom, equality, individualism, and democracy.

275

and lack of individualism and personal attention reflected in this attitude of college education as a business. They felt they were merely numbers. The students organized peaceful protests, and when Chancellor Kerr ordered the square in Berkeley where students had gathered to argue and debate closed to them, students defied the order. Arrests and riots resulted. To call attention to their concern that the university pay more attention to the individual, in keeping with the American ideals of individualism and democracy, the students seized the administration building. The Governor sent in state police. More arrests were made.

Berkeley stands as the symbol of student protests of the 1960s, but protests and building seizures occurred at many other campuses as college students attracted to the American ideals of freedom and equality were frustrated by the limitations they found both in United States society and on college campuses. The Students for a Democratic Society (SDS), a group organized to give leadership to the student movement, articulated these frustrations in their Port Huron Statement. The Port Huron Statement condemned racism and poverty amidst plenty, the power of corporations and the military/industrial complex, and the Cold War. The Port Huron Statement called for a return to the great American ideals of freedom, equality, and democracy. The student movement that became identified with the New Left was active on the college campuses, in the anti-Vietnam protests, and in the political campaigns of 1968 and 1972. While student protests led to violence at times, the movement at first was modeled on the work of Dr. Martin Luther King, Jr. Like the Civil Rights Movement, it fragmented in the late 1960s and some factions turned to violence. The movement lost influence in the 1970s.

The War on Poverty

A growing awareness of the amount of poverty in America leads Johnson to propose a War on Poverty.

It was not only African-Americans and students who were concerned about poverty in America. President Johnson was also. In 1962 Michael Harrington published a book, *The Other America*, in which he documented the prevalence of poverty in the United States. According to Harrington and government statistics, over 20 percent of the population lived in poverty. Kennedy, the millionaire, read the book and was ready to address the issue when he was assassinated. Johnson did address the issue with a comprehensive legislative program. Johnson's War on Poverty and related legislation provides another one of those reform periods that occur with cyclical regularity throughout American history.

The War on Poverty began with the Economic Opportunity Act of 1964, which established a job corps for training those without skills, a work experience program for unemployed parents, Project Headstart for preparing children of low income families for first grade, and Upward Bound to help bright but impoverished and poorly prepared high schoolers for college. Project Headstart is considered the most successful program of the War on Poverty. Volunteers for Service to America (VISTA), a domestic Peace Corps, was established for those who wished to work with the poor to help alleviate problems of rural and urban poverty. Other acts came after Johnson's election as president in 1964.

Election of 1964

In the 1964 election Republicans nominated Barry Goldwater, Senator from Arizona, who represented the very conservative side of the party. Johnson chose as his running mate the liberal Senator Hubert Humphrey of Minnesota. They won a one-sided victory, and Johnson then introduced his Great Society Program, which incorporated the War on Poverty.

Johnson overwhelmingly wins election in 1964.

The Great Society

Legislation rolled through Congress in 1965, all aimed at creating what President Johnson called the Great Society. In addition to the Civil Rights Voting Act, there were environmental, educational, and cultural laws passed. The first Water Quality and Air Quality Acts establishing Federal clean water and air standards were passed in response to the first burst of environmental awareness the nation experienced.

The Great Society program includes a wide range of legislation to improve many aspects of American life.

An elementary and secondary school act, the first providing direct aid ($1.3 billion) to this age group, and a higher education act providing federally funded college scholarships were passed. Education in America had always been supported and operated by local authorities, and the federal government had not been involved in direct financing until the Great Society legislation.

The National Foundation for the Arts and Humanities was established to provide funding for artists, writers, musicians, and scholars in the humanities as opposed to the sciences. The National Science Foundation had previously been endowed by the government to support scientists.

An Omnibus Housing Bill (OHB) provided support for home building. The establishment of the Cabinet-level Housing and Urban Affairs Department (HUD) was an acknowledgment that our cities were as important as our agriculture. The Department of Housing and Urban Affairs was to administer the government housing and urban programs designed to solve urban problems such as the lack of affordable housing.

A new immigration law abandoned the national quota system established after World War I. It set a total number for immigrants from the Western Hemisphere (120,000) and the rest of the world (170,000) with no more than 20,000 from any one country. The dislocations caused by wars since 1965 have led to many more immigrants coming to America than set in the law.

Finally, in 1965 the first national health insurance measure, the Medicare Act, was passed. It combined hospital insurance for retired people with a voluntary plan to cover doctors' bills. Medicaid was established to give grants to the states to administer medical aid to the poor who were not retired. Medicaid was another part of the War on Poverty.

The Medicare Act establishes the first nationally funded health insurance measure.

In the next three years Congress passed other legislation including the Highway Safety Act and National Traffic and Motor Vehicle

Safety Act, both of them inspired by Ralph Nader, who became the nation's most articulate spokesperson for national consumer rights. Also passed was a raise in the minimum wage, the establishment of a Cabinet Department of Transportation, and a Clean Water Restoration Act.

The War on Poverty is replaced by the Vietnam War as Johnson's primary concern.

However, the war in Vietnam became more and more the focus of the nation, and Johnson was faced with the economic dilemma of how much more could be spent on domestic policies when money was needed to fight the war. The dilemma has been described as "deciding between guns and butter." Johnson's response was to keep domestic programs but to create no new ones. Fortunately, the Gross National Product (GNP) grew rapidly, stimulated by the 1964 tax cut, and government revenues increased. These revenues helped finance the War on Poverty.

The expanding economy provided jobs that helped reduce the number living in poverty. Both the absolute numbers and the percentage of those living below the poverty line decreased dramatically, from almost 25 percent in 1962 to less than 12 percent ten years later, but the War on Poverty put a strain on the economy.

In retrospect, some scholars question its effectiveness, suggesting that it was the improving economy that changed the situation for the poor, and that legislation aiding impoverished families has perpetuated the pattern of poor education and adolescent pregnancies. However it is judged, the War on Poverty was motivated by those American values of concern for others and a desire for equality.

Meanwhile, during the Kennedy and Johnson years the Cold War continued, and money had to be spent on United States defense.

Kennedy and Cuba

Kennedy inherited from the Eisenhower administration a new situation in Cuba. In 1959 after years of guerrilla warfare, Fidel Castro defeated the Cuban dictator, Batista. Castro had received some of his education in the United States, and it was hoped he would establish a democratic government for Cuba. Instead he moved to break the power of American business over the Cuban economy by nationalizing foreign industries and establishing a Communist government. Eisenhower authorized the CIA to train Cuban refugees for invasion of their country. Kennedy accepted the plan to have the refugees land at the Bay of Pigs on the southern coast of Cuba in April, 1961, only three months after his inauguration.

The Cuban Missile Crisis brings the world to the brink of nuclear war.

The Bay of Pigs invasion was a disaster—the Cuban people did not rise up to support the invaders. The planning had been poor, and the invaders were captured. Castro turned to the Soviet Union for support. The CIA then planned to assassinate Castro, but the plots failed. The Soviet Union agreed to send missiles and nuclear weapons secretly to Cuba. On October 14, 1962, a U-2 spy plane spotted missile sites being set up in Cuba.

The administration saw the missiles as a threat to United States security. As a response to the Soviet show of force, Kennedy's advisors suggested everything from a United States invasion of Cuba to peaceful negotiation in response to the threat. A naval blockade of Cuba was decided upon to prevent Russian ships from delivering missiles. Kennedy announced this decision on national television on October 22 as ships went into position and planes loaded with nuclear weapons circled the sky. It has been said that Kennedy and Nikita Khrushchev, leader of the Russians, were eyeball to eyeball and Khrushchev blinked. When the United States stopped a Soviet ship, Khrushchev offered to withdraw the missiles if the United States would guarantee Cuba's sovereignty. Later he added the United States should remove United States missiles from Turkey.

Kennedy agreed to guarantee the sovereignty of Cuba; Khrushchev removed the missiles; the United States ended the blockade; war was averted. Later the United States withdrew its missiles from Turkey.

A telephone hotline between Moscow and Washington was agreed upon soon after the crisis to aid communication between the two capitals in case of another crisis. It is generally agreed that in the last two weeks of October, 1962, the world came closer to a nuclear war than at any other time in the Cold War.

The Cuban Missile Crisis was considered a great success for Kennedy. In the 1980s, as the Cold War ended, Russian, Cuban, and United States scholars of the crisis discussed their findings together. The Cuban scholars said their research showed Castro would not have asked for missiles if there had been no Bay of Pigs or CIA attempts on his life. It is clear United States reliance on military force to counter Communist force bears some responsibility for the Cuban Missile Crisis. Likewise, Khrushchev and Castro share responsibility for their collaboration on missile placement and their testing of the United States' resolve to stand up to a Communist threat in the Western Hemisphere.

New information released in the mid-1980s gives a different perspective on the Cuban Missile Crisis.

The crisis showed that the young Kennedy, a Democrat, could be tough on Communism, as tough as the Republicans. Kennedy had stood up to those people who were different. He had confronted the devil. The Russians, however, felt humiliated and increased their arms buildup.

A debate still continues on whether the United States should have taken the world to the brink of nuclear war over the Cuban missiles. What do you think? There is a large amount of information on the topic if you wish to pursue the issue.

The Berlin Wall

Prior to the Cuban Missile Crisis there had been another crisis in Berlin. With the election of Kennedy, the Russians asked for new negotiations on the status of occupied Berlin. The United States declined and Kennedy called up the National Guard for federal military service. The Russian reaction to this show of force was to

The Berlin Wall intensifies the Cold War and symbolizes the division of Europe.

build a wall separating their sector of Berlin from the area occupied by the three western Allies. The wall went up essentially overnight in August, 1961. The wall confirmed the separation of Europe into East and West.

Nuclear Arms

Nuclear testing is resumed.

In 1958 the United States and the Soviet Union had both stopped nuclear testing, but in 1961 after the Berlin crisis, the Russians resumed testing. Then the United States also resumed underground testing. The arms race was on again. In July, 1963 a treaty banning atmospheric testing was finally signed by the major powers except France and China, who were still developing their nuclear capacity. This was the first agreement to begin reduction on nuclear weapons.

The Peace Corps and Alliance for Progress

Kennedy's idealism is evident in the establishment of the Peace Corps.

Kennedy's idealism and desire to have Americans "ask what they can do for their country" led to the establishment of the Peace Corps. Young Americans volunteered to use their skills in Third World countries. After brief orientation they worked on projects designed to help local conditions in rural and some urban settings abroad. Thousands of Americans served. The Peace Corps was an excellent example of the good heartedness and concern for others of the average American.

Kennedy's policy towards Central and South America was to have the nations of the Western Hemisphere work together in an Alliance for Progress in the hemisphere. The concept of the Alliance for Progress was excellent, but the funding, $20 million, was inadequate to address the hopes raised by the project. As has happened often in United States relations with its southern neighbors, good intentions were not fulfilled. In the 1960s the southern neighbors of the United States were not considered central to the Cold War as was Vietnam.

Kennedy and Vietnam

Kennedy increases United States involvement in Vietnam.

Kennedy, in his years in office, increased the number of United States troops in Vietnam from approximately 2,000 to 16,000. However, the history of United States involvement in Vietnam begins long before Kennedy. Vietnam is the most important single issue the United States faced in the 45 years after the end of World War II and ranks with the Depression and World War II for its impact on 20th century American history.

KEY POINT TO REMEMBER

John F. Kennedy brought idealism and youthful vigor to the nation but achieved little in domestic legislation and was slow to embrace the Civil Rights Movement. After his assassination, Lyndon B. Johnson led the nation into another great period of reform with his War on Poverty and concept of the Great Society.

PEOPLE TO REMEMBER

Stokeley Carmichael A leader of the Civil Rights Movement, organizer of the Student NonViolent Coordinating Committee, later accepted the need for violence to achieve full rights for African-Americans; joined the Black Panthers.

Malcolm X Most noted spokesperson for the Black Muslin movement; assassinated by fellow Black Muslim in 1965; Malcolm X inspired inner city African-Americans with a sense of purpose and self-confidence. His approach to civil rights was very different from that of Martin Luther King, Jr.

John F. Kennedy Naval war hero, Senator from Massachusetts; as President during the Cuban Missile Crisis he led the United States in a confrontation with the Soviet Union that came close to nuclear war; began the escalation of the war in Vietnam; his youth and charisma inspired confidence; he instituted the Peace Corps; he called for civil rights legislation before his assassination in 1963.

LINKS FROM THE PAST TO THE PRESENT

1. Relations with Cuba and Fidel Castro continue to be a foreign policy issue for the United States.
2. Legislation has provided important guarantees of civil rights since the Civil Rights laws under Johnson.
3. The problem of poverty in America remains unsolved.
4. United States involvement in Vietnam led to a war that still has effects on American society.

QUESTIONS

Identify each of the following:

Civil Rights Act of 1964	Peace Corps
SCLC	Cuban Missile Crisis
Black Muslims	Economic Opportunity Act
Watts	Medicare

True or False:

1. President Johnson waged a war on poverty.
2. President Kennedy was assassinated in Dallas, Texas on November 22, 1963—an event that traumatized the nation.
3. Only African-Americans participated in the March on Washington in 1963.
4. Black Muslims believed in seizing freedom by any means including violence, a philosophy that opposed the non-violence preached by Martin Luther King, Jr.
5. After Martin Luther King, Jr. wrote "Letter from a Birmingham Jail" and TV showed children attacked by police dogs and firehoses in Birmingham, Alabama, President Kennedy called on Congress to pass a major civil rights act.
6. The Democratic Party was pleased to accept the members of the Mississippi Freedom Democratic Party (MFDP) as delegates to the party convention of 1964.
7. Beginning in 1964, there were race riots in the ghettos in Harlem, Watts, and many other American cities.

8. The Student Movement of protests in the mid-1960s had no connections with the Civil Rights Movement.
9. The Great Society was President Johnson's name for his program of domestic reforms.
10. The Bay of Pigs was an unsuccessful attempt by Fidel Castro to attack the city of Miami.
11. The United States and the USSR called on Cuba to offer solutions to the Cuban Missile Crisis.
12. The Peace Corps is an example of President Kennedy's idealism.

Multiple Choice:
1. The following organizations provided important leadership of the early, non-violent Civil Rights Movement:
   a. SCLC, NAACP, and the Black Muslims
   b. SCLC, CORE, and SNCC
   c. CORE and the Black Panthers
2. The main purpose of the Civil Rights Act of 1965 was to guarantee the right to
   a. vote
   b. pay for accommodation in hotels and restaurants
   c. sit-in
3. The following measures were part of President Johnson's Great Society:
   a. Project Headstart, VISTA, Job Corps
   b. Medicare, Upward Bound, National Endowment for the Arts and Humanities
   c. all the above.
4. Kennedy's relations with Cuba included all of the following except
   a. U-2 spy plane finding missiles and a blockade of Cuba
   b. sending U.S. troops to attack the Bay of Pigs
   c. allowing the CIA to plot attacks on Fidel Castro's life

ANSWERS
True or False: 1. T, 2. T, 3. F, 4. T, 5. T, 6. F, 7. T, 8. F, 9. T, 10. F, 11. F, 12. T.
Multiple Choice: 1. b, 2. a, 3. c, 4. b.

II.   THE VIETNAM WAR

Background

The United States supports Ho Chi Minh against the Japanese during World War II.

United States interest in Vietnam did not begin with Kennedy or even Eisenhower. United States interest in Vietnam, then French Indochina, was one of the reasons the Japanese attacked Pearl Harbor in 1941. After the fall of France in 1941, the United States had warned the Japanese to stay out of the French colony. Negotiations got nowhere, and the Japanese seized the colony. United States-Japanese relations deteriorated and led to Pearl Harbor.

During World War II the Office of Strategic Services (OSS), the United States intelligence service, aided the Vietnamese nationalists led by Ho Chi Minh in their attacks on the Japanese. After the war Ho Chi Minh asked for United States support in establishing an independent Vietnam, but he was ignored. The United States officially supported the French as they tried to reestablish control over all of Vietnam.

War broke out between the French forces and Ho Chi Minh's Vietminh Movement. Ho Chi Minh had studied in Moscow, and, in the context of the Cold War, the United States saw the Vietminh as another manifestation of the devil, the Communists, who were slowly taking over all of Asia.

The Communists under Mao Zedong had just gained control of mainland China, and the Korean War began in June, 1950. Following the containment policy, Truman determined to block the Vietminh from gaining control of Indochina and sent military aid but not troops to support the French in their war.

In retrospect Ho Chi Minh appears first a nationalist fighting for independence and secondly a Communist, but it was difficult to make such distinctions in 1950. The French, even with United States aid, were unable to defeat the Vietminh, and when French forces at the mountain outpost of Dien Bien Phu were surrounded and captured, the French began negotiations at Geneva for a peaceful settlement.

The French fail to defeat Ho Chi Minh and the Vietminh.

The Geneva Accords granted independence to Vietnam as well as Laos and Cambodia. Vietnam was "temporarily" divided at the 17th Parallel into a North Vietnam ruled by Ho Chi Minh's Vietminh and a South Vietnam ruled by Ngo Dinh Diem. The Communists supported the North and the United States supported Diem in the South. The Geneva Accords called for elections to unite the nation. Diem, supported by the Eisenhower administration, rejected that provision in 1955.

In 1956 Diem began a crackdown on those in the South who questioned his authority. In 1957 those opposing Diem began terrorist attacks on his troops and in 1959 North Vietnam began sending aid to them. In 1960 Diem's opposition organized as the Vietcong or National Liberation Front. In the meantime Eisenhower sent military advisors to support the Diem government.

The Vietcong are organized to fight the government of Ngo Dinh Diem.

By the time Kennedy became president, the United States had been involved directly or indirectly in Vietnam for 20 years. We were giving military aid and had 2,000 advisors there. As a Cold War warrior who was determined to win the war, Kennedy decided to increase United States aid. He sent more advisors to help the Diem government in what had become a war against the terrorist attacks of the Vietcong.

Before Kennedy was assassinated, it became clear that the Roman Catholic Diem did not have the support of the South Vietnamese people. In 1963 several Buddhist monks protested Diem's undemocratic tactics by immolating[1] themselves. The incidents were shown on United States television.

---

[1]*immolate*   To kill as a sacrifice; the Buddhist monks set themselves on fire as a public sacrifice.

Television in the decade of the '60s had become a very important factor in American politics as Americans viewed incidents such as the attack of police dogs on civil rights workers or Buddhist monks burning themselves alive and reacted with horror. The public's reaction as they saw freedom loving people like themselves being attacked had to be considered by political leaders.

A coup supported by the United States overthrows Diem.

Kennedy's response to the South Vietnam situation was to approve a coup organized by the CIA to overthrow Diem. It was successful, but the United States was now committed to finding a successor to Diem who could rally the South Vietnamese people and defeat the Vietcong. The United States was never able to do so, and that was the tragedy of Vietnam. The North Vietnamese and the Vietcong were fighting for their freedom and independence from oppression. No South Vietnamese leader could inspire his people the way Ho Chi Minh did. When the United States sent massive aid to the South, it was to support a regime which never won the masses to its side. The South Vietnamese government was seen by many Vietnamese as a puppet of the United States and not a national government. This was the situation President Johnson faced when he became president.

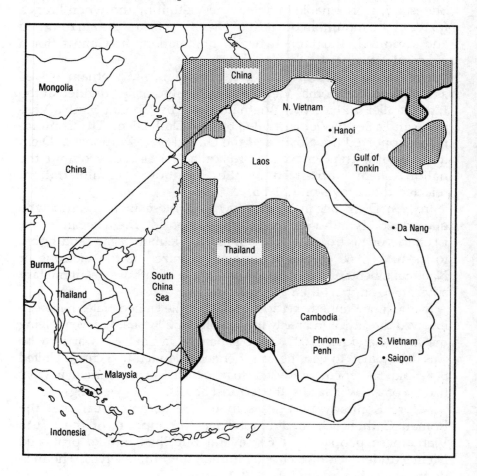

Americanizing the War

With South Vietnam in turmoil after the Buddhist protests, there were calls for compromise and a coalition government of Vietcong- and United States-supported groups. Like Kennedy, Johnson, a novice in foreign affairs, saw the war in Vietnam as a Communist threat. Johnson would not compromise. Johnson adhered to the Domino Theory first expressed during the Eisenhower administration in the 1950s. The Domino Theory held that if one Southeast Asian nation fell to Communism, the others would all fall like a line of dominos.

Johnson sees the war in Vietnam as a Communist threat and subscribes to the domino theory.

Johnson wanted victory in Vietnam and in 1964 began a huge buildup of American forces. In August it was reported that a United States destroyer in the Tonkin Gulf off North Vietnam had been attacked by small North Vietnamese gunboats. No clear evidence was submitted, but Johnson went to Congress with a request to use force against any North Vietnamese attacks. In the emotion and confusion of the moment, the Gulf of Tonkin Resolution was overwhelmingly passed by Congress. While not a declaration of war, Johnson used it as a justification for Americanizing the war. More troops were sent, fighting escalated[2], and the bombing of Vietcong supply routes in Laos and of North Vietnam was begun.

Congress passes the Gulf of Tonkin Resolution, and Johnson increases America's involvement in the war.

Johnson overwhelmingly won the 1964 presidential election, which seemed an endorsement of his Vietnam policy. After the Vietcong won a victory in February, 1965, the Joint Chiefs of Staff asked Johnson for more military forces. This meant further escalation. After discussions, the decision was made to increase American forces rather than negotiate. Assistant Secretary of State George Ball, who in all the consultations had supported negotiations, declared in his memoir, *The Past has Another Pattern*, "our protracted involvement in the Vietnam War was an authentic tragedy—perhaps the most tragic error in American history."

George Ball's advice to negotiate was not followed. More troops were sent, reaching almost 600,000 by the end of Johnson's presidency. Massive bombing attacks on the North could not break the will of the North Vietnamese people.

George Ball's advice to negotiate an end to the war is not followed.

Fighting conditions in the jungles of the South and the hills of central Vietnam were horrible. There was no battle line. The Vietcong enemy could be anywhere or anyone. The United States dropped a defoliation agent, Agent Orange, to kill forest growth that hid the Vietcong camps, but this did not help and only harmed the agriculture of the South Vietnamese. Few United States troops could communicate with the Vietnamese, and many Americans viewed them as ignorant peasants. Americans' feelings of superiority and intolerance for others not like themselves were manifested. American troops found their identity in priding themselves on being different from the Vietcong, the "gooks." In frustration,

---

[2]*escalate* To increase or intensify; steady escalation of the United States war effort became the Johnson policy in Vietnam.

the United States forces committed atrocities both against their own officers who might force them into combat and against Vietnamese who might be an enemy.

The My Lai Incident

The massacre at My Lai shocks Americans and makes clear the horrors of jungle warfare.

The most shocking incident took place at My Lai, where troops on a search and destroy mission against the Vietcong massacred men, women, and children in the village of My Lai. The incident was not reported in the United States press for over a year, but when it was, it shocked the American nation. Yet it merely reflected the horrors and frustrations of a war where there was no clear line between the enemy and the defenders.

United States television reported daily on the war, which seemed to be getting nowhere. More troops were being sent; more bombs dropped—by the end of the Vietnam War more bomb tonnage was dropped on Vietnam than had been dropped throughout the world in World War II—yet the enemy would not surrender. Finally, Assistant Secretary of State George Ball and Secretary of Defense McNamara realized there was no way to victory, but they could not persuade the President of that. They resigned from the Johnson government in protest over the continued policy of escalation.

The Tet Offensive

The Vietcong launch a Tet Offensive that illustrates the vulnerability of the United States forces.

By the start of 1968 the United States could claim a few minor successes, but the Vietcong forces still occupied almost half of South Vietnam as they had in 1964. After three years of fighting, the United States seemed to be nowhere. Then in January the Vietcong launched a nationwide offensive, the Tet Offensive, that rocked United States forces.

While the cities lost to the Vietcong were recaptured, the Tet Offensive showed how vulnerable United States forces were. The Joint Chiefs asked for 200,000 more troops but would not promise victory with them.

In early March Senator Eugene McCarthy, who ran as an anti-war candidate, made a surprisingly strong showing in the New Hampshire Democratic primary. The Senate Foreign Relations Committee held hearings on whether the war should continue. Anti-war protests were increasing. Some 500,000 protesters gathered in New York City in the spring of 1967, and many of them burned their draft cards. Young men were leaving the country to avoid the draft. The mood of the nation, which had been strongly supportive of the Tonkin Gulf Resolution in 1964, was shifting.

Hawks and Doves express different opinions on the war.

Those opposing the war were called doves; those in favor, hawks. It was reminiscent of 1812, when the War Hawks from the West wanted war with England. At the end of March, 1968, President Johnson announced he would not be a candidate for reelection and that he was stopping the bombing of North Vietnam and would seek a negotiated settlement. Johnson had come to see the war was unwinnable by military effort but was not prepared, nor were the American people prepared, to simply withdraw and let the Vietnamese people negotiate their future.

The Vietnam War had taken Johnson's time and the government's money away from his plans for the Great Society and the War on Poverty. The Vietnam War had tragic consequences for the United States.

1968: Election and Protests

1968 is one of those years that can be viewed as a watershed in history. The Tet Offensive signaled that the United States would eventually withdraw from Vietnam. In April Martin Luther King, Jr. was assassinated, marking an end to one phase of the Civil Rights Movement. Rioting followed in over 150 cities. The race for the Democratic Party's presidential nomination was full of protest and violence. College youth had become active anti-war protesters, and many of them supported Eugene McCarthy's campaign. When Johnson withdrew, the race was wide open. Robert Kennedy, former Attorney General and brother of President John F. Kennedy, had strong support from African-Americans and former Kennedy supporters. He became the leading contender but was assassinated in June on the eve of his victory in the California presidential primary. He was shot by a young Palestinian upset by Kennedy's pro-Israel position.

1968 stands as a watershed in American history.

With two political assassinations in three months, with riots in the inner cities, with anti-war protests growing, the nation seemed to be falling apart. Student protests, which had begun at Berkeley with the Free-Speech Movement, continued. Students at Columbia University, protesting the university's support of military-oriented research and the recruitment of students by such industries, the CIA, and the military, seized the administration building. Police forcefully removed them and 150 were injured. Protests occurred at two other colleges.

Student anti-war protests increase.

Then at the Democratic Party convention in August in Chicago, anti-war student protesters, poor people led by Ralph Abernathy, Martin Luther King, Jr.'s successor, and Yippies from the Youth International Party, all gathered in Chicago to express their views before the Democrats. The contest for the nomination was between Eugene McCarthy, the anti-war liberal Senator from Minnesota, and Hubert Humphrey, Johnson's Vice-President. Humphrey carried the stigma of having been in the administration that had escalated the war. In spite of his liberal record on domestic issues, there was no indication he had ever opposed the war. The situation around the convention hall was tense. Finally, the police and National Guard were called in to break up the protesters. Again Americans watched the actions on television.

The Democratic Convention in Chicago is beseiged by protesters but nominates Hubert Humphrey, Johnson's Vice President.

Humphrey won the nomination but in the campaign was unable to separate himself from Johnson's war. George Wallace, Democratic Governor of Alabama and a strong segregationist, ran as a third party candidate opposing the Democrat's stand on civil rights. The Republicans nominated Richard Nixon, Eisenhower's Vice-President. Nixon and his Vice-Presidential candidate, Spiro Agnew of Maryland, won the election but with a minority of the popular vote as Governor Wallace received 13 percent of the votes

Richard Nixon wins the presidency.

cast—a strong showing for a third party and a clear indication there was still strong anti-civil rights feelings in the nation.

Nixon had first gained prominence with his anti-Communist positions. He was prepared to negotiate a Vietnam settlement, but he was not prepared to "lose the war." As a minority president, Nixon in his victory speech called on the country to come together. 1968 had revealed a great split in the nation. It took a long time for the division to heal, and the scars are still there.

Vietnamization

Nixon orders an invasion of Cambodia and provokes more student protests.

Nixon and his Foreign Policy Advisor, Henry Kissinger, began secret negotiations with the North Vietnamese and announced a slow withdrawal of United States forces. Nixon's policy was to train the South Vietnamese army to take over the war. It met with limited success since the South Vietnamese were not fully behind their government. In 1970 Nixon ordered the invasion of Cambodia where the Vietcong had established safe camps and supply bases. Students on college campuses staged protests. At Kent State University in Ohio, National Guard forces fired on the student protesters and killed four. Protests erupted on over 500 college campuses. The CIA undertook assassinations of South Vietnamese civilians who supported an immediate end to the war.

The End of the War

The war and negotiations dragged on. Congress repealed the Gulf of Tonkin Resolution, yet Nixon and Kissinger were convinced they had to apply military pressure on Vietnam to prove the United States would not simply withdraw. They mined the harbor of Haiphong, a major port, and resumed the bombing of the North in 1972. After years of private talks during which thousands more Americans were killed, formal negotiations began in 1972 and a cease fire was reached in January, 1973, soon after Nixon had won re-election. The negotiated terms called for a coalition government in South Vietnam including the Vietcong.

An end to the war is negotiated, and its terms suggest the tragedy of the Vietnam conflict.

If the Geneva Accords had been adhered to in 1956, the government that would have been established by elections most likely would have been a coalition government for all Vietnam, but Dulles and Eisenhower saw the North Vietnamese as the enemy and would not compromise. A coalition government could also have been had in 1963 if Kennedy had undertaken negotiations and again in 1969 if Johnson had done so. Part of the tragedy of the Vietnam War is that what it achieved could have been achieved years before through negotiation and without war. It suggests the importance of understanding your capabilities and the history of your allies and enemies. This is one of the great challenges of any war situation.

The 1973 agreement also called for the withdrawal of all United States troops as soon as all United States prisoners of war were released. Prisoners were released, though some soldiers are still listed as "Missing in Action," and the last United States forces were withdrawn on March 29, 1973.

Violations of the Cease Fire

There were violations of the cease fire on both sides. The new President, Gerald Ford, asked Congress for more arms for the South, but Congress refused. The Communists mounted an attack. Vietnamization proved unsuccessful. In April, 1975 South Vietnam's capital, Saigon, fell to the Communists. The war was over.

The strains the war placed on American society are still felt. The cost of the war in killed and wounded (over 350,000 Americans and many thousands of Vietnamese) and money (over $150 billion to the United States alone) was staggering, but the cost of the war cannot be measured only in those terms. The division the war created between hawks and doves, the disillusionment it created in the young, the anger it created among African-Americans and poor, many more of whom fought in Vietnam than did wealthy whites, the horror and terror of the fighting conditions, and the lack of appreciation felt by disillusioned veterans are still part of the American experience and affect life in the United States as the nation approaches the end of the 20th century.

Vietnamization proves unsuccessful as Saigon falls to the Communists.

The Vietnam War still affects us today.

KEY POINT TO REMEMBER

United States involvement in Vietnam was an "authentic tragedy" that divided the United States and achieved little for the Vietnamese people. The tragic consequences and "lessons" of Vietnam continue to be important in the development of United States domestic and foreign policy.

PEOPLE TO REMEMBER

Lyndon Baines Johnson United States Senator from Texas, Senate Majority Leader, Vice-President under John F. Kennedy; became president after Kennedy's assassination; declared a War on Poverty and set the goal of a Great Society both to be achieved through legislation and the leadership of the federal government; the success of his domestic programs was jeopardized by the increasing involvement of the United States in the Vietnam War which led to his decision not to seek reelection in 1968.

LINKS FROM THE PAST TO THE PRESENT

1. The "lessons" of Vietnam for foreign policy makers still affect decisions.
2. Failure of massive carpet bombing to bring victory is one "lesson" of World War II and Vietnam.
3. It is always important when conducting foreign policy to have an understanding of your enemy, as the Vietnam War illustrates.

QUESTIONS

Identify each of the following:

Geneva Accord 1954	My Lai
Vietcong	Tet Offensive
Tonkin Gulf Resolution	Kent State

True or False:

1. United States interest in the Vietnam region of Southeast Asia began before the attack on Pearl Harbor in 1941.
2. Ho Chi Minh was a Vietnamese nationalist who wanted the French to remain in the country.
3. The Vietcong was organized as a National Liberation Front in South Vietnam.
4. President Johnson opposed the buildup of United States forces in Vietnam but was persuaded to change his mind by his advisors.
5. Secretary of Defense Robert McNamara and Undersecretary of State George Ball resigned from the government in protest over further escalation of United States involvement in the Vietnam War.
6. After the Tet Offensive President Johnson was convinced the United States could win the war in Vietnam.
7. Student and anti-war protests, political assassinations, and inner city riots rocked the United States in 1968.
8. President Nixon finally negotiated an end to the Vietnam War and withdrew United States forces in 1973.

Multiple Choice:

1. The Geneva Accords in 1954 called for
    a. withdrawal of United States forces after prisoners of war were returned
    b. division of Vietnam at the 17th Parallel and later elections to unite the country
    c. the French to remain in the country to preserve order.
2. The Diem government lost the support of the United States government when
    a. it attacked North Vietnam
    b. it turned to Russia for aid
    c. it attacked Buddhist monks who responded by burning themselves to death
3. The United States escalated the war by bombing
    a. North Vietnam and Vietcong supply lines in Laos
    b. Saigon, the capital of South Vietnam
    c. Vietcong bases in Southern China
4. After the United States withdrew its forces from South Vietnam
    a. the South Vietnamese invaded North Vietnam
    b. Saigon fell to the North Vietnamese in April, 1975
    c. peace reigned throughout South Vietnam
5. Nixon's policy in the Vietnam War was to
    a. Americanize the war
    b. withdraw United States forces from Cambodia and stop all attacks on the North
    c. Vietnamize the war

ANSWERS

True or False: 1. T, 2. F, 3. T, 4. F, 5. T, 6. F, 7. T, 8. T.
Multiple Choice: 1. b, 2. c, 3. a, 4. b, 5. c.

III. THE PRESIDENCIES OF RICHARD NIXON AND GERALD FORD

The Cold War and Detente

After years of brinkmanship and containment, President Nixon and Henry Kissinger, at first Nixon's National Security Advisor and later Secretary of State for both Nixon and Ford, began a new approach to the Communist world known as detente[1]. The policy of detente acknowledged the differences between the United States and the USSR but sought through negotiations and meetings to achieve limited agreements on issues of common concern. Nixon had gained his reputation as an anti-Communist Republican Congressman from California in the late 1940s even before the era of McCarthyism. As a result, he was able to conduct negotiations with both the People's Republic of China and the Soviet Union without the threat of being called "soft on Communism"—a charge often leveled by American conservatives at Democrats.

Nixon and Kissinger embark on a policy of detente with the Soviet Union and the Communist world.

Negotiations led to a trade agreement that provided for large amounts of surplus grain to be sold to the Soviets at low prices. The agreement helped United States farmers and helped the USSR feed its people. It was mutually beneficial. It was another approach to the perpetual farm problem of overproduction in America. Negotiations on arms control led, in 1972, to the signing of the Strategic Arms Limitation Treaty (SALT), which limited the number of anti-ballistic missiles (ABMs) each side could have. Negotiators also agreed to a freeze on the number of offensive weapons each side would hold.

Relations with China

The most dramatic move made by Nixon and Kissinger as part of detente was to open talks with the Communist leaders of the People's Republic of China, often referred to in the United States as Red China in order to distinguish it from "Free China," established on the island of Taiwan by Jiang Jieshi. After the Chinese communist victory in 1949, the United States had refused to recognize the government of Mao Zedong and both the Korean and Vietnam wars strained United States-China relations.

Nixon establishes diplomatic contacts with the People's Republic of China.

Although China and the Soviet Union were Communist nations, they had many differences, and these became intensified in the 1960s. By negotiating with the People's Republic, Nixon hoped to encourage the split. The Chinese welcomed United States support and more particularly the opportunity to trade with the United States. Henry Kissinger conducted secret negotiations with the Chinese leaders for several years, culminating in a visit by Nixon to Beijing, the capital of the People's Republic of China, in 1972. The United States agreed to support the entry of the People's Republic into the United Nations and its taking over the Security Council seat reserved for China. In 1979 formal relations between the two nations were established with the exchange of ambassadors.

---

[1]*detente* A relaxing and easing of tensions between nations.

President Ford continues Nixon's policies of detente.

While detente did not end confrontations between the Soviets and the United States, relations seemed less tense. Nixon visited Moscow and Leonid Brezhnev, the new Soviet leader, came to the United States for summit meetings. President Ford continued the Nixon policies of detente and kept Henry Kissinger on as Secretary of State. Ford went to China, held two summit meetings with the Soviet leaders, and agreed to further arms limitations. Kissinger clearly believed the United States-Soviet relations were at the center of international affairs, yet there were other international crises to be handled in the Nixon years.

Africa and South America

Ford militarily supports anti-Communist forces in spite of detente.

As African nations became independent in the 1960s and South Africa intensified its enforcement of Apartheid, the United States sought allies and attempted to block any possible Soviet influence in the area. President Ford supported anti-Communist guerrillas in the civil war that broke out in the Portuguese colony of Angola. United States investments abroad were large and, according to the Nixon-Kissinger policies, had to be protected. Aid, both economic and military, continued to be sent abroad, but the former did little to redress the greatly increasing gap between the poor nations, referred to as the Third World[2], and the traditionally rich, industrialized nations of Europe, North America, and Japan. When a Marxist, Salvatore Allende, was elected President of Chile, the CIA intervened, and a military junta overthrew Allende. The United States was not going to tolerate another potential Castro in the Americas in spite of detente.

The Middle East

Wars between Israel and the Arab states fail to resolve the political problems of the Middle East.

After the Suez crisis of 1956, peace did not come to the Middle East. In 1967 Israel successfully attacked its Arab neighbors in a dramatic Six Day War. Israel more than quadrupled its size. The Arabs were shocked. They refused to sign a peace treaty. The Arabs who had fled Israel during the 1948 and Six Day wars organized under the leadership of Yassir Arafat the Palestine Liberation Organization (PLO), pledged to retaking their homeland and destroying Israel. In 1973 in the Yom Kippur War, Egypt and Syria attacked Israel. To support the Arabs, an embargo was placed on the exports of oil to the United States by the recently formed Organization of Petroleum Exporting Countries (OPEC).

Nixon sent Kissinger to the Middle East to find a peaceful solution. A cease fire was put in place, and then Kissinger undertook for the United States a year of "shuttle diplomacy," flying frequently between Middle Eastern capitals seeking agreements between the Arabs and Israel. The result was that in 1975 Kissinger finally got Egypt and Israel to agree to a United Nations peace-keeping force in the Sinai Peninsula. The United Nations force separated the two armies, but Israel refused to withdraw from the occupied territories.

---

[2]*Third World:* Undeveloped or developing countries that are not aligned with either the Communist or non-Communist blocs; first used in the 1950s by French President de Gaulle.

OPEC ended the embargo in 1974, but not before oil prices had more than tripled worldwide and inflation began. The resulting impact on world development and poverty in the non-oil producing nations is still apparent. OPEC still exercises strong control over world oil prices.

The world economy is affected by OPEC.

Kissinger's diplomacy failed to bring peace. In 1990 these issues are still unresolved.

Nixon's Domestic Policies

Nixon's view of domestic government was clearly that of a conservative who did not want changes and preferred the way things were in the past. Nixon attempted to block the renewal of the Voting Rights Act of 1965 and to delay integration of the Mississippi school system ordered by the federal courts. He supported an anti-busing law to block the use of buses to integrate schools, but Congress failed to pass the legislation. When Chief Justice Earl Warren retired, Nixon appointed a more conservative Chief Justice, Warren Burger. Later two of Nixon's very conservative, Southern, Supreme Court appointees were rejected by the Senate.

Nixon introduced a program, the New Federalism, to give more power to the states. He asked Congress to revise the way federal programs were financed by distributing $30 billion to the states for their use without the federal government prescribing how the money should be spent. Nixon also proposed that states take responsibility for most welfare payments, but the proposal was not pushed through Congress.

Nixon presents a conservative program of New Federalism.

In 1969 Nixon persuaded Congress to cut spending and raise taxes. The economic situation in the United States had deteriorated due to growing international competition, the cost of the Great Society, and the Vietnam War. Federal deficits had grown in order to finance both guns and butter. Congress gave Nixon authority to regulate prices and wages, but he was reluctant to enforce strong measures. Inflation grew and the situation worsened after the OPEC oil embargo.

Nixon persuades Congress to raise taxes and cut spending.

During the Nixon years Congress passed several laws not supported by the administration. These included the strengthening of the Clean Air and Water Pollution Acts in response to growing environmental concerns exemplified by the organization of Earth Day 1970. Congress extended the vote to 18-year-olds.

Domestic Protests and the 1972 Election Campaign

During Nixon's first term, the 1968 mood of protest continued. Radical groups bombed business offices. Black protests and city crime increased. In spite of his statements that he wanted to bring the country together, Nixon's policies and views of government increased the divisions. Students rallied against the escalation of the Vietnam War, and the death of four students at Kent State symbolizes these divisions.

Nixon planned a re-election campaign for 1972 based on a Southern strategy, designed to attract traditionally Democratic voters to

In spite of continuing anti-war and student protests, Nixon appeals to "the silent majority" and wins re-election in 1972.

the Republican party. His civil rights proposals and Supreme Court appointees were part of this strategy. Nixon appealed to what he termed "the silent majority" of middle America who wanted "law and order" and not the permissiveness he claimed was the policy of the Democrats, who were soft on crime and drugs, and who supported civil rights, black militancy, and student radicals. The strategy worked, and Nixon and Spiro Agnew won an overwhelming victory over the liberal Democratic candidate George McGovern.

The Watergate Break-In

A break-in at the Democratic Party headquarters in the Watergate apartments reveals Nixon's fears of radicals and becomes the start of the Watergate scandal.

In spite of his brilliant moves in foreign policy, Nixon did not trust either the American people or his own abilities to appeal to them. He resorted to underhanded and illegal measures, apparently convinced they were the only way to protect the nation from those he perceived as radicals and un-American—the student protesters, the civil rights leaders, the Hippies, and those not part of the "silent majority." Nixon even had an "enemies" list—a classic example of dividing the world into "us" and "them."

"....PHONES TAPPED, MAIL OPENED, DOORS KICKED DOWN....I GUESS ALL THIS IS THE PRICE WE GOTTA PAY FOR LIVING IN THE FREE WORLD."

Mauldin in this cartoon makes a comment on the activities of the Nixon administration. Note the title over the door suggesting a connection with Watergate. What type of society do you think of in connection with phone tapping and opened mail?

On June 17, 1972 during the beginnings of the Presidential campaign, five men were caught after breaking into the Democratic Party headquarters at the Watergate apartment complex in Washington. On June 22, Nixon said his administration was in no way involved in the Watergate break-in. Thus began the Watergate scandal and cover-up. It unwound slowly over the next two years and culminated in the resignation of President Nixon.

After the break-in Nixon ordered his Chief of Staff, H.R. Haldeman, to keep the FBI from investigating. At first the cover-up worked. Little attention was paid to the Watergate break-in during the campaign, and the voters ignored it. However, President Nixon's cover-up was revealed eventually, and Watergate ranks as one of the worst scandals in the history of the nation.

Resignation of Vice President Agnew

While the Watergate cover-up was being exposed, Vice President Spiro Agnew resigned his office after he was accused of taking bribes while serving as an official in Maryland. He was also accused of income tax illegalities. At the same time Nixon was assessed $500,000 in back taxes by the IRS for failure to pay all his taxes between 1969 and 1972 and for using federal money to improve his private homes. The government appeared bogged down in scandals and disgrace. Following the provisions of the recently adopted Amendment XXV on succession, Nixon nominated and the Senate confirmed Congressman Gerald R. Ford of Michigan as Vice President.

Vice President Spiro Agnew is accused of taking bribes and resigns.

The Watergate Case

In March, 1974 the Watergate case reached its climax. The Watergate grand jury handed down indictments against White House staffers Haldeman and John Ehrlichman, former Attorney General John Mitchell, and four White House aides. President Nixon was named a co-conspirator but he was not indicted. During the investigation, it was learned that Nixon had tape recordings of all conversations in his office. Nixon at first refused to release the tapes. When he was forced to do so by court orders, the tapes—despite an 18-minute blank—revealed White House involvement in the cover-up. Calls for impeachment grew.

Tape recordings of conversations in Nixon's office reveal White House involvement in the Watergate scandal.

On August 8, 1973, Richard Nixon announced his resignation as President of the United States effective the next day. He is the only President to be forced to resign his office. President Gerald Ford in September, 1974 pardoned Nixon, believing it was time to put Watergate behind the nation. Nixon was never indicted for a crime and never admitted any wrongdoing. In the years since then he has regained some stature as historians acknowledge his important foreign policy contributions.

The reaction of Congress to Watergate and the Nixon resignation was to pass legislation to address the perceived reasons for the Watergate scandal. Congress acted to limit Presidential power with the War Powers Act in 1973. This controversial act required Congressional approval if combat troops are committed for longer than

Congress moves to limit Presidential power.

90 days in any situation. Congress also set limits on the amount of financial contributions and expenditures allowed in Presidential campaigns—remember, Watergate began as a campaign issue. Congress also extended the Freedom of Information Act, requiring the government to act promptly when information is sought by the public and to prove the need on national security grounds whenever classifying information as secret.

Whether the measures have been successful or addressed the true reasons for Watergate is debatable. The mood of the nation as a result of the Vietnam War, the frustrations over the failure to attain the Great Society, the deterioration of the economic situation, and the personality of President Nixon were all factors in the Watergate scandal. No legislation could address these issues. While Watergate dragged on for two years, it weakened the President's credibility and effectiveness as leader of the nation. Finally, 29 members of Nixon's administration were indicted, pleaded guilty or convicted in the Watergate scandal.

The Ford Presidency

President Ford continues Nixon's domestic policies.

When Nixon resigned, Gerald Ford became President, the first not elected by the Electoral College. He nominated Governor Nelson Rockefeller, long time spokesperson of the more liberal wing of the Republican party, as his Vice President. Ford continued Nixon's domestic policies.

The economy worsened and unemployment rose. The OPEC oil embargo pushed inflation from 3 percent in 1972 to 11 percent in 1974. Baby-boomers needed jobs at a time when Americans were rejecting gas guzzling cars made in Detroit because of high oil prices. Increased foreign competition, particularly from Japan in autos and electronics, hurt the economy. Many new jobs were added, but they were in service industries—restaurants and selling—rather than in heavy manufacturing. American productivity, or the amount an individual produced, did not keep pace with the Japanese and Europeans. As a result, profits did not rise as wages did. The economic picture of the nation was changing.

Ford's response was to call for voluntary restraints on wages and price increases to combat inflation. He called for tax cuts, which, according to theory, would stimulate industry. Ford did not want to spend for the programs of the Great Society.

Ford's economic policies prove unsuccessful and the nation enters a recession.

Ford's policies were not successful. The nation was in an economic recession—the post-New Deal term for what had been termed panics or depressions. The New Deal had ended laissez-faire as a federal government economic policy and had established that the federal government should act to affect economic conditions of inflation and recession. The Kennedy/Johnson tax cuts had stimulated the economy, but conditions were different in the mid 1970s, and it was not until the Reagan presidency that inflation was reduced and the economic situation improved.

Election of 1976

Governor Ronald Reagan of California, a strong conservative, contested the Republican primary with Gerald Ford. Ford won the nomination. Jimmy Carter, Governor of Georgia, worked hard for over two years to win name recognition and in the Democratic Party primaries did well enough to gain his party's nomination. He ran as an outsider—one who was not linked to Washington and so would bring a new spirit and integrity to the Presidency. Carter and his Vice President, Walter Mondale of Minnesota, defeated Ford and Rockefeller.

Jimmy Carter, an outsider, wins the Democratic nomination and the presidency.

To suggest the new spirit and mood he would bring to the nation, Carter and his wife, Rosalyn, after his inauguration at the capital, walked at the head of the traditional parade down Pennsylvania Avenue from the Capital to the White House. The nation was ready for this new spirit. Unfortunately, the Carter presidency for many reasons was unable to achieve its goals of a more democratic and just society.

KEY POINTS TO REMEMBER

Nixon's policy of detente relaxed Cold War tensions and led to agreements with the Soviet Union and the recognition of the People's Republic of China. Domestically, the Watergate break-in and resulting scandal destroyed Nixon's credibility and forced his resignation.

PEOPLE TO REMEMBER

Richard Nixon Congressman from California, Vice President under Eisenhower, 37th President of the United States; he was forced to resign the presidency as a result of the Watergate break-in and resulting scandal; he negotiated an end to the Vietnam War and achieved major foreign policy successes through his policy of detente with the U.S.S.R. and by his recognition of the People's Republic of China; his policy of "New Federalism" attempted to give more power to the individual states.

LINKS FROM THE PAST TO THE PRESENT

1. Scandals in the federal government recur periodically and have an important impact on the nation.
2. Disarmament negotiations have been held throughout this century and continue.
3. It is always important to be prepared to negotiate with "the enemy" regardless of who it is.
4. The importance of the American legal system for maintaining honesty and integrity in government has been important in our history from the *McCulloch v. Madison* decision to the Watergate Case to the Iran-Contra Affair.

QUESTIONS

Identify each of the following:

SALT	OPEC
Southern Strategy	Watergate

True or False:

1. The policy of detente acknowledged differences between the United States and the U.S.S.R.
2. After Nixon's trip to China, the United States prevented the People's Republic of China from taking the Security Council seat assigned to China.
3. The CIA intervened in Chile to support the overthrow of President Allende.
4. Israel more than quadrupled its size by seizing Arab lands in the Six Day War.
5. OPEC continues to exercise control over world oil prices.
6. President Nixon's conservative views can be seen in his attempts to block the renewal of the Voting Rights Act, his Southern Strategy for re-election, and his appeal to the "Silent Majority."
7. The Watergate scandal began because Nixon was overconfident of re-election and of his support by all groups in the United States.
8. President Nixon was indicted for his role in the Watergate scandal and pardoned by President Ford before his conviction.
9. Governor Nelson Rockefeller was nominated to the Vice Presidency by President Ford and his nomination was approved by the Senate.
10. President Ford continued President Nixon's foreign policy programs and tried unsuccessfully to control the inflation precipitated by the OPEC oil embargo.

Multiple Choice:

1. President Nixon and Henry Kissinger worked through detente to improve relations between the United States and
    a. Leonid Brezhnev of the U.S.S.R.
    b. Jiang Jieshi of the People's Republic of China
    c. Yassir Arafat and the Palestine Liberation Organization
2. Henry Kissinger undertook shuttle diplomacy in the Middle East in order to bring a settlement to
    a. the Six Day War
    b. the OPEC embargo and the Yom Kippur War
    c. the poverty in the area
3. The Nixon concept of government was called
    a. the New Frontier
    b. the New Federalism
    c. the Pentagon Papers
4. Among those involved in the Watergate break-in and cover-up were
    a. Nixon's attorney and White House aides H.R. Haldeman and John Erhlichman
    b. Vice President Spiro Agnew
    c. all of the above

ANSWERS

True or False: 1. T, 2. F, 3. T, 4. T, 5. T, 6. T, 7. F, 8. F, 9. T, 10. T.
Multiple Choice: 1. a, 2. b, 3. b, 4. a.

IV. LIFESTYLE OF THE '60s AND '70s

The New Left and the Counterculture

Two movements, the New Left and the counterculture, best represent the changing expectations and lifestyles of the 1960s and early '70s. The New Left, in which the Students for a Democratic Society (SDS) was most significant, believed in changing the political system. Members of the New Left believed their goal of a more democratic society would best be achieved through participatory democracy, in which all members of society—rich and poor; African-American, Hispanic, Native American, white—would be heard in any decision making.

Members of the New Left were strong anti-anti-Communists, and many were committed to the teachings of Marxism and the anti-war radicalism expressed in Europe in the 1920s. The New Left began by using the model of non-violence established by the Civil Rights movement, but it slowly slipped into the use of violence, especially after 1968. At the same time, many New Left members, especially those in SDS, became more radical, founding groups like the Weathermen, committed to the violent overthrow of existing institutions. Several of the founders then abandoned the New Left, and it quickly lost political impact.

The counterculture movement was not only non-political but anti-political. Those who were part of the counterculture are known as Hippies. They were mainly young people. As a result of the post-war baby boom, by the mid-1960s over half the United States population was under 30. The counterculture was another manifestation of the youth culture of the post-World War II years.

The Hippies were alienated by bureaucracy, materialism, and the Vietnam War. They encountered bureaucracy in the ever-growing size of universities and the government that was conducting the Vietnam War. They were exposed to materialism in the lives of their parents, who had lived and often suffered as youngsters in the Depression years and had become adults during the war and postwar years of conformity and business success under Eisenhower. The Hippies accused this older generation of measuring success in terms of what they could acquire. It was another case of identifying yourself as what the others were not.

Hippies were angered by the Vietnam War, which they were expected to fight and of which they disapproved. The New Left and the counterculture united in opposition to the Vietnam War. In 1965 the largest anti-war rally brought together 80,000 people in New York; in 1967, 500,000 members of the New Left and counterculture gathered in Central Park in New York City for an anti-war rally. Draft resisters were supported by the counterculture movement. Over 30,000 went to Canada. In 1968 what for most began as peaceful demonstrations at the Democratic Convention turned into riots. Some of the more violent leaders had planned for violence from the start, and this helped split the New Left. After 1968 the New Left became more and more violent and essentially died out.

The New Left and counterculture movements reflect changing attitudes of some Americans.

The Hippies reject bureaucracy and materialism and protest the Vietnam War.

The Hippies of the counterculture continued. They focused their lives on new approaches to love and life.

Love, Drugs, and Rock 'n' Roll

Members of the counterculture experiment with non-traditional life styles.

The center of the counterculture was the Haight-Ashbury district of San Francisco. In their attempts to find new patterns for living to replace traditional approaches they found restricting and alienating, Hippies tried various experiments in communal living in both urban and rural settings. They experimented with drugs, seeking new experiences and new values. Their emphasis on love and peace earned them the name of "flower children."

Rock 'n' roll and folk artists express the sentiments of the counterculture movement.

Music, especially rock 'n' roll, provided an outlet for the ideas of the counterculture. The United States tour by the English rock group, the Beatles, popularized rock among the young. The lyrics of folk artists Bob Dylan and Joan Baez expressed the concerns and alienation of the Hippies. The rock music of stars such as Janice Joplin and Jimi Hendrix brought them together. The rock concert at Woodstock, New York, in August, 1969 brought over 400,000 members of the counterculture together in an atmosphere of rock, sun, joy, love, and drugs. Woodstock become synonymous with the counterculture and its values, which American traditionalists viewed as dangerous and subversive. The counterculture movement, together with anti-war sentiment on college campuses and among some Democratic party members, led to Richard Nixon's fear for his re-election and his concern about loyalty, patriotism, and support for his Vietnam policy. The result was Watergate.

The Sexual Revolution

Several factors lead to an apparent sexual revolution.

Another aspect of cultural change in the 1960s is seen in the so-called Sexual Revolution. The awareness that sexual patterns differed and many men and women experimented with pre-marital sex, combined with the attitudes expressed by the counterculture, laid the foundation of the sexual revolution. The discovery and availability of "the Pill," a female contraceptive that lessened the possibility of pregnancy, affected the changing moral and ethical behavior of young Americans who saw themselves as "liberated" from the "old morality." Many young people lived together as their attitudes towards pre-marital sex changed.

The publicity given to such behavior may be responsible for its seeming to be a revolution since there had always been several standards for morality in America. While female promiscuity was frowned upon in the past, male infidelity and loose behavior had been tolerated. It was only with the publicity given to sexual behavior of males and females by the Kinsey reports and the availability of the Pill that a new morality was shared by both sexes and was seen as a revolution.

Fundamentalist churches and the Roman Catholic church decried the new morality. Many Protestant churches responded with the concept of situation ethics, in which one's moral behavior was to be based on the situation, not on an established univeral principle. Situation ethics became popular with the younger generation and was discussed in college classrooms.

Women's Liberation

The Civil Rights movement not only provided a model for the SDS, it awakened other minorities to their subordinate status. The largest group so inspired were women, who actually formed a slight majority of the population but who shared with minorities a place in the economic and political structure subordinate to the white male.

Betty Friedan in her 1963 book *The Feminine Mystique* first expressed views that became the focus of the women's liberation movement. Friedan claimed middle class values stifled women, who were expected to spend their days with children with no stimulation from other adults. A woman was to fill the position of housewife and companion to her husband, who left home daily to meet the challenges of the world. Many women agreed with Friedan's criticism, and in 1966 the National Organization for Women (NOW) was organized.

NOW focused attention on the job discrimination women faced in companies run by white males where women rarely had executive positions. NOW argued for equal pay for equal work done by men and women, for greater job opportunities, and for day care facilities. In 1972 Congress passed and sent to the states for ratification an Equal Rights Amendment (ERA) to the Constitution which would guarantee equality of the sexes. The states failed to ratify the amendment within the ten year time limit and the time was extended in 1982 but the amendment has not passed. NOW leaders suggest this failure confirms their analysis that white men in positions of power discriminate against women. The debate over ERA and women's liberation was intense and raised such questions as, "Would women be drafted into the armed services if the ERA passed?"

The women's movement created a greater awareness of the place of women in American society and raised the consciousness level of both men and women. Its membership and the concerns it addressed were largely middle class issues, which limited its success and appeal. However, in the 25 years since NOW was founded, job opportunities for women have greatly increased and some progress has been made in equal pay and in the availability of day care.

All three issues became very important for American women as the divorce rate climbed in those years and more and more single women became heads of families. These single heads of families need job opportunities, better pay, and day care if they are to raise their families.

Unfortunately for the effectiveness of the women's movement, the focus of the National Organization for Women was blurred in 1969 when lesbians, who were organizing for their rights, were kept out of the organization. The question raised was, should NOW support only political and economic rights or all rights of women? In 1971 the anti-lesbian policy was reversed and NOW accepted all women without regard to sexual preference.

In The Feminine Mystique *Betty Friedan expresses views that become the focus of the women's liberation movement.*

The Women's Movement addresses primarily issues of concern to middle class Americans.

The Roe v. Wade decision by the Supreme Court makes abortion a major controversy in America.

NOW's fight for a woman's right to abortion in cases of unwanted pregnancy was won in the Supreme Court decision of *Roe v. Wade* in 1973. The Roe decision expanded the Court's interpretation of the right to privacy and removed state restrictions on abortion during the first three months of pregnancy.

The abortion decision created great controversy in America and has split the women's movement. A pro-life group emerged claiming abortion was murder because the fetus was a human life; a prochoice group countered that until the fetus could survive outside the womb, it should not be considered a person and that a woman should be in charge of her own body—not a man, a court, a church, or the legislature.

The abortion controversy still rages in the United States as prolife and pro-choice forces battle for political and judicial power. The abortion controversy diffused the focus of the women's movement as many of its leaders devoted full time to it and not to the many other issues of concern to American women.

Gay Rights Movement

The Gay Rights Movement achieves some results.

Lesbian and homosexual Americans also organized to secure their rights as minorities who shared a different lifestyle. Many laws making certain sexual practices illegal were changed. Men and women came "out of the closet" to state openly their sexual preferences. While homophobia is still prevalent in American society, as a result of the Gay Rights movement it is now possible for gays in some communities to work openly as teachers, police, and public servants, to marry, and to raise children. The Gay Rights movement was another spin-off of the Civil Rights movement and another aspect of the Sexual Revolution which began in the 1960s.

American Indian Movement

The American Indian Movement makes limited progress in changing the status of Native Americans.

Native Americans organized the American Indian Movement (AIM) to secure their rights as a minority. Just as the Civil Rights Movement turned to violence when the Black Power groups became important, so did the Native Americans seeking their rights to tribal lands turn to violence. In 1973 members of AIM took hostages and seized a trading post on the reservation at Wounded Knee, South Dakota, site of a massacre of Indians by the United States Cavalry in 1890. After a two-month seige the United States government agreed to examine the treaty signed with the Sioux. In 1971 the federal government returned a sacred lake in New Mexico to the Indian members of the Taos Pueblo. Through cases brought in the federal courts, Indian groups have been able to get native tribal lands returned and to gain hunting and fishing rights. While significant, these gains have still left the majority of the Native American population as the most depressed group in the country.

American Agriculture

The New Deal began subsidizing American agriculture, and subsidies continued in the post-war period. Farms were consolidated and more and more run like large businesses. Small farmers suffered and continued to leave the farms they sold to the large conglomerates. Nixon's grain deals with the USSR benefited the large wheat farmers of the Midwest. Government-acquired farm surpluses were distributed to needy countries as part of Cold War policy to win them to the American side.

In spite of increasing mechanization, farm workers were needed at harvest time. These migrant workers, many of them illegal immigrants, were often exploited. Their living conditions were as poor as any in the country.

In California, Cesar Chavez organized agricultural workers to gain for them greater economic power and human dignity. Chavez' work on behalf of the poor farm worker parallels the work done by the Civil Rights leaders in gaining rights for the minority. Chavez created a greater awareness of the lot of the farm workers by organizing boycotts of produce produced on non-union farms. The non-violent technique proved successful, and some working conditions and pay scales did improve.

Agriculture becomes a large business, and Cesar Chavez organizes agricultural workers to gain economic advantages for them.

The Supreme Court

The Supreme Court under Chief Justice Earl Warren, who was appointed by Eisenhower, handed down several significant decisions in the area of civil and individual rights. Besides the *Brown v. Board of Education* decision in 1954, which declared unconstitutional "separate but equal" schools, the Warren court upheld the Civil Rights legislation of the 1960s. Two cases, *Gideon v. Wainwright* in 1963 and *Escobedo v. Illinois* in 1964, protected the rights of criminal suspects. In the Gideon case the Court held that a lawyer must be supplied for any accused prisoner who could not afford a lawyer. In the Escobedo case the Court declared the police had to inform a suspect of his or her legal rights. If this were not done, the case could be dismissed.

The Warren Court extends individual rights.

Some Americans reacted that the Court was "soft on crime." This became an issue in Nixon's 1968 election campaign when he appealed for "law and order" in America.

These Supreme Court cases illustrate that the Court shared the 1960s concern for the poor. When Earl Warren retired, Nixon appointed a more conservative Chief Justice, Warren Burger, but the Court under Burger continued to interpret the Constitution to extend American's right to privacy and to protect the rights of the poor. The most important and yet controversial decision of the Burger Court was the *Roe v. Wade* decision on abortion in 1973. In another controversial decision, the Bakke case, the Burger Court declared unconstitutional quotas that were used to establish equal opportunities for minorities in hiring and schooling. Quotas had been established by federal legislation to gain greater access for minorities to the business and economic life of the nation.

The Burger Court declares quotas unconstitutional.

American Business

Postwar prosperity continued through the 1960s, stimulated by the Kennedy/Johnson tax cut and the spending for both the Great

In the post-World War II period until the 1970s the government appeared able to control swings in the business cycle through fiscal and monetary policies.

Society and the Vietnam War. There had been mild economic recessions during the Eisenhower presidency, and business and economic growth was not entirely untroubled during the 1960s, but the federal government through its fiscal and monetary policies seemed to have control of the business cycle. Fiscal policy is controlled by Congress under the President's leadership and involves government spending and the raising and lowering of taxes at the proper moment. Monetary policy is controlled by the Federal Reserve Board and government agencies and involves increasing and decreasing the amount of money in circulation and controlling the interest rate. At times the President and Congress disagree, and both may disagree with the Federal Reserve Board, but overall until the 1970s the system worked quite effectively.

The shift in the economy to service industries and away from heavy industry deeply affected the strength of labor unions as most service industries were non-union. The electronics industry began to grow, bringing rapid growth to some regions such as the peninsula south of San Francisco, California, dubbed Silicone Valley because of its heavy concentration of electronic companies, and Route 128 around Boston, Massachusetts. Later challenges from Japan would affect these growth industries of the 1970s.

The OPEC oil embargo brings an end to the postwar boom and begins a period of high inflation.

The excessive spending on the Great Society and Vietnam created economic problems for Nixon. He asked for price controls and a tax cut, using the traditional techniques to combat recession. While the economic situation was not good in the Nixon years, it was the oil embargo of 1973 that brought an end to the postwar boom. The economic situation was different from the usual recession, when jobs were lost and prices fell. As a result of the embargo, jobs were lost but prices rose. Ford and later President Carter struggled with the situation, but neither was able to stop effectively the inflationary cycle. The auto industry suffered and pulled other industries down with it.

American heavy industry has not yet recovered from the economic crisis of the mid-1970s. Yet American industry continued to be highly important and visual in American policy-making circles. The need for defense and military goods in Vietnam kept one side of American industry producing. This combination of military need and industrial power became a powerful force in American life after the Cold War began. In his farewell address to the nation, President Dwight Eisenhower warned of the power and potential danger of this "military industrial complex," which could dominate the United States economy. While the economic problems of the 1970s seemed to suggest Eisenhower was wrong, the need to support United States industry and to keep it strong for defense became an important factor in the Reagan presidency.

Entertainment and the Arts

Films, literature, and art reflect the views of the counterculture.

Several of the more distinguished movies of the 1960s reflected the changing values of society. The life of the counterculture was portrayed in 1969's *Easy Rider,* the story of a drug-using motorcycle rider who travels the country with no particular goals. *Who's Afraid of Virginia Woolf* with Elizabeth Taylor and Richard Burton in 1966 and *The Graduate* with Dustin Hoffman in 1967 were brilliantly acted. Both stories questioned the traditional social and sexual values of America as did Tom Wolfe's novel, *Electric Kool Aid Acid Test* (1968). John Updike commented on the spiritual malaise and sexual adventures of middle-class suburbanites in works like his Rabbit series: *Rabbit Run* (1960), *Rabbit Redux* (1971), and *Rabbit is Rich* (1981). Thomas Pynchon's *Gravity's Rainbow* (1973) explored new areas of literary understanding and gained him a wide following. American literature was becoming more and more diverse. Andy Warhol and Ray Lichtenstein used items from the popular culture—tomato soup cans and comic strips—to create a new world of art. Their art reflected the same questioning of materialism and its values seen in the counterculture and the Sexual Revolution.

Hundreds of movies and television series were produced, and the number of hours children and adults watched "the tube" increased. *Sesame Street,* a television program designed to prepare youngsters for school, became a hit and illustrates one attempt to use the media for educational purposes. The Presidential election debates of 1960, the news coverage of the Civil Rights Movement, the Vietnam War, and Watergate illustrated the power of television to impact American political life and to present social issues. For the most part, however, movies and television provided escape and entertainment. More and more professional athletic contests were covered by television, and sports viewing became a major pasttime of the American public.

Television has a major impact on American society.

KEY POINT TO REMEMBER

American culture in the 1960s and early '70s was dominated by a counterculture movement, which supported love, drugs, and an anti-war policy. Different minorities organized to gain their "rights" as the long post-World War II economic boom finally came to an end.

PEOPLE TO REMEMBER

Betty Friedan   Reformer; founder and President of National Organization for Women and National Woman's Political Caucus; author of *The Feminine Mystique*, which analyzed the role of women in American society.

Cesar Chavez   Founder of National Farm Workers Association; organized migrant farm workers in California and other regions; started a national, non-violent boycott of California grapes to force farm owners to improve conditions and wages for migrant workers.

LINKS FROM THE PAST TO THE PRESENT

1. Abortion, first raised as an issue by the women's movement, continues as a major issue in American politics.
2. Rock 'n' roll, television, and art all play important roles in contemporary American life.

Equality and Freedom—The basis of America's Ideology

Equality

The Declaration of Independence states that "all men are created equal" and throughout American history some people have struggled to make this literally true. Many others have interpreted the phrase to mean all men (and women) should have an equal *opportunity* in life. These two views of equality are often in conflict. To achieve either view of equality, laws are needed and these laws restrict the freedom of individuals.

Freedom

Throughout American history many individuals have emphasized freedom as being the basis of American life. They emphasize that we fought England in the Revolution to defend our freedom and have continued the struggle to the present. While many would support equality as an ideal, they love their freedom more and so oppose laws and other methods used to create equality of all people or situations of equal opportunity. They believe that only by allowing full freedom for individual actions can we achieve our best in society.

---

3. The various minority movements for civil rights—Gay Rights, NOW, AIM, Farm Workers—continue to be significant and reflect Americans' concern for individual rights.

QUESTIONS

Identify each of the following:

Counterculture	*Sesame Street*
NOW	Military Industrial Complex
AIM	*Roe v. Wade*
Escobedo v. Illinois	

True or False:

1. The Civil Rights Movement was established by the counterculture.
2. Hippies believed in drugs, violence, and the Vietnam War.
3. Rock 'n' roll provided an outlet for the ideas of the counterculture.
4. The Pill had little effect on the moral and ethical behavior of Americans.
5. Situation ethics was based on established universal principles of sexual behavior.
6. The Equal Rights Amendment was passed by Congress and ratified by the states in 1982.
7. Betty Friedan's work, *The Feminine Mystique*, argued against women's role as housewife and caretaker of children.
8. Native Americans seeking their rights seized hostages at a trading post at Wounded Knee, South Dakota.

9. Cesar Chavez organized boycotts to create a greater awareness of the condition of farm workers and to gain for them economic rights.
10. In *Gideon v. Wainwright* the Supreme Court ruled that accused felons who could not afford a lawyer must be supplied one.
11. *Sesame Street* was designed to replace kindergarten.
12. President Eisenhower in his farewell address warned of the potential of a military industrial complex.

Multiple Choice:
1. Woodstock became synonymous with
    a. the Gay Rights movement
    b. Women's Liberation
    c. the counterculture movement
2. Among the groups formed to advance their rights as minorities were
    a. the Gay Rights movement and NOW
    b. SDS and AIM
    c. all of the above
3. The counterculture and the New Left were united in their attitudes towards
    a. the Vietnam War
    b. the importance of rock 'n' roll
    c. drugs

4. The Kinsey Reports revealed that
    a. Americans strictly adhered to the teachings of all churches on morality
    b. American women were more promiscuous than American males
    c. neither of the above
5. Andy Warhol and Ray Lichtenstein found inspiration for their art in
    a. tomato soup cans and comic strips
    b. movies
    c. stories from Tom Wolfe's *Electric Kool Aid Acid Test*
6. Fiscal policy involves
    a. increasing and decreasing the amount of money in circulation
    b. raising and lowering government taxes and spending
    c. controlling the interest rate

ANSWERS
True or False: 1. F, 2. F, 3. T, 4. F, 5. F, 6. F, 7. T, 8. T, 9. T, 10. T, 11. F, 12. T.
Multiple Choice: 1. c, 2. c, 3. a, 4. c, 5.a., 6.b.

CHAPTER 13

The Recent Past: 1977–1990

APPROACHES TO HISTORY
Current Events or History and The Need for Revision

As you are aware, historians interpret history in many different ways. No matter what perspective an historian takes, all historians deal with events in the past, events that can be investigated and analyzed over time, events that can be shown to have had significance. As historians study events closer to the present, they lose the perspective they have on the more distant past. Historians are called upon to make decisions about what events are significant without time to analyze the full impact of an event over a period of years.

All people face a similar problem in their own lives. How do you decide in your own life what is important in a given year? If you look back to when you were five or ten, you will recall a few events you can say were important in making you who you are today, but how do you decide what events of the past year will be included in your biography written 30 years from now? An athletic victory, ending a close relationship, an illness may seem very important now, but time may change that understanding. So it is with recent events with which historians must deal.

Some historians suggest that the events of the most recent ten to twenty years should be considered current events and not history. They suggest that only with time will we truly understand what events were significant and be able to effectively analyze them. To illustrate this, these historians refer to "revisionist" history.

All historians, regardless of their basic viewpoint, continually analyze and reanalyze the information from the past. At times new information from the distant past or the application of new analytical skills or new assumptions about human nature will be applied to the distant past and lead to revisions of old interpretations, but these situations are rare.

What is more common is to have revisions made of recent history—of the last 100 years.

In the past ten years, historians have presented revisions of the accepted views of the origins of the Cold War, the role of Presidents Truman and Eisenhower, and the Cuban Missile Crisis, all because they have gained a perspective on those times and have had access to new information. Earlier explanations no longer appear as valid. The historian recording recent events and the students of them must realize they are dealing with current events and the historical perspective is therefore lacking. What events of the past 15 years will appear in a textbook on American history 200 years from now? That is the challenge faced as the Carter, Reagan, and Bush presidencies are studied.

To illustrate this point consider three events: the Iranian hostage crisis during Carter's presidency, the invasion of Grenada by Reagan, and the intervention in Panama by Bush. All appeared major events at the time. However, while realizing the events were very hard on the individuals involved, their importance is fading in comparison to other actions taken by these three most recent American presidents. On the other hand, Carter's establishment of large wilderness areas in Alaska, Reagan's inability to balance the budget, and Bush's commitment of forces to Saudi Arabia appear more and more important.

As you read the following pages, keep in mind that many historians would consider this chapter an account of current events, which will require careful analysis by historians in the years ahead to determine just how significant they are in the long history of the United States. Perhaps you will be one of those historians.

I. DOMESTIC POLICIES OF CARTER, REAGAN, AND BUSH

Domestic Issues Under Carter

Carter was the "outsider" in Washington. He was a "born again" Christian and wished to conduct the government on moral principles. He introduced legislation to deal with complex energy and economic problems but failed to push his programs consistently. It was said Carter became entrapped in the details of issues and was unable to focus on the broad goals. Carter had no "program" for his presidency but did act in several areas.

Carter began the move toward deregulation of industry, which was accelerated by Reagan. Environmental legislation under Carter included the creation of a "superfund" to clean up hazardous toxic waste dumps, which were being identified as

Carter introduces no major program for reform but attempts to deal with environmental issues, energy conservation, and economic problems.

environmental hazards, and the establishment of a wilderness area of 100 million acres in Alaska, an act some environmentalists have praised as the most important conservation act since Theodore Roosevelt. A Department of Energy and a Department of Education were added to the Cabinet thus acknowledging the importance of these two areas and the changing role of the federal government in education.

Responding to continuing concerns about United States' use of oil and the power of OPEC, Carter attempted to establish an energy policy, but oil pressure groups in Congress and Carter's own lack of consistency on what he wanted made the attempt unsuccessful. Carter was no more successful in combating the economic problems of inflation and recession. Like Ford and Nixon, he followed a voluntary approach to wage and price control, setting guidelines only. The Federal Reserve Board, exercising its control over monetary policy, tightened the money supply, which increased interest rates. High interest rates reduced car and house sales, which affected employment levels. By the time of the 1980 election, the annual inflation rate was 12 percent, interest rates were 21 percent, and unemployment levels were high.

Election of 1980

The Republicans nominated Ronald Reagan, former movie star and former Governor of California, as their candidate. As an actor in Hollywood, Reagan had been a Democrat and expressed liberal ideas, but his views changed and as Governor of California he became a spokesperson for the conservative wing of the Republican party. Reagan believed less government was better. He advocated deregulation of industry, less government expenditure on social welfare, lower income tax rates, and the buildup of United States military defenses.

What seemed to appeal most to the American public were Reagan's sincerity and his appeal to the traditional values of American life—religion, family, and patriotism.

Reagan chose as his Vice President George Bush, a New Englander who had made a fortune in Texas oil before turning to government service. Bush had served as Congressman from Texas, director of the CIA, United States liason officer in the People's Republic of China, Ambassador to the United Nations, and head of the Republican Party. He was one of the most qualified candidates on the basis of offices held who had ever run on a National ticket.

John Anderson of Illinois, a more liberal Republican, had contested the primaries against Reagan and ran as an Independent. Carter and Mondale were renominated. They went into the campaign handicapped by the hostage crisis, the economic situation, and the nation's swing to conservatism. Reagan and Bush won overwhelmingly in the Electoral College, and the Republicans gained control of the Senate and made gains in the House of Representatives.

Ronald Reagan, espousing traditional American values, wins the presidency and the Republicans gain control of the Senate.

Reagan's Economic Policy

Reagan was ideologically commited to conservatism. Some saw his program as an attack on the whole New Deal and its restructuring of United States society, but Reagan made no changes in the New Deal's Social Security legislation and promised to maintain a "safety net" of welfare benefits for the most needy. He did, however, push through Congress massive budget cuts affecting all types of domestic programs from food stamps to college loans.

Reagan supports supply-side economics and pushes Congress to reform the tax code.

Reagan believed in "supply side" economics. Supply side theory holds that if taxes are reduced, people will not spend the extra money for goods but will invest the extra money. These investments will create new jobs in industries. Everyone will benefit, the nation will prosper and thus the government will collect more in taxes in spite of the lower tax rates. To many, supply side economics was a new way of describing the old 19th century "trickle down" theory that held that helping the rich will ultimately help the poor.

Following supply side economics, Reagan pushed through Congress two major bills reforming the tax code. The graduated income tax[1] rates were an important part of New Deal social policy, by which the gap between the rich and the poor was to be narrowed by using income and inheritance taxes to take money from the wealthy for the government to spend on programs to benefit the poor and less wealthy. The top tax rate was now cut from 70 percent to 28 percent, greatly benefiting the wealthy. An increase in deductions helped middle class families, but the middle class as a whole benefited very little. Many poorer Americans paid no taxes as a result of the changes. At the time the Reagan policy was widely acclaimed.

The Economy

The economy, battered by high interest rates and the oil crisis at the end of Carter's administration was in recession by late 1981. Blue collar workers of the "old" industries and blacks were hardest hit. Slow improvement came as non-OPEC oil producing nations increased supplies and the rate of inflation declined to 4 percent. The Federal Reserve responded by lowering interest rates, and economic conditions improved, helped by the tax cuts that gave people money to spend. However, the rise in government revenue expected after the tax cuts never occurred. The federal deficit grew tremendously. It reached $195 billion in 1983, and it continued at very high levels during the Reagan administration. While some taxes were increased under Reagan, both Reagan and Bush were reluctant to do so. Bush finally agreed to some tax increases on gasoline and liquor in late 1990 but the agreements did not include the cost of the Savings and Loans "bailout" (see page 314) or the Persian Gulf crisis.

The country emerges from recession.

---

[1]*Graduated income tax* An income tax policy in which there is a different tax rate for differnet levels of income, with rates as high as 95 percent on the highest incomes and no tax on those with lowest incomes. The opposite policy is to have a flat rate, which all people pay regardless of income level.

The trade deficit turns the United States into a debtor nation.

Making the economic situation more complex was the huge trade deficit that developed in the 1980s as Americans bought more goods from overseas than they exported. During the Reagan presidency the United States became a debtor nation, owing more than it earned for the first time since World War I. These conditions persisted as the last decade of the century began.

The cartoonist Marland comments on the growing recession in the New England states in this 1989 cartoon. What "line" are the man and woman in? Since the New Deal, the states and the federal government have provided unemployment payments for those who are out of work. It lasts for a limited time but it provides some help to those who lose jobs when recessions occur.

Reprinted with permission of the artist, Mike Marland, Concord Monitor, Concord, N.H.

The stock market and business takeovers attract large sums of money.

During these Reagan-Bush years the gap between the rich and poor widened. The pay of top business executives grew on a percentage basis much more rapidly than did that of daily wage earners. Much of the money released by the tax cut found its way into the stock market and other speculation and not into new industry. Established companies bought other companies in a great wave of consolidation and takeovers. All of this buying and selling of corporations did not address the basic problems of American industries: lack of efficient productivity, aging plants, and foreign competition.

Homelessness

The number of homeless increases in urban centers.

Meanwhile the numbers living in poverty in America increased and reached percentages similar to those before Lyndon Johnson declared a War on Poverty. Homelessness grew and by the end of the 1980s was a major problem in American cities where men, women, and often whole families lived on the street in cardboard boxes or in shelters for the homeless. George Bush spoke of a "kinder and gentler" America and referred to "a thousand points of light" provided by private individuals who aided the poor, but in his first two years in office he took little initiative in addressing at the federal level issues of education, day care, taxation, debt, and poverty.

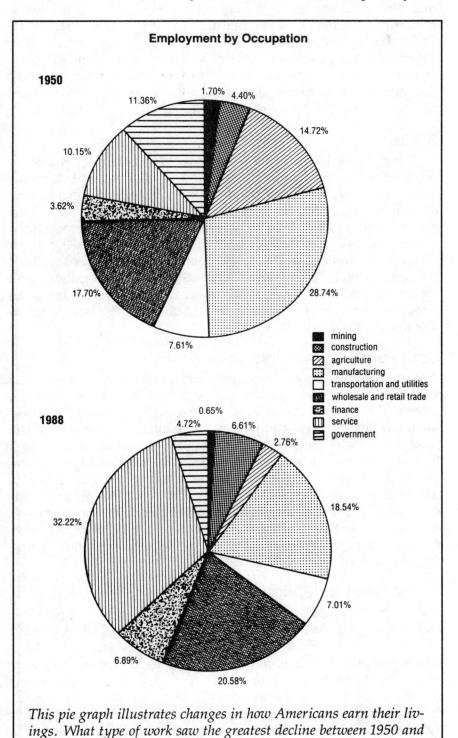

Employment by Occupation

1950

1.70% 4.40% 14.72% 28.74% 7.61% 17.70% 3.62% 10.15% 11.36%

mining
construction
agriculture
manufacturing
transportation and utilities
wholesale and retail trade
finance
service
government

1988

0.65% 4.72% 6.61% 2.76% 18.54% 7.01% 20.58% 6.89% 32.22%

This pie graph illustrates changes in how Americans earn their livings. What type of work saw the greatest decline between 1950 and 1989?

Prosperity is unevenly distributed.

While some enjoyed prosperity under Reagan, it was not evenly distributed. Farmers, who had suffered so often in the United States history, had borrowed heavily in the Carter years and were unable to repay loans when farm prices fell in the 1980s. The oil industry in Texas was hard hit by the drop in oil prices in the mid-1980s and the region experienced a recession that led to the bankruptcy of many Savings and Loan Associations (S&Ls). By 1990 Texas had recovered somewhat, but the Northeast was hurt by a decline in the computer industry and a major drop in real estate prices, which led to several banks declaring bankruptcy. To most analysts the American economy did not appear healthy at the end of 1990 and a major recession seemed likely.

S & Ls

Deregulation allows S & L managers to speculate. This leads to many bankruptcies.

Government deregulation is considered in part responsible for the continuing Savings and Loan (S&L) problems. S&Ls are like banks and receive from the public deposits that the owners and administrators of the S&Ls invest. They had been under federal government regulation. With deregulation many S&Ls speculated with loans, and after the recession in Texas in the mid-1980s many S&Ls went bankrupt. The government has since appropriated billions of dollars to buy the bankrupt S&Ls, reorganize them, and return money to creditors. What the cost will ultimately be to the American taxpayer is not clear, but it will be a major factor when dealing with the federal deficit.

Strategic Defense Initiative

Reagan's military build-up includes funds for SDI.

Reagan cut back social programs and used the money saved as well as other funds borrowed by the government to increase the size of the United States armed forces. This military build-up included new missiles and planes, more aircraft carriers, and the Strategic Defense Initiative (SDI), popularly called "Star Wars." SDI was to provide a shield over the United States against any possible Soviet nuclear attack. Some scientists claimed it was a daydream; others claimed laser technology could achieve it. Congress partially funded the plan and SDI became an important issue in arms negotiations with the Soviet Union, which saw it as a way for the United States to destroy the Soviet Union without being destroyed itself.

Environmental Policy

Environmental concerns are largely ignored.

Reagan believed the environmental legislation establishing water and pollution controls saddled American industry with unnecessary expenses. Congress overrode Reagan's veto of a Clean Water Act, but Secretary of the Interior James Watt and others responsible for enforcing environment regulations often ignored them. Scientists warned of the dangers of Acid Rain, and at the end of Reagan's administration they began speaking of the "greenhouse effect" created by increasing carbon gases and of a hole in the ozone layer. The United States refused to support a move for international controls to attack the possible "greenhouse effect." How significant these decisions were will not be clear for a number of years.

The Supreme Court

Perhaps the greatest impact President Reagan will have on United States history is through his Supreme Court appointments. His four appointees, including Sandra Day O'Connor, the first woman appointed to the court, were conservatives and changed the balance of what had been a liberal court under Earl Warren and Warren Burger. Reagan raised conservative Associate Justice William Rehnquist to be Chief Justice. Bush appointed conservative David Souter to the court. How the Rehnquist Court will interpret issues of privacy, abortion, civil rights, and the rights of the accused is not yet clear and will affect all Americans in the years ahead.

Appointments appear to create a more conservative Supreme Court.

Reagan's Popularity

Like Nixon, Reagan opposed renewal of the Voting Rights Act. He was also opposed to NOW's goal of "equal pay for equal work." Reagan did not appoint as many minorities and women to positions in his administration as had Carter. Over 100 Reagan appointees, including his Attorney General Edwin Meese, were accused and indicted on charges of corruption and misuse of power, but these accusations did not affect Reagan's popularity. Reagan was an excellent communicator, and the public supported this man who came to symbolize all the good and traditional values of America—family, religion, and patriotism.

Reagan, an excellent communicator, remains popular and wins re-election, carrying all but one state and the District of Columbia.

In 1984 Reagan and Bush overwhelmingly defeated Democrats Walter Mondale and Geraldine Ferraro, the first woman to run for national political office as a candidate of a major political party. Reagan and Bush carried every state except Minnesota and the District of Columbia. The nation had voted for Reagan's economic policies and conservatism.

Election of 1988

With the approach of the election of 1988, it appeared the Democrats would have a good chance for victory given the economic situation, the disaffection of women and African-American voters, and the problems created by the Iran-Contra Affair.

George Bush defeats Michael Dukakis for the presidency.

Michael Dukakis, governor of Massachusetts, and the Reverend Jesse Jackson emerged from the primaries as the leading contenders. Jackson was the first African-American to attain such national prominence in a presidential campaign. Dukakis finally won the nomination and, to appeal to the Southern voters, picked Lloyd Bentsen, senator from Texas, as Vice President. Bush won the Republican nomination easily and picked Dan Quayle, a young, little-known but conservative congressman from Indiana as Vice President. Dukakis, far ahead in the polls at the start, ran a poor campaign while Bush made Dukakis' liberalism an issue. Bush promised "no new taxes." Some analysts deplored the negative campaigning[2] in the election, but American politics has been full of such tactics through the years. Bush and Quayle won a strong victory. The Democrats retained control of both the House and the Senate.

Bush continued Reagan's economic policies. In 1990 he was forced, as a result of the continuing huge budget deficit, to break his "no new tax" pledge, infuriating the strong conservative Republican right. In the 1990 Congressional election the Democrats gained one more Senate seat and increased their strength in the House, but by the end of 1990, there were still no announced Democratic presidential candidates for 1992. This was an unusual situation and political analysts were not certain what it meant.

KEY POINT TO REMEMBER

In spite of tax cuts, lower inflation, lowered interest rates, and apparent prosperity in the Reagan years, the United States economy was not healthy, as farmers faced foreclosures, the Texas oil industry suffered from a recession, S&Ls failed, trade deficits increased, and the national debt grew dramatically.

LINKS FROM THE PAST TO THE PRESENT

1. Recent United States attitudes towards taxes and tax policy have their roots in the pre-Revolutionary cry of, "No Taxation Without Representation."
2. Issues of recession and government spending policy which began with the Panic of 1819 continue in spite of the New Deal legislation.
3. Efficiency and productivity of United States business has been and continues to be the key to United States economic prosperity.

QUESTIONS

Identify each of the following:
"Supply side" economics   "No new taxes"
"Greenhouse effect"

True or False:
1. President Carter considered himself an outsider in Washington politics.
2. President Carter set aside a wilderness area in Alaska, an action environmentalists have praised.
3. President Carter was unable to establish a uniform energy policy but was very successful in lowering inflation and high interest rates.
4. In the election of 1980 Ronald Reagan appealed to the traditional values of American life—religion, family, and patriotism.
5. President Reagan was a supporter of environmental legislation.

---

[2]*negative campaigning*   The use of political ads and announcements that emphasize the opponent's weaknesses and points they believe the voters will dislike rather than emphasizing their own candidate's positions on issues.

6. Large sums of money in the 1980s were spent buying corporations rather than in creating new industries and improving old ones to create new jobs.
7. Homelessness and poverty grew in the 1980s.
8. Sandra Day O'Connor was nominated to the Supreme Court, but the Senate failed to approve the nomination.
9. Geraldine Ferraro was the first woman to run for national political office as a candidate of a major party.
10. During the 1988 campaign the press continued its long-established policy of not commenting on the social behavior of political candidates.

Multiple Choice:

1. Supply-side economic theory holds that if taxes are reduced
   a. the money saved will be invested to create new jobs
   b. companies will consolidate and small companies will be bought
   c. the poor will be helped and ultimately this will help the rich
2. President Reagan pushed through Congress two tax reform bills that
   a. increased the top tax rate from 28% to 70%
   b. ended the New Deal use of income tax rates to make social policy
   c. created special loopholes for the rich
3. Reagan and/or Bush appointed and the Senate approved the following judges for the Supreme Court:
   a. Robert Bork and William Rehnquist
   b. Sandra Day O'Connor and David Souter
   c. Geraldine Ferraro and John Anderson

ANSWERS
True or False: 1. T, 2. T, 3. F, 4. T, 5. F, 6. T, 7. T, 8. F, 9. T, 10. F.
Multiple Choice: 1. a, 2. b, 3. b.

II. FOREIGN POLICY UNDER CARTER, REAGAN, AND BUSH

Carter's Foreign Policy

President Carter had won his election victory as an outsider in Washington politics but he was also an outsider in foreign policy. His approach to foreign policy was grounded in his belief in peace, democracy, and human rights for all people, but he was inconsistent in its application. In calling on the Soviet Union to allow free emigration of its Jewish population and to release all dissidents and political prisoners, he antagonized Leonid Brezhnev and detente lost its momentum. A second Strategic Arms Limitation Treaty (SALT II) was signed but never approved by the Senate after the Soviet Union sent troops into neighboring Afghanistan to support its communist government against guerrilla attacks. Carter

Detente loses momentum as Carter stresses human rights in his foreign policy.

responded by stopping grain shipments and barring United States athletes from competing in the 1980 summer Olympic games in Moscow. These actions worsened relations but had little impact on Soviet policy. After eight years of inconclusive warfare the Soviet Union finally withdrew from Afghanistan, dubbed the Soviet's Vietnam since Afghanistan had the same impact on the USSR as Vietnam had had on the United States. Guerrilla warfare continues in Afghanistan and no resolution appears in sight.

Carter completed the process of recognition of the People's Republic of China begun by Nixon. Ambassadors were exchanged, and the official recognition of the government of Taiwan was ended. Carter resolved growing conflicts with Panama by negotiating a treaty that will transfer the United States owned and operated Panama Canal to the Republic of Panama in 1999. Over strong opposition from conservatives, Carter gained Senate approval of the treaty.

Camp David Accords

In the Camp David Accords Egypt recognizes the independence of Israel, and Israel returns the occupied Sinai Peninsula to Egypt.

The seeming high point of Carter's foreign policy was the Camp David Accords. Addressing the issue of peace in the Middle East, Carter invited President Anwar Sadat of Egypt and Prime Minister Menachem Begin of Israel to Camp David in Maryland, where Israel agreed to return the Sinai Peninsula to Egypt and in return, Egypt officially recognized Israel as a nation, the first Arab country to do so. In 1978 the Camp David Accords seemed a major step to peace, but the hopes it generated have yet to come to fruition as no other Arab nation has recognized Israel.

Iranian Hostage Crisis: 1979–1980

The Iranian Hostage Crisis paralyzes the Carter presidency.

The low point of Carter's presidency was the Iranian hostage crisis. In 1953 the CIA had arranged the overthrow of a popular nationalist government in Iran, which had moved to seize control of foreign oil companies. The monarchy under the Shah was restored. Ignoring the oppressive methods used by the Shah to stay in power and adhering to the containment policy, the United States sent Iran large amounts of military aid to help the Shah maintain stability in the area on the southern border of the USSR. In 1978 a popular uprising forced the Shah to flee Iran, and a Muslim religious leader and nationalist, the Ayatollah Khomeini, established an Islamic Republic based strictly on the laws of the Koran.

Carter allowed the Shah to come to the United States for medical treatment. In anger young Iranian militants broke into the United States embassy in Teheran, made the staff hostages, and demanded the return of the Shah for trial. Carter refused and the resulting 444 day crisis captured the attention of the American people and almost paralyzed the Carter presidency. An attempt to rescue the 52 male hostages—the Iranians had released women and black hostages—failed when helicopters malfunctioned.

Carter seized Iranian assets and appealed to the U.N. The Shah died of cancer, but the crisis continued. Finally, negotiations did take place and Carter agreed to release Iranian assets in return for the hostages, but they were not released until Reagan's inauguration day in January, 1981.

During the crisis the television news each night had a special report on the crisis and counted the days since the crisis began, thus keeping the issue before the public. Iranian students carrying signs in English demonstrated before TV cameras in what sometimes looked like an international advertising campaign to convince the world of the evils of the United States, which Khomeini declared to be Satan[1]. The crisis illustrated the power of television, the growing use of terror and hostages to achieve goals in international affairs, and the difficulty a great power has imposing its desires on small nations.

In 1980 war broke out between Iraq and Iran. The origins were complex. The war made more difficult the creation of permanent peace in the Middle East.

Television plays an important role in the Iranian Hostage Crisis.

In this 1980 cartoon MacNeely made a comment on the war between Iran and Iraq which appears to have been prophetic. Note the ball and chain attached to the leg of the character representing the United States. What is MacNeely suggesting about the ability of the United States to remain neutral?

Relations with the Soviet Union under Reagan and Bush

Reagan came to the White House convinced the Soviet Union was an "evil empire." His view reflected the attitude of many Americans who were frustrated that the world was not just like

---

[1]*Satan* Another term for the devil, used particularly in the world of Islam.

Reagan considers the Soviet Union the "evil empire."

America, whose values of freedom, equality, and democracy were obviously good. These views illustrate the nationalistic interpretation of history and the sociological understanding of identifying yourself as being different from "the others."

Reagan was convinced United States military weakness encouraged Communist aggression and that by strengthening United States defenses, he could defeat the "evil empire" around the world. In spite of his views of the Soviets, the Reagan administration began talks on arms limitations. These collapsed in 1983 but began again when Gorbachev came to power in 1985.

The Soviet Union was moving through a period of transition in the early 1980s as the older generation of leaders died. A rapid turnover of leadership among old and ailing men provided little direction for the USSR as the nation struggled with economic problems.

Glasnost[2] and Peristroika[3]

Gorbachev and Reagan hold several meetings.

In 1985, Mikhail Gorbachev took control of the government and introduced domestic reforms and shifts in foreign policy in an attempt to address the problems of a stagnating economy. Gorbachev's policy of glasnost and peristroika changed eastern Europe and ended the Cold War. Reagan and Gorbachev met several times, their personal relationship grew warm, and they agreed to talks on arms control.

Soviet domestic crises present a new challenge to the United States.

As the Soviet and Eastern European economies worsened in the late 1980s, Gorbachev made it clear the USSR would no longer force the Eastern European nations to remain Communist or members of the Warsaw Pact. The Soviet occupied Baltic States, led by Lithuania, declared their independence of the Soviet Union. While this was not granted by Moscow, the Soviet Union appeared on the verge of disintegration. This was a challenge for United States policy. Should the United States encourage the break-up of the USSR or was it better to help maintain its integrity? As Communist regimes fell in Eastern Europe in 1989, the Soviets negotiated withdrawal of their troops and in August, 1990 the Soviet Union supported the United States policy in the Persian Gulf crisis.

When food shortages occurred as a result of a bad distribution system and the desire of farmers to hold their crops until Gorbachev introduced a capitalist free market system, Gorbachev, in December 1990, asked the United States and Western Europe for food aid. The United States offered $1 billion in credit for technology and food purchases. United States-Soviet relations had dramatically reversed themselves in the ten years since 1980. Whether Gorbachev's plans to restructure the Soviet Union would succeed was uncertain at the end of 1990, when Gorbachev was granted

---

[2]*glasnost* An opening up; it has been used to describe both the economic and political opening of the Soviet society and the opening in foreign policy which affected eastern Europe and ended the Cold War.

[3]*peristroika* A rebuilding; it has referred to the rebuilding of the Soviet economic system; it does not imply a movement in the political area towards democracy but a restructuring of the economy.

extraordinary powers to rule by decree. Most Americans were relieved that the Cold War was over and the "evil empire" was now an ally, but the future of USSR-United States relations was impossible to predict.

United States in Europe: 1981–1990

During the decade Europe moved closer to economic unity and set 1992 as the date for all tariffs and other economic barriers to disappear among the European Community (EC). The European Community will become the largest trading block and economic power in the world. How this will affect the United States is unclear. Many United States companies bought European companies during the 1980s to be sure of access to this European market in case the EC establishes tariff barriers against non-members.

The European community will become the largest economic power in 1992, when all economic barriers are scheduled to be removed.

Since World War II, the General Agreement on Tariffs and Trade (GATT) guided world trade policy. Tariff barriers were reduced and trade prospered, but in 1990, GATT negotiations broke down on the issue of government subsidies paid to European farmers. This has created great uncertainty over the future of world trade.

1989 in Europe

Since the start of the Cold War, Eastern European nations had been ruled by Communist governments with Soviet backing. The USSR used its army to crush revolts in Hungary in 1956 and in Czechoslovakia in 1968. Matters changed when Gorbachev indicated the USSR would not use troops to stop change in Eastern Europe.

Communist governments fall in Eastern Europe.

In 1989 Czechoslovakian students protesting their oppressive Communist government were joined by workers and intellectuals, and the Communist government fell. East Germans leaving their country were allowed to cross the border into the West. Thousands left for West Germany. In November East Germany opened the Berlin Wall, which had stood as a symbol of divided Europe and the Cold War. In October, 1990, less than a year after the fall of the Berlin Wall, Germans voted for union and the Chancellor of West Germany became the leader of a new German state with its capital in Berlin. Germany is now the largest single economic power in the European community.

The Berlin Wall is opened and Germany is united.

New non-Communist governments were established in other Eastern European countries. Vaclav Havel, the new president of Czechoslovakia, had been in prison six months earlier, and Lech Walensa, leader of the banned Solidarity Union, was elected President of Poland. President Bush promised economic aid to Poland and Hungary but the amount was small. The United States could do little more, considering its own huge budget deficits. By the end of 1990 the last Communist nation in Europe, Albania, was subjected to student protests and riots calling for change.

These new governments of Eastern Europe were not finding adjustments to capitalism easy to make. Old nationalist feelings emerged. Whether nationalist feelings would seize the people and destroy the countries and how the United States should react to this rising nationalism was another issue facing policy makers as

1990 ended. Gorbachev had often referred to the "common European home." What place this would leave for the United States in Europe as the United States and the USSR build a "new world order" is a major question for the future.

In this cartoon Toles uses the symbol of the Liberty Bell to comment on the year 1989 in Eastern Europe. What is Toles suggesting happened in Europe?

United States and Latin America

The Reagan administration fights the Cold War in Central America.

In 1980 in El Salvador revolutionaries were challenging the military dictatorship supported by large landowners. Reagan believed the rebels were agents of Cuba and the USSR and asked Congress to aid the government using the old domino theory as his argument. Congress sent aid but often attached conditions. Some Americans urged negotiation and saw the rebels as nationalistic, democratic liberals who were trying to achieve a better life for the poor people of El Salvador. Ten years later the war continues, with killings of civilians and other atrocities on both sides. The United States appears powerless to affect the situation.

In neighboring Nicaragua the military dictator had been overthrown by a group called the Sandinistas before Reagan was elected. The Sandinistas asked for help from Cuba to improve health and education in the country. Reagan believed the Sandinistas were committed Communists. He ordered the CIA to train a group of Nicaraguans that became known as the Contras to attack the Sandinistas.

After Congress cut off aid to the Contras, members of Reagan's administration developed a secret plan to aid the Contras. When discovered, the Iran-Contra Affair (see page 324) became another national scandal and split the nation. While Nicaragua's neighbors sought a negotiated solution, Reagan preferred a military victory.

Finally, in 1988 a cease fire was signed, elections held, and the Sandinista government lost. The transition of power has not been easy and the government is shaky, but some slight progress has been made in Nicaragua towards peace. What the future holds for both El Salvador and Nicaragua and the rest of Latin America, which suffers from poverty, overpopulation, and the lack of a strong economic base, and what impact the United States can have on the region are debatable.

Invasions and Drugs

The United States did intervene militarily in two Latin American nations in the decade. Reagan invaded the island of Grenada in October 1983, ostensibly to protect United States medical students from internal political strife. The Leftist government of Grenada was friendly to Cuba, and there were rumors it was building a large airstrip that bombers could use. After the invasion a new government friendlier to the United States was established, and United States troops were slowly withdrawn. Many Americans responded favorably to this show of strength and patriotism but the U.N. passed a resolution condemning the United States' intervention.

Military force is used in Grenada and Panama.

In 1989 President George Bush ordered United States troops into Panama to seize the dictator, General Manual Noriega, who was accused of aiding drug smugglers. He was captured and brought to the United States for trial. The man who had won a previous election but who was kept from the presidency by Noriega was put into office.

The question of drugs from South America was an issue throughout the decade. Fortunes were made in the world-wide drug trade, and the United States attempted to curtail it through international efforts. As supplies from Turkey and Asia became less available, trade shifted to South America. The United States gave governments money to wipe out the production, but poor farmers benefited greatly from the drug trade. Colombia waged a war on drug lords and it almost destroyed the nation.

Drugs are an issue in international relations.

Some Americans doubt that attempts to control the supply of drugs will be successful if the demand for drugs remains high in the United States. What the impact of drug lords and drug money will be on the world's economy provides another point of uncertainty for the 1990s.

Civil War in Lebanon: 1982–1990

The other Arab nations refused to accept the Camp David Accords, and no negotiations on the Palestinian homeland question were held as called for in the Accords. The PLO resorted to terror attacks against Israel, and in 1982 Israel invaded Lebanon to destroy PLO bases. Despite a United Nations peace-keeping force, civil war raged in Lebanon until the end of the decade.

Terrorism becomes a tool in the PLO's struggle to create a homeland for the Palestinians.

Frustrated, the PLO and the Arab nations turned to more international terrorism as a means to draw attention to their situation. After United States and other Western hostages were seized in Lebanon and numerous terrorist attacks were carried out in Europe, President Reagan, who had declared he would never negotiate with terrorists, claimed Mu'ammar al-Gaddafi, President of Libya, was behind many terrorist attacks. He ordered United States planes to bomb Libyan military bases, and one of Gaddafi's children was killed.

The use of terrorism then waned, although hostages are still held in Lebanon, and at the end of 1990 a solution to the Arab-Israeli conflict still appears far away.

Iran-Contra Affair

The Iran Contra Affair divides the country.

In 1985 while Reagan was declaring he would never deal with terrorists, members of his administration—including CIA director William Casey, National Security Advisor John Poindexter, and White House Aid Lt. Col. Oliver North—arranged to sell arms to Iran in return for Iran's support in obtaining release of the American hostages in Lebanon. The money made from the sale of arms

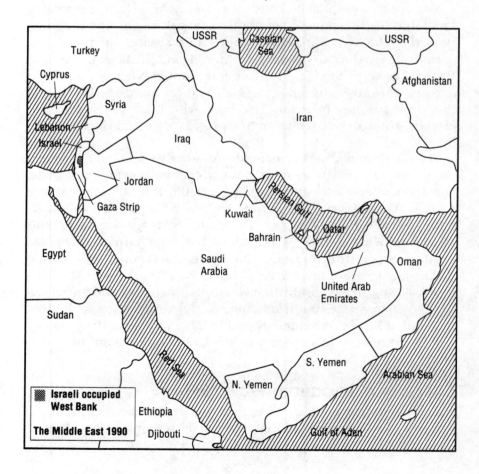

was to be used to support the Nicaraguan Contras. Thus began the Iran-Contra affair, which rocked the country for the next three years. American opinion was split over the Affair, with many viewing Lt. Colonel North as a hero and patriot and others seeing him as one who ignored the basic concept of constitutional government. Throughout the investigations and trials, Reagan maintained he knew nothing of the plan. Some saw parallels between Watergate and the Iran-Contra Affair and the unconstitutional use of executive power, but Reagan's great popularity with the voters kept all suggestions of his involvement from sticking.

Persian Gulf Crisis

The Iran-Iraq War began in 1980 and ended in 1988, but Iraq had a huge debt. To pay the debt Iraq needed to keep oil prices high to pay it. Iraq's dictator, Sadaam Hussein, believed that OPEC was not doing so and that Iraq's neighbor, Kuwait, was both over-producing and pumping oil from an Iraqi-owned field. When negotiations between Kuwait and Iraq broke down in July and the United States, which had supported Iraq in the Iran-Iraq War, suggested through its Ambassador that the United States had no special interest in the issue, Iraq soon invaded Kuwait. Within three days Kuwait was occupied, and President Bush reacted by sending troops to defend Saudi Arabia, whose oil was essential to the economies of United States allies.

Iraq invades Kuwait.

Bush turned to the United Nations for support, and the world came together to condemn the Iraqi aggression, to establish sanctions stopping all trade with Iraq, and finally to support the use of force by a coalition of nations to push Iraq out of Kuwait if Iraqi troops were not withdrawn by January 15, 1991. As the deadline neared many nations attempted to negotiate an end to the crisis. There was concern that President Bush had not clearly articulated all of America's goals. Administration leaders gave as reasons for their position oil, American jobs, the need to stop Hussein (who was described as "another Hitler"), and the creation of a "new world order," where "aggression would not pay." Bush received the strong support of the American people as he made one last attempt to negotiate.

The Persian Gulf crisis pulled together the many strands of the complex issue of peace in the Middle East. These issues include: the conflict between the rich and poor Arab nations; the size of each nation's armaments including their nuclear and biological arsenals; the antagonisms between the different Islamic sects; the need of Japan and the European nations for a stable supply of oil; the struggle of the PLO for a homeland; and the future of Jerusalem and the recognition of Israel by the Arab nations. Compounding the crisis is the Islamic belief in Jihad used by Iraq's Hussein to describe the conflict with the United Nations coalition and by many Arabs to describe the conflict with Israel; Israel's refusal to accept a general peace conference to discuss all Middle East issues; and Israel's refusal to withdraw from occupied Arab lands in spite of United Nations resolutions. While at the end of 1990 world atten-

The Persian Gulf Crisis pulls together many complex issues in the Middle East.

tion was focused on the issue of Iraqi withdrawal from Kuwait, these other issues needed to be addressed. As 1990 came to an end, the United States had many interests in the Middle East and it was understood the United States would be involved in any peace process adopted in the region.

Africa and Asia

Reagan began the 1980s supporting non-Communist forces in the civil wars in Angola and Nambibia. The decade ended with the United Nations negotiating settlements that still need to be fully implemented. The United States responded to severe famines in the Sudan and Ethiopia with food aid, but civil war in those countries kept aid from the people, and drought, overpopulation, and the resulting environmental degradation made the problems appear insurmountable unless new methods of food production could be developed and taught.

The United States supports sanctions to end Apartheid in South Africa.

A world outcry led by the United States against the policies of Apartheid[4] in South Africa led to international sanctions. African Nationalist leader Nelson Mandela was released from prison and negotiated with the government, but outbreaks of violence between rival factions stalled movement toward a new government arrangement as 1990 ended.

Student and worker protests in China fail to bring democracy.

In China a crackdown on dissident students and workers in June, 1989 ended an attempt to bring greater democracy to that Communist nation. Congress passed moderate sanctions against China, but by December, 1990 relations were back to normal.

Elsewhere in Asia in the 1980s countries such as Singapore, Hong Kong, Taiwan, South Korea, and especially Japan experienced great economic growth and increased trade with the United States. United States trade deficits with these countries grew, and in 1985 under United States pressure Japan put quotas on the number of cars that would be shipped to the United States market. Japanese business responded by building or buying auto plants in the United States. Similar developments occurred in the microchip industry in 1987. The purchases of large United States corporations by Japanese industrialists strained United States-Japanese relations. Loss of United States jobs and a growing recession at the end

Nations of the Asian Rim prosper in the 1980s.

of 1990 led to talk in the United States of tariffs and a trade war with Japan. How to resolve the trade imbalance between the United States and the Asian Rim[5] nations appeared to be one of the major issues for United States policy in the 1990s.

One Asian nation, the former United States colony of the Philippines, did not benefit from economic growth in the 1980s. A popular revolution in 1987 overthrew the dictator, Ferdinand Marcos, whom the United States had supported. His popular successor, Corazon Aquino, has not been able to resolve the many economic and political problems she inherited from Marcos. The

---

[4]*apartheid* The policy of legalized race separation practiced in South Africa.

[5]*Asian Rim* Those nations on the western edge of the Pacific Ocean who have developed their economies in the post-World War II period.

United States had large military bases in the Philippines, and as 1990 ended, new leases on the bases were being negotiated. There are many international situations that may become the major issues of the 1990s but at the time of writing the Persian Gulf crisis appears the most troubling and the most likely to take space in future history books.

KEY POINT TO REMEMBER

Events in all parts of the globe affected the United States in the 1980s, and the United States was involved in many different situations but was not able to exercise total control in any of them. As the Cold War ended and Communist governments fell in Eastern Europe, the United States and the USSR worked to establish a "new world order."

PEOPLE TO REMEMBER

Jimmy Carter   Peanut farmer, Governor of Georgia, 39th President of the United States; he achieved the Camp David Accords which brought peace to Egypt and Israel; his ideals of international human rights led to tensions with the Soviet Union and the Iranian hostage crisis prevented his focusing on domestic issues; after his defeat in 1980 he established a foundation that deals with international peace and homes for the homeless.

Ronald Reagan   Radio broadcaster, Hollywood movie star, Governor of California, 40th President of the United States; believed in supply side economics and put through two major tax reforms; cut back on the New Deal and social programs; built up United States defenses; saw the Soviet Union as an "evil empire" but ended his presidency by negotiating arms and trade agreements with the USSR.

George Bush   New Englander, pilot in World War II, founder and President of Zapata Petroleum Corporation, Congressman from Texas, United States Ambassador to the U.N., Chairman of the Republican National Committee, head of the United States Liaison Office in Beijing, head of the CIA, Vice President under Ronald Reagan, 41st President of the United States; made a fortune in Texas oil; began his presidency promising no new taxes but as the budget deficit grew he accepted limited tax increases; committed United States troops to defend Saudi Arabia and worked to create an international coalition against Iraq.

LINKS FROM THE PAST TO THE PRESENT

1. The Cold War began immediately after World War II with the division of Europe into East and West blocs and ended with the fall of communist governments in Eastern Europe in 1989 but its effects are still important.
2. Disarmament negotiations continue to be important in U.S.-USSR relations.
3. Tensions in the Middle East are complex, deep rooted, and dangerous for world peace as seen in the Persian Gulf crisis.

4. Tariffs and trade policies still have a major impact on the world economy as illustrated by OPEC policies.
5. United States armed interference in Latin American nations is still an important element in U.S. policy as seen in Grenada and Panama.

QUESTIONS

Identify each of the following:

Camp David Accords	Contras
SDI	Kuwait
European Community	Apartheid
Sandinistas	

True or False

1. President Carter negotiated a treaty with Panama giving the United States perpetual control of the Panama Canal.
2. For 444 days the Iranian hostage crisis became a major issue on nightly television news.
3. President Reagan considered the USSR to be an "evil empire."
4. As the older generation of leaders died in the early 1980's, the USSR lacked strong leadership until Gorbachev became leader.
5. The United States refused to supply aid to the USSR when requested by Gorbachev in December, 1990.
6. GATT has guided world trade policies since World War II.
7. The Polish labor union, Solidarity, was stopped by the Communist government but later helped achieve the overthrow of that government.
8. The fall of the Berlin Wall symbolized the end of the Cold War.
9. Reagan believed the Sandinistas were agents of Cuba and the USSR.
10. Reagan forbade the CIA to train the Contras for warfare in Nicaragua.
11. Lt. Colonel Oliver North and others used a secret plan, funds from the sale of arms to Iran, to aid the Contras in violation of a law of Congress.
12. Reagan invaded Grenada to force out the government, which had refused the United States request to build a large airstrip.
13. United States planes bombed Mu'ammar al-Gaddafi's headquarters in Libya because he had invaded Lebanon.
14. In December, 1990 it was not clear if there would be war between United States forces and Iraq as a result of Iraq's invasion of Kuwait.

Multiple Choice:

1. President Carter reacted to the invasion of Afghanistan by the USSR by
   a. signing SALT II
   b. sending grain to Afghanistan
   c. boycotting the 1980 summer Olympics in Moscow

2. The policies of reform, openness, and change in the Soviet Union were
    a. begun by Chairman Brezhnev
    b. called perestroika and glastnost
    c. used to discredit Gorbachev in the United States
3. Changes in Eastern Europe were helped by
    a. Gorbachev's statement that the U.S.S.R. would not stop them
    b. the strength of United States forces in Europe
    c. the crisis over Kuwait.
4. President Bush invaded Panama because of
    a. a need to keep the canal open
    b. attacks on the government by Communist rebels
    c. General Noriega's involvement in drug traffic
5. President Reagan refused to accept the Latin American nations' plans for a negotiated end to the Nicaraguran war because
    a. he wanted to defeat the Sandinistas who he believed were supported by Cuba
    b. he believed the Contras were freedom fighters
    c. he wanted to cover up the Iran-Contra Affair
6. Asian nations that underwent great economic growth in the 1980s include
    a. South Korea, Japan, and Hong Kong
    b. China, the Philippines, and Singapore
    c. all of the above.

ANSWERS

True or False: 1. F, 2. T, 3. T, 4. T, 5. F, 6. T, 7. T, 8. T, 9. T, 10. F, 11. T, 12. F, 13. F, 14. T.
Multiple Choice: 1. c, 2. b, 3. a, 4. c, 5. a, 6. a.

III. SOCIAL CHANGES IN THE UNITED STATES

The "Me" Generation

The altruism and idealism instilled by Kennedy was dissipated by the Vietnam War and Watergate. Carter was unable to reinspire the people. The mid-'70s to the mid-'80s are looked back on as the "Me" decade, when the love and peace attitudes of the Hippies were replaced with self-improvement efforts by people of all ages and most economic backgrounds. Disillusioned by foreign and domestic events, the "Me" generation turned inward to improve themselves through athletics (especially jogging), psychological experiments with group therapy and meditation, and Eastern religions with their emphasis on self inspection. These attitudes continued into the mid-'80s and to them were added the goals of personal wealth and self-gratification.

The 1980s saw a very different group of young people from that of the 1960 Hippies. Born during the Civil Rights Movement and the Vietnam War, the young, white, middle- and upper-class youth

The "Me" generation turns inward and pursues goals of personal wealth.

329

were now seeking a share of the economic wealth as quickly as possible without regard to traditional ethics. A generation of young people who fought for Civil Rights and rejected the establishment was replaced by a generation dubbed the Yuppies, who worked within the system to make as much money as possible. Donald Trump, who made millions in real estate and Atlantic City casinos, and Michael Milken, who made billions in junk bonds, exemplified the values and goals of the Yuppies. New York and Wall Street became their mecca.

Junk Bonds

The Reagan tax cuts and general philosophy of support for the wealthy reinforced this attitude among the young Yuppies. After the Iran-Contra Affair, the indictment and conviction of Milken for insider trading[1] on the stock market, and the near bankruptcy of Donald Trump, by the end of the 1980s there appeared a slight shift of values among young college graduates as fewer headed towards Wall Street and more chose professions such as teaching. It is too early to tell just how widespread this shift in attitudes will be and how it will affect United States society in the 1990s.

The Peace Movement and the Environment

Going against the self-centered attitude of the "Me" generation, a strong peace movement developed in opposition to Reagan's defense build-up in the early 1980s. Focusing on the threat of a "nuclear winter"[2] following any use of nuclear weapons—Reagan administration spokespeople had suggested the United States could fight and win a nuclear war—there were protests around the country.

After the Cold War ends, the anti-war movements focus on environmental issues.

When Gorbachev and Reagan agreed on arms limitations and the Cold War ended, many of the peace groups such as Beyond War, the Physicians for Social Responsibility, and the Union of Concerned Scientists focused their attention on environmental issues. The Bush administration was slow to respond, suggesting that recycling and enforcement of clean air legislation would be poor for business. In April, 1990, on the 20th anniversary of the first Earth Day, a second Earth Day was celebrated throughout the world. People's attention was called to various environmental concerns from toxic waste dumps to global warming to a lack of space in landfills.

---

[1]*insider trading* Using information the general public does not have about business changes that would affect the price of stocks and bonds to allow the person with the information to make money; the practice is illegal under federal law.

[2]*nuclear winter* The concept supported by many scientists that after a nuclear war the fall-out dust would shield the earth from the sun and create permanent winter conditions on the earth.

Environmental issues have been of concern to some Americans since the conservation efforts of President Theodore Roosevelt. Others have not been concerned. In this cartoon what view is Toles expressing on the issue of the Greenhouse effect and American's response to it?

Religious Fundamentalism

The 1970s and '80s saw another religious revival in America. Many Americans turned to religious fundamentalism. Billy Graham, a revivalist speaker and friend of post-World War II presidents gained in popularity. Evangelists turned to television to reach the people. Thousands responded, and one evangelist, Jerry Falwell, became a major political factor in the Republican Party. These religious leaders preached conservatism and adherence to traditional values. They opposed the ERA, abortion, drugs, pornography, and the sexual revolution and strongly supported defense and patriotism. Falwell and other evangelists supported Reagan. Falwell himself ran in Republican primaries as a presidential candidate in 1988, but by then sex scandals involving two other television evangelists weakened his support. The "religious right," as it was called, continues as an important factor in American political and social life. In the 1970s Eastern religions had had a strong appeal to many, but interest in these waned in the late 1980s.

Religious evangelists turn to television to bring their message to Americans.

Population Changes

The population of the United States underwent several important changes in the Carter and Reagan years, changes that will be of major significance in the 1990s and after. The Sun Belt states continued to grow as New England and the Midwest continued to shrink in relative size population. The Sun Belt states tend to be more politically conservative. As the number of representatives from states is changed after the 1990 census, this population shift may have an important impact on the United States House of Representatives and its voting patterns.

The population of the Sun Belt continues to grow more rapidly than that of other regions.

The United States birth rate declined in the 1980s, and as the Baby Boomers aged, so did the average age of Americans. Social Security will be affected as there are fewer young workers to pay Social Security taxes to support older, retired workers. The birth rate drop was particularly sharp among middle- and upper-class whites, where women, enjoying the liberation gained in the 1960s and early '70s, followed careers and had fewer children or had children later.

The Hispanic percentage of the population grows rapidly.

On the other hand, the Hispanic population, which increased 61 percent in the 1970s, continued to grow rapidly through births and immigration, both legal and illegal. Illegal immigrants came to escape revolution, poverty, or both, in Central America. It was clear that by the 21st century the Hispanic-American population would be the largest minority group in the United States. It would form a majority of the population of California. Poor educational background and lack of job opportunities kept many Hispanics in poverty. Their frustrations led to several riots in Miami reminiscent of the black ghetto riots of the 1960s.

The black population in the inner city ghettos continued to suffer from poor education and lack of jobs. Drug use increased in the ghettos and drug-related killings skyrocketed as young and Hispanics fought for a piece of the illegal drug business that offered one of the few hopes for quick riches. Statistics suggested that one out of every four urban preteen males could expect to be shot.

The Reagan and Bush administrations waged a war on drugs. City mayors increased police units, but the use of drugs in the inner cities saw little decrease in spite of the declared war on drugs and the appointment of a federal Drug Czar who was charged with coordinating the war. Drugs also continued to be a problem in the suburbs, but with the increase in AIDS[3], there seemed to be a slight drop in hard drug usage while more young people used alcohol. Car accidents, usually connected with alcohol, were the largest killer of adolescent whites. These differences in the causes of death between black and white youth reflect the continuing separation of America into rich and poor, suburb and city.

Asian immigrants adapt to American life.

One group of immigrants, Asians, were often able to bridge the gap between rich and poor. Many Vietnamese fled at the end of the war and they, as well as Asians from South Korea, Taiwan and Hong Kong, came to the United States in large numbers.

[3]*AIDS* Acquired Immune Deficiency Syndrome is a fatal disease first diagnosed in 1981.

These new Asian immigrants illustrate how diverse and complex American society has become as the 21st century approaches. The 19th century concept of America as the melting pot, in which all immigrants will be Americanized, was replaced in the post-World War II period by the concept of pluralism, where each individual's cultural background will be respected under the umbrella of American democracy. Establishing a balance between pluralism and separatism, between American freedom and American equality, will require great sensitivity and skill from the political leaders of the next century.

Urban Problems

Besides urban problems of drugs and crime, the rise of AIDS put great pressure on city budgets. Transmitted only through the exchange of bodily fluids, AIDS first appeared in the United States among intravenous drug users and the homosexual population of the major cities. As the homosexual population shifted its sexual practices, the spread of AIDS has slowed within that group but little impact has been made on the drug-using population with particularly disastrous results for their babies, for themselves, and for the health care programs for the urban poor. AIDS has spread into the heterosexual population and more cases are being found among the college age population, suggesting that adolescents are exposing themselves to this disease which has a long incubation period and for which there is no cure as of the end of 1990. The number of potential victims and the cost of caring for them is staggering. Without an inexpensive cure, AIDS will be among the greatest problems cities face in the 1990s.

AIDS becomes a major health problem.

Another great problem of urban life at the end of the 1980s was the number of homeless people in America. At one time Americans thought only drunks and mentally disturbed individuals lived on the street without homes, but increasingly people are aware that at least some of the homeless are simply poor, and many blame the increase in the problem on Reagan economic policies. The problem has intensified in the Bush years and homeless families are found in communities throughout the nation. Some have jobs but at the low end of the wage scale and cannot afford to pay rent. They work, send their children to school, but sleep on the street or in shelters. Former President Carter has begun a project, Habitat for Humanity, to help build low-cost housing and there are many other projects but a great need exists throughout the country for inexpensive and affordable housing.

Homelessness illustrates the gap between rich and poor.

Suburbs and Farms

Suburbs continued to grow in the 1980s and "going to the mall" became one of the most accepted adolescent activities. Many older people went to the mall, where they could exercise in air conditioned or heated spaces without concern for the weather. More small farms were sold in the 1980s as agriculture became more and more run by agribusinesses[4]. American farm production was high, but

---

[4]*agribusiness*   Large-scale farms run by corporations.

GATT negotiations stall and add to the uncertain future of America's farmers.

New inventions and the goals of the "Me" generation increase the pace of life in the nation.

world farm prices dropped in the early 1980s and many Midwestern farmers went bankrupt. As the GATT talks stalled at the end of 1990 over the issue of farm subsidies paid by European nations to their farmers, it is not at all clear whether United States farmers will ever be able to survive without government subsidies, which Republican administrations have tried to reduce but with only moderate success.

The Pace of Life

The pace of American life increased during the 1970s and '80s. The Yuppies of the "Me" generation jogged and did aerobics to improve their health, taking time away from home life. The VCR made movies of your choice a nightly possibility, and cable television opened up as many as fifty new channels for those in large urban areas. TV channels devoted to one subject—sports, news or weather—made such information instantly available at all times to everyone. Home video cameras replaced home movie cameras and allowed for instant replay of what one had produced. Federal Express and other companies guaranteed overnight delivery of mail, but the FAX machine was even faster, immediately sending printed information around the world. Satellites allowed for live radio and television broadcasts from anywhere in the world as well as for instant telephone communication. Computers became available in all sizes and capacities and instantly provided the recall of information and the rewriting of papers. Microwave ovens increased the speed at which frozen dinners could be prepared or meals cooked so that each member of a family could prepare a hot meal almost instantly. Many workers had to moonlight[5], putting an added burden on them and increasing the pace of their lives as they carried two jobs.

Some psychologists and members of the older generation worried about how this ability to achieve instantly whatever one wanted would affect the American values of hard work and effort. In spite of concerns and growing evidence of tension and stress-related disorders, all indications are that the pace of life in America and ultimately throughout the world will increase in the 1990s.

Entertainment

The number of professional athletic teams increased and TV watchers could find a game on at almost any time. Salaries of professional athletes skyrocketed, as did those of movie and rock stars, all of whom justified their salaries by the fact their earning period was "limited" and they had to make their money fast. The salaries and celebrity of these stars made many young people aspire to making their fortunes in these fields, but the number of opportunities for success were very limited, adding to the frustrations of inner-city basketball players, who saw their heroes in televised games, and suburban rock 'n' roll musicians, who watched theirs on MTV.

---

[5]*moonlight*   Work at a second job, often at night, in order to make extra money.

Movies continued to be a source of entertainment and social commentary. Although the Vietnam War was over, movies like *The Deer Hunter* (1978), *Apocalypse Now* (1979), *Platoon* (1986), *Good Morning Vietnam* (1987), and *Born on the Fourth of July* (1989), addressed the issue of the war and its effects on the individuals who had been involved in it.

The crime, drugs, and sexual violence found in American life were portrayed vividly and more and more explicitly in movies. It was hard to find a movie that was not rated "R" (Restricted—anyone under 17 must be accompanied by an adult), and in 1990 a new listing was added, "R-17" (No one under 17 admitted), to identify movies that were sexually explicit and violent but did not deserve the "X" rating given to pornographic movies. The lyrics of rock 'n' roll and rap music (music based on talking to the beat and rooted in the inner city) also became more and more explicit.

With the increasing variety in and fragmentation of the world of the arts, it has become harder to judge what works will be the classics of the future.

KEY POINT TO REMEMBER

The "Me" generation and Yuppies focused on self-improvement and making money while problems of drugs, AIDS, and homelessness and the pace of life for all Americans increased. Violence and crime seemed a natural part of American life and were reflected in movies, rock 'n' roll music, and literature.

LINKS FROM THE PAST TO THE PRESENT

1. Periodic swings in American attitudes from idealism to personal concerns is most recently reflected in the Me Generation.
2. Revival religion in America began with the first Great Awakening in the 18th century and continues with TV revivalist preachers and Born-Again Christians.
3. Music for young people continues to reflect American culture.

QUESTIONS:

Identify each of the following:

Me Generation   Habitat for Humanity
War on Drugs   AIDS

True or False:

1. The "Me" generation was disillusioned by foreign and domestic events and concentrated on self-improvement.
2. The Hispanic population was growing but it was far from being an important minority group in the late 1980s.
3. Jerry Falwell, a TV evangelist, opposed Ronald Reagan's views and ran as a Democrat in the 1988 primaries.
4. President Reagan began and President Bush continued a War on Drugs.

5. In post-World War II America the concept of pluralism replaced the concept of the United States as a melting pot where immigrants of all nations came together.
6. AIDS and homelessness are two major problems facing American cities as the 1990s begin.
7. American farm production dropped during the 1980s.
8. Satellite communication, computers and FAX machines have had little effect on the pace of American life.
9. Athletes and rock stars argue they deserve high salaries because they give money to the homeless.
10. Peace groups such as the Union of Concerned Scientists turned to environmental issues after the end of the Cold War.

Multiple Choice:

1. Prominent examples of "Me" generation members who made great wealth are
    a. all who are called Yuppies
    b. Donald Trump and Michael Milken
    c. Oliver North
2. In the late 1970s and 1980s population changes included
    a. continued shift in population from the North to the Sun Belt states
    b. an increased birth rate for whites
    c. both of the above
3. Television evangelists and members of the Religious Right opposed
    a. abortion, pornography, and the sexual revolution
    b. the ERA
    c. all of the above
4. AIDS (Acquired Immune Deficiency Syndrome) can be
    a. caught only by homosexuals
    b. found only on college campuses
    c. disastrous for the health care programs for the urban poor
5. Movies which presented aspects of the war in Vietnam included
    a. *Good Morning Vietnam* and *Platoon*
    b. *Apocalypse Now* and *Born on the Fourth of July*
    c. all of the above

ANSWERS

True or False: 1. T, 2. F, 3. F, 4. T, 5. T, 6. T, 7. F, 8. F, 9. F, 10. T.
Multiple Choice: 1. b, 2. a, 3. c, 4. c, 5. c

Important Dates of American History

Date	Significance
1492	First voyage to America by Columbus
1607	Founding of the first English settlement at Jamestown
1620	Pilgrim's arrival at Plymouth in New England
1763	Peace of Paris ends French and Indian War
1776	Declaration of American Independence
1789	Ratification of United States Constitution and start of new government
1800	Election of Thomas Jefferson transfers power to new political party for first time
1850	Compromise of 1850 delays Civil War for ten years
1860	Election of Lincoln; secession of states of the deep South and establishment of CSA
1861	Start of Civil War
1865	End of Civil War; assassination of Lincoln; Reconstruction begins
1896	Election of McKinley marks end of Populist Movement
1898	Spanish-American War
1914	World War I begins in Europe; United States neutrality
1917	United States enters World War I
1929	Wall St. Stock Market Crash starts the Great Depression
1941	Pearl Harbor; United States enters World War II
1945	V-E and V-J Days end World War II in Europe and Pacific
1954	Armistice ends fighting in Korean War
1968	Tet Offensive in Vietnam; anti-war demonstrations; riots at Democratic Convention
1974	Resignation of President Nixon after Watergate scandal
1980	Election of Reagan marks conservative political swing
1989	End of Cold War; fall of Berlin Wall and political changes in Eastern Europe.

The United States with Date of Entry into the Union

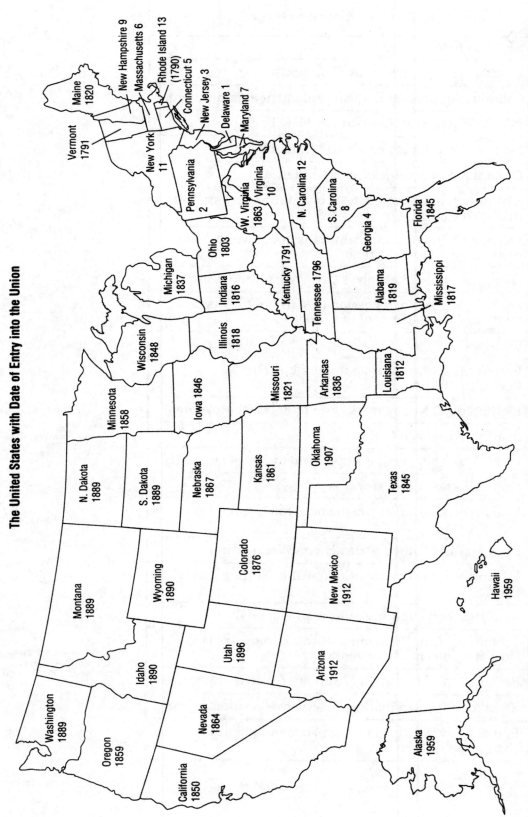

Maine	1820
Vermont	1791
New York	11
Pennsylvania	2
New Hampshire	9
Massachusetts	6
Rhode Island	13
(1790) Connecticut	5
New Jersey	3
Delaware	1
Maryland	7
W. Virginia	1863
Virginia	10
N. Carolina	12
S. Carolina	8
Georgia	4
Florida	1845
Ohio	1803
Michigan	1837
Indiana	1816
Kentucky	1791
Tennessee	1796
Alabama	1819
Mississippi	1817
Wisconsin	1848
Illinois	1818
Minnesota	1858
Iowa	1846
Missouri	1821
Arkansas	1836
Louisiana	1812
N. Dakota	1889
S. Dakota	1889
Nebraska	1867
Kansas	1861
Oklahoma	1907
Texas	1845
Montana	1889
Wyoming	1890
Colorado	1876
New Mexico	1912
Idaho	1890
Utah	1896
Arizona	1912
Washington	1889
Oregon	1859
Nevada	1864
California	1850
Hawaii	1959
Alaska	1959

Note : For the original 13 states the order in which they ratified the Constitution is given.

Index

Index

Grange, 149, 173
Grant, Ulysses S., 128, 129, 136, 139
Gravity's Rainbow (Pynchon), 305
Great Awakening, 103–105
Great Compromise, 54
Great Depression, 220–222, 239
Great Gatsby, The (Fitzgerald), 216
Great Society, 277–278
Greece, 245–246
Greeley, Horace, 139
greenbacks, 171
"greenhouse effect," 314–315
Greenland, 8
Grenada, 323
Grenville, George, 32
Grimke, Angelina & Sarah, 106
Gross national product (GNP), 262
Guatemala, 246
Gulf of Tonkin Resolution, 285, 288

H

Habitat for Humanity, 333
Haight-Ashbury, S.F., 300
Haldeman, H.R., 295
Hamilton, Alexander, 46
    Bank of United States and, 61
    Constitutional Convention and, 53–55
    economic program, 60–61
    French Revolution and, 64
    loose construction view of government, 61–62, 101, 222
    as Secretary of the Treasury, 57
Hancock, John, 39
Hanna, Mark, 176, 177
Harding, Warren G., 214, 215
hard money, 172, 173, 177
Harlem Renaissance, 216
Harper's Ferry, VA, 124
Harrington, Michael, 276
Harrison, Benjamin, 175
Harrison, William Henry, 76, 90–91
Hartford Convention, 78
Harvard College, 25
Havel, Vaclav, 321
Hawaii, 187–188, 211
hawk, 76
hawks, 286
Hawley-Smoot Tariff, 219
Hayes, Rutherford B., 139–140
Haymarket Massacre (1886), 155, 156
Hayne, Robert Y., 87
Hayne-Webster debates, 87
Hearst, William Randolph, 165
hegemony, 30
Heller, Joseph, 267
Hemingway, Ernest, 216
Henry, Patrick, 33, 35, 37, 54, 61
Henry the Navigator, 10
Henry VII, 11
hippies, 270, 299–300
Hiroshima, 237
Hispanic-Americans, 332
Hispaniola, 15
Hiss, Alger, 255–256
historian's method, 1–2
history:
    cause and effect analysis, 29
    cyclical view of, 170–171
    economic determinism and, 119
    enemy concept and, 269–270
    ideology and, 196–197
    influence of individuals on, 50
    multi-causal approach to, 13
    revisionist, 308–309
Hitler, Adolf, 208, 221, 235–236
    aggression in Europe, 209–210
Ho Chi Minh, 283, 284
holding company, 152–153
Holocaust, 209

homelessness, 312–314, 333
Homestead Act (1862), 131, 148–149
Hoover, Herbert, 200, 219, 221–222
horses, 15
House of Burgesses, 17, 26, 33, 35
House of Lords, 38
House of Representatives, 54
House Un-American Activities Committee, 240, 255
Housing and Urban Affairs Department (HUD), 277
Howe, Sir William, 44
Hudson, Henry, 15, 18
Hudson River, 15
Hughes, Charles Evans, 199
Hull House, 160
Humphrey, Hubert, 277, 287
Hungary, 248
Hussein, Saddam, 250, 325
hypothesis, 2

I

ideology, 196–197
Illinois, 149
immigrants, 277
    after 1880, 157–158
    Asian, 332, 332–333
    Chinese, 150
    to English colonies, 24
    Europeans, 8–11
    Hispanics, 332
    Irish and German, 114–115
    Native Americans, 3–6
    restriction of, 215
immolation, 283
impeachment, 136
imperialism, 187, 189–190
impressment, 65, 75, 76
Incas, 4
indentured servants, 17
India, 252
Indigo, 23
Indochina, 212, 282
industrialization, 112
Industrial Workers of the World (IWW), 155
industry:
    before 1850, 115–116
    between World Wars, 215–216
    during World War II, 239–240
    end of World War II to 1960, 262–263
    shift to service industry, 303–304
infrastructure, 261
insider trading, 330
integration, 258
interchangeable parts, 116
internal taxes, 35
internment camps, 240–241
Interstate Commerce Act (1887), 173
Interstate Commerce Commission (ICC), 149, 173–174
Intolerable Acts (1774), 37
inventions, 115–116, 150, 152
Invisible Man (Ellison), 267
Iran, 245, 250, 318–319
Iran-Contra Affair, 324–325
Iranian hostage crisis, 318–319
Iran-Iraq War, 325
Iraq, 250, 325–326
Irish immigrants, 114–115
"Iron curtain," 244
Islam, 9
isolation, 194, 203–205
Israel, 249, 292, 318

J

Jackson, Andrew, 78
    Bank of United States and, 87
    domestic policy, 88

    elected President, 84–85
    personality conflicts and, 88
    secession and nullification issues, 85–87
Jackson, Helen Hunt, 147
Jackson, Jesse, 315
James, Henry, 164
James I, 17–19
Jamestown, 17
Japan, 142, 192–193, 204, 221
    Cold War in, 251–252
    economic disagreements with U.S., 326
    Indochina and, 282
    World War II and, 208, 212, 235, 237–238
Japanese-American internment camps, 240–241
Jay, John, 54, 57, 65
Jay's Treaty (1795), 65
jazz, 265
Jazz Singer, The, 216
Jefferson, Thomas, 38, 60, 149
    Barbary pirates and, 73
    as Declaration of Independence author, 39
    economic policy against England, 76
    elected President, 68
    French Revolution and, 64
    Louisiana Purchase and, 74
    Napoleonic Wars and, 74–76
    as Northwest Ordinance author, 51
    as Secretary of State, 57
    strict construction view of government, 61–62, 222
Jiang Jieshi, 252, 291
job relief, 226–227
Johnson, Andrew:
    becomes President, 135
    impeachment of, 135–136
Johnson, Lyndon B., 260
    becomes President, 272
    elected President, 277
    Great Society, 277–278
    Vietnam War and, 285–287
Johnson, Richard, 88
Johnson, William, 54
Jolson, Al, 216
judicial review, 99–100
judiciary, 53
Judiciary Act (1789), 57
Judiciary Act (1801), 69, 73
Jungle, The (Sinclair), 179
junk bonds, 330

K

Kansas, 123
Kansas-Nebraska Act, 123
Kansas-Nebraska territory, 122–123
Keat, John, 264
Kellogg-Briand Pact (1927), 205, 208
Kennan, George F., 246
Kennedy, John F.
    Alliance for Progress and, 280
    assassination of, 271
    elected President, 260
    New Frontier, 270–271
    Peace Corps and, 280
    Vietnam and, 280, 283–284
Kennedy, Robert, 287
Kentucky, 68, 74, 127
Kentucky Resolutions, 68, 86
Kerouac, Jack, 267
Kerr, Clark, 275–276
Khomeini, Ayatollah, 318, 319
Khrushchev, Nikita, 248, 279
King, Martin Luther Jr., 258–259, 272, 275, 287
Kinsey, Albert, 264